60

FARRAR
STRAUS
GIROUX

LOVE,

LIFE,

GOETHE

LOVE,

LIFE,

GOETHE

*Lessons of the Imagination from
the Great German Poet*

JOHN ARMSTRONG

Farrar, Straus and Giroux

New York

Farrar, Straus and Giroux
19 Union Square West, New York 10003

Copyright © 2006 by John Armstrong
All rights reserved
Distributed in Canada by Douglas & McIntyre Ltd.
Printed in the United States of America
Originally published in 2006 by Allen Lane, Penguin Group, Great Britain,
as *Love, Life, Goethe: How to Be Happy in an Imperfect World*
Published in the United States by Farrar, Straus and Giroux
First American edition, 2007

Library of Congress Cataloging-in-Publication Data
Armstrong, John, 1966–
    Love, life, Goethe : lessons of the imagination from the great German
poet / John Armstrong.— 1st American ed.
        p.   cm.
    Originally published in 2006 by Allen Lane, Penguin Group, UK, under
the title: Love, life, Goethe: how to be happy in an imperfect world.
    Includes bibliographical references and index.
    ISBN-13: 978-0-374-29968-2 (hardcover : alk. paper)
    ISBN-10: 0-374-29968-4 (hardcover : alk. paper)
    1. Goethe, Johann Wolfgang von, 1749–1832—Criticism and
interpretation.   2. Happiness.   3. Self-actualization (Psychology).
I. Title.

PT2177.A76 2007
831´.6—dc22

                                                            2006034072

www.fsgbooks.com

1   3   5   7   9   10   8   6   4   2

*This book is dedicated to my grandfather, John Marsh,
and to the happy memory of my grandmother, Elizabeth.*

Contents

List of Illustrations

1. *Mephistopheles and the Pupil*, 1828, from Goethe's *Faust*, Eugène Delacroix (Bibliothèque des Beaux-Arts, Paris, France/photo: Bridgeman Art Library, London)
2. *Goethe*, 1828, Joseph Stieler (Neue Pinakothek, Munich/photo: akg-images)
3. Woodcut after drawing by Gottfried Franz (1846–1905) by Johannes Scherr (Coll. Archiv f.Kunst & Geschichte/photo: akg-images)
4. *Das Haus zu dem drei Leiern*, 1824, Friedrich Wilhelm Delkes-kamp (Goethe-Museum, Frankfurt am Main/photo: Stiftung Weimarer Klassik/Ursula Edelmann)
5. The 'Peking' Room, Goethe house, Frankfurt (Freies Deutsches Hochstift)
6. *The Goethe Family in Arcadian Dress*, 1762, Johann Conrad Seekatz (Goethe-Museum, Frankfurt am Main/photo: akg-images)
7. *View from a back window*, Karl Reiffenstein (Goethe-Museum, Frankfurt am Main/photo: Stiftung Weimarer Klassik)
8. *The poet in his study*, 1768/70, Johann Wolfgang von Goethe (Goethe-Museum, Frankfurt am Main/photo: Stiftung Weimarer Klassik)
9. *Herder*, 1775, Johann Ludwig Strecker (Hessisches Landes-museum, Darmstadt/photo: akg-images)
10. Strasbourg Cathedral (photo: DK Images)
11. *Charlotte Kestner*, 1782, Johann Schröder (Goethe-Museum, Frankfurt am Main/photo: Stiftung Weimarer Klassik)

12. *Lili Schönemann*, 1782, Franz Bernhard Frey (Krautergersheim, Alsace/photo: akg-images)

13. *Cornelia Goethe*, Johann Wolfgang von Goethe (Goethe-Nationalmuseum, Weimar/photo: akg-images)

14. *Goethe*, 1775/6, Georg Melchior Kraus (Stiftung Weimarer Klassik/photo: akg-images)

15. *Carl August Sachsen* (photo: ullstein bild)

16. *Goethe*, 1779, Georg Oswald May (Yale University Art Gallery, New Haven/photo: akg-images)

17. The garden-house, Weimar (photo: ullstein bild)

18. The bedroom of the garden-house (Goethe-Museum, Frankfurt am Main/photo: Stiftung Weimarer Klassik)

19. *St Catherine of Alexandria*, 1507/8, Raphael (National Gallery, London/photo: Bridgeman Art Library, London)

20. *Goethe reading leaning back in a chair*, 1786/7, Johann Heinrich Tischbein (Stiftung Weimarer Klassik/photo: akg-images)

21. *Goethe at the window of his apartment by the Corso in Rome*, 1787, Johann Heinrich Tischbein (Goethe-Museum, Frankfurt am Main/photo: akg-images)

22. *The cursed second pillow*, 1786/7, Johann Heinrich Tischbein (Stiftung Weimarer Klassik/photo: akg-images)

23. *Goethe in the Campagna*, 1787, Johann Heinrich Tischbein (Staedelsches Kunstinstit, Frankfurt am Main/photo: akg-images)

24. *Goethe*, 1787/8, Angelica Kauffmann (Stiftung Weimarer Klassik/photo: akg-images)

25. The Roman Capitol with the statue of Marcus Aurelius (photo: DK Images)

26. *Christiane wearing a shawl*, 1788/9, Johann Wolfgang von Goethe (photo: akg-images)

27. *Bacchanal before a Herm*, Nicolas Poussin (National Gallery, London/photo: Bridgeman Art Library, London)

28. *Bestrafung durch eine Priap-Herme*, Johann Wolfgang von Goethe (Goethe-Museum, Frankfurt am Main/photo: Stiftung Weimarer Klassik)

29. *Friedrich von Schiller*, c. 1786, Anton Graff (photo: akg-images)

A Note on Pronunciation

Goethe's name is something of a problem. At least for English speakers it raises a tricky issue of pronunciation.

Growing up in Glasgow I occasionally heard of a German writer called 'Go-th'. It's not a bad attempt and carries interesting resonances: Gothic architecture and the Goths – always linked with Vandals and Huns. My mother sometimes spoke of someone called 'Gerter' or 'Gerder' – tentatively acknowledging the 'otherness' of the name. It has no 'r's in it so perhaps, by the perverse logic of a foreign tongue, you stress them precisely because they're not there. It does sound quite Germanic. My mother is the perfect audience for the Dublin building-site joke. A new construction worker is a bit confused and asks: 'Joist? Girder? What's the difference?' The foreman patiently explains: 'Joist wrote *Ulysses*, Girder wrote *Faust*.'

I was still following the construction-site usage when I happened to mention Goethe while teaching English as a foreign language. A German student assumed I was talking about someone he hadn't heard of until I commented that, of course, this writer's best-known work was *Faust* – at which point he said: 'Oh, you mean "Goo-t'h".' (Say 'ou' while thinking intently about the letter 'r'.)

'Goo-t'h' it is: in my opinion less pleasant than some of the mispronunciations. It's an additional, if perhaps minor, obstacle to the reception of the man and his work. I still feel anxious when I mention his name to people who have heard of *Faust* but are entirely unsure who this 'Goo' person might be.

Although this is the settled modern pronunciation, it was not such

Faust and Mephistopheles having fun

a clear-cut matter in Goethe's own day. There is a letter by the lovely Caroline Flachsland, who later knew Goethe very well, referring to 'Gede' – a young poet all her friends are talking about. So they must have been pronouncing the great man's name in a way that would upset today's sophisticates.

My encounter with Goethe had a slow and awkward beginning. I first came across 'Go-th' or 'Gerder' in a children's encyclopaedia I used to skim while waiting for my mother to finish singing to my brother – with whom I shared a bedroom – and come over and tuck me in. There was a picture of Faust and Mephistopheles, both with little Shakespearian beards. It looked like a slapstick comedy along the lines of Laurel and Hardy.

There was also a picture of Goethe in his later years looking exceptionally stately: in fact, really quite like my grandfather.

What is maturity?

Through my turbulent childhood my grandfather was the representative of maturity; my parents, while fascinating, were distressed bohemians and not obviously in control of life. My grandfather stood for the ideal of the person who has overcome life's complications and is now on stable, secure ground: someone who never gets angry, never fusses, is always sensible, kind, reliable; I couldn't imagine my grandfather ever being late or in a panic: conditions which dominated my early existence. The picture of Goethe became the repository of this fantasy of maturity – one I could neither attain nor renounce. And an undercurrent in this book has been my attempt to reconsider this ideal, to distinguish a genuine vision of maturity from this earlier idealization. There was no received, oppressive Goethe to escape from; rather, Goethe was something one might try to escape to.

PART ONE

Luck

*People who want to grow large in spirit have to pull
    themselves together quickly:*
*Mastery shows itself, first, in how you cope with restricted
    circumstances.*

Goethe, from the poem 'Nature and Art', *c.* 1800

I

The Beautiful Ambition

Goethe's name is one of the most famous in literary and cultural history. He has long occupied a place in the high ranges of the educated imagination: Carlyle called him 'the wisest of our time'; Ruskin rated him alongside Homer and Dante; Nietzsche, Freud and Wittgenstein were fascinated admirers of his work. James Joyce placed Goethe in 'The Holy Trinity' of literature, together with Dante and Shakespeare. In a famous television series Kenneth Clark described Goethe as 'one of the chief heroes' in the story of civilization.

But for all this Goethe's actual achievements and real human worth remain shadowy. What did he do that was supposed to be so important? What was the nature of his literary or cultural contribution? Should we take a special interest in him? Or does Goethe have merely antiquarian value?

Goethe found fame as a writer at the outset of his adult life. *The Sorrows of Young Werther* – his story of fatal romantic passion – was published in 1774 when he was only twenty-five. It made him, almost at once, a celebrity across Europe. His position as one of the leading figures of world literature was secured by his ambitious and complex drama *Faust*, which he worked on all his life and completed only in the months before his death, at the age of eighty-two, in March 1832.

Goethe's achievement was not just literary or intellectual, compelling and profound though some of his writing was. (It should be admitted from the start that some of his vast output is neither of these things.) In equal measure it was his life, his character, the way he lived, the kind of person he was, which was impressive. Trying to do the impossible and sum up his work, Goethe once declared that all his writings were 'fragments of a great confession'. 'Confession' claims an intimate connection between life and books, between experience and art. In his writings, Goethe was trying to understand his own life. Goethe was not primarily 'confessing' his private failings; he wanted to do something more risky and more valuable: confess his strengths and grasp what had gone well: how he had been happy and successful. He thought, as most writers secretly do, that we could learn from him how to lead better our own lives.

It would be a pity if Goethe were to remain a mere name associated only with an intriguing novel and a famous but not-much-read play. Not because we need to be better informed about the past. Rather, Goethe is worth listening to now. Although he was an outstanding intellectual and artistic figure, Goethe was very much a 'Weltkind' – to use one of his favourite words: 'a creature of this world'. He had an appetite for engaging with the world as it is – for facing the realities of authority, for 'getting on', for finding out how things work, for concrete success. He wasn't intimidated by the material world, or by the largely philistine powers that hold sway within it.

The opposite of the 'Weltkind' is the albatross: the poet-intellectual of whom Baudelaire was to write so movingly. The huge bird soars magnificently in the empty skies but when brought down by an arrow on to the deck of a ship it can hardly move its great bulk. The creative artist becomes a fool – comic, tragic and useless – on the stage of ordinary life. Goethe was interested in developing the capacity to soar and wanted to survive on deck: he wrote *Werther* and was a conscientious minister for roads and mines in the Duchy of Weimar; he had a pleasant social life and he wrote *Faust*; he was financially prudent and amazingly imaginative. Through his representative life, Goethe invites us to connect things that are dislocated in our society as well as in ourselves – creative freedom and emotional stability; profundity and practicality; refined taste and power. To live well, we have to thrive in the imperfect world we have.

Goethe is trying to find a way past a thought that has tempted and seduced people down the ages: that there is an inescapable conflict between mental culture and material success. It is not just that he wants both, that he rejects the tragic 'either–or' for a hopeful 'both–and'. The ideal is more interesting: intellectual sophistication needs to come into practical and fruitful contact with responsibility and the everyday world; otherwise it remains pointless and abstract. At the same time, wealth and power need to be educated and refined; otherwise they are like blind giants. The marriage of depth and power – which is a good definition of civilization – was not something Goethe merely wrote about or advocated: he tried to be that ideal himself.

Broadly, Goethe's view of life focuses on two things: growth and wholeness. His ideal is of the balanced individual who integrates apparently divergent demands: open to sensuous pleasure, yet rigorous and disciplined; learned, yet pragmatic and wise.

'Close thy Byron, open thy Goethe' – Carlyle's advice is quaintly dated: 'thy Byron' isn't very likely to be open; nevertheless the phrase gestures at something serious. It illuminates the first of Goethe's two principal concerns: growth. Goethe admired Byron, but when he introduced the poet into the second part of *Faust* in the guise of a little boy called Euphorion (Faust's son) Goethe has the child die young. This was not so much to record the actual death of Byron – in 1824 at the age of only thirty-six – as to point to his hatred of getting older. For Byron, twenty-two was the perfect age: to get any older is a tragedy. The hint from Carlyle is that there is something unusually sane and helpful about the way Goethe thinks of life. To 'open thy Goethe' is to be invited into a world in which it is exciting – rather than sad – to grow up.

Like most people, Goethe developed his philosophy in and through the course of his existence; the purpose of this book is to follow that course and draw from it – as Goethe himself did – his sense of the meaning of life.

2

Inheritance

Goethe nearly had no life at all. After a wretched labour he was born blue and cold at midday on 28 August 1749. The midwife pummelled him and, at last, he started breathing. Wolfgang, as the family called him, was the first child of Catharina and Caspar; they had been married just over a year; she was only eighteen, he was nearing forty.

In his autobiography, Goethe makes the fantastical claim that the planets were in a supremely favourable alignment at the precise moment of his birth. Rather than seeing this as a spurious explanation of his life it can be seen as an acknowledgement of an extraordinary degree of good fortune. It is an admission that he was lucky.

This was particularly evident in economic terms. Caspar's father – Wolfgang's grandfather – had been an enterprising tailor; after a stint in France he married a wealthy Frankfurt widow and set himself up as the proprietor of one of the city's largest and grandest inns. The ex-tailor died in 1730 leaving a fortune of ninety thousand florins: in purchasing power, the equivalent of several million pounds today. Caspar, who was only twenty years old and still a law student, could live very comfortably without ever earning a pfennig. In fact these funds were the bedrock of the family finances for well over a hundred years – a portion passing to the tailor's great-great-grandsons in 1832. And the background security it provided was a crucial element in Goethe's encounter with the world.

Caspar went on to complete a doctorate in jurisprudence and gain practical experience at the Imperial Law Courts in Vienna and Wetzlar. He made a Grand Tour, mainly in Italy. Returning to his native Frankfurt in his early thirties, Caspar's position was complicated. By education and fortune he belonged in the highest of five carefully defined social classes. However, his late father's basic, if remunerative, trades and comparatively recent citizenship excluded him from the inner circle of the patrician elite. He was 'new money', a parvenu; the city was deeply traditional. His seemingly reasonable hopes of obtaining a prominent appointment in the civil administration – for which his education perfectly qualified him – came to nothing.

Caspar's difficulties were increased by a political drama within the Holy Roman Empire unfolding just when he returned to Frankfurt. In 1740 the Hapsburg estates had passed to Maria Theresa. The Hapsburgs were the most powerful family in the Empire and succession by a woman was a delicate matter; complex negotiations had supposedly secured international agreement. Nevertheless, the youthful Frederick II of Prussia – later to be known as Frederick the Great – took the opportunity to deny the legality of Maria Theresa's inheritance.

At the close of that year, 1740, Frederick marched into Silesia, a wealthy province belonging to Maria Theresa; he soon collected a wide range of allies – most importantly France – all of whom had something to gain from the weakening of the Hapsburgs. At this point Carl Albrecht, King of Bavaria, saw a great opportunity. With Maria Theresa and the Hapsburgs in a state of military embarrassment, and so many forces arrayed against them, Carl Albrecht advanced his own claim on the vacant Imperial title and managed to get himself elected and crowned – in Frankfurt (as tradition dictated) – as Emperor Charles VII. Being Emperor was the ultimate honour, the summit of the feudal imagination and ambition. But pleasures of the imagination turned out to be all it provided Carl Albrecht.

Caspar, recently returned to Frankfurt and more recently denied an administrative post, decided to purchase the title of Imperial Councillor. Despite being bought, such a title would normally secure considerable social standing; so it might have eased Caspar's social insecurity. However, by ill luck – or by some vague self-harming impulse – his timing was disastrous. A title granted by Carl Albrecht aligned Caspar with the anti-Hapsburg faction. This made things difficult in pro-Hapsburg Frankfurt.

While the new Emperor was still in Frankfurt, busy selling titles to the likes of Caspar, the Austrians made a tactical peace with Prussia and attacked Bavaria. Austrian troops seized Munich, Carl Albrecht's own capital city. The homeless Emperor died soon after and the Hapsburgs regained their traditional honours with Maria Theresa's husband being elected as the next Emperor.

Caspar's side was completely out. He never made any serious attempt to pursue a career after this debacle. This reveals something distinctive about Goethe's father: awkward though the situation undoubtedly was, it would not have proved final to anyone of flexible spirit or urgent ambition.

Whatever the reasons for his non-career Caspar did make a very shrewd marriage a few years later. His young wife, Catharina, was a daughter of Johann Wolfgang Textor, who had recently been appointed as Schultheiss – the chief official of the Frankfurt city council. The Textors were a legal family; the grandfather of the chief official had been the senior judge in the city. But public service had not made the Textors wealthy and their daughter certainly did not aspire to an aristocratic marriage. From a pragmatic point of view, Caspar could not have found a better partner. Catharina had that desirable quality which eighteenth-century moralists called 'complaisancy': she was able to get along pleasantly with all sorts of people – most importantly, of course, her rather touchy husband – while still enjoying, and being, herself.

On marriage, Catharina joined Caspar in his mother's large house, located in a street called the Hirschgraben. It had been formed from two old houses, both opening directly on to the cobbled street. Together they made a very picturesque composition of steep gables, chimneys and irregularly placed windows.

It was in this house that Wolfgang was born. Within a few months Catharina was pregnant again. A daughter, Cornelia, was born on 17 December 1750.

Caspar's mother, now very elderly, kept to her large and comfortable room on the ground floor of the house. Wolfgang recalled her as looking rather haggard, but she was well cared for and always wore

The house where Wolfgang was born.

perfectly laundered white gowns; she was gentle and friendly to the children, who took their toys into her room and played round her bed.

3

The Mother

Charming though the old house must have been it had its drawbacks for four-year-old Wolfgang and little Cornelia. They were frightened of its many gloomy corners, especially at night. Their parents wanted them to overcome their irrational fears and the children were made to sleep alone – that is, without a maid – in the nursery. The anxious little pair used to creep out of their dark room late in the evening to seek the reassuring company of the servants. To put a stop to this Caspar, dressed only in his nightshirt, would suddenly step out from the shadows, block their way and terrify them back to bed.

His strategy, of course, was less than helpful. The imaginary horrors of the dark were merely outweighed by real horrors in the corridor. Catharina had a wiser approach. She promised each child a treat (a ripe pear) in the morning if they stayed in their room through the night. For the sake of this reward they managed to master their anxieties and everyone was happy.

This problem and the way it was resolved struck Goethe in later life as dramatizing something at once extremely simple and deeply important. Each parent wanted to achieve the same thing: one strategy compounded the difficulty; the other was kindly and successful. Caspar was an intellectual man; Catharina was uninstructed in higher learning. He got it wrong; she made everything right. All of his life Goethe was appalled at the possible gulf between learning and practical wisdom.

Wolfgang was a quick, lively, confident little boy, very much attached to his sister, Cornelia. He was the leader; she was always deeply devoted to him. Wolfgang was a great favourite with grown-ups and not very interested in children of his own age, Cornelia apart. Perhaps, to children who are much loved by tender and imaginative mothers and grandmothers, grown-ups simply seem nicer and more fun than other children.

Catharina had a cheerful disposition; she avoided dwelling on problems if there was nothing of practical use she could do to alleviate matters. She liked formulating little rules for a contented existence. Her style is vivid, if grammatically imperfect. 'I never *bemoralize* anyone, always seek out the good that is in them, and leave what is bad to Him who made mankind, and knows how to round off the angles. In this way, I make myself and others comfortable.'

Goethe's outlook was deeply affected by the example of his mother – he saw her as a model of what a person should be like. Throughout his adult years he regarded a sunny character like hers – a 'Frohnatur' – as the mark of a good person. He never embraced the idea that it is somehow deeper and better to find a home for the sorrows of the world in one's own heart. The mother's happy attitude might be expected to go with a dreamy avoidance of reality. But Catharina was, in fact, a woman with a decidedly practical turn of mind: always active, always getting things done efficiently.

Here is how she saw herself: 'Order and quiet are my principal characteristics. Hence I dispatch at once whatever I have to do, the most disagreeable always first, and I gulp down the devil without looking at him. When all has returned to its proper state, then I defy anyone to surpass me in my good humour.' She is the sort of woman who is revered in Dutch genre painting: warm-hearted, efficient, wise without erudition, emotionally civilized.

Catharina loved inventing tales for her children. The stories had an allegorical turn: she would personify natural elements – air, fire, water – as princes and princesses. She described travelling to the stars and the godlike spirits who lived there. She was not merely inventing things to entertain the children; she was expressing her own beliefs, trying to express in terms a child could grasp what she felt about nature, morality and life.

Little Wolfgang was a passionately involved listener and would get cross if he didn't like how things were going for a favourite character. He was easily moved to tears and outrage. 'But, mama, the princess won't marry the nasty tailor, even if he does kill the giant' – was an outburst that particularly struck the young mother.

When she broke off for the day, Wolfgang would be desperate to know how the story would continue and full of speculations. He would trot downstairs and chat with his grandmother, telling her what he thought would happen next. Later, in an exercise of loving diplomacy, Catharina would pick up these hints from her mother-in-law and shape the narrative in line with the boy's hopes, building on his suggestions.

The next day the story would continue, Wolfgang longing to discover how things would turn out. He was ecstatic when the story advanced in just the way he had hoped. The secret between the women was faithfully guarded and revealed by Catharina only in old age to one of Goethe's friends.

'In a well-run, neat and ordered house, the experience of children is rather like that of rats or mice. They are curious about every little crack or hole where something secret or interesting might be hidden; they take what they can find with a kind of guilty glee.' So Goethe later wrote of one of the major pleasures of childhood. In the big old house with its many locked cupboards and storerooms, he sometimes had to wait weeks or months before his mother's household operations would lead to certain intriguing doors being opened. He kept a special watch on the larder door. When his mother called him to help her in there his highest ambition was to steal a golden plum.

Goethe passed the whole of his life up to the age of sixteen in Frankfurt. Given its status as a major urban centre, it was almost unimaginably small by modern standards. The population was around thirty thousand, roughly the same as present-day Whitstable. That an important city could be this size tells us a good deal about the scale and character of the world into which Goethe was born. The Empire – covering most of what we now think of as Germany as well as Austria – was a diffuse, decentred entity. Frankfurt owed its significance to trade; on the banks of its river, the Main, were large cranes for handling cargo to and from the Rhine; like many small boys Wolfgang loved them. There were periodic, large trade fairs that brought merchants from around Europe and contributed to the cosmopolitan atmosphere. The city was entirely surrounded by huge military walls and moats: tightly packed old houses and narrow streets within; orchards and market gardens beyond.

Frankfurt was a Free Imperial City not subject to any direct political control save that of the Emperor. Since the Empire was neither pro-active nor demanding Frankfurt was to a large extent self-governing; effectively, it was a city state. However, the city had an intimate connection with Imperial ceremonies. By tradition, the nine Electors who chose the Emperor had to make their election in Frankfurt, and the coronation also took place there.

A Free Imperial City was very different from a Court, or Residence, City, which is what most of the larger urban centres of the Empire were – like Munich, Vienna or Dresden. These cities were not merely ruled by a prince, the whole system of government and culture was an appendage of the court; the leading administrative officers were usually nobles. Such cities looked to France and particularly Versailles as their model of what a modern state should be.

In Frankfurt Goethe grew up in a strictly hierarchical society but one in which his non-noble status did not count as a handicap. The city administration was almost monopolized by affluent lawyers: the class to which his father and maternal grandfather – and indeed his great-great-grandfather – belonged. The two children liked going to the Town Hall, which was a focal point of civic pride, and were extremely impressed that their grandfather (whom they usually saw wearing tattered old gloves tending his garden) was the only one in the council chamber with the privilege of a desk.

4

Home

After his mother's death, in 1754, Caspar had the two Hirschgraben houses reorganized internally and a smooth, more imposing but perhaps less charming, façade erected.

The family house as rebuilt during Wolfgang's childhood

The main door opens directly from the street and a wide, tranquil hallway goes through to the pretty paved courtyard at the back. An elegant stone staircase with wrought-iron balustrades leads to the upper floors. One floor up is a gracious, formal salon known as the Peking Room. The wallpaper is decorated with Chinese motifs and there are delicate rococo mouldings at the corners of the ceiling. The chairs are upholstered in rose-coloured silk – similar to the swagged curtains of the four windows, which look out directly on to the Hirschgraben. With its elaborate chandelier and wall-mounted candelabra the room is opulent, certainly, but it stands as an accent, a point of concentrated grandeur against a much simpler general style of the house: the wide, restrained and bright hallways, the wooden floorboards, the absence of clutter. There is a charming music room and a very large cellar – in Goethe's day holding a huge stock of wine, which constituted a significant portion of his father's wealth.

On the floor above the Peking Room is the picture cabinet, hung from floor to ceiling with paintings. Many of these were commissions from local painters working either in a gentle Italianate landscape manner or in the Dutch domestic idiom. Opening from this gallery is the father's lovely library. The scale of the rooms is nicely judged: they have an intimate but dignified character. It was not a show house designed to awe visitors; it was a comfortable house for a family – but one in which comfort was enhanced by taste and learning.

On the walls of the hallways were prints of the great monuments and architecture of Rome. Reference to international culture, especially to France and Italy, was part of the fabric of Goethe's childhood. Caspar taught Cornelia Italian; and young Wolfgang – although not the official recipient of this instruction – managed to pick up the language. The Italian tutor who helped Caspar in the extremely slow preparation of his travel journal joined the family in making music.

Among the many reminders, or anticipations, of Italy, was a toy gondola the father had brought back from Venice. As an occasional treat Wolfgang was allowed to play with it. This domestic image of the son playing with the boat has particular poignancy because of its link to his later life. One of the most magical moments in Goethe's *Italian Journey* occurs on a night in Venice: cradled in his gondola he hears the boatmen singing far away, one voice answering to another across the great expanse of water.

Caspar was a highly cultivated man, devoted to the arts but in a passive, almost timid, manner. He was what Proust would call a 'celibate of art'; his admiration found no echo in any creative undertakings of his own. He confessed himself to be something of a plodder: mastering the law by endless cramming; obsessed by routine and order, easily irritated by any deviation.

Reflecting on his first visit to Goethe's childhood home, Thomas Mann remarked that Goethe was the great representative figure of what he called the 'burgerliche Zeitalter' – 'the bourgeois epoch'. He saw Goethe as the culmination of a long development of German urban and domestic life. The phrase is apt; for Goethe domestic life was a central concern through which he imagined many other complex issues. The ideal of the well-run home and of the life lived within it was, for him, emblematic of human fulfilment.

This orientation of Goethe's mind might be taken as showing how narrow, even philistine, he was. The exciting thought runs in the opposite direction. Goethe shows us that, properly considered, domestic economy is a major human good, continuous with our most noble and serious aspirations. Part of what makes him attractive and important as a figure in world culture can be seen precisely in the way in which his ideals are not foreign to everyday existence.

When we think about Goethe – as when we consider any major writer – we are looking for hints on how to live. Keeping the house clean, arranging the kitchen cupboards and balancing the books, all have their real dignity illuminated by Goethe's loving regard. What might have seemed like low-grade, repetitious labour is brought into contact with the noble purposes of thinking and creation. That helps us see the way in which arranging a cupboard, or filing bills and warranty records – when done well – draws upon the same principles as the creation of a work of art: it seeks to bring clarity where there was confusion, to introduce elegance and coherence into the potential mess of daily life. Undertaking these tasks well requires taste, discipline and intelligence.

The competent, prudent – ordinary – aspects of Goethe make him a slightly odd figure in the pantheon of great dead artists and thinkers.

There is a tendency to assume that high art and magnificent ideas are produced at terrible personal cost; and that such creativity is connected to financial incompetence or (ideally) bankruptcy. Admittedly, there is a lot of evidence to support this point of view.*

If we long, as Cyril Connolly did, 'to have written *Les Fleurs du Mal* or the *Saison en Enfer* without being Rimbaud or Baudelaire, that is without undergoing their mental suffering and without being diseased and poor', we can at least console ourselves with the thought that it is impossible to write a masterpiece and be healthy and comfortable. If it really is a case of 'either/or' it's probably wise to opt for a pleasant life. Goethe is unusual: he did not 'pay' for his enormous creative drives and successes.

This may explain a recurrent motif of Goethe scholarship: the attempt to prove that Goethe was unhappy or psychologically disturbed. Goethe is made to fit the desired pattern: one that consoles us for our uncreative lives. But this is the wrong lesson to teach. Goethe is important because he integrates material and emotional stability with an astonishingly fertile creative life.

---

* *Mozart*: no idea about money, pauper's grave; *Beethoven*: his friends had to take his money away from him because he was so irresponsible; *Balzac*: dressed as a monk, drank forty cups of coffee a day, economic basket case; *Baudelaire*: drug addict, compulsive gambler, squandered his inheritance; *Wagner*: insanely egoistic, borrowed from all his friends, never paid his debts; *Tolstoy*: wanted to be a penniless serf; *Nietzsche*: didn't make a penny from writing, later royalties went to his horrible sister; *Proust*: didn't know how to open a window or boil a kettle, lost lots of money through extravagance and inept speculation; *Wittgenstein*: tormented ('If just one person could understand me I would be satisfied'), ate mainly bread and cheese, gave away all his money – to his rich siblings so as not to corrupt the poor; *Jackson Pollock*: everyone else made money out of him ('If I'm so famous why ain't I rich?').

5

Education

Goethe and Cornelia were educated mainly at home and very much under their father's direction, although their tutors were sometimes drawn from local schools. Caspar was clearly ambitious for the children but he pursued this ambition in an enlightened and kindly way. The curriculum was extensive, rather than intensive; there was an emphasis on languages, which Wolfgang found congenial. Latin was obligatory – not just for access to the classics but as a living language of legal scholarship and philosophy. French was important as the international language of civilization; he learned some English and picked up Italian. He spent some time on Greek – as the language of the New Testament – and found himself a tutor in Hebrew so that he could study the Old Testament more carefully.

There remained traces of the happy, diligent schoolboy right through Goethe's life. He was certainly not a prodigy, but Caspar was understandably proud of his son's early literary productions. He had the boy's efforts bound and treated seriously; Goethe's later ability to take himself seriously was surely fostered by this paternal admiration: he didn't have to struggle too hard to feel that his father not only loved him but also respected him.

Most importantly, Caspar ensured that learning was fun: Wolfgang wrote witty Latin dialogues, pasted together little paper models of the regular solids (as a way of learning geometry) and as an adolescent wrote a novel about a family scattered across Europe who write to each other in the language of the countries they are in – integrating lessons in geography, economics, composition and languages.

*

Nietzsche – whose educational experience was so very different (rigorous boarding school, brilliant at exams) – once wistfully quoted Goethe: 'I hate everything I've merely learned – learning which doesn't immediately enliven my thinking or enhance my capacity for action.' In fact Nietzsche saw the kind of education Goethe had as an important defence against an overestimation of the value of knowledge for the sake of knowledge – an antidote to the cult of learning. Nietzsche was no doubt irked by a school system which was officially in awe of Goethe but which provided the kind of teaching the great man would have hated: perversely forcing boys to learn by rote effusions against learning by rote.

It is ironic that Goethe is the champion of personal relevance as the valuable thing in learning. For his life is now the focus of an academic, impersonal industry. The question Goethe might have asked is: why do you want to know so much about me? Does studying the details of my doings immediately enliven your thinking and enhance your capacity for action? When he came to write his autobiography Goethe freely reshaped events to better stimulate and help others. His father, on the other hand, would have relished every little puzzle: on which day of the week was *Werther* started? What was my son's exact income in such-and-such a year?

The more that we can know about Goethe, the more pressing becomes the question: what do we really want to know and why? The greater the quantity of information, the more important it becomes to identify a principle of quality. The answer Goethe himself makes is clear: whatever will make a genuine contribution to how you live your life. Goethe can be approached from many angles of inquiry: what can he tell us about the world in which he lived? What can we learn about the development of German literature? But the question – for non-academics – is why do we want to know about these things?

The aim of this book is more intimate: to consider how getting to know Goethe might enrich life. This friendship-model of investigation reminds us of something quite strange in the modern tradition of biography: when we know another person, when we are friends with them, there are often large blank spaces in their history, as far as we are concerned. We may have only a sketchy – and probably one-sided

– grasp of what occurred over substantial stretches of that person's life. And yet our encounter with them is not puzzling or missing something. As we grow into a friendship, aspects of how the other person thinks and acts become part of the fabric of our life – part of how we see things, what we regard as possible, desirable, interesting or worthwhile. The path of this book is that of an imaginary friendship.

In 1755 – when Wolfgang was six – Caspar gave the children a puppet theatre as a Christmas present. In one of Goethe's later descriptions of happy childhood, clearly inspired by his own, there is an account of the growth of a child's interest in drama. It starts when the boy sees a puppet show at home. At first the little theatre seems magical. The child has no idea how the figures come to move or speak; he is entranced. He sneaks round behind the curtain and is shocked to find a man pulling the strings and putting on the voices.

Disappointment turns to excitement when he realizes that he can work the puppets himself. From being the spectator he becomes a creator. He makes puppets and costumes, recruits the help of his sister and friends; he writes a little play and directs the whole thing. Later he turns to his father's library, leafing through the famous dramatists for scenes of slaughter: his favourite part of any play. Eventually this leads to an interest in the plays as a whole. He reads Racine and Corneille not because he has been told to study the French classics but because he wants to steal their plots. The moral is simple: don't just stare at my life as if it were a puppet show: create your own life, and feel free to take your plots from me.

We get an insight into young Goethe's character from an anecdote he relates about his attitude to religion. Aged seven, he took it upon himself to make up a religious ceremony. He got together various small stones and arranged them on a music stand. At sunrise he used a magnifying glass to focus the first rays and light a candle: the flame – originating in the sun – symbolized the soul's upward movement towards the deity. It is one of those apparently quite trivial incidents which, seen retrospectively, is indicative of the man. It unites serious-ness and independence. The greatest themes of the human condition can be enacted in your own home. And, of course, in his private religion, Wolfgang could be the high priest.

Caspar's great care for his son's education was not disinterested. From early on he had mapped out a course for Wolfgang's life. He would study law, obtain a doctorate in jurisprudence, undertake the Grand Tour, gain experience and useful contacts at one of the Imperial tribunals and return to join the Frankfurt city council – in due course replacing his grandfather as head of the administration. He would, ideally, write a few books of well-regarded poetry and generally move the family on a little further up the social scale – not too far though: the last thing Caspar wanted was to lose his son to an aristocratic world in which he himself could never be comfortable. Wolfgang was supposed to be a better version of Caspar not a completely different kind of person.

Reflecting on his father's character, Goethe was to write much later: 'For any father it is a happy wish that he might see his son complete what he has begun; it is as if, in this, the father can live a second time around; and the wisdom that the father has acquired in the course of his life can be put to use.' Caspar's attitude allowed him to delight in his son's progress and to welcome – rather than fear – being surpassed. It made him especially appreciative of the qualities he saw in Wolfgang and which he himself lacked. And, to an extraordinary degree, we see the tastes and concerns of the father developed and fulfilled in the life of the son.

This scheme of life illuminates Goethe's doubts about 'being a writer'. To be, primarily, a writer was a sign of failure rather than of success in life. There's a terrifying line in Plato when he says: 'Who would merely write about a general or a statesman, if they had the ability to be one?' This was very much the prevailing view. Writing stories and poems, however finely, was an elegant accompaniment, but the real thing was the exercise of power.

Goethe was to regard his father's house in Frankfurt as his home base until his late twenties. After that he became rather detached from his parents. In fact he hardly saw his parents at all after he finally left home. But this apparent distance may actually reflect something very different: Goethe 'internalized' his parents to a remarkable degree. They were so alive and real in his imagination that their physical presence was secondary.

There was, however, an ambivalent aspect in Caspar's attitude to his son. 'My father often used to tell me – sometimes in the most serious tones, sometimes jokingly – that if he had had my talents he would have put them to better use.' The father acknowledges the son's superiority of mind and ability, but then undercuts the recognition by a maddening and illogical – but utterly normal – sleight of hand. If I were you I'd be better than you.

Young Goethe returned his father's ambivalence in an equally natural way. Occasionally, he was teased by other children about his artisan grandfather – the tailor-turned-innkeeper. There was even a rumour that Caspar was the illegitimate son of an illustrious nobleman. Wolfgang became very excited when he heard about this and took to looking very carefully at the portraits of local aristocrats which he often saw in the homes of family friends.

For all Goethe's fantasies about a mysterious aristocratic grandfather, he was very obviously the child of both his parents. He united, in the clearest way, the virtues of both – and of his wider family. And he was, in fact, quite aware of this and later wrote a poem about it. Put into prose, it goes like this:

'I get my build, and my serious side, from my father; I've got dear mama's happy ways – and just like her I love to invent stories. My grandfather (on my father's side) was always a favourite with women; well, that goes for me; my grandmother was pretty stylish and loved a bit of display – that's in the blood too. These qualities are fused in me: there's nothing that's actually new.'

This poem is a testament to Goethe's early good fortune. At the time of his departure for university at Leipzig, he was clever, rich and (fairly) handsome and little had happened to distress or vex him. Considering him at this point we may think of Goethe not merely as lucky but – in a curious way – too lucky. The depth and degree of his good fortune has something almost embarrassing about it; for it may suggest that the lucky individual is cut off from the ordinary experience of life. Hence his thought will be less relevant to us; the pattern of experience will be – if enviable – remote.

This is particularly pressing in Goethe's case. For he wanted to see himself as 'representative'. Once when he was in Italy he remarked that a good friend, the writer Carl Philipp Moritz, was 'me – only born poor'. It's a sweet comment, gently creating common ground across a merely economic divide. But it is misleading. Moritz wrote a celebrated autobiographical novel called *Anton Reiser* that describes his horrible early years. His parents were fanatical and hard; they hated one another and fought constantly; they never displayed any tenderness towards him; he was torn apart by the fact that his mother, whom he loved, often seemed to be explicitly in the wrong with respect to his father, whom he feared. He was very lonely; he loved reading but his parents possessed only two books – a Bible and a manual on how to read. The contrast with Wolfgang is dramatic. It wasn't just the family wealth: it was his mother's warmth and wisdom; his father's imaginative ambition for him; it was the fine collection of books, the prints and paintings – these were the things that constituted Goethe's luck.

But Goethe was luckier than most people – and, of course, he lived in a particular kind of society: so we might still wonder about his 'representative' status and his longing to use his own experience to illuminate that of others – including ours. Goethe's good fortune did not preserve him from suffering – from unhappiness in love, from anxiety about what to do with his life, from the death of people he loved, from the horror of war, from loneliness or frustration. However, he was healthy and strong enough to face these facts and problems without flinching too much. His good fortune was not of an inhuman fantasy kind: a life without troubles. It was good fortune in the sense that he was well equipped to face trouble, to acknowledge the difficulties of life and try to think about them clearly.

As a writer Goethe is 'universal' in the sense that he addresses themes and issues that were not in any way unique to his time. He is concerned with elemental themes: love, distress, growth through experience. It is striking how, as a writer, Goethe tends not to dwell a great deal on the specific, material details. In *Werther* and *Faust*, to take only the most famous examples, there is comparatively little descriptive detail tying the works to the period in which they were written. Goethe's urgent interest was in fundamental problems of existence not in whether a character was wearing a periwig or writing with a quill.

One of Caspar's idées fixes was that poetry ought to rhyme. This conviction led him to an aversion for the most exciting poet of the day, Friederich Gottlieb Klopstock. Klopstock's reputation with the public derived from a blank-verse religious epic, *The Messiah*, published in sections from 1749, the year of Wolfgang's birth, until 1773. As a child Goethe was very taken by an episode in which Christ descends into Hell, and he learned the verses by heart, despite his father's strict opposition to the work.

One evening, while Caspar was being shaved at home, Wolfgang and Cornelia were in the same room, secreted behind the stove, quietly reciting the forbidden stanzas. In her excitement, Cornelia suddenly cried out and startled the barber, who emptied a bowl of water over Caspar. Such upsets were unbearable to him and on discovering the cause he banished the poet (or at least the poetry). But when, about fifteen years later, his son's growing reputation led to a visit from Klopstock – intended and received as a public benediction – Caspar had the grace to be heartily pleased.

6

The Seven Years War

At the beginning of 1759, when Goethe was nine years old, the smooth order of family life was disturbed by war. The Seven Years War was a continuation of the antagonism between Prussia and Austria, between Frederick the Great and Maria Theresa. It had long been a settled policy of France that Austria was its major rival in Europe. Thus the French had been supporters of Frederick in his early battles.

The Austrian chancellor, Kaunitz, persuaded the French king – Louis XV – that Prussia was more of a problem to France than Austria. French policy was not dictated by hatred of Austria but by the desire to keep rivals weak. As Frederick expanded his territories the balance of power changed: so too should French policy. Such arguments led, in May 1756, to the formation of an extensive secret alliance of Austria, Russia, France and Sweden against Prussia. (The alliance was marked by the betrothal of the future Louis XVI to a young Austrian archduchess called Marie Antoinette.)

Frederick soon discovered that the French had changed sides and that forces were being assembled to attack him. He immediately invaded Saxony – his neighbour in the west – partly so as to control its resources and also to enlist its troops in his army. Thus began the Seven Years War. French troops entered the Empire as allies; some way into the conflict, in January 1759, they descended on Frankfurt.

The occupation of Frankfurt – though not aggressive – had intimate consequences for the Goethe family. The French governor of the city chose to reside in the best rooms of their fine new house and he directed his official business from there, which naturally entailed great disturbance with equerries, messengers and visitors coming and going at all hours. Caspar loathed the intrusion; and while not in principle anti-French he could not help but resent the whole purpose of the campaign. The French were fighting on the same side as the Hapsburgs and against Prussia. Yet it was the reascendency of the Hapsburgs that had caused Caspar difficulties; and they were attacking his hero, Frederick.

The occupation brought to a head tensions within the extended family. Goethe's maternal grandfather – old Textor – was a Hapsburg supporter. More than that, as the leading official of the city, he was responsible for cooperation with the French forces. A rumour went about that he had gone beyond his duty and actually encouraged the French to hold the city – and that he had been well rewarded. Although the French were allied to the Empire, there was no special obligation that troops should be billeted in Frankfurt, and some people thought that this could have been avoided, but for the rapacity of the likes of Textor. Caspar was angry enough to repeat this accusation to his father-in-law at a family lunch. Goethe's grandfather threw a knife; Caspar drew his sword. Bloodshed was avoided but relations were permanently strained.

For Wolfgang it was all a demonstration of the domestic location of power: if (as his father said) old Textor had betrayed the city, the centre of authority had merely shifted from Grandpa's desk at the Town Hall to his parents' drawing room.

The French governor, Comte de Thoranc, was – to Caspar – an exceedingly unwelcome intruder; to the children he was more interesting. He introduced them to ice cream, sending it up to the nursery from his table. A portrait of the time shows him as combining sensitivity and maturity with slightly dreamy, sad eyes: a rather wonderful self-image for a highly responsible public servant.

While in Frankfurt de Thoranc commissioned a large number of paintings including a series of twelve pictures of the life of St Joseph. Wolfgang had to give up one of his rooms to serve as a studio for the local painter Johann Georg Trautmann. Wolfgang was a regular visitor, observing the painter's working practice and suggesting subject

The most formal room in the family home

matter and details for the presentation of the story. The pictures were taken to France and much later acquired for the Goethe Museum in Frankfurt.

7

Adolescence

One of the pictures Caspar commissioned was a family portrait, dating from 1762. It shows Caspar and Catharina in an Arcadian setting among ruined columns and urns overgrown with weeds. Wolfgang and Cornelia act out the roles of shepherd and shepherdess with some friendly sheep.

In the background, five naked infants play beneath the graceful trees: conventional putti, perhaps, or a pitiful reference to the five infants who did not survive. Only one of these, Hermann, lived beyond the age of three; he died of dysentery in January 1759, not long after his sixth birthday, when Wolfgang was nine.

From adolescence onwards, Goethe's bedroom and study were in the extensive attics, on the third floor of the house. He spent a lot of time on a balcony formed at this level at the back of the house, between two gables. 'He would gaze out over the neighbouring gardens, watch the sun going down, the stars coming out and the night deepening. Listening to the sound of the crickets he would recite favourite bits of poetry to himself.'

However beautiful the sunset, there was something profoundly frustrating about the view. He could see the lovely gardens in the cool of evening – but he couldn't go there. The family house had only a small paved and high-walled courtyard. They had a pleasure garden and a kitchen garden a little way out of town, but nothing to equal the town gardens he could see all around him.

The poetry he recited reveals something of his adolescent sexuality. He was especially excited by Tasso's *Jerusalem Delivered* (1580–81)

The family as they liked to imagine themselves

– his father's favourite work, as it happened. Wolfgang relished the description of a fight between Clorinda and Tancred. There is an underlying erotic theme here: Clorinda – as Goethe was acutely aware – has a rather masculine, or ambiguous, character: she is the woman who puts on armour and fights to the death (her death) with Tancred whom she loves and who loves her. In part it is a reflection on a theme Oscar Wilde was to make his own: 'yet each man kills the thing he loves'. Perhaps more importantly it was an image of the confusion of gender and the shady ground between love and violence.

During early adolescence Goethe – though sociable – didn't have any really close friends. He preferred to order people about, to be in charge

The neighbours' gardens: inaccessible beauty

– he wanted troops, subordinates, but not equals. Like all youths of his class he dressed very grandly; a complete gentleman in miniature, with powdered wig and silver sword.

Somehow, in his wandering around the town and his frequenting of the stage door (he had a free pass courtesy of his grandfather), he fell in with a group of rather wild youths: lawyers' and merchants' clerks. They were slightly older and from much less respectable homes. They met in a local inn and had a scheme for forging bills of exchange. Their wine was served by a pretty waitress; unsurprisingly she took a rather tender and protective attitude to Wolfgang – an elegant, lively boy obviously out of his depth among these ruffians. And it is equally unsurprising that he mistook her kindness for love.

Remembering her in later life, he called her 'Gretchen' – the name of Faust's desperately unfortunate mistress. Goethe was always fond of 'meeting his characters'. This was a matter of personality, not plot. To be 'a Gretchen' was to be innocent but open to flirtation, naive and attracted to material things rather than to be condemned to death – as happens to poor Gretchen in the play.

His happiest time with 'Gretchen' was spent during an Imperial coronation – when there were lavish ceremonies and fireworks. Young Goethe was not at all cynical or dismissive about such things. Indeed the excitement he felt at the grand displays left a clear mark on his later views of society. He thought that public ceremony should play an important role in stressing the difference between the ruler and the ruled; to make it obvious to the people who they were ruled by. The grandeur of the ceremony is a kind of exhibition of authority so you know who to blame if things turn out badly. Goethe would have hated – and regarded as a dangerous trick – the modern tendency for rulers to cultivate a homely, modest demeanour.

Goethe spent a lot of his life around people who exercised political power. He wanted to persuade us that power should be explicit. Of course showing the real wielders of authority to the public isn't sufficient for good government, but it does counteract the bureaucratic nightmare of Kafka in which one can never find out who is actually responsible for anything, there are only layers and layers of subordinates. During Goethe's lifetime public administration became much better organized and more extensive – and often more surreptitious, with the deployment of secret police. It was all the more important, therefore, that it should be made obvious who is actually in charge and upon whose shoulders responsibility finally rests.

It was around the time of the coronation that the youths' fraudulent scheme was discovered; they were quickly dealt with. Wolfgang, though slightly implicated, was not prosecuted – he had not been an active participant, though he must have known what his companions were up to. He was seriously upset by the parental anger that followed the exposure of his naive involvement, which indicates how rarely he had been disapproved of at home.

The wider world – as it presented itself to the adolescent Wolfgang – seemed well arranged: 'religion, morals, law, rank and habits rule over the surface of society. Streets of magnificent houses are kept clean; everyone outwardly conducts himself with propriety'. Yet he was acutely aware that this was not the whole story: 'The disorder within is often only the more desolate; and a polished exterior covers many a wall which totters and falls with a crash during the night. How many families had I not more or less distinctly known in which bankruptcy, divorce, seduction, murder and robbery had wrought destruction. Young as I was, I had often, in such cases, lent my succour; for my frankness awakened confidence, and my discretion was known; and my activity did not shun any sacrifice – indeed rather preferred the most perilous occasions – I had frequently to mediate, console and try to avert the storm; in the course of which I could not help learning many sad and humiliating facts.'
    Goethe never came to regard this gap as hypocritical. He didn't conclude that nice houses and clean streets were a sham because the lives indoors were distressing and confused. Dirty streets and squalid buildings wouldn't make things better.

Rather a lot is known about Goethe's early years, largely because – fairly late in life – he wrote about it in the first, and most substantial, part of his autobiography, the full title of which is *From My Life: Poetry and Truth*. What is arresting about that enterprise is that Goethe didn't concentrate on his achievements – on the remarkable things he did once he was famous – but on the fairly ordinary things that happened prior to his public achievements. In fact his is the first childhood and boyhood to have been narrated in detail.
    Why was Goethe so interested in his own childhood? You need to see how things begin in order to understand what they become.

8

Leipzig

In accordance with his father's educational scheme, Goethe was sent at sixteen to study law at the University of Leipzig. His university teachers were uninspiring and he was never a diligent student but he was able to pursue other interests with considerable freedom. He was very well prepared for his legal studies; Leipzig seems to have offered little that had not already been covered at home with Caspar. He was given a generous allowance and letters of introduction to the most useful people – who often treated him with great kindness.

The letters of his we have from this period reveal a delightful young man of great vitality and amazing charm. Here he is writing to one of his friends back in Frankfurt:

'Today I have heard two lectures ... that'll do, eh? ... I haven't seen Gottsched [a well-known writer] yet. He's married again. She's nineteen, he is sixty-five. She is four feet, he is seven feet; she is as thin as a herring; he's as broad as a bed. I make a great figure here. But as yet I am no dandy. I never shall become one ... In society, concerts, theatre, feastings, promenades, the time flies. Ha! It goes gloriously. But also expensively. The devil knows how my purse feels it. Hold! Rescue! Stop! There go two louis d'or. Help! There goes another. Heavens! Another couple are gone.'

He practised drawing with an accomplished master, became interested in medical science (his dining club was composed mostly of medical students) and flirted with love. Leipzig, which was closely associated with the great Royal Court of Saxony at Dresden, had a reputation for elegance and sophistication. Here, Goethe became aware of his own provincialism. In reaction he became self-consciously smart.

Courtly culture was, in the middle of the eighteenth century, the focus not only of fashion but also of intellectual life in Germany. Such a culture did not disdain writing but it repudiated publication. Its ideal was the 'occasional' work written for a few individuals known to the writer, rather than for anonymous middle-class readers. For example, Gottfried Leibniz, the outstanding philosophical figure of the previous generation, presented his theories and ideas in letters to his circle of mainly aristocratic correspondents. The image of the court poet writing verses for an intimate circle of friends held a deep, lifelong appeal for Goethe.

Goethe made friends with a rather louche character called Behrisch, thirty years of age and (until fast living got him sacked) tutor to a local young aristocrat. Behrisch lived – and drank, often enough with Wolfgang – in a place called Auerbach's Cellar. Goethe was to send Faust there for a riotous session, as his first encounter with the world of pleasure after the power of Mephistopheles has freed him from his academic job.

He kept up a correspondence with Cornelia, much of it written in French. She was still at home in Frankfurt and not very happy. In the absence of Wolfgang, Caspar's oppressive need to organize other people focused on his rather awkward daughter. What was to become of her? No one, least of all Caspar, had any good ideas.

In Leipzig, Goethe became attached to Käthchen Schönkopf – whose family owned the inn where he took many of his meals. She was slightly older: twenty to his seventeen. 'Good full figure; a friendly, round face – not an amazing beauty – but a gentle, open, captivating expression. She's very confident, but not a coquette; beautifully intelligent, but without having had all that much education.'

There was an unpassable social divide between them – Goethe was an educated young gentleman, she was the daughter of an innkeeper. Both must have been quite aware that they were acting out – however sincerely – a generic romance: the student affair. Goethe was wholly under his father's rule – legally as well as economically; it was inconceivable that Caspar would consent to a marriage. Goethe forced himself to break up with Käthchen, and did so at the end of April 1768. He explained to Behrisch that he loved Käthchen and couldn't bear to separate but he had to because he could not marry her and he must not let her think that he might. He clearly managed the break delicately and well because not so long after – when he was back in Frankfurt – he was writing in his most genial style to the whole family.

'Your servant, Herr Schönkopf! How do you do, Madame? Good evening, Mademoiselle; Peterkin, good evening!

'N.B. You must imagine coming in by the little parlour door. You, Herr Schönkopf, are sitting on the sofa by the warm stove. Madame in her little corner, behind her desk; Peter is on the floor under the stove. And if Käthchen is sitting in my place at the window she only has to stand up to make room for the visitor. Now I begin to orate.[. . .]

'By the way, you will surely have forgiven me for not saying farewell. I was in the neighbourhood, I was actually at your door, I saw the light burning and went as far as the stairway, but I did not have the heart to go up. The last time, how could I ever have come down again?

'So I'm now doing what I should have done then, I am thanking you for all the love and friendship that you so constantly showed me and that I shall never forget.'

Over the next few months, Goethe wrote a play about Käthchen and himself, called *Partners in Guilt*; rather than analyse the relationship – which was later to be his speciality – he projects into the near future, developing a common fantasy: that of returning to someone you have ditched. A young nobleman by the name of Alcest comes back to the inn he had frequented in his student days (Goethe took this role himself in the first performance of the play nine years later). He finds his old girlfriend, Sophie, is now married to a boorish drunkard. Goethe was no stranger to the casually cruel hope that those we leave will be unhappy without us.

Alcest receives a letter and the nosy old innkeeper, Sophie's father, decides to sneak up to Alcest's room and find out what the letter is

about. The drunken husband, however, immediately takes advantage
of Alcest's absence to enter his room and steal his purse full of gold.
Later the old man goes up to Alcest's room to find the letter and while
he's there he hears the sound of a woman's footsteps. The father hides
and Sophie and Alcest come in. Before she leaves, Sophie realizes that
her father is hiding in the room. Alcest retires and the innkeeper makes
his escape.

The next morning Alcest realizes that his purse has been stolen and
alerts the old man. Sophie hears about the theft and of course assumes
that her father has taken the money – since she knows he was in the
room the previous evening. Finally all is revealed. It's a reasonably
witty derivation from the comedies of Molière – and very loosely
inspired by Shakespeare's fondness for deception and confusion
among the characters while all is clear to the audience. However, the
circumstances are so contrived and the denouement so predictable
that it is hard to feel any deep admiration for the play.

Its biographical interest lies in the way in which Goethe uses drama
to approach a fantasy. He would like to go back and find Käthchen
still in love with him – but married to someone horrible. He could
then be loved and yet safe from the consequences of love: responsibility
for the welfare of another, marriage.

Goethe did not complete his studies; falling seriously ill at the end of
his third year and leaving Leipzig on his nineteenth birthday he
returned home without a degree for a long convalescence. He had
some kind of nervous collapse; there was damage to one of his lungs
('I spewed blood') and trouble with his bowels. The months of recuper-
ation at home in Frankfurt were difficult. This was not at all what his
father had expected. Young Goethe was supposed to be racing towards
a distinguished civic career. And here he was not yet twenty and
apparently at death's door. Emotionally it was too complicated for
Caspar: the harshness of disappointment competing with a natural
anxiety about his son's health.

These months, for Goethe, were marked by an intensely religious
attitude – fostered no doubt by the gravity of his illness and encouraged
by some pious friends of his mother who were, understandably,

attracted to this pale and interesting young man; especially one Frau von Klettenberg whose religious ardour, in turn, fascinated Goethe. For a while he took up her Pietism; it was a widespread movement in Germany at that time, striving towards an inward, spiritual Christianity. Pietism took some of the established Protestant tenets to a logical extreme. It made the quality of the individual's relation to God, as experienced in the movements of their thoughts and feelings, the essential basis of salvation. One is saved, ultimately, by the depth of one's heart. The value of an action depends entirely upon the motive which inspired it.

The central thing Goethe took from Pietism was its 'inwardness'. It paid close attention to the secret drama of feelings: the complex transitions of doubt, hope, despair and shame; the dawning of faith, the grandeur of certainty – as well as the infinite possibilities of spiritual pride and self-deception. Goethe was to discover here a great reserve of artistic capital. He applied this style of self-awareness to his relationships – not with God and the Devil but with girls.

Goethe, here, provides a model of how we might regard those parts of our past from which we have 'moved on'. Rather than consign our earlier enthusiasms to the dustbin we should try to see what the underlying attachment was. This is a vision of how we might preserve life from episodic fragmentation. We will not have the same overt interests across the whole of life – so how can we make life feel coherent and continuous? Our early passions are imperfect sketches of maturity; if we throw them away we are continually starting at the beginning. If we are too nostalgic – on the other hand – we cannot see these as errors, only as lovely things we have lost. In effect, Goethe is asking: how do we learn from our mistakes? Which means admitting that they are mistakes, but not merely stupid. The suggestion is that mistakes are only partial – an error is a truth badly expressed. But to make use of this we have to look with a mixture of generosity and unsentimental clarity at our past loves and enthusiasms.

In *Partners in Guilt* Goethe showed himself as a highly competent technician, an adept at naturalistic observation of real people. He can move them about from scene to scene in a convincing way. But it is all external; the drama deals only with a sequence of events. Goethe was – over the next three years – to take his first steps as a great literary artist when he learned to combine this technical facility with an astonishingly sensitive delineation of the inner processes of the heart and mind.

The perfect place

As he recovered his health Goethe shook off the pietistic attitude, and was soon calling himself a 'pagan'; but this religious episode provided him with experience of which he could later make use – he did so particularly in *Wilhelm Meister*, which is the central work of Goethe's oeuvre precisely because it digests the widest range of his own experience. Goethe was basically indifferent to all accepted forms of religious practice but he didn't find it difficult to get on with religious people; he sustained close relationships for many years with intensely religious characters. He didn't repudiate his own experience – although he passed on from it; he didn't come to despise this ill self who had been so moved by discussions of divine love.

A drawing from this period – almost certainly a self-portrait – shows Goethe in his attic room at the top of his parents' house. The young man is seated on a high-backed chair at a writing table by the window, concentrating on his work. Behind him we see an easel supporting a landscape painting. Near to hand there is a table with a bottle of wine and a glass; his coat has been thrown over a chair, his sword hangs from a peg. On the walls there are sketches and drawings. It's an amateurish sketch but it presents a beguiling image of a young man full of his own projects and energetically getting on with them.

9

Strasbourg

When he finally recovered his health Goethe was sent to Strasbourg to undertake a doctorate in law, arriving there early in April 1770. Although essentially a German city and situated not far from the Rhine, Strasbourg was then, as now, in France; with a population of some forty thousand it was of broadly similar size to Frankfurt.

Goethe, now twenty, with his years at Leipzig and his illness to give him polish and depth, was a handsome youth. He was a little above average height and held himself well; he was very keen on fencing. His high spirits, dramatic brow, magnificent eyes and huge self-confidence made him a natural favourite and leader among his fellow students.

He gave little time to his official studies and eventually received only a less prestigious 'licence' granted on the basis of disputation rather than a dissertation (his dissertation was rejected). This was disappointing to his father, who had looked forward to having the manuscript published. But the time at Strasbourg was extremely important to Goethe. It was there, in September 1770, that he met Herder, one of the most powerful personalities and most original thinkers of eighteenth-century German culture.

Born in 1744, Johann Gottfried Herder was five years older than Goethe. He was a charismatic figure, an ambitious cleric and a prophet of Romanticism. He argued for the equality, but mutual incomprehension, of different cultures and epochs. In implying that French culture was not superior to all others, that the ancient Greeks were, in fact, rather mysterious, Herder was reversing the assumptions of his day. He claimed that each culture has its own particular character and strengths: what he called 'its own centre of happiness'.

Herder: he admired all societies – except the one he happened to live in

An underlying aim of Herder's thesis was to encourage respect for societies and eras that might otherwise have been regarded with condescension. Herder, for example, encouraged Goethe's interest in Gothic architecture – thoroughly out of fashion at the time. Goethe was to give Herder's historical generosity a more intimate and personal application. We can understand something of Goethe's character as a poet if we think of him as not condescending to many of the aspects of life that had been disowned by preceding German poets. Goethe takes themes like childhood, sex, flirtation and selfishness seriously.

Herder was a difficult man to be friends with. This was partly due to continual suffering – he was actually in Strasbourg only so that an operation could be performed on his eye. He was confined to a dark room; Goethe was a regular visitor to the sick bed.

Herder had a marked dislike of France and aristocrats: the two were closely associated in his mind because of the widespread adoption of French manners and style in the courts of the German states. In principle, Herder argued, French culture was valid – in France, where it was connected to a whole multitude of specific facts: the climate, traditions, social structure, schools, language. But transplanted to Germany, it became an absurdity – a mere aping of a foreign way of life that could never really be successful. Unfortunately, French culture developed a kind of pride: the assumption of the Enlightenment philosophers was that 'reason' could solve all human problems – and that the 'solution' would not need to vary from one place to another. Voltaire, for example, would dismiss as superstition the very myths and traditions which Herder thought had to be the foundation of human satisfaction – as achieved in a particular historical society.

The Voltaire-led drive against superstition and myth was an attempt to replace all obscure beliefs with clear and precise explanations: hence the image of 'enlightenment' bringing lucidity to the dark realms of error and confusion. By contrast, Herder – and soon Goethe – retained an admiration for a kind of inarticulacy, for those inchoate emotions and sensations which resisted explanation or simple statement but which were none the less felt to be central to experience. Goethe was to christen such attitudes 'dumpf': dull and muffled.

Visually the city of Strasbourg was dominated by its twelfth-century cathedral, which was the inspiration for Goethe's first public essay, 'On German Architecture', a vivid and journalistic little piece, written in 1771 when he was twenty-two and published in Frankfurt three years later.

At that time, 'Gothic' was the name given to architecture outside the classical tradition; it was dismissed as barbarous and inept. Contemporary French architecture was, by contrast, regarded as rational. Goethe defends the Gothic style of the Strasbourg Minster as the expression, or manifestation, of feeling. It cannot be justified according to rules, he says. Devotion to rules and reason has withered the capacity for feeling in the modern era. Reversing the hierarchy of mind and heart – but employing its crude terms – Goethe denigrates reason and elevates feeling. It is a 'dumpf' building: it cannot tell you its message in clear sentences: it is too deep for that. It was later to become clear that the medieval architect of the cathedral, Erwin von Steinbach, had actually carried out a highly intellectual project integrating sophisticated theories of proportion and complex principles of engineering.

Goethe glories in his own unorthodox enthusiasm, predicting (in fact, hoping) that many readers will feel disgusted by his attack on the

Strasbourg Cathedral: a 'dumpf' building

highly esteemed classical tradition. In Rome the local populace relieve themselves in the colonnades of St Peter's, he jeers. He revels in the possibility of offence: 'If this makes an unpleasant impression on you, or none at all, good luck to you, harness your horses and be off to Paris.'

It does make an unpleasant impression – but not for the reasons Goethe intended. The weakness of the argument sits badly with the swagger of the prose. Nevertheless there was something here that was genuine. He wants to admit passion and inarticulate love; he is resistant to petty rules and routine admiration. But in this early essay he can only assert what he cares about by cheaply denigrating other things. Goethe had never been to Paris, there is no personal experience behind his attack on classical buildings – why on earth should he hate the colonnades of St Peter's? It's just a pose borrowed from Herder. By the time he was forty Goethe was rhapsodizing about Palladio – the most un-Germanic of architects by the standards of this essay – and blissfully casting off all northern gloom.

In addition to inspiring this immature outburst, the cathedral was to figure in one of the core representative occurrences of Goethe's life. He wanted to climb up to the top of the extremely high tower to enjoy the view but the thought of standing on such a small space so high up terrified him – very understandably so as there were no protective railings around the platform. Goethe set himself to conquer this fear and gradually, by repeated attempts, completely overcame his fear and was able to enjoy the wonderful prospect without anxiety.

In itself this sounds like a rather trivial achievement but for Goethe it was hugely important. He was firmly attached to the idea that we can deliberately make improvements in our lives: we can master ourselves even though our initial resistance is quite intense. But the point of self-mastery is not the avoidance of evil – Goethe did not think it was morally wicked to be scared of falling off a tower. Simply, he was held back from doing something he really wanted to do. The point of self-mastery here isn't to keep oneself good or pure or to resist temptation; we may need to overcome our fears to do some of the things we most want. Self-mastery, here, is the means to pleasure, not the mechanism for resisting its allure.

The appeal of 'dumpf' was not confined to buildings. A human version of it turns up in English literature, particularly in Goethe's favourite novel at the time: *The Vicar of Wakefield*, written in 1766 by Oliver Goldsmith. The vicar is an honest-hearted, kindly – rather simple – man; menaced by several misfortunes he none the less stays true to his traditional and decent convictions. A typically English hero of modesty (like Trollope's Mr Harding in *The Warden*), he has a naive, wholesome character quite alien to the spirit of Voltaire.

The most charming scenes of that novel describe the happy domestic life in the parsonage. And this sensibility is the key to Goethe's next really significant romantic attachment – there were to be many more over the years. Riding out from Strasbourg he became a frequent visitor of Friederike Brion in nearby Sessenheim. She was the daughter of an intelligent and cultivated pastor, the German equivalent of the vicar of Wakefield.

As with the Schönkopfs in Leipzig, Goethe got on very well with the whole family. The day of his first visit he pretended to be a poor theology student and charmed the father with his interest in divinity. The next morning he dressed in his smartest clothes, appearing as the perfect young plutocrat – except he used a burnt cork to extend his eyebrows, making them meet in the middle. He thought this would make a more imposing impression. Friederike sounds like an early Jane Austen heroine – lively and sharp witted. She and Goethe danced and went for walks in the moonlight. She was eighteen, Goethe twenty-one. Whether or not they slept together, it seems clear that Friederike and her family thought that Goethe would marry her.

Perhaps Goethe himself thought that in the brief time when he was with her in the country and their life was confined to the pleasant parsonage, the local meadows, country-dances and picnics. But when Friederike came to Strasbourg and he saw her there she made a much less favourable impression. Town Friederike was no match for the more urbane girls he was meeting.

Goethe simply abandoned Friederike by heading back to Frankfurt, probably not even taking leave in person. This abrupt exit seriously compromised her; the Brion family eventually had most of the letters relating to the matter destroyed. Friederike was never to marry.

One of Goethe's best poems of this period describes the departure of a lover. The last two lines run: 'I went, you stood, your eyes on the ground; you gazed after me through your tears./But what a joy it is to love and, my God, what joy to be loved.' Whether or not this is a description of a parting from Friederike, it is suggestive of the spirit in which Goethe took off. The ease with which he won her love seems to have made him aware of something powerful in himself; as if to say: if she loves me, who else might I find?

It wasn't exactly an abstract question – Strasbourg was not short of young women who found Goethe deeply appealing. His dancing master – Goethe was learning to waltz – for example, had two lively daughters who acted as partners during the lessons. Emilia, the younger, was particularly appealing, but she was already attached to another man. Her elder sister, Lucinda, fell in love with the handsome pupil – and became jealous, of course, of her sister.

The pleasant triangle of flirtation came to grief when a fortune-teller visited the house after one of the lessons, while Goethe was still chatting with the girls. Emilia was keen to learn what her lover was up to. When Lucinda was told her fate the news was grim: you love, but are not loved; the one you love loves another. Lucinda naturally enough regarded her sister as 'the other' and rushed from the room.

When Goethe got up to escape this unpleasant situation Emilia drew him towards her. Despite her other beau, she confessed she was half in love with Goethe; since they were alone at last she took the opportunity for a quick kiss. At this point Lucinda dashed back in, grabbed Goethe from her sister's embrace, cursed him for ever and kissed him in the wildest passion. Goethe had to abandon his lessons and never mastered the waltz.

10

Dr Goethe

After finishing his studies and receiving his licence – which rather generously carried the title of 'Doctor' – Goethe headed back in August 1771 to his parents' house, just in time to be admitted to the Frankfurt bar as an advocate on his twenty-second birthday.

He occupied himself rather fitfully with legal work – practising from an office at home alongside another literary-minded lawyer called Georg Schlosser, who was eventually to marry Cornelia. But much more of Goethe's efforts were devoted to writing. The cathedral essay came to the attention of a wider audience through being reprinted in a collection of essays brought together under Herder's direction and entitled *Of German Style and Art*. This collection came to be regarded as the 'manifesto' of the Sturm und Drang movement – the cult of Storm and Stress.

The movement got its name from the title of a play by Goethe's friend Friedrich Klinger, although the play *Sturm und Drang* wasn't actually written until a few years later, in 1776. The movement was an attempt to break out of what was seen as the unduly narrow confines of both the small-scale world of prudent practicality and the Enlightenment vision of reasonableness. To give it a personal turn, it was directed against the likes of Caspar and against Voltaire. It was an essentially youthful, almost adolescent, cult: not only in its adulation of energy and 'breaking through' and 'breaking down', and its diffuse, ardent longing for 'change'; but also, and more so, in that it had no positive vision of what things might be like after the cataclysm. Primarily its adherents wanted to be free to pursue wine, women and song, to stamp about the countryside. This was pretty much what they were doing at present – the problem was that they were going to have to stop: the transition from student life to adult responsibility (respectable employment, marriage, children) was what they feared.

Goethe was regarded as a champion of this cause – and it is not hard to see why. He got involved in a new periodical, the *Frankfurter Gelehrten Anziegen* – a kind of 'Frankfurt Review of Books'. The editor was Johann Heinrich Merck – eight years older than Goethe, a trained lawyer, connoisseur of the arts and man of business. Merck was fascinating: he had a brightly destructive wit, adept at mocking the falsehoods, confusions, errors and pretensions of others.

The best thing Goethe wrote for the *FGA* was a satire on Christoph Martin Wieland, a very respectable writer living in Weimar. Wieland had portrayed the visit of Hercules to Hades, from where he rescued Alcestis – a woman who had sacrificed herself to save her husband. What the young men of Frankfurt objected to were the genteel attitudes and delicate manners given to the heroic characters – could this foppish, polite and refined person really be the great Hercules who spent his time wrestling with lions and clubbing bears?

Sitting down one afternoon with a bottle of claret at his elbow, Goethe wrote the perfect satirical review – in the form of a miniature play. Wieland is snoring in his bed when he suddenly awakes to find some ruffians in his room. Who can they be? 'We're Hercules and the rest of the gang.' And, of course, he cannot recognize them – since his image is so inadequate to their heroic qualities.

This lively, pointed article went down well and everyone had a laugh at Wieland's expense – including Wieland, who was an extremely good-natured man with whom Goethe was later to establish a very cordial friendship.

A much more substantial contribution to the cause of Storm and Stress and the dream, or nightmare, of 'authentic' German literature came in Goethe's first really successful drama: *Götz von Berlichingen* (1773). Herder was the major influence on the play. He had called for a German Shakespeare who would write historical dramas to forge a sense of national identity and destiny.

Goethe's 'History Play' picks upon actual events but transforms them to suit his dramatic needs. The story is set in the sixteenth century in the early days of the Reformation; Martin Luther has a walk-on role. Götz is the representative of the traditional Teutonic virtues: he is forthright, courageous and loyal to the Emperor but otherwise ferociously independent. One of his hands, having been severed in battle, has been replaced with an iron fist. But for all his merits Götz is not able to adapt to the demands of the emerging modern state, which requires diplomacy and bureaucratic administrative ability.

The play was well received – a publisher asked for ten more just like it – but has largely been forgotten. Despite its encouraging reception, *Götz* didn't bring Goethe any money; in fact he lost money because he had it printed privately, borrowing from Merck to raise the funds. It had, however, a belated impact. Twenty-five years later, in 1798, the play was translated by young Walter Scott. *Götz* was an important model for his own incredibly successful historical romances.

In effect Götz is the vicar of Wakefield transposed to the heroic plane. Their virtues are essentially simple and appealing; yet success in life requires adaptation to the way the world is; you need to be diplomatic or cunning or devious to keep up. The core idea is this: to be good, to be a hero, is – in essence – incompatible with flourishing in the modern world. This is an ideology of failure: I am bad because I am good; other people are to blame for my troubles. It is hardly surprising that this attitude – so generous to our troubles – has always had its devotees.

Martin Luther plays a very small part in the play: he meets Götz in the woods for about five minutes – just long enough to sound off against sexual abstinence. But he is quite a helpful point of reference. Luther was not really a great thinker: his impact upon his countrymen did not come from sophisticated theology or compelling argument.

Luther's position, baldly stated, comes to this: religion has to make sense in straightforward emotional terms. His famous declaration 'Here I stand, I can do no other' is absorbed into the Sturm und Drang view of life. The great things are not done by calculation, the great moves in human culture are not the product of careful reasoning: they are the firm assertions of faith: this is what I am; don't weary me with argument. Sincerity and passion are what count.

Götz is a troubling kind of hero: he stands for authenticity and individuality but he cannot hold out against a more powerful social order. The centralized bureaucratic state is determined to bring him to heel. Although Götz is a figure from the past he speaks to the modern sense of being alienated from one's time, worn down by petty demands. Shuffling his legal briefs – and all too often laying them aside – Goethe created a character who speaks to our fears: all that is fine or noble in us will be of no help in 'getting on'. Our longing for personal fulfilment and the demands of the world are on a collision course.

In choosing Götz as a hero for his first major work, Goethe was trying out one way in which he himself – as a writer – could be a hero: the heroic writer creates the dramas of national identity. Ironically Goethe was not very good at this, and precisely because he was already on the way to being a great writer. For Goethe gives Götz a fate which cannot ground a specifically national story, for it is universal in its implications. The fine loyalties by which Götz lives his life are not adequate to the demands of living in the emerging modern world. Thus Goethe broaches the question that was to dominate his work for the rest of his life: if we don't want to be tragic heroes, how are we to live in a very imperfect world: the only world we have?

PART TWO

Love

Love, my love:
The golden beauty of daybreak
Firing over the misty hills.
Goethe, *May Song*, May 1771

I

Wetzlar

In line with Caspar's plan for his son's career, Goethe's next step was a stint at the Imperial Court of Appeal, located in Wetzlar – only thirty-two miles north of Frankfurt – where he went in May 1772, a few months short of his twenty-third birthday. Wetzlar itself was tiny – a mere six thousand inhabitants, of whom about one fifth were directly involved in the work of the court. It was an ancient town, the old Gothic houses were connected by steeply stepped streets; it was notoriously dirty, with very little in the way of public sanitation (something on which Goethe always had strong views).

The court had been established to resolve disputes between the individual states that constituted the Empire. Inadequately funded and lacking in authority, its proceedings had become unbelievably entangled. A backlog of sixteen thousand cases – some of which had been up for review for over a century – were adjudicated at a rate of about one hundred per year.

If the cause of justice was little advanced at the Imperial Court of Appeal, Goethe's time in Wetzlar provided the material for his next literary success – the greatest public success of his life: *The Sorrows of Young Werther*. Officially there to further his legal career, Goethe made no secret of his preoccupation with the poetry of Homer and Pindar. His father's wealth was well known, as were Goethe's literary achievements, and the other young men attached to the court were eager to seek his acquaintance.

With the drama of Götz, Goethe had spoken to a nostalgic inclination in the rising generation of successful young professionals. The men who went to Wetzlar were either wealthy or nobly born and saw the move as a step towards senior administrative positions. Perhaps for this very reason they admired Götz and imagined themselves as being just like him, rather than as they really were – just like his enemies.

Shortly after his arrival, on 9 June, Goethe attended a ball, for just twelve couples, at Volpertshausen, a small village not far from Wetzlar. The group he went with included a very pleasant young woman – nineteen-year-old Charlotte Buff. She was lively and physically attractive in a rather conventional style.

Lotte: the unavailable object of love

Goethe was rather taken with her and the next day he called at her family home. Her father was the regional administrator of the Order of Teutonic Knights, a wealthy, aristocratic society. The Buffs occupied a sort of grand farmhouse with an appealing mixture of rustic and sophisticated features.

Goethe was enchanted by the whole, big family and soon discovered that Charlotte was informally engaged to a certain Johann Christian

Kestner. Kestner, at thirty-one, was eight years Goethe's senior: he was a serious and industrious man, cultivated and obviously intelligent. Like Goethe, he was attached to the Imperial Court. Unlike Goethe, Kestner was diligently pursuing his career. He used to find it half-amusing, half-irritating to drop in after long hours drawing up legal documents to find Goethe sitting with Charlotte shelling peas in the kitchen garden. But Kestner need not have worried. Charlotte was sensible enough to see that Goethe could spend time being sweet and interesting because there wasn't anything else he had to be. She didn't hold Kestner's absence against him because she understood that he was working hard to establish himself comfortably so that they could get married.

The events of the next few weeks were to fix the three of them – Goethe, Kestner and Charlotte – in the public imagination for the rest of their lives and indeed down to the present day. Goethe and Kestner quickly became friends. Kestner was conscious of his advantage in age. He was sensitive to Goethe's character; he liked his young friend's imaginative verve, his complexity and intensity, his independence of mind, his ease with women and children.

Kestner and Goethe took long walks together and enjoyed wide-ranging, speculative conversation. In a tantalizing entry in his journal, Kestner records how one evening they spent hours walking through the moonlit streets of Wetzlar, talking of everything, finally leaning against a wall helpless with laughter.

Then Goethe fell in love with Charlotte. He was thrilled if she sent him a note; he needed to see her every day – and that was all he needed – nothing else mattered. His passion for Charlotte was like a lamp, illuminating everything else in his life; without that light everything would be bleak and pointless. That, at least, is how it seemed to Goethe at the time; but it wasn't easy to see how the lantern could continue to burn – since Charlotte obviously was going to marry Kestner.

Kestner knew of Goethe's obsession but he never took Goethe seriously as a rival. He was quietly – and rightly – confident that his Lottchen, as they called her, was not in love with the young writer.

Goethe quickly acknowledged that Lotte would never offer him more than friendship; she knew just how to behave so that hope, for more, was given no encouragement.

If this situation was painful, Goethe soon had the sharp and sceptical Merck – on a flying visit to Wetzlar – to give him advice. Merck put things plainly: Lotte was lovely but Goethe would not be able to prise her away from Kestner. Even if he could, it would be an extremely stupid thing to do. If she were to break her engagement, it could only be for the sake of marrying Goethe. Did he want to get married? More than likely he would bolt off to Switzerland or somewhere and repeat, in even more serious fashion, the trauma of Sessenheim and Friederike: devastation for a girl he liked, guilt for himself.

Merck brought word that Goethe's sister, Cornelia, had just become engaged to Schlosser. Schlosser, Goethe's legal partner and colleague on the *FGA*, was like Kestner: cultivated, conscientious, older than Goethe but highly appreciative of the younger man's qualities. Nevertheless, Goethe was not at all pleased by this news. He was worried – with some justification – that the proposed marriage would not be a success. This was not a criticism of Schlosser, though; rather, it was Goethe's firm view that Cornelia should never marry.

Goethe thought of his sister as being, essentially, a spiritual leader of women – he called her an 'abbess'. This was also how Cornelia saw herself. Things were going badly for her at home. Caspar's controlling grip – so evident in his 'life-plan' for his son – had tightened on his daughter during the years Wolfgang had been away in Leipzig, Strasbourg and now Wetzlar. Cornelia – her brother knew – didn't want to get married. But she had come to see marriage as a necessary means of escape. Decent, unloved Schlosser was the lesser of two evils.

The increasingly tense triangular relationship of Goethe, Charlotte and Kestner fell apart. Goethe wanted something impossible: everything to stay as it was – Kestner always the prospective husband, himself the permanent lover. He did not even need to be Charlotte's lover in a sexual sense; he wanted to be the privileged object of her amorous regard. While such arrangements might seem enticing in theory their chances of success in reality are obviously slender. Goethe wanted something very specific from Charlotte: intense romantic friendship, intimate conversation, kisses in the moonlight, holding hands. He sought to make permanent the fleeting experience of falling in love.

The problem was that Charlotte did not share such tastes. She was fairly straightforward and conventional, not a romantic virtuoso. She wanted a successful, respectable husband, plenty of children, a fine house. And in fact this is what she got with Kestner. The pain for Goethe was that he was attracted to women like Charlotte: he loved her domesticity, her simplicity and wholesome normality. Of course, it was just those qualities – the absence of erotic or emotional complexity – that made her want just the kind of relationship that Goethe could not offer. He wanted a sophisticated relationship with a simple woman.

Eventually, Goethe did the right thing. He made himself put out the lamp. On 11 September 1773, at seven in the morning, having sent a brief farewell note to Charlotte and Kestner, Goethe left Wetzlar. He had been there only five months. This departure was the moral equivalent of going up the tower of Strasbourg Cathedral – forcing himself to renounce a longing in this case, rather than face a fear. That he parted from it in good grace is evident from the fact that he was soon in friendly correspondence with Kestner.

2

Werther's Passion

Two months later, back home in Frankfurt, Goethe received a long letter from Kestner. It told of the suicide of a mutual Wetzlar acquaintance – Carl Jerusalem. Neither of them had known him well; but his face had been familiar to Goethe for several years; they had been at Leipzig together; as it happened Jerusalem had been at the very same Volpertshausen ball where Goethe had met Charlotte. He was from a wealthy family and had a considerable aptitude for philosophy, some of his essays being published posthumously under the editorship of Gotthold Ephraim Lessing.

Jerusalem, it turned out, had been secretly in love with the wife of one of his colleagues but she had rejected him. She told her husband and forbade the young man to see her. Kestner had become entangled in the tragedy. Jerusalem said he was going on a journey and borrowed a pair of pistols from Kestner – an unremarkable precaution at the time. Young Jerusalem then blew his brains out.

Kestner's letter was of great importance to Goethe. Three months later, when he started writing *Werther*, he lifted many details directly from the account. The novel is closely derived from its main sources: Goethe's attachment to Lotte who is contentedly engaged to Kestner and the events leading up to and surrounding Jerusalem's suicide. So much so that to tell the story of these sources is largely to reveal the plot of the novel.

A short note from a fictional editor prefaces the story of Werther:
'I have carefully collected whatever I have been able to learn of the story of poor Werther and present it to you, knowing that you will

thank me for it. To his spirit and character you cannot refuse your admiration; to his fate you will not deny your tears.

'And you, good soul who suffer as he did, draw comfort from his sorrows; let this little book be your friend, when by fate – or through your own fault – you can find no more intimate companion.'

This is really a kind of artistic creed. A book can aspire to play the role a friend might; and this is a precious service because sometimes we are too weighed down by our troubles to find and sustain the sympathetic companionship of other people.

Werther is a young man of considerable ability and natural charm. He has arrived in the countryside to secure a legacy that has been withheld from his mother – and also, we are given to understand, to escape from an unfortunate romantic intrigue. It is May: the countryside is beautiful; the simple, traditional rural life, which Werther observes, enchants him. He is invited to a ball and his party includes a lovely young woman called Charlotte. The very first thing he hears about her – before he even sees her – is that she is engaged to an admirable man called Albert, who is currently away on business. At the ball Werther dances with Charlotte; they discover a shared taste for English novels; during a brief thunderstorm, Charlotte displays presence of mind, common sense and a pleasant, social grace.

Over the next days Werther falls in love with Lotte – as Charlotte is familiarly called. He plays with the younger brothers and sister – to whom Lotte has acted as a mother since her own mother's death. Werther visits her every day. For six weeks his attachment to Lotte grows. Werther hopes, perhaps believes, that she loves him, but nothing in her behaviour suggests that she feels more than friendship towards him.

The greater part of the novel is presented as a series of letters that Werther writes to a friend called Wilhelm – whose replies we never see. Thus we seem to be inside Werther's mind as he recounts, as it occurs, the process of falling in love. This sequence of letters is among the finest things Goethe ever wrote. The gradual deepening of the attraction is perfectly portrayed, so that Werther seems to be living through not just his own experience but a universal sequence of emotions. Attraction soon becomes devotion and there is a brief, blissful interlude of perfect contentment. But soon Werther requires more of Charlotte – if he doesn't see her for a day, if she neglects to send him a message or is slow in replying or doesn't pay him special attention, he is reduced to despair. She occupies all his thoughts: all his hopes and fears are focused on her.

It is a portrayal of the condition in which romantic love appears to be the meaning of life: the relationship with this person is the only thing that counts; when it is going well life seems wonderful; but this is a desperately unstable situation. The slightest hint of difficulty takes on the grandest proportions. It is not merely an attachment that is at risk: the meaning of life is in danger. If it is love that gives life meaning, any threat to love seems to make life pointless.

Eventually Albert, Lotte's husband-to-be, returns from his long business trip. He is 'a fine worthy fellow, whom one cannot help liking'. Werther begins behaving badly whenever he finds Albert and Lotte together. 'I am unable to bear it; behave like a fool; commit a thousand extravagancies. "For heaven's sake," said Charlotte today, "let us have no more scenes like those of last night."'

A few days later, Werther gets into an absurd dispute with Albert. Werther decides to spend a few days in the mountains and asks to borrow Albert's pistols – a simple and reasonable request. Albert agrees but mentions that he keeps his guns unloaded following an accident – when a servant fooling around with a gun which was believed to be unloaded ended up shooting one of the maids in the hand.

Werther takes up a pistol and holds it to his forehead. Albert is horrified: 'I cannot comprehend how a man can be so mad as to shoot himself.' Werther launches into a slightly hysterical defence of suicide, goaded by Albert's view that suicide is beyond the bounds of sympathy.

After six increasingly strained weeks Werther finally agrees to take a step his mother has long been recommending. He accepts an offer of a diplomatic post in a distant town.

*

Werther is intelligent and industrious; a fine career is open to him. But he encounters two obstacles. He does not get on easily with the ambassador, his employer, whom he considers a man of mediocre talents. Then on one occasion he is exposed to social humiliation: he inadvertently attends an aristocratic reception, a dreary occasion but one at which he has no right to appear, due to his non-noble birth. His host is obliged to ask him to leave. Soon Werther learns that this little incident is being talked about.

Rather than accommodate the imperfections of the world – imperfections that are irksome but far from fatal – Werther withdraws. He resigns his post. He hears of Albert's marriage to Charlotte. He toys with the idea of a military career. He visits the place where he lived as a child but it brings only melancholy thoughts about a time, now impossibly distant, when he was innocent and free.

Having been away for about ten months, he returns to live near Charlotte. He is now continually in a strained and miserable state. He thinks he sees some imperfections in the union of Albert and Charlotte. Everything in nature and in the fabric of society seems to reinforce Werther's desperation and his despair about life in general.

Werther's problem is not merely to do with Lotte. His experience with her seems to suggest something terrible about life. He regards love as sacred – as the most important emotion. However, there is no guarantee that love, however ardent, will be returned: that the world will meet it and reward it. He feels as if the most valuable thing that he has is useless in the world as it is. Existence is perverse.

Werther's misery is obvious to Lotte and she confronts him with a dose of common sense. She suggests that his devotion to her is exaggerated because she is unavailable. If she were unattached to Albert, Werther would soon have tired of her and moved on. In any case, she cannot be the only woman with whom he could be happy. His abilities and character are such that many courses of action are open to him; obviously he could form a new and more satisfying relationship.

These words are lost on Werther. But they are central to the novel. What Lotte says is obviously right, but Werther cannot make use of these simple truths. This reveals the central tension of the novel.

The extraordinary finesse with which Goethe has revealed Werther's passion for Lotte makes us sympathize deeply with him – in fact identify with him. His love is our experience of love. Yet Werther's life is collapsing, and it is his passion that is the cause of this. He prefers death to life without her.

Goethe made several additions to the text for a second edition of the novel (undertaken a decade or so later when it was included in an early edition of his collected works). One addition is particularly revealing. Werther is made to write a couple of lines amplifying the idea that Lotte loves him. This is striking because, in general, we hear very little about Lotte's feelings. Further, the addition is placed just after two letters in which Werther describes instances of self-deception. The authorial message seems clear: Werther is deceiving himself. This little insertion underscores a crucial feature of the whole work. We are not, in *Werther*, reading a story about lovers who are kept apart by a cruel or harsh society. It is not convention or propriety that stands in the way of Werther's love for Lotte. It is just that she does not fully reciprocate his love even though she likes Werther and wants him as a friend.

The tragedy is, therefore, more internal than we might initially have suspected. Werther is on the road to ruin, not because of the faults of the world, but because of some flaw in his inner condition. Werther's letters to Wilhelm open with a question: 'What is the heart of man?' A devastating answer is now proposed: it is a tragic organ that, in seeking fulfilment, destroys itself.

In one of his letters (dated 22 May) Werther suggests what this flaw is. The letter comes before the meeting with Lotte and is designed to intimate Werther's character apart from his relationship with her.

'It's occurred to many people that life is merely a dream – and I'm drawn to that feeling. When I see the narrow boundaries of action and thought within which we are confined; when I see how so much human effort is directed merely at satisfying our basic needs – and has no other ambition or aim; serving only to prolong one's poor life; when I see that the only comfort intellectual knowledge can bring us is a lesson in resignation (the most sophisticated teaching of literary philosophy is only this: put up with things) while the best art can do is decorate the walls of the prison house in which we live – all these thoughts leave me speechless, utterly dumb.

'I draw back upon myself and find a world within ... my dreams are real, but the world is a dream.

'...I know very well you will say that the happiest people are those who live like children. Children live only for the day, carrying their dolls around ... reserving the deepest respect for the cupboard where Mummy keeps the biscuits and cakes ... these are the happy creatures.'

In other words, the capacity to think and understand is fatal to human satisfaction; to search for meaning and depth and purpose in life is a sure route to depression; the best condition is to never think, never question, to be made happy by the simplest things – by biscuits and cakes.

This isn't a problem with social arrangements, with injustice or blocks to one's career. Rather, there is something fundamentally wrong with the human condition (Schopenhauer – who was much impressed by Goethe – called it the 'design fault' theory). We are given to reflection, to searching for meaning and purpose – but these are the very things that make satisfaction impossible.

This puts a rather different light on Werther's problems when he works as secretary to the ambassador and is taught some painful lessons about social hierarchies: he has to obey the ambassador, not because the ambassador is more intelligent or more wise, but simply because it is his job to do what he is told to do; he is unwelcome at an aristocratic party not because he is impolite or lacks merit – but simply because he was not born into the right sort of family.

These frustrations are so glaring that they appear to play an explanatory role. It can look as if what is unbearable to Werther is social injustice – at least so far as that impinges upon him. They provide a temporary 'alibi', a more reassuring explanation of his unhappiness. They play up to a Rousseau-inspired interpretation of life's problems – all is well with 'natural man' – it's just that 'artificial' social arrangements prevent us from living according to nature. And many readers would certainly have read *Werther* that way.

But we know that Werther's problems are of a different order – are problems which would not disappear were he to be made welcome at the party or receive an apology from the ambassador.

Thinking and feeling – intelligence and love – are the things we look to for meaning and through which we hope to be happy. And in a horrible, and horribly plausible, way, it is precisely these capacities that make Werther's world so bleak and empty.

3

Werther's Death

The problem Werther lives with and dies by – the problem that Goethe is presenting through Werther – can be understood by comparison with Rousseau. Like Rousseau, Goethe is deeply alive to the problems of civilization – to the ways in which social arrangements can frustrate us: why can't Werther and Albert share Lotte? Why can't Werther be appointed ambassador? Why does he have to have a job at all? But Goethe's difficulty is that he doesn't think these problems are the only ones we've got. It's not as if, by nature, we are free and happy and yet tragically society enslaves us. We are also unhappy 'by nature': the course of existence frequently denies us the things we long for – mutual love and the sense that life makes sense. But this looks like a problem with existence, rather than a problem with particular societies.

Charlotte's advice is the first glimmer of a solution. It comes to the demand that Werther must grow up. But what does it mean for someone like Werther to 'grow up'? What process of development or maturation is being invoked? This was the question that guided much of Goethe's later work; it provides the connecting theme that allows his later work – especially *Wilhelm Meister* and *Faust*, which are epics of personal growth – to be read as responses to *Werther*.

We can also apply the theme retrospectively to see the way in which *Werther* is a development from *Götz*. Götz is at odds with his world – but the problems, so far as the play is concerned, are all to do with other people. Götz is just fine as he is – he is loyal and courageous; the wickedness of others turns these virtues into liabilities.

However engaging the story that results from this assumption of the good person in a bad world, it cannot be humanly deep. The most potent problems we have do not stem from the wickedness of the world but from flaws within us. Since we cannot remake society to suit ourselves we have to acquire the capacities to flourish in the only world we have – this very imperfect, but perfectly real, one.

The novel changes its narrative form towards the end. Werther's letters give way to the fictitious editor's narrative – which is, in fact, very closely copied from Kestner's description of Jerusalem's last days and death.

Just before Christmas Werther, by now deeply distressed and beset by thoughts of suicide, calls on Lotte while Albert is out at work. He reads to her from Ossian. Goethe makes the mistake of reproducing several astonishingly tedious pages of this fake Gaelic epic. They weep. Werther falls at Lotte's feet then kisses her; she breaks from the embrace and locks herself in another room declaring that she will never see him again. The next day, Werther writes a note to Albert asking to borrow his pistols. Albert sends them and the next night Werther shoots himself. His servant discovers him in the morning and Werther dies at midday on Christmas Eve.

The closeness of the novel to its sources easily encourages the view that it is a mere transcription of experience: one is tempted to the view that it must have been rather easy to write.

Formally speaking, the novel is a perfect tragedy. It rigorously conforms to Aristotle's analysis of the best way in which to provoke fear and pity in the reader. Werther is clearly very likeable: intelligent, warm hearted, engaging. His demise comes about through a flaw in his character – his inability to break free from an impossible attachment. It is a flaw with which we can easily sympathize. His fall from happiness to misery is brought about by a succession of small steps, none of which is in the least implausible. It is not some malign force that strikes him down; it is just the normal conditions of life: a pretty girl already has a lover; one's talents are not fully appreciated at work; society contains exclusive but essentially petty cliques. Werther's fate is intimately shocking because it is so understandable as something that could happen to oneself.

Hearing only Werther's voice we are drawn into his world; and rather than imagining ourselves as the recipient of his letters, the 'you' to whom Werther's 'I' makes its address, we become the writer.

There is a species of vanity evident in Werther's suffering. He is proud of his suffering even as he communicates his despair. As if to say: I suffer because I am so fine.

And it must surely be this which lies behind the 'danger' of the book – and its power to draw unhappy lovers in. Werther provides an interpretation of unhappiness – a kind of ideology of misery – in which suffering is seen as more noble than contentment.

Thus it can be a bit of a shock to hear Goethe's own later one-line summation of the second, and tragic, part of the novel. Werther, he says, is a young man who loses himself in groundless speculation and self-absorption. In other words, Goethe didn't see Werther's tragedy as turning on thwarted love. It hinges on the condition of mind in which Werther faces what is after all a very normal experience – loving but not being loved as much in return. It isn't that Werther is the victim of an exceptionally unfortunate sequence of events. There is a fatal problem with the way he thinks and feels and this converts a series of rather ordinary difficulties into a personal catastrophe. Far from being admirable in his ways of thinking, Werther is himself a representative of a dangerous cultural decadence: sentimentalism.

Goethe writes with an intimate sympathy for extremes of despair and confusion; but he doesn't hold these up as glamorous or noble. He never loses sight of a commonsense proposition – that, after all, we are better off getting on with life. He displays a deep commitment to overcoming, rather than wallowing in, problems. We can understand how Goethe came to be seen as a champion of the Storm and Stress movement – even though this was a role he was uncomfortable with. With genuine Romantics he shared an interest in despair, passion and wildness; he didn't share their admiration for these extreme states.

It was therefore deeply ironic – though understandable – that the story of Werther should itself become the focus of a sentimental cult. It was absorbed into the very cultural attitude to which it is subtly, but seriously, opposed. No one would have loved the novel more than Werther himself: that is part of his tragedy.

Werther dies – as Jerusalem had – with a copy of Lessing's play *Emilia Galotti* open on his desk. This is, in part, a symptom of Werther's condition, as is his extended reading of Ossian. Far from recommending Ossian, Goethe privately remarked that Werther starts getting keen on it only once his mind has given way; in other words, a passion for Ossian is not in itself a good thing; rather, that passion is itself the symptom of an already disturbed state of mind.

Four decades later Goethe received a heart-rending letter from his very dear friend Carl Friedrich Zelter, the Berlin composer. Zelter's stepson had committed suicide, shooting himself in the mouth sitting on his bed in the family home. In his grief Zelter bitterly contrasts himself with Caspar – Goethe's father – whose son grew to be as substantial and fine as the family house in Frankfurt. And Zelter pleads: 'send me a healing word'.

In a long and loving reply, Goethe reverts to the period in which he wrote *Werther*. He himself suffered acutely the 'natural-unnatural' symptoms of suicidal despair. 'It took the greatest determination and effort to pull myself from the engulfing waves.'

4

Fame

The Werther novel was published at the Leipzig book fair in October 1774. By the end of the year Goethe, at twenty-five, was the most famous – although not the most respected – writer in Germany. In the next years he was to become – entirely on the strength of this single book, which was widely translated – the best-known German writer across Europe. That *Werther* immediately attracted a great deal of attention is not really surprising – the narrative is gripping and the style of writing is exceptionally attractive; it appears hardly to have been written at all but reads as the transcript of Werther's soul miraculously made public.

The story of Werther is written as if from the inside, and written with such immense plausibility that Werther appears to be the vehicle for Goethe's own emotional history. Werther *is* Goethe – up until the moment the bullet enters Werther's skull. If that's the case, then surely Lotte and Albert are real too. It was not long before Charlotte and Kestner, now married, were identified as characters in the novel. To be 'an Albert' (or a Kestner) became an insult: a byword for insensitive, philistine complacency. People thought that Lotte had been Goethe's mistress, or that if she hadn't she should have been.

Understandably, the Kestners were less than happy about this. In a letter written in November that year, just a few weeks after the book had been published, Kestner wrote to a friend outlining the actual situation.

'In the first part of "Werther", Werther is Goethe himself. Lotte and Albert borrow certain features and characteristics from my wife and from me. Many of the scenes are completely true, but quite a few are altered; others are completely alien to our experience with Goethe. To provide presentiments of Werther's eventual death, Goethe has added various things to the early sections which certainly never happened. Charlotte, for example, was never as close to Goethe, in the way the book describes Lotte's relationship to Werther – in fact she's never been that intimate with anyone. In general we take this rather ill, because quite a number of the incidental details are quite true and well known, so people can hardly help connecting those characters with us.

'The second part of the book has nothing to do with us; in that part, Werther is Jerusalem; Albert is drawn from the secretary to the Pfalsich legation; Lotte is the secretary's wife. I knew Jerusalem only slightly – my wife knew him even less; he kept very much to himself most of the time; he visited me only twice. He did actually write me the letter which Goethe included in the story; without thinking, and simply out of politeness, I sent him the pistols as he requested. They weren't loaded – I'd never even fired them. I discovered quite a bit about this singular business and wrote to Goethe about it when he was in Frankfurt.

'I'm quite sure Goethe didn't mean any harm; he has too high an opinion of my wife – and of me – for anything like that. That much is clear from his letters to us and from the rest of his behaviour. He really acted in a far more noble way than he describes Werther as doing.'

The book was well received by leading writers – Wieland and Klopstock admired it – as well as by the wider reading public. Parodies of the novel quickly followed: there was *Joys of the Young Werther* and *Sorrows of a Young Wertheress*. Goethe himself wrote a very short 'Joys of Werther': it turns out that Werther didn't kill himself, he merely damaged his eyes and singed his eyebrows; Albert took pity and gave Lotte to him. Werther and Lotte chat pleasantly about the novel: 'Remember what happened on page 29?'

For many years Goethe was plagued by the attention the book received. He was known everywhere as 'the author of Werther'. He recounts how this haunted him even in an isolated town in Sicily – at the furthest point of his wanderings.

Goethe's own ambivalence about this work is well illustrated in a conversation which his servant, Philipp Seidel, recorded. A member of the Frankfurt city council declares to Goethe that *Werther* is too extravagant. Goethe then likens the work to an episode of drunkenness. Most people can sleep it off and try to forget what they have said; only he has committed it all to paper in this novel. But though he makes this disparaging comparison he can't bear it when the councillor continues his attack, maintaining that *Werther* is dangerous. Goethe explodes and Seidel records him word for word: 'Dangerous! What do you mean dangerous? It's beasts like you who are dangerous, who contaminate everything around you with putrefaction, who beslobber and besmirch everything that is beautiful and good, and then try to convince the rest of the world that nothing is any better than their own excrement.'

Such outbursts, which were not untypical of Goethe, are an important antidote to the received image of him as the sage of Weimar, serene and wise and utterly self-assured. Nevertheless we might think that Goethe's rage on this occasion was fuelled by a real anxiety – or rather frustration. His book was indeed dangerous, but dangerous not because of its actual character but because of the ways in which it could be misunderstood – and evidently was being misunderstood, by many of those who most intensely admired it.

Young men took to wearing the 'Werther' costume: a blue coat, yellow waistcoat, white breeches and riding boots – the clothes that Jerusalem had been wearing at the end. Scenes from the story were illustrated again and again. The fame of the novel was commercially exploited: fashionable people might use 'Eau de Werther', drink tea from a 'Werther' cup; they could take long walks through the woods, muttering bits of Homer and Ossian, and generally enjoy a bout of 'Werther fever'. Desperate young men and women were reported to have followed Werther's example, dying with a copy of *Werther* before them – open at the page where he kills himself. (In fact no such cases have been authenticated.)

Half a century later, Goethe's friend – and chronicler of his last years – Johann Peter Eckermann was to offer what is perhaps the truest explanation of the public success of *Werther*. At all times, there is a great deal of private, unacknowledged misery in the world; all Goethe did was to bring this to the surface in a sympathetic manner.

5

Lili

Not long after he had – inadvertently – made himself a celebrity by drawing upon the intimate history of his relationship with Charlotte Buff, Goethe fell in love again, this time with a local Frankfurt girl, Lili Schönemann. They met in the early days of January 1775, about three months after the publication of *Werther*. Lili was the sixteen-year-old daughter of a Frankfurt banker – her father was apparently very wealthy and the family lived in grand style. She was charming, accomplished and clearly very attracted to Goethe.

Lili was rather different from the girls Goethe had previously been involved with. The recent Charlotte and the earlier Friederike were essentially country girls – well brought up and very civil to be sure, but not sophisticated. They were nice looking, but nothing special. In those cases, it seems clear that Goethe was the emotionally active partner to begin with – he was the one working his way into the heart of another person. By contrast, Lili was self-consciously seductive.

Her look is full of erotic knowledge. And her charms were not limited to her appearance. She had a passion for sharing little secrets with men – and such confidences, she playfully admitted, necessarily included the revelation of her intimate weaknesses. One of these, she confessed, was the need to toy with potential admirers. She could hardly help herself: she needed to gain the love of men and then exercise the power of rebuffing them.

Of course in admitting this to Goethe she was entering delicate territory. Was she using this revelation itself to draw him in, with the intention of casting him off once she was sure she had him? Was she, perhaps, gently hinting that she understood him – for, to any

Lili: what did her raised eyebrow mean to Goethe?

unsympathetic outsider, it might well have looked as if she was describing Goethe's own emotional pattern. Had he 'done a Lili' on Charlotte, Friederike and Käthchen? But then there was another possibility: Lili was identifying common ground – they were both rather predatory, rather wicked, and hence, perhaps, the perfect partners: partners in guilt, she might have said, drawing on the title of Goethe's earlier play. Or was she meeting in Goethe a kind of retribution? She exercised her powers of attraction on the young celebrity, promising herself the rare pleasure of casting him adrift, only to discover that she was unable to ditch him.

Such layers of interpretation could hardly have come from straightforward girls like Charlotte or Friederike. Goethe was certainly enchanted and in old age he liked to say that Lili was the one true love of his life. This can hardly mean that he loved Lili more than the others; but it does pick up on something: Lili was perhaps someone he really could have married.

In fact, he nearly did. At Easter, in April 1775 – having known each other for about four months – he and Lili got engaged. This step, however, introduced too much reality into the fantasy of life together. For one thing their respective families were not at all enthusiastic. The Goethes certainly considered themselves the social equals of the Schönemanns but these were just the sort of showy people Caspar loathed. Lili's brother – the driving force of the firm – was not impressed by the young novelist. How were novels going to help the bank? The brother was determined that Lili should make a good match to a wealthy business associate.

Goethe set himself earnestly to the task of building up his legal career as a condition of making himself more eligible; an act which tells us something extraordinary about the state of publishing at the time – how far it was from Goethe's mind, despite having written the most celebrated novel of the era (and one which was immediately very successful), that he might be able to make a good living from writing. In this endeavour he was much helped by his father.

Because of his official standing as an Imperial councillor Caspar was ineligible to practise as a lawyer in Frankfurt. However, he was quite widely respected for his legal learning and ability. He had built up an honorary practice in which he produced legal documents for his associates and friends, although these documents had to be signed by a practising lawyer. This benefited his friends since they had only to pay for endorsement – rather than for advice or drafting. And it left a neat hole for the son to fill. Young Goethe was able to take on this role and to verify the documents his father produced; they also acted as agents in various business enterprises.

Goethe was at least sufficiently industrious to be short of time – he experienced the very familiar conflict whereby his devotion to establishing himself in a career actually prevented him from spending much time with the girl he had in mind. 'Out of love for her I was trying to manage my business affairs and broaden their scope and as this expanded my visits to Offenbach [where Lili and her extended family lived in great style] became so infrequent that they caused a certain painful embarrassment. Obviously the present was really being neglected and sacrificed for the sake of the future.'

*

Legal work, however, was not the only thing keeping Goethe away from Lili. From the start of his days with Lili, Goethe was discussing the relationship in letters to another woman, Augusta ('Gustchen') von Stolberg, whom in fact he was never to meet, although her brothers – the youthful Stolberg counts – were soon to play a hectic role in his life.

Augusta, in raptures over *Werther*, wrote a fan letter to the young author; he wrote back and the correspondence became intimate. She became the confidante of Goethe's self-analysis. He tells her about the tensions in his character: the struggle between two very different versions of himself. There is 'Carnival' Goethe, dressed from head to toe in the most elegant clothes – silk stockings, breeches, braided tailcoat. Carnival Goethe lives by the light of chandeliers, flitting from the card table to the ballroom. To Augusta he characterizes Lili as just another pretty blonde, someone in whom his interest is frivolous.

There is also 'Boots' Goethe – boots being the material antithesis of ballroom attire. Boots devotes himself to his creative life, he lives for himself and his art. This Goethe gets on with what he is interested in: developing his own nature, without trying to please. And certainly Boots isn't interested in spending his life running a provincial legal practice in order to keep an elegant woman in carriages and silk dresses. He likes tramping across open heaths in the wind and rain, shouting poetry to himself above the storm.

There's a flirtatious aspect to the way Goethe presents himself to Augusta – my fiancée doesn't know or care for the real me; but you do – I'm closer to you than to her.

6

Switzerland

In early May – only a fortnight or so after Goethe's engagement to Lili – Augusta's brothers turned up at the Goethe home in Frankfurt with another young aristocrat, Count von Haugwitz, in tow. They were on their way to Switzerland and desperate to have Goethe join them. One of the brothers, Leopold, had recently had an unhappy love affair with an English girl and – acting out a cliché (his speciality) – he was travelling to forget his woes. They were incredibly enthusiastic about *Werther*; Goethe was their 'brother'; his mother, Catharina, was the universal mother – the symbolic mother of all geniuses. To her delight they called her 'Frau Aya', perhaps referring to an obscure fertility goddess or, more likely, picking upon an old Byzantine term for the governess of princes.

The three counts spent a lot of their time at the Goethes' drinking. On one occasion, after a few bottles of wine the young men started expressing in the loudest terms their hatred of tyrants, baying for the blood of such terrible monsters. Old Caspar looked on indulgently; he much enjoyed the lively company of his son's friends.

Catharina was initially startled; she didn't know anything about tyrants but she did know when things were starting to get out of hand. As the counts got more and more worked up she quietly headed down to the cellars and chose some of the very best wines from the great vintages going back to the earliest years of the century. She set out the wines in beautiful decanters. 'This is the true blood of tyrants! Enjoy it, but all thoughts of murder are unwelcome in this house!'

It was an elegant gesture, much appreciated by her son – the rebuke was effective and without a sting. But Goethe could not resist the rather obvious remark, and in the case of the Stolbergs a highly apposite one: 'The grapevine is the worst tyrant of all . . .'

Caspar keenly supported the suggestion that his son join in the Swiss adventure. Why not extend the tour into Italy? It was very important to the father to think of his son enjoying the place he had spent so much of his own life thinking about. And, in any case, it might just put an end to the engagement to Lili – about which Caspar was not at all enthusiastic.

And so it was arranged. The four set off by way of Darmstadt, where Goethe's friend Merck was living. Merck's attitude to the Stolbergs was merciless. 'Your aim,' he said to Goethe, 'your unalterable course, is to give poetic form to reality; the Stolbergs of this world are trying to give reality to their so-called poetic ideas . . . and that only results in non-sense.' In other words they are merely actors, pretending that what they make up is real. They have dreamed up some fantasies of what life ought to be like: shouting down tyrants, running about mountains feeling lovesick and cavorting with celebrities.

The problem with Merck was that he combined such acuity with malice – he could see to the heart of human folly, he could sum up perfectly what was silly and contemptible about the counts, but he had no 'kindness', as Goethe put it. Merck's insight was, in the end, too sharp for the human condition. Writing about it afterwards, Goethe calls it 'Mephistophelean'; in fact, 'Mephistopheles Merck', as he was often called, was an important contribution to Goethe's view of the Devil as it emerged in *Faust*. Merck (who later killed himself), judges the world rationally and as it is – but, like the Devil, he sees it without love. And such a world is indeed disgusting and intolerable. Mankind is hateful, viewed in this light.

Having read too much Rousseau, the Stolbergs decided they ought to try to return to the state of nature. Did man, in the state of nature, wear clothes? They must, if possible, dispense with such artifice. There was a fishpond in the neighbourhood of Darmstadt and they annoyed the locals by jumping in and splashing about naked in this public place. They weren't doing it because they felt the need to bathe, but because they were acting out a part they had taken on. They wanted

to scandalize, because this provided confirmation of their own originality. Far from being oblivious to the reaction of the honest burghers,
the counts craved their response; like naughty children seeking
attention by being irritating.

Leopold kept going on about how unhappy he was; about how
much he had loved the girl he had parted from. Goethe supposed he
might know something about this kind of pain from his own experience; in any case the entire educated world now regarded him as the
most insightful writer there had ever been on such matters. But this
wasn't a comfort to Leopold. The more Goethe tried to reason with
him, the more von Stolberg insisted that nothing in the world could
equal his grief. No woman in the world could be as beautiful as the
one he had had to renounce.

'. . . when we arrived in Mannheim, we stayed in some nice rooms
at a respectable inn. During the dessert of our first noon-day meal, at
which wine had not been spared, Leopold demanded that we drink to
his fair one's health, which we did amongst considerable clamour.
When the glasses were empty, he exclaimed: "But now not another
drink may be taken from these hallowed goblets. To drink a second
health would be a desecration, and so let us destroy these receptacles!"
Thereupon he threw his long-stemmed glass against the wall. The rest
of us followed suit, while I imagined I could feel Merck pulling on my
collar.' What he didn't have to imagine was the addition to the bill for
the damage.

Parting briefly from his rather trying aristocratic companions, Goethe
made a detour to visit Cornelia and Schlosser at Emmendingen, where
Schlosser had been appointed to the lucrative and responsible post of
high-bailiff. The Schlossers occupied a fine – even magnificent – house.
But the little town of Emmendingen was a backwater and Cornelia
found herself isolated and deprived of the civilized and highly cultivated social circle that had been important to her in Frankfurt. She
now had a baby daughter, Maria.

Goethe we know saw Cornelia as a woman who would have been
the ideal mother superior of a convent; she was intellectually able and
well educated; more specifically: 'she exercised an altogether irresistible

influence over feminine souls: she lovingly attracted young persons and dominated them through the spiritual force of her inner merits'. But in the world in which she lived such a vocation was not open to her; the family was Lutheran and there were no convents in that Church. In any case, Goethe's point isn't a religious one: it's not that he saw Cornelia as a deeply religious woman, but rather as a leader of serious women – and there simply were no relevant institutions. In later times he might have imagined a career for Cornelia as headmistress of a girls' school or within a university.

Goethe loved his sister but hated her hairstyle

Cornelia had fine qualities of mind, but physically she was not very attractive; indeed Goethe thought that she was positively unattractive. She had – like him – an unusually large forehead, unpleasantly accentuated by the current fashion, which dictated that a woman's hair must be swept back and piled up in a great dome. Cornelia's imperfections were left cruelly exposed and heightened. She also suffered from blotchy skin, brought on by any kind of social expectation: an invitation to a ball or a party or even just a small gathering would cause her to come out in disfiguring red spots. Cornelia, Goethe thought, was entirely devoid of sensuality. She comes across, in his descriptions, as high-minded, awkward, rather stubborn and certainly unhappy. She entirely lacked the flexibility, the capacity to let things wash over, that so eased her mother's passage through life.

Given his view of Cornelia's temperament and character it is not surprising that Goethe was anxious about seeing her. He knew that she and Schlosser could not be very comfortable together – and indeed they were not. It is perhaps telling that Cornelia strongly urged her brother not to marry Lili, not to marry at all. For her, marriage was the only available – although very imperfect – route of escape from home, Frankfurt and Caspar. Since Goethe did not need to make such an escape why should he be thinking of getting married?

It was to be the last time he saw her. Two years later Cornelia died of a fever that seized her in the weeks following the birth of her second child, Elizabeth Catharina – named after her grandmother.

Finally reaching Switzerland, Goethe met up with Johann Caspar Lavater – the founder of phrenology. Lavater worked with the intuitively plausible idea that character is legible in a person's face. We do, after all, often feel that just on looking at someone, we can form some approximate conception of what they are like. Lavater extended this in intriguing – though hardly, as he thought, scientific – ways. He focused on the silhouette and published matching plates of lovers, rivals, enemies. This was a charming game: a great many fashionable people enjoyed playing it and Lavater became a great celebrity. His rapturous description of Goethe's profile had certainly helped bring the young man to the admiring notice of cultivated Germany.

In Geneva, the Stolberg brothers continued their practice of nude bathing – inciting a number of locals to throw stones as they cavorted in a pond. At which point they finally realized they were not wanted.

Heading off into the mountains for a few days on his own, Goethe paid a visit to a large pilgrimage church, which had been constructed around the remains of a little hut, where – almost a thousand years before – a hermit called Meinrad had lived. The otherwise desolate valley was now popular with pilgrims, despite being so difficult to reach. 'Here a single spark of morality and piety had kindled a gleaming and ever burning little flame to which throngs of believers would make the arduous journey so that they might ignite their little candles at this sacred fire. Be that as it may, this is an indication that mankind has a boundless need for the same light and warmth which the saint had nurtured and enjoyed with the profoundest feeling and surest conviction.'

This is one of the moments in which we see Goethe's view of his own life being displayed. A very normal reaction for a non-believer like Goethe would be depression – look how much enthusiasm is wasted on misguided beliefs; see how people search for salvation in the oddest, least promising places. This is how Voltaire would have responded – should some misadventure have taken him to such a place. It would have seemed to him to show the appalling ignorance of the people. But Goethe's response stresses the need – not the folly. They need something. And the success is inspiring – an idea can touch people: one individual life can, a thousand years on, inspire.

We are with Goethe on his 'arduous journey' to the shrine of Meinrad, but for us the object of interest is not the lonely hermit of the Dark Ages. The question that hangs in the air is whether Goethe is an inspiration for us.

Returning to Frankfurt in July, Goethe was now convinced he could not marry Lili. The cost of life with Lili – in terms of his necessary devotion to business – was too great; he was hardly ready to commit himself to a woman who would have had great expectations not only for material life but also of the kind of emotional devotion her husband would have to provide.

It was, perversely, the very plausibility of the marriage that probably caused Goethe to break off the engagement. Even a happy marriage would have constrained his existence; it would have brought the necessity of setting up a home of his own; it would have tied him to Frankfurt. Goethe's loyalty to a developing vision of his future was stronger than his desire for Lili's love.

Fortunately a fairly painless dissolution of their relationship came about; it was a resolution in harmony with the essence of Lili's character. She had, as they both knew, a great power over men, and up to now had enjoyed dismissing her admirers – apart from Goethe. Among her suitors-in-waiting were several business associates of the family firm. These associates tended to pass through Frankfurt for the large commercial fairs. When that time of year came round again in the autumn of 1775, Lili was able to reanimate an old love and within a few months she was married to the wealthy Baron von Türckheim.

She was just in time; almost immediately after the wedding the family bank collapsed. Lili's brother had been falsifying the accounts; but he had managed to secure a safe, rich haven for his sister before the deception unravelled and he shot himself. Lili, now a baroness, moved to Strasbourg, where her husband became mayor.

7

Genius

There was a special name for the kind of trip Goethe took with the Stolbergs: a 'genius journey'. This was just one application of the term 'genius' which had come into vogue and was prone – in Goethe's opinion – to serious abuse. 'When anyone undertook something preposterous, to no purpose or profit, it was a "genius prank".'

Every energetic young man wanted to be a genius. It was a species of inflation: a term of praise originally used with caution and reserve and applied only in cases of the most outstanding poetic excellence was now brought into common currency. Used in this promiscuous fashion, 'genius' changed its meaning. It was no longer the term for a special kind of achievement: it became the name of a manner. Genius 'manifested itself by transgressing against existing laws, overturning accepted rules and declaring itself free of all restraint'.

Goethe was very much a beneficiary of all this talk about genius. Broadly, what it did was direct attention to the person, the personality and life of the creative person, seeing every detail as somehow manifesting their admirable spirit. So, if Goethe admired blue coats worn with yellow waistcoats – the Werther uniform – then it was felt that somehow these items of clothing must encapsulate the intelligence and originality of Goethe himself. By dressing this way one could participate in the creative life.

At the same time, Goethe was very much opposed to the cult of genius. For one thing it had a very one-sided view of creativity. In *Werther* and *Götz* Goethe breaks what in those days were regarded as the rules of literature. One might think that what's important about those works is merely that they are unconventional, that they break the rules. This view was immensely annoying to Goethe because it completely fails to identify the positive achievements of his writing. It suggests that any novel which included a suicide would be just as good as *Werther*, any play which included some vigorous and crude expressions would be the equal of *Götz* (which famously introduced the phrase 'lick my arse' to high art). The necessary question goes unasked: why is it good to break the rules? It might be, but only if there is some worthwhile project that requires such innovation; on its own, transgression is pointless.

Goethe saw the overestimation of transgression, and the cult of genius, as attempts to disguise envy. If it's easy to be a genius, then there is no anxiety about superiority. This is the underlying theme of the encounter with the Stolbergs. They hadn't written anything remotely comparable with *Werther* but they could put themselves on a par with Goethe by defining his achievements in a way that made them easy to equal. If what's good about *Werther* is just that it expresses the deep feelings of an individual then you can do your own version of this by flinging a glass against a wall. For that too expresses the intensity and impotence of passion.

Like the Stolberg brothers, we are not geniuses. If setting up as a spectacular creative spirit is the wrong way of trying to be like Goethe, what should the brothers have taken from their beguiling friend? They should have paid more attention to the gap between the character in the novel and the writer of the book. What was brilliant about Goethe wasn't that he – like many other people – had had an unhappy love affair but that he had been able to write superbly about it: he had transformed his experience into art. And to do this he had to be much more than merely passionate. As the writer of the novel Goethe reveals qualities that Werther himself does not have – Goethe can know the value of Charlotte's advice; Werther cannot. The achievement of writing was founded upon coming out of the passion and understanding it. To write the book, Goethe had to grow out of the emotions in which the hero is trapped; he had to integrate his passionate sensibility and his artistic drives to clarity, coherence, discipline, and regard for the reader, who needs to be able to follow what is going on in Werther's heart.

*

Goethe had his own, very specific, view of his creative ability. 'I found myself most at home, and most satisfied – it was the thing that brought me the greatest joy – when a poetic creation came to me spontaneously – irrespective of my wanting it – sometimes even against my will.'

This often happened at night. He would wake up with stanzas ready formed in his mind. Without lighting a candle he would get out of bed and put on a sort of dressing gown he'd had specially made for such a purpose. Feeling his way in the dark he'd go over to his writing stand and take up a pencil – much more practical than the spluttering and unreliable pens of the period. This was a lesson learned of experience – the scratching of the pen brought him out of his drowsy reverie and this would be enough to destroy the thought.

In a letter to his Leipzig friend Behrisch, Goethe tells of just such a dream. They'd been out drinking all evening and on arriving back at his rooms Goethe fell into a drunken slumber. 'I soon had stupid dreams of elongated people, feather hats, tobacco pipes, acrobats, card tricks. I finally woke up and sent it all to the Devil. After that, a peaceful hour – lovely dreams. The usual: a girl beckoning, a quick kiss. Then *ftt* – she pulls a sack over my head. You know they trick guinea pigs into sacks? But a fine gentleman, like me? Unheard of! I knew it was odd. Well, in the sack I do a bit of philosophizing, then I begin moaning poetry – about a dozen allegories in the style of Shakespeare, the rhyming bits. Then she disappears but I'm still in the stupid sack.

'Then I woke up – and with all the champagne we'd had it felt as if there really was a damned sack stuffed inside my head.'

8

Jung-Stilling

Goethe became something of a connoisseur of intellectual character. He was at this period easily moved to friendship and sympathy, and had a ready response to anyone with an original and interesting view of life. And he made the painful discovery of the multiple deformities of the intellectual character – which sometimes seems maddeningly and inextricably interwoven with virtues.

There was, for example, one Jung-Stilling (his real name was Jung, but he published a biography under the pseudonym Stilling); Jung-Stilling had been a tailor, a village schoolmaster, a hermit. He was obviously rather odd; Goethe was both repelled by and deeply interested in him. After studying at Strasbourg – where he had been in awe of Goethe – he had become a modestly successful doctor specializing in the new and risky business of removing cataracts. This undertaking had an especially pathetic feature – sometimes in the immediate aftermath of the operation the patient would have his sight restored, only for this to gradually fail as the eyes healed.

Jung-Stilling stayed for some time in the Goethe house in Frankfurt – not long after Goethe's return from Switzerland and the break with Lili. He was there to perform a complex eye operation for which a large fee was to be paid (something of which he was in considerable need).

What was fascinating to Goethe was Jung-Stilling's incredibly heightened and dramatically intense view of life. He believed that God was watching everything he did and intervening at every point. When he was good he earned God's favour and things would go well; if God were displeased all his efforts would be brought to ruin. This epic of the meaning of life was being played out – and at a particularly critical moment – before Goethe's eyes. For the cataract operation was inherently risky; it really wasn't under Jung-Stilling's control whether the treatment would be successful or not.

The situation developed in an all too probable way. The well-publicized operation that Jung-Stilling carried out in Frankfurt was entirely unsuccessful; his professional reputation was crushed – and the faith and investment his wife and her family had made in him was destroyed (so he would be returning to an extremely awkward domestic situation). His general outlook made this bad situation much worse: obviously God had made the operation fail – God was punishing his wicked servant. Jung-Stilling was emotionally incapable of adopting the sane view that medical science was as yet imperfect.

Someone like Jung-Stilling reveals a horrible tension in how we experience life. His beliefs had the attractive consequence that life is filled with meaning – every apparently minor occurrence could be seen as hugely significant (Why did so-and-so smile at me? Why did I find a thaler in my shoe?) because they are not random events but the work of God. Yet, at the same time, such a view becomes extremely depressing if things happen to go badly.

9

Stella

At around this time, Goethe wrote a short play of five brief acts entitled *Stella*. The plot is rather improbable. A mother and daughter arrive at an inn; they are upper-class women but have fallen on hard times since the disappearance, many years before, of their husband and father. Much distressed by his absence they nevertheless retain love and admiration for him. The daughter has come to take up a position as the paid companion of a noblewoman whose house lies across the square from the inn. This noblewoman, Stella, it turns out, had herself been abandoned a few years before by her long-established lover. The same day an officer called Fernando arrives at the inn and is noticed by the daughter.

The mother and daughter go to meet Stella, the future employer; they find her very pleasant and sympathetic. Soon she shows them a picture of her departed lover – one Fernando. The mother immediately recognizes this man as her own departed husband, but says nothing. The daughter, who had been too young to know her father, exclaims that it is a portrait of the officer who has just arrived at the inn across the square. He is sent for and is rapturously received in private by Stella. They vow never to leave one another.

Before long Fernando finds himself alone with the mother. He exclaims that she is his wife, his true love. He has, he says, been looking for her for years: that was why he left Stella. Stella learns of this and is desolate. The situation appears hopeless: whichever of the women he goes with Fernando will leave the other – whom he loves and who loves him – in despair. But then the mother has a happy thought. Why don't they share him? He belongs to both – why not 'one house, one bed, one grave' for the three of them? In a few ecstatic lines everyone agrees and the play ends.

The play is rather ridiculous because of the extremely laborious way in which the central situation is set up. A great deal of the action involves getting people into the right room at the right time, and establishing who knows what and who doesn't know what. The drawn-out process contributes nothing to the central issue that can be stated in one line: Fernando loves equally and is equally loved by two women. Having spent an age getting to the problem Goethe provides only a bare assertion of his ideal solution. It is how you respond to the problem itself (being confronted by the impossible choice between two loves) rather than how you get into it that is interesting.

Stella, perhaps, should not be judged as a play to be performed. It is not designed primarily for public reception at all. One can see the play as providing an excuse for intimate conversation. Goethe can use the process of writing, which is a relatively respectable undertaking, to bring into discourse with women and perhaps with his male friends too something which was clearly very important to him, and yet hardly a polite topic – the sharing of lovers: two men sharing one woman or two women sharing one man. One can imagine: 'What are you writing now, dear Doctor – another *Werther*?' And Goethe – eyes gleaming – saying, 'Not exactly, it's a play, well it's like this . . . And how do *you* think it should end, my dear?'

When revising the play for the 1806 edition of his collected works, Goethe changed the ending. The lovers are unmoved by the suggestion of a ménage à trois, Fernando shoots himself and Stella dies. This is a rather boring denouement – and an admission that he's brought the play to an impasse and can't think how to end it. Nothing in the development of the characters remotely hints that they might turn to self-slaughter, nor explains why they should find life unliveable in the circumstances.

Like *Werther*, *Stella* identifies a terrible problem that may occur in life, one that occurs because we love. But, within the worlds of these works, there is no adequate response to such problems – there is only a fantasy solution (let's all love one another) or death. It is not until much later – especially in *Wilhelm Meister* – that Goethe finds the way out of these problems. In that novel he places his hero in similar situations: Wilhelm loves passionately and is rebuffed; later he has to choose between two women. The difference is that Wilhelm has other concerns in his life. Although love matters to him – and his life is shaped and scarred by love – romantic difficulties are not fatal because he is devoted to other tasks and enterprises and because he has the support of other people with whom he is not in love.

10

The Lesson of Voltaire

The publication of *Werther* – adding to his reputation as the writer of *Götz* and as a critic for the *FGA* – brought Goethe to the attention of the princely courts. A character such as Goethe would be welcome as a celebrity, as a stimulus and as an entertainer. One minor prince wrote excitedly to his sister after meeting the young hero:

'In the afternoon, I was sitting in my room when a servant came in to say there was some Frankfurt Doctor downstairs who wanted to speak to me. Imagine my surprise when Doctor GOETHE marched in. Yes it was really him . . . well, I made him to sit on the sofa with me and we had a very intimate chat. He only stayed half an hour. This unexpected visit gave me so much pleasure – I really like Goethe, he's so natural.'

Goethe was immensely charming to a particular kind of German prince. He was famous and clever and sympathetic to the delights and difficulties of the upper world. Thus a new kind of career presented itself – perhaps Goethe could take up an appointment at one of the many princely or ducal courts. In fact an invitation did come from the young Duke Carl August of Weimar, whom Goethe had briefly met in Carlsruhe in May 1775, during his 'genius journey', and then again in Frankfurt in September. Carl August was determined to get Goethe to visit Weimar, and promised to send a carriage for the longish journey to the other side of Germany.

Such a career was not at all to the liking of his father. Partly this was to do with the fact that it did not fit into the plan of life he had sketched for his son – which was to culminate in leading the city of Frankfurt. But there were practical dangers, too, in his eyes. And to illustrate these he pointed to the disastrous experience of Voltaire at the court of Frederick the Great.

Caspar was a 'Fritzian' – he admired the personality and character of Frederick the Great and the principles of his government. Prussia under Frederick was emphatically non-nationalist and was at odds with the Empire – within which, in fact, only about half of its lands lay. Frederick aimed at creating a much more efficient state, with a unified code of law.

Frederick was a devotee of the philosophy of the Enlightenment. The aim of this philosophy was practical: it did not seek merely to understand the world but, through understanding, to reform and improve practice. Voltaire was the most prominent intellectual on the European stage in the middle of the eighteenth century. In 1751 he was invited by Frederick the Great to reside at his Sans Souci Palace at Potsdam near Berlin. This was an invitation that had been made repeatedly in the past, and up to then Voltaire had always refused. But in that year his long-term companion, Madame du Châtelet, died and Voltaire agreed to go and help Frederick with his poetry – apart from which duty he would be free to pursue his own interests under extremely luxurious circumstances.

Voltaire, however, cannot in any ordinary way be said to have needed money. He was an obsessive speculator and investor and had built up a substantial fortune. Yet it was clearly very attractive to him to be offered a vast pension by Frederick as well. Once in Potsdam he soon found a way of making even more money – one that, unfortunately, was illegal.

He heard that the neighbouring Saxon government was to be forced to pay off some bonds held by Prussian citizens – at great profit to the Prussians. Voltaire was not entitled to purchase the bonds but the opportunity was irresistible. He found an intermediary to purchase them, secretly, on his behalf, handed over the money, took possession of some jewels as security and waited for the cash to roll in. But the bonds were not procured and Voltaire could not get his money back. He then discovered that the jewels were not as valuable as he had supposed. He took the case to court – always his favourite pastime – and won. But the proceedings brought embarrassing publicity and revealed to Frederick the fundamentally deceitful character of the whole business.

Things were patched up between Frederick and Voltaire – but only for a short time. And it was not long before Voltaire decided to leave the Prussian court. When he left he took with him a volume of poetry written by Frederick, despite a very pointed request that it be returned prior to departure. Frederick ordered Voltaire's arrest. The Prussian officers, however, did not catch up with him until he reached Frankfurt. Since the manuscript was with his luggage, which was being conveyed separately, Voltaire was held under house arrest for two weeks until the volume finally arrived and was handed over. Frankfurt certainly did not lie within the jurisdiction of Frederick, and the action of his officers – who were, after all, seizing the most famous writer of the era – created a public scandal. Voltaire lost no time in letting the world know his wildly exaggerated version of what happened. It was a farcical outcome, showing princely patronage at its most absurd and humiliating.

The great lover – around the time he left Frankfurt for Weimar

Whatever the rights or wrongs of the affair they seemed, to Caspar, to point a simple moral. Writers should not take up positions at the courts of princes. The underlying problem was the dramatic inequality of patron and poet. The patron had no real need of the poet, except as an amusing guest, a companion, a wit: hardly a proper foundation for the dignity and security of the writer.

The carriage promised by the Duke of Weimar somehow failed to arrive and as Goethe was all prepared for travelling Caspar took the opportunity to persuade his son to head for Italy instead. Even though he was a rather controlling father, it has to be admitted that his plans were highly attractive. Goethe was very unclear about what he wanted to do and where he wanted to go but set off from home with the vague intention of getting to Italy eventually.

Within a few days a message arrived from one Major von Kalb, a highly cultivated Prussian who had left the army and was now chamberlain to the Duke of Weimar. He had been sent to accompany Goethe to the court and had been chasing him around the country in the carriage. Eventually he caught up with Goethe in Heidelberg; as the coach horn sounded Goethe made up his mind, jumped in and headed straight for Weimar.

PART THREE

Power

Wanted to buy
Small dog:
Mustn't bark or bite;
Must feed on broken glass
And shit diamonds.
Goethe, *c.* 1812

I

Ambition

Goethe's 'spur of the moment' decision to go to Weimar turned out to be the decisive move of his life. The invitation was merely to visit the duke; but Weimar was to become Goethe's home for the rest of his long life – with only one significant break: his two years in Italy after ten years of service at the court. To see why the little town of Weimar and its small court were so important to Goethe we have to consider the ambitions that were driving him at this stage in his life: the hopes, fears and longings that were contending within him.

In the last months in Frankfurt prior to his departure for Weimar, writing to Augusta von Stolberg, Goethe described the state of his soul. It is, he says, 'like a sock that is being turned inside out': 'the outer becoming inner; the inner, outer'. At first glance it is a disarmingly banal analogy; nevertheless it is a revealing statement of his personal ideal of life; and an avowal of a strikingly original ambition. The second point is to do with expression. His thoughts and feelings seek external manifestation: the inner is to become outer. And through externalization, his inner states will – hopefully – lose their fleeting, private and capricious character and be made precise, ordered and available to others.

But this desire is twinned with a longing to absorb what is out there in the world: what is outer becomes inner. It is obvious that we can encounter great objects – like Strasbourg Cathedral – or great individuals – like Herder – and yet be untouched by them; they remain 'outside' us. Admiring them, saying that they are great, doesn't automatically enrich your inner world. Goethe is alluding to the most intimate, and elusive, aspect of experience: that in which we take possession of the things we encounter and make them our own.

A mutual exchange between the inner life of an individual and the external world is what is at stake here. What is so important is that both are mentioned, and mentioned together; the neatness of the language being used to suggest the deepest connection between the two. And yet we know how easily they fall apart; how each is diminished when pursued alone. The urge to communicate what is going on 'inside' becomes a boring egoism, unless what is expressed is substantial and serious. On the other hand, exhaustive taking in – visiting all the famous places, reading everything – is a sterile occupation unless what is absorbed becomes personally enriching. Goethe wants to become more receptive and more creative; and sees the two projects as needing one another for their proper fulfilment.

In a simple sentence Goethe is sketching an ideal which was not only important to him – one to which he devoted his life – but which also reveals two kinds of failure: the overemphasis of self-expression, when the quality of the self being expressed is not considered; and the overemphasis on learning and scholarship, when little attention is paid to inner transformation.

Later, Goethe was to expand on these ideas in a letter to his old Swiss friend, the fashionable phrenologist Lavater. Goethe was now writing in the light of his early Weimar experience: his submission to public responsibility and the demands of many administrative duties.

'The daily task that is assigned to me, that becomes easier and harder for me every day, demands my attention waking and dreaming. This duty becomes dearer to me daily, and in this I should like to prove the equal of the greatest men, and in nothing greater. This desire, to raise the pyramid of my existence, the base of which is given and founded for me, as high as possible into the air, outweighs everything else and hardly allows of a moment's forgetfulness. I have no time to lose, I am already well on in life, and fate may break me off in the middle, and the Babylonian Tower will remain blunt and unfinished. At least they shall say: it was boldly planned, and if I live, I hope, with God's help, to have the strength to finish it.'

It is striking, here, that Goethe employs – as a metaphor of his own aims in life – the Tower of Babylon, which was the incarnation of folly, confusion and misplaced pride. It was the tower with which man attempted to reach the heavens – and this presumption was punished with the separation of languages: the workers could no longer cooperate. Goethe thought that he could reverse this conclusion: building the tower could be a legitimate aspiration. The languages of poetry, government, science and love could be brought back into a wonderful harmony.

Goethe is determined to bridge the gaps between creative art and what is called 'the real world'. For much of the nineteenth and twentieth centuries artists have withdrawn their sympathy from the normal conditions of comfortable existence. The artist is at odds with – and critical of – 'bourgeois life'. But what 'bourgeois' means is something like this: the material condition of life to which most people aspire – more subtly, it indicates the complex set of relations between effort and reward, responsibility and security, within which a great many people live their lives.

Goethe's immense hope was that there need not be – should not be – a spiritual loathing or artistic contempt for that life. Which, after all, is normal life, broadly speaking. If depth of thought, maturity of passion and grace of feeling are to be central to a society, these spiritual qualities have to coexist with the normal demands of life. And Goethe suggests more than coexistence; he is looking at the ways in which the discipline of 'the real world' – the demands of power and responsibility – might actually offer special opportunities for personal growth and development. While we often say that power corrupts, Goethe is here suggesting that the exercise of power – when it is taken seriously – might be a maturing and refining experience. The poet might become a better poet, the artist a better artist, if they could lovingly engage with what is called 'the bourgeois experience'.

It was once suggested that Goethe's move to Weimar and his embrace of public duty was as if Byron – having become the darling of rebellious youth across Europe – had suddenly decided to join the civil service. But for Goethe the move does not appear in this light – as a sell-out. Goethe's underlying ambition was concerned with personal growth, with the mutual exchange of inner and outer. He did not long to write more and more successful novels, but to become a particular kind of person. Weimar was to offer him a great opportunity. It was his chance to 'get real'. The imaginative and expressive powers so evident in the writing of *Werther* might be raised to even higher worth if they could somehow be integrated with a deep appreciation of everyday life.

Goethe's ambition is highly personal – it is focused on his own character. It contrasts with the more usual list of desiderata: status, money, power, possessions, sexual satisfaction. Goethe pursued all of these as well, and with some success. But they are not really what he was primarily aiming at. He wants these external things as means to – as vehicles for – his emotional and intellectual development. We tend to think of spiritual growth as a shedding of worldly attachments. Goethe's beautiful idea is of a fine cooperation of inner and outer. He can be more fully himself through exercising significant responsibility, through the deployment of the resources of wealth, through travel and collecting and setting up wonderful homes. And the proper exercise of power and the good use of wealth rests upon the inner excellence of the individual.

The attempt to lead the perfect inner life, to become the best possible kind of person, had of course been pursued before; but almost always in a religious connection. Goethe takes seriously the idea of the condition of one's soul, but he doesn't link this to loving God or the avoidance of sin or the purity of one's intentions. Instead this ideal of inner quality has been brought back into connection with the world of experience, with intellectual curiosity, with politics and administration, with art and history and travel. He's suggesting to himself that there is no necessary opposition between the world and the spirit.

It is significant that Goethe was exploring this ambition through his early years in Weimar. For these years – his late twenties and into his thirties – represented his first real break with home and with the world of his parents. The relationship with Lili brought money and personal development into conflict: he would have had to make a good living, not so that he could be a better person, but so that Lili could live in her accustomed affluence. Now he was beginning to think of an alternative scenario.

2

The Court of Weimar

For many writers, the most enviable moment of Goethe's life was his invitation, in 1775, to the court at Weimar. Carl August, Duke of Saxe-Weimar-Eisenach, was eighteen and had just made a calculated marriage to Princess Louise of Darmstadt. She held no personal charm for the young duke, but brought useful family connections: one of her sisters had been selected by Catharine the Great as a bride for the grand duke (Louise herself had been rejected as lacking in physical charm). Carl August had only just come of age and was on the lookout for sympathetic young courtiers to balance the older group of advisers and administrators he inherited.

Weimar had developed a reputation as a centre for culture under the patronage of Anna Amalia, the duke's mother and regent during his long minority – his father, the previous duke, having died when Carl August was a baby. The 'Musenhof' (court of the muses), as Weimar liked to think of itself, was impressive only by comparison with other tiny courts. It was an impoverished and undeveloped little state. Due to the vagaries of inheritance its territories were separated into four mini-states several miles apart; it had almost no industry and a scattered rural population of about one hundred thousand, of whom only six thousand lived in the town of Weimar itself. The roads were bad, in fact they were mostly just tracks; the court was overspending and in need of extra funds to repair recent, extensive fire damage to the main palace. The duke had a problematic interest in keeping up an army – an exceptionally expensive hobby and hardly a practical one. Nearby Prussia, infinitely stronger in the field, effectively dominated Weimar's foreign policy.

The big village of Weimar was, really, an appendage to the duke's castle, servicing the needs of the ducal family and their courtiers. The state was not easily distinguished from the private property of Carl August himself – and might be seen rather like a vast family estate. The estate was largely autonomous; although in principle appeal could be made above the duke to his feudal lord, the Emperor.

On arrival in November 1775, the twenty-six-year-old Goethe was hailed as a kind of god in human flesh; his John the Baptist was Wieland – who held no grudge for the memorable satire in the *FGA*. He was extravagant in his praise: Goethe is simply the finest human being who has ever lived: amazingly intelligent, charming, handsome, bursting with vitality. 'I love Goethe more than anyone in the world; no, that's absurd and wicked, let's just say that after my wife and children I love Goethe best.'

Born in 1733 – hence now in his early forties – Wieland was an attractive individual and representative of the best side of German culture upon which Goethe was now making such an impression. He had come to Weimar about three years before in 1772, at the invitation of the dowager duchess and regent, Anna Amalia, as tutor to the teenage duke-in-waiting Carl August and his younger brother, Constantin. Wieland got the post on the strength of a 'Fürstenspiegel' or 'Mirror of Princes' – a kind of educational manual for rulers – that he had written. He tried to show how young men of the ruling class need not grow up as either boorish country squires or fops – the two seemingly standard results of education – but could become both elegant and wise. It remains an urgent task.

In one of his poems Wieland describes a serious young man, devoted to high ideals. He meets a charming young woman and starts explaining to her how human beings will attain the loftiest spiritual planes if they will only refrain from sex and live on a diet of beans. As he's saying this, the girl lets her dress fall ever more open, revealing her cleavage to the best advantage. She knows what is wrong with him.

The presence of a distinguished young literary figure at the Weimar court quickly drew other young writers, friends of Goethe, to the town to try their luck. They were in search of patronage: the necessary condition for a successful literary career in late eighteenth-century Germany. The Stolberg brothers were the first to turn up. In their favourite style they held a rowdy dinner during which they ordered some urns to be brought in from the local cemetery and delivered drunken orations to the ashes. They then had the urns filled with wine and passed round the company.

Anna Amalia encouraged their excesses. They were having dinner with the duke's young brother, Constantin, at Tiefurt, a nearby farm which had been extended and improved for use as an occasional summer residence.

'Suddenly the door opens and in came the old duchess with the wife of the chief equerry – she's a splendid person: good and pretty. They've both got huge old swords in their hands – they proceed to knight us. We stayed in our seats while the ladies went round pouring and pouring the champagne. After supper we played Blind Man's Buff and kissed the equerry's wife . . . At what other court could you do things like that?'

One of the Stolbergs, Fritz, was offered a post as a courtier by the duke. But he was swiftly ordered to turn down the job by Klopstock, the most serious and eminent of German poets. Klopstock sought to exercise paternal control from Frankfurt over the literary world and to mould it to his own fairly austere and high-minded image. He was not entirely unsuccessful in his search for influence: he started a craze for skating by writing an ode on its spiritual benefits. Goethe did not particularly want Fritz around, but he resented this interference and abruptly told Klopstock to keep his nose out of Weimar. It was a declaration of independence.

Goethe's transition from Frankfurt literary celebrity – from leader of the Stormers and Stressers – to friend and adviser of a reigning prince with a dukedom to organize, was marked by the casting off of old bonds and alliances. The Stolbergs soon left. Other wild friends who turned up were greeted coolly; their hopes of obtaining patronage from Carl August were not supported by Goethe. This was his new world and he did not want to carry the baggage of his earlier existence.

3

The Wild Days

Goethe arrived in Weimar as a guest. For the first few months – from November 1775 to April 1776 – he had no fixed position; he was simply the duke's best friend.

Carl August was a coarse, sensual, stubborn young man: snub-nosed, stocky, energetic and very self-confident. His passions were sex – with peasant women, not his wife – hunting and soldiering.

In old age, Goethe reminisced about the early days: 'We certainly led a rather mad life. The duke was like a fine wine, still in a high state of fermentation. He did not know how to expend his powers, and we often nearly broke our necks. Fagging all day long on horseback, over hedges and ditches, through rivers, up hill and down hill; and then at night, camping in the open air, by a fire in the wood – this was what he liked. To have inherited a dukedom was to him nothing; but to have taken one by storm he would have considered something.'

Typically, after a breakneck ride through the mountains, Goethe, Carl August and their companions would set up camp for the night, making huts out of the branches of fir trees, cooking their supper over a fire. They smoked their pipes – except Goethe who loathed tobacco but out of deference to the duke never complained. They passed round the wine flasks, and would drink and dance with the peasants, the duke relieving his sexual needs with any local girl who happened to be to hand. He fathered many children this way; as they grew up he would acknowledge them with the intimate 'Du' – while the rest of the country folk were addressed in the third person, as 'he' or 'she'. But that verbal distinction was as close as these children got to acceptance into the ducal family. The boys were later sent to work in the forests and the girls placed in domestic service.

There was some disquiet about Goethe's influence. Wasn't he merely encouraging the duke in his bad ways, giving the young sovereign's irresponsible behaviour a glamorous veneer?

Klopstock – still observing from a distance – was indignant. Why doesn't Goethe educate the prince – that's what he's there for: to refine and make noble this wild young man. Klopstock was not alone in his anxieties; the duke was the keystone of the state, he didn't have a legitimate heir yet – in fact it was to be seven years before one was born; if he broke his neck – as seemed more than likely – what would happen? Frederick the Great had a distant claim by marriage: the Prussians would come in and take over.

These worries were real enough, but what was Goethe to do? A wiser observer commented that Goethe had to win the trust of the duke, had to meet the sovereign on his own territory, before any good influence could be exercised: 'I confessed to him that I myself wished he would drop some of his wild ways, that make people misjudge him here, though at bottom they amount to nothing more than that he goes shooting, careering about on horseback and cracking a long whip in the market place all in the company of the duke. These are certainly not Goethe's own tastes; but he must carry on like this for a time to win over the duke and to be able to exert a good influence. That (at least) is how I think about it.'

This observer was a middle-aged woman to whom Goethe had been introduced in the first days after his arrival: Charlotte von Stein, the 'splendid person: good and pretty', and wife of the master of the horses, the chief equerry, as he was rather grandly called. Von Stein was a pleasant man much occupied with court matters, but a husband only in name. They had seven children though only three – all boys – survived babyhood, but Charlotte was not particularly maternal towards them. Quite soon her emotional life was to find a new focus.

The duke, almost inevitably, did not get on very well with his wife. He had married her for openly prudential reasons. She had been brought up in the refined atmosphere of the Darmstadt circle – and did not find it easy to live with the much rougher, coarse Carl August (it especially maddened her when he brought his hunting dogs into her boudoir).

Goethe made it his business to support and hopefully educate her. One stratagem was to make a cult of her birthday, thereby designating her as an especially important person and encouraging others to show her the greatest respect; Goethe employed the well-established tradition of aristocratic amateur theatricals to this end. In January 1778 he directed and acted in a deviously charming piece called *The Triumph of Sensibility*. The term 'sensibility' had overtones of excess – of sentimentalism. A charge Carl August might have laid at his wife's door.

However, to make the play more palatable, Goethe turns the tables and portrays a husband who is in the grip of this spiritual sickness. He professes a deep reverence for nature, so deep, in fact, that he has procured a 'Reisenatur' – a travelling nature kit. He has cardboard trees and backcloths and an artificial stream stowed in packing cases so that any room can be turned quickly into a meadow or a forest –

and it's better than reality since, being indoors, there are no flies and it never gets too windy. He is also in love – with a large doll; far less trouble, of course, than attempting to sustain relations with a real woman.

But reality is revealed when the doll breaks open – and is found to be stuffed with fashionable writing: pages from Rousseau and some of Goethe's earlier pieces. It is this material, now strewn around the stage, that has sustained the self-delusion.

The underlying message to the young duchess is simple: don't judge your husband by the standards of behaviour to be found in fashionable books. But the moral is presented in such a witty, farcical manner that it is easier to take than any direct admonition.

4

Charlotte von Stein

Goethe's meeting with Charlotte von Stein had been prepared in a manner which could hardly fail to excite their mutual curiosity. By the end of 1774 Charlotte, like everyone else, had read *Werther*. She was so agitated by Werther's suffering and death that she was incapacitated for a week. She was unable to take pleasure in any of her usual diversions. Her friends teased her for her excessive sensitivity. Charlotte sought advice from Johann Georg Zimmermann, an extremely successful society doctor (he also wrote a classic study of loneliness in four volumes).

Writing to Charlotte on 19 January 1775 he mocks those who mock her. He goes on to feed her curiosity about the young novelist, painting a highly flattering – indeed exaggerated – portrait: Goethe has a masterly understanding of music, drawing, painting, engraving; is well versed in every art and science; and is an excellent barrister as well. Zimmermann also reports a bit of gossip: 'A society lady who has often met him told me that Goethe is the most beautiful man, the most lively, the most original, the most ardent, the most tender, the most seductive – and the most dangerous for a woman's heart – that she has seen in her entire life.' He enclosed with this letter portraits of Goethe and the Kestners, as the prototypes of Lotte and Albert in the novel. It was people like Zimmermann who were driving the poor couple to distraction.

This is how Zimmermann saw 'new' Charlotte: 'Her eyes are very beautiful – large and dark; her voice is soft, yet impressive. Her cheeks are rather red; her hair is quite black; she looks rather Italian. Her disposition is gentle and serious; she knows the social art of pleasing other people – her courtly manners have been refined to a point of complete naturalness; everyone can see the deep sensitivity evident in her face; she is very good humoured but retains a soulful aspect; her movements are light and graceful – from the way she dances you'd never guess her poetic and religious sensibility. She is in her early thirties; she has four children – and weak nerves. The keynote of her whole character is elegant simplicity.' Charlotte was a measured woman; without affectation; not at all given to outbursts of emotion. But nor was she cold or harsh.

Later on, in the summer, Zimmermann ran into Goethe and showed him a silhouette of Charlotte von Stein. On examining the image Goethe had taken up a pencil and written beneath it: 'She sees the world as it is, and yet through the medium of love.' Zimmermann was careful to let Charlotte know of this flattering interpretation of her outline.

Whether or not this phrase was true of Charlotte – and Goethe could not possibly have known – it neatly expresses an ideal that was extremely important to him. 'To see the world as it is' sounds like a recipe for disenchantment. While the 'medium of love' is one that often distorts, love makes us blind. 'To see the world as it is, and yet through the medium of love' sounds like a paradox; as if to say: now I'm wearing rose-tinted spectacles I see things for what they are. But we can read the statement in a more interesting way. Realism – seeing things for what they are – tends to produce cynicism, but needn't. Love often involves blindness to the faults of the beloved, but needn't. Thus 'to see the world as it is, but through the medium of love' can be to attain an ideal – without illusions and yet without disillusionment: objective and yet generous and tender.

This ideal is Goethe's aim for himself as a writer. The two great passionate characters of Goethe's early writings, Götz and Werther, were blinded by their emotions: neither could come to terms with reality, and it was precisely their noble emotions which prevented them from seeing how things really were. Thus the capacity Goethe assigned to Charlotte – or to her shadow portrait – is one that could make the difference between life and death.

The integration of love and realism is also Goethe's aim as a human being – and perhaps it is a common one, though not often stated in quite these terms. We try to steer a path between cynicism, which is realistic about life and full of loathing, and sentimentalism, in which life is found lovely only because it is seen through rose-coloured spectacles.

Once in Weimar Goethe quickly drew close to Charlotte; she was quite different from the other women to whom he had been passionately attached. Friederike and the first Charlotte were not only much younger, but they were also pleasing in their simplicity, in their inno- cent good nature. Lili had been worldly and flirtatious but hardly Goethe's match in culture or experience. New Charlotte, at thirty- three, was seven years older than Goethe. She was well educated, knowledgeable about art, courtly life and the ways of the aristocratic world – and not available for marriage. This must have helped, for if Goethe had learned anything from the Lili episode it was that he shouldn't be thinking of marriage.

Charlotte became Goethe's mentor. Their relationship was platonic. It was almost certainly so in the relatively trivial sense that they didn't sleep with each other. This was a matter that deeply interested the local gossips and has preoccupied a few literary historians as well. But the relationship was platonic in a more important way: Charlotte didn't love Goethe just as he was; she loved a conception of what he might become. And in order to keep her love Goethe developed in the light of her vision. The genuinely platonic love isn't one that is merely non-physical but one in which the object of desire is the personality of the loved one made perfect.

Because, at this stage, Goethe was such a striking figure – such a commanding and exciting presence – most people were attracted to him as he was. A bit like his father, Charlotte was interested in his future, although not in the clear, curriculum vitae mode of old Caspar. Charlotte worked with the concern that Plato makes so central to the character of Socrates: she wanted Goethe to know himself.

Goethe elaborated this theme in a poem in which he tried to capture the quality of his relationship to Charlotte the Second. It was included in a letter dated 14 April 1776 and so written within six months of their first meeting. Like so many of Goethe's poems the diction is unnervingly simple. It opens with a question – to God or to the unknowable forces that govern life. One well-meaning translation of the first line runs: 'Why with insight deep did you endow us?' But Goethe didn't write a word like 'endow', with its self-conscious 'poetic' tone. And 'insight deep' inverts the normal sequence of English words. In any case, insight is always deep. What did Goethe actually write? His words are: 'Warum gabst du' – 'Why did you give': the most utterly normal turn of phrase, straight from everyday life. Give what? 'Die tiefen Blicke' – literally 'the deep look'; meaning, here, the ability to look below the surface; in short: 'insight'. So the opening line reads: 'Why did you give us insight?'

What Goethe is getting at in the poem is this: there is a tension between love and knowledge. To know and understand another person is not usually (as an over-optimistic proverb has it) to love them. It is more likely that you will realize you don't really love them – or that you won't be very happy with them, and won't be able to make them happy. Insight gives you the capacity to see how you really stand with another person: to see past your projections, your fantasies of the other. Insight may be a gift from God or the divine powers – but it is also the enemy of romance.

Most people, Goethe continues, drift through life without knowing themselves or those they profess to love. For them life is 'light'. In their romantic lives they pass from unrealistic hope to sudden unexpected misery. But they lack insight: they don't understand how or why the relationship turned sour. They continue to believe in love and put failure down to bad luck. So they are free to exult again when the next passion comes along.

We – Goethe and Charlotte – however, cannot share those illusions. We don't 'see in the other what they never were, what they never will be'. And he goes on to say: 'Oh, it's as though you were, in an earlier life, my sister or my wife.' I know you already in a familiar way, and know that we will not be romantic lovers now.

And yet it is precisely this 'knowing' that has allowed Charlotte to be so good for him. For, to be good for another person is, in such cases, precisely not to go along with their illusions about themselves: it is to see past the fantasies and daydreams of who that person thinks he is. But this kind of love – care for the good of the other – cannot be romantic love. It is more like the love between brother and sister, between friends, or a long-married couple.

Charlotte did have a real impact on Goethe's character. Under her guidance, and certainly under her critical gaze, he moderated his tone; he became more measured, more statesmanlike.

Goethe at thirty: the point of maximum allure

A portrait of Goethe from this period shows him in his thirtieth year. His face is lean and long and sensuous; his forehead is unusually high but rather elegant. His fine nose and mouth suggest vitality, but his enormous eyes are languid. It is hard not to read into the picture what we know of his character. He was certainly very good-looking.

5

Tasso

Charlotte never quite succeeded in making the perfect courtier out of Goethe – he remained somewhat awkward and uneasy in courtly company. He never acquired the gracious ease of the ideal aristocrat – Goethe wasn't quite like them and everyone could see it. Nor, in the end, did Charlotte succeed in retaining Goethe's love. She had invented a personal role for him as her chaste lover: the knight who is infinitely devoted and yet content to be given the occasional handkerchief (or, in her more practical way, some soup or a pie from her kitchens).

Artistically, however, she made a great impression. For if Goethe could not quite manage to live according to Charlotte's ideals he could understand them and admire them and embody the qualities of kindness, dignity and refinement in a work of art – which may, in fact, be the only place where they can really come to perfection. Charlotte's vision of coming to terms with the world was decisive for Goethe's gradual maturation as an artist.

All through his early years in Weimar Goethe was working on a play about his father's favourite writer: the sixteenth-century Italian poet Torquato Tasso. Tasso had lived at the Renaissance court of Alfonso II d'Este, Duke of Ferrara. This setting is central to the play: Goethe makes a study of the relations between the poet and the duke, under whose patronage Tasso wrote his long verse epic, *Jerusalem Delivered*, which has survived as the great literary classic of the period.

When, in Act I, Tasso introduces his poem to the duke, he comments that the poem really belongs to the patron: it is the duke's achievement. Tasso had a difficult life: his parents lost their money and as a young man he was very gloomy – his literary talent was corrupted by an excessively morose and anxious way of life. The duke has freed him from material worry; by bringing him to live among the noble people of the court, he has restored Tasso's dignity. Tasso has been able to produce his best work: he belongs to the class of writers who do not thrive in adversity but need luxury, calm and material security in order to develop well and to write well.

When a writer chooses as his subject a situation parallel to his own, it is tempting to think that he is making the central character (in this case a poet at court) into a vehicle for himself. It is natural to assume that Tasso is Goethe, lightly disguised. Is this a literary self-portrait? It is deeply personal, but Goethe is defining himself against Tasso. As if to say: you may think that I'm like that but really I'm not. And the person it is most important to say this to is Goethe himself. Tasso is who he fears he may be, who he is terrified he could become. Tasso is a part of Goethe, a problematic but precious aspect of his own character. But what is wonderful about Tasso – namely that he can write great poetry – is on its own insufficient as a basis for a happy and constructive life.

The text was not completed until quite a number of years later and much of its extraordinary finesse derives from the later 'classical' period when Goethe was striving – very successfully – to make the surface of his works as beautiful and lucid as possible.

The play opens with two women, the princess – the unmarried sister of the duke – and her friend Leonora, a countess, sitting in a pleasant garden. They are weaving wreaths to decorate the busts of the great poets Virgil and Ariosto: the revered dead.

When Tasso approaches they praise him highly, saying that he is fit to join this company, and they crown him too. This is difficult for Tasso to accept: he is delighted but also disturbed. He is highly conscious of the imperfections of his own long poem; awkward about being placed on a level with his heroes. At the same time he is immensely proud of his own achievements.

They are expecting the arrival of Antonio, the duke's ambassador, who has been on a mission to Rome. The princess, who is deeply attached to Tasso, conceives the idea of linking these two admirable men in friendship. Antonio is somewhat older: a man of considerable experience, known for his tact and interest in poetry; he is even something of a poet himself in an amateur way. She strongly recommends to Tasso that he become more closely acquainted with Antonio; in doing so she conjures up an image of an intimate alliance: a group of men of the highest calibre, all 'faithful' to her and themselves close friends. Presented with this prospect Tasso becomes very excited.

When he meets with Antonio, Tasso is exuberant and direct: so, we are to be close friends; we are to be, as it were, spiritual brothers. The older man, however, is much more cautious: I cannot just give you my friendship; trust and affection have to grow over time, have to be proved in experience. Tasso appeals to his achievements as a poet, but Antonio is not yet convinced; he points to Ariosto and Virgil: the acclaim of generations shows their worth; Tasso is not yet in their league. The comment has, for Goethe's audience, an ironic edge – since Tasso was indeed to be recognized as the outstanding literary figure of his era. Yet, Antonio's words are reasonable: his trust is not, and should not be, something he can deliver on demand.

Tasso is put out by this unexpected rebuff. In his pride he thinks that his offer of friendship has been turned down because he is only a servant. Countering this, Tasso asserts that he has no master; not even the duke. The duke has no rights over him, except the rights that come from brute force. This ungenerous interpretation of patronage and attack on the established order – of which both men are beneficiaries – outrages Antonio, who rebukes the impudence of the young poet. His retort drives Tasso to frenzy; he draws his sword and challenges the diplomat. Antonio mocks him: they are guests of the duke, duelling is strictly forbidden; even to draw one's sword carries a mandatory punishment. And at this moment the duke himself appears. He has no choice but to imprison Tasso, which he does in the lightest possible fashion: the poet is ordered to keep to his own room.

The next brief scene, in which the duke and Antonio discuss what has happened, sets the character of the piece and reveals its refined morality. Obviously, says the duke, Tasso is technically in the wrong; nevertheless the fault lies with the older man: Antonio is experienced in the ways of the world, he is prudent, self-control is part of his diplomatic trade. He should have known what he was doing; he must have seen how his words would enrage the poet. He had no business pressing a point – however correct – which could induce a young and valuable man to draw his sword.

Antonio apologizes: the duke has put the matter in such a way that Antonio sees his fault. And this, he adds, is the fine art of government. He does not merely obey the duke: he is convinced, and therefore his obedience is not forced. We see what Tasso – now locked in his chamber – cannot see: the kindness and intelligence with which these worldly men judged him. The frightened, anxious Tasso does not know, cannot let himself know, how much sympathy and wisdom there might be in men who are not poets but are sovereigns or agents of practical affairs. He assumes that the duke holds him as a criminal and that Antonio is plotting against him.

When the princess and Leonora in their turn discuss what has occurred, they too are loving and generous in their opinions; they admire Antonio; why could the two not be friends? They have so much to offer one another. If only nature could blend one person from the two, what a wonderful creation that would be. And this line, this vision, is the centre of the play. Goethe himself is attempting precisely to be Antonio-Tasso; the character of Tasso in the play represents who Goethe might be if his Antonio side were not developed.

6

Poet and Politician

In *Tasso* Goethe conveys a particular ideal: as the women put it – how wonderful it would be if Tasso, the poet, and Antonio, the ambassador – the man of political skill – could be one single individual rather than rivals. In the later sections of the play, Goethe makes great dramatic use of the hostile misconceptions the poet and politician have of one another.

Tasso has his own explanation of Antonio's hostility: Antonio, he is determined to think, is motivated by envy of Tasso's native poetic inspiration. What does the diplomat really want? Tasso asks himself – and gives the most flattering answer.

> Status, possessions, honours – not these;
> These come with effort, cleverness and luck.
> But that which only nature can bestow
> No effort, no ambition can make attainable
> Not gold nor sword nor clever scheming
> Nor persistence wins – that, he never can forgive.
> How can he bear it . . . ?

This is brilliantly put, but it cannot be the whole story. There is a great deal to be said for the qualities that Tasso is discounting. It may indeed be that Antonio longs for something he doesn't have – but it doesn't follow that his merits are unreal. And a man who has acquired these capacities and exercised just these virtues of patience and intelligence is right to be annoyed when they are scorned.

In a wonderful cross-cutting of themes, Goethe has Tasso display precisely his own envy of practical knowledge and experience. Why do they never ask my opinion on matters of state, Tasso furiously asks himself – it's always: let's hear what Antonio has to say; we can't discuss this until Antonio is here; we'd better seek advice from him. Tasso envies the trust accorded and the deference paid to the ideas and words of the diplomat – but he never asks himself why people do listen to Antonio. And, of course, the answer is only too obvious – however magnificent Tasso's inspiration may be (and no one doubts this for a moment) it will not reveal how they should treat matters of state, how they should carry on a negotiation, how they should conduct their business affairs. They listen to Antonio and seek his advice for the simplest of reasons – he really knows what he is talking about.

Voltaire made just such self-aggrandizing complaints against Frederick the Great in Potsdam – he felt unfairly left out when matters of government or the dealings of the army were discussed. But Frederick was merely being reasonable – the philosophical and literary brilliance of his friend was not in doubt, only it gave no grounds at all for seeking his advice on practical matters of state business.

As quite often happens in his works, Goethe is presenting as two distinct characters what are really two parts of his own personality. He has his Tasso side and his Antonio side. And in Weimar, these were both considered important – he was there, in the first place, as an imaginative, creative genius; but what he was also there to do was to exercise political responsibility. In the eyes of Carl August there was no contradiction.

But to achieve this, to fill the role which was there for him, Goethe had to overcome in himself the conflict between these two drives: the drive to freedom – to do what he liked when he liked, to give voice to his poetic ideas, to be set apart from others; and the drive to power – which could be enacted only through cooperation, diplomacy and holding his tongue.

Back in the play, his friends urge Tasso to control himself, to moderate his passions, to liberate himself from his obsessive introspection, to broaden his horizons. In a sense the theme of the play is 'the education of Tasso' and the moral is the failure of that education. But it does

not fail for want of tact or intelligence on the part of those who seek
to help. Tasso stands at the outer edge of Goethe's imaginative world
– on the edge of the abyss. For Tasso is deep and creative; and yet the
whole business of living seems to be beyond him. His problems with
living can be seen in his raging appetites, his longing to gorge himself,
his refusal of any medical advice (how can I take medicine, it tastes
horrible); his need to see anyone who disagrees as an enemy ('don't
take my hate from me, I love my hatreds'). He experiences these
life-destroying aspects of his character as one with his poetic talent.

> In vain I pit my will against the urge
> That flows and ebbs in me, by day and night.
> If I am not to ponder and compose
> I have no life to lead, my life's no life:
> As soon forbid the silkworm its cocoon,
> Though closer to its death it spins itself
> Out of its inmost being it has drawn
> That precious web, and never will desist
> Till it has locked itself inside its coffin.

He knows he is spinning himself to death and yet not to spin would
be to make life worthless.

Tasso is a paradox in that he can produce the most beautiful, refined
and moving poetry, and win for hundreds of years the admiration of
cultivated audiences. And yet he cannot cultivate himself, and he
cannot live at his ease in a civilized society. Tasso, then, is a tragic
figure precisely because he is unable to learn the kind of lesson that
Charlotte von Stein was trying to teach Goethe.

A related problem is displayed in Tasso's relationship with the princess. She is deeply devoted to Tasso and movingly describes their
friendship: 'how all our talking still increased the need . . . daily better
our two minds were tuned to the pure pitch of richer harmonies'.
Tasso is her only 'true and pure possession'. This is loving friendship
at its most enviable and rare; for the princess, it has nothing at all to
do with marriage. She has completely accepted – not willingly, but
with a clear eye – the prevailing social order, upon which so much

that is good in her life depends. She recognizes that she is not free to follow her inclinations with respect to marriage; in her world, marriage is a political act; to deny that is to renounce the world she inhabits. And she has no intention of doing that. So when Tasso embraces her, close to the end of the play, she sees this as a violation of their relationship rather than its consummation. And everyone else regards his passionate clutching at her in this light. It is a second fall: Tasso, like Adam, has seized the forbidden fruit and must be expelled from the beautiful garden, to live among 'thorns and thistles'.

The play closes with a long speech that Tasso makes to Antonio, in which Tasso finally recognizes his need for the other man. Tasso is the wave that breaks on the rock of Antonio. And at the same time he is the poor boatman who has lost his way, whose vessel splits on the rock to which he must then cling for survival.

This is education at its most cataclysmic: it is only the shipwreck of Tasso's personality that holds out any prospect of survival. If Werther had to die, Tasso is able to survive only by approaching as close as possible to moral and social suicide. Tasso can learn only in extremis; nothing less can get through to him.

The most obvious distinction between Goethe and his character is this: it is clearly out of the range of that imagined figure – the Tasso of the play – to have written such a play. Tasso the character is defined by the way he sees the world, whereas the play is as much concerned with how other people see Tasso, and their views are presented in a way incompatible with his own.

Charlotte von Stein would have wanted to take Tasso in hand. But she would have done so in a loving way. And, of course, he might have been beyond her reach. The Goethe who wrote *Tasso*, however, has internalized her: he, as the writer of the play, is his own Charlotte. For he, the writer, is employing in his treatment of his characters the very qualities Charlotte was exercising on him.

In the long run, things did not turn out well between Goethe and Charlotte. She could never have been utterly pure and disinterested in her relation to Goethe – she quietly resented his admissions of flirtation with all the pretty girls at court. The 'Misels', as he called them, were fascinating to him, and he told Charlotte rather too much about it. She was just able to bear this while he was still around and unattached. Her relation to Goethe was the great achievement of her life; she felt that she had had a hand in making him what he was. Goethe paid conspicuous attention to her and his esteem for Charlotte was hugely important to her.

When, eventually, Goethe went off on his long trip to Italy he gave her no adequate warning; he didn't write to her for three months, although they had been in the most regular correspondence for years. This assertion of independence – of the fact that he didn't need her – was bad enough, but when he returned and took up with an uneducated Weimar girl, this was beyond endurance. It would, perhaps, have been difficult for Charlotte to have accepted any permanent relationship between Goethe and another woman – but this young woman was almost a personal insult to Charlotte, for (as we shall see) she was about as different from Charlotte as it is possible to be.

Nevertheless, in so far as Charlotte was able to help Goethe live with the inner tension between the poet and the politician, she contributed something important and impressive to his life.

7

To Govern

Goethe didn't go to Weimar and stay there simply to chase about the country after wild boar or write entertaining little plays – although he did plenty of both – nor even to learn the ways of the courtier at the feet of Charlotte von Stein. The appeal of Weimar was clearly to do with his desire to rule. In a rather offhand note to Merck in the early days he comments that he's now got a dukedom to play with.

Power wasn't a sudden new interest – Goethe had been brought up with the expectation of running Frankfurt. That was attractive, but the drawbacks were obvious: it would take an extremely long time to rise to the position of his grandfather; in any case, 'running' Frankfurt was a matter of endless compromise, negotiation and majority votes. The city was an oligarchy and no one person could really be said to govern it. Weimar was much more appealing. The state – small though it was – was in practice the private kingdom of Carl August.

Weimar provided a very specific kind of opportunity for Goethe. He was the personal friend of the duke – and the duke was the only person who really mattered in the state. Every decision concerning the forests or roads or pensions – indeed everything and anything – was in his hands. Still, it was his own property that was at stake, and Carl August was sane enough to take very seriously the advice of people qualified to give it.

There was always court etiquette to consider – and on this the duke was fairly rigid. For example, it was considered inappropriate for any non-noble, however famous or intelligent or charming, to sit at dinner at the duke's table. That social right was reserved for those with titles.

And so, for several years, until he was granted a patent of nobility in 1782, Goethe dined at the lower table.

From the beginning of Goethe's Weimar days – even when they were dashing over the hills – decisions still had to be made and Goethe was there to talk things through with the duke; they often stayed up late into the night discussing not only their love affairs, of which the duke had a great many, but also matters of state. There was a new superintendent of the clergy to be appointed – a post which involved responsibility for education as well as the churches. Goethe suggested Herder and an offer was made. After some hesitation, Herder accepted and arrived in Weimar in the middle of 1776. In fact Goethe found he could no longer get on so well with his old mentor and the presence of Herder was to cause quite a few strains in Weimar. Nevertheless it was a very significant move. Herder was a major intellectual figure with a real public following. Weimar was rapidly becoming the literary capital of the German-speaking world.

This was power, although of an informal kind. The duke, however, quickly took steps to create a permanent position for Goethe and decided to make him a member of his 'secret' or private council: the cabinet of four advisers with whom he discussed all matters of state. Although he could in principle appoint whomever he liked, the duke could not, of course, control the reactions of his existing administrators. And he had to avoid alienating them since they were the ones who knew how everything worked.

On 24 April 1776, von Fritsch – the president of the council – wrote to the duke offering, as he had been requested to do, his thoughts on the appointment of Goethe to the cabinet. Von Fritsch was clearly not at all happy; without going into specifics – and stating that he did not disrespect Goethe and had no doubts about his sincere affection for and devotion to the duke – he simply says that he could not continue to be a member of the council if Goethe is appointed and suggests that such an appointment would make Weimar a laughing stock.

The duke's response is exemplary in its confidence and clarity. He knows that he can appoint Goethe and, we may suspect from the tone of the letter, he knows that von Fritsch is unlikely to resign. What lies behind this is his confidence that Goethe will behave very well –

seriously, responsibly, intelligently – in respect of council business; that von Fritsch's anxieties are misplaced:

'You will yourself see that a man such as he [Goethe] would be wasted in tedious and mechanical service at a lower, subordinate level. When a man has great talent you must employ him so that those talents can be used – otherwise you abuse him. The world judges by prejudice; but I don't – and nor should anyone who does his duty properly.'

A few days later, Anna Amalia, the duke's mother, whom von Fritsch had long served, wrote to the president encouraging him to get to know Goethe properly. The outcome of which, she was sure, would be a change of opinion. In fact Goethe and von Fritsch were able to work together amicably – and with growing mutual respect – for many years.

Goethe was well looked after by the duke. In addition to his substantial salary he was given a little garden-house just outside the city, only a few minutes' walk from the palace. Carl August wasn't just being generous to a friend. The drawbacks to being in Weimar were only too obvious – small, out of the way, lacking in resources. The duke was anxious to keep Goethe in Weimar and to do so he knew he had to make conditions attractive. Goethe had the modest garden-house repaired and furnished. This was a striking undertaking for a man who had the option of a more opulent life.

The small house was located in a large garden just across the river Ilm from the ducal palace. The interior was extremely simple, but elegant in its simplicity.

'I have a lovely garden beyond the town gates in a valley of beautiful meadows by the river. There's an old cottage which I'm having repaired. All is in bloom and the birds are singing . . . At night in my garden, I will sleep here alone for the first time . . . it is a wonderful sensation to sit alone in the field and be at home. I hear the ticking of my clock and the sound of the wind and the millstream from afar.'

Here he secured the possibility of solitude, in an age of continuous sociability; he had personal contact with nature, as opposed to the domination of nature in the formal garden. In these ways he exhibited

a particularly modern sensibility. Goethe often used the garden to entertain children: his specialities were making pancakes and organizing Easter-egg hunts. His solitude was not complete: Goethe's servant, Philipp Seidel, often shared the small bedroom with his master. This has encouraged speculation on Goethe's sexuality, although it is impossible to draw firm conclusions from such evidence. Sharing a bed was much more common practice then than now and was not generally regarded in an erotic light. Seidel was certainly devoted to Goethe, copying his master's distinctive manner of walking and taking up his enthusiasms for natural science, poetry and flirtation. But his devotion did not prevent him from engaging in free discussion with Goethe. They often talked late into the night. Seidel records: 'We continued in the most heated set-to until nearly four o'clock in the morning. The question we fought over with such vehemence and learning was this: whether a nation is not happier when it is free than when it is under the authority of a sovereign lord.' The master is on the side of authority, the servant argues for freedom.

*

The overriding problem in Weimar was money – the revenues that came to the state were insufficient to cover its expenses. Goethe was troubled by the fact that ultimately the state finances derived from the peasantry, who had to be hounded to pay their taxes. Goethe wasn't opposed to a hierarchical society – he didn't at all mind that there were peasants and princes living radically different kinds of life. But he did think that the relations between these different parts of the social organism needed to be made more harmonious. The peasants needed to live well if the state were to flourish; grinding down the peasants could extract a bit more cash in the short term but could hardly be a sustainable policy.

A remedy, which deeply appealed to Goethe, was suggested by the existence of defunct silver mines in the Ilmenau district, some distance from the main Weimar territories. Goethe argued that the mines should be reopened so that a further – and substantial – source of income could be developed. Goethe's first official duty was to oversee the opening of the mines.

Late on in his life, Goethe once tried to calculate how much – in financial terms – his complete works had cost. How much money did he have to spend to get the experience that went into his books? With perhaps a touch of bravado he arrives at the almost preposterous sum of two million thalers – with quite a lot of it being money he had spent on behalf of the state.

For example, in *Faust* there's quite a lot of talk about mining. How did Goethe come to know so much about that? How much did that cost? Rather a lot as it turned out. The Ilmenau silver mine was prone to flooding; it was hard to get hold of anyone with sufficient expertise to solve the technical problems; the rights to the mines were actually shared among several different interested parties and they all had to agree before operations could proceed. And when they eventually did try to extract silver, the ore wasn't rich enough to be commercially viable. The whole enterprise – which dragged on for many years – was an economic disaster. Goethe was not unwise or incompetent in this undertaking. The saga of the mine revealed only the pain of responsibility: a reasonable policy, properly executed, can still fail.

Goethe's areas of responsibility gradually widened; he was asked to be in charge of the roads; then the army; and later – at the high point of his duties – the finances. These responsibilities were not quite as large as they might sound: the roads were mainly tracks; the army was very small. One of Goethe's best results was to persuade the duke – who was passionately keen on military matters and loved army life – to reduce the number of troops from about five hundred to about two hundred.

However, it was in connection with army recruitment that Goethe had the most difficulties. In general 'recruitment' was by force; criminals were frequently made to serve, but there weren't enough criminals. It was standard practice in the German territories for larger states to buy or extract troops from less powerful neighbours.

Battles and wars were not national. Kings and princes were not conducting military campaigns on behalf of their people. They had no particular concern where their troops came from. Frederick the Great was happy to press Weimar peasants into his army; at one point Carl August – and Goethe – agreed to sell some prisoners to the British army in America. Such a sale was not all that unusual for the times; nor, by the standards of the day, was it morally dubious. It would be quite unfair to draw the conclusion that Goethe was cruel or exploitative. He certainly got his hands dirty in government, but only in ways which were pretty much inescapable as part of governing while keeping a small, financially precarious state going.

Goethe's position in Weimar in this period (1775–86) is particularly interesting because of the way it blended – not always comfortably – intellectual, creative, administrative and governmental aspects. Retrospective views of Goethe's life have, understandably, been ambivalent about this. And one can understand attitudes to this period as symptomatic of the condition of later intellectuals and academics. Thus, for example, in periods when intellectuals are supposed to occupy a pure and somewhat removed position – when the ideal is 'research' or creation and being left alone to do it – Goethe's practical functions look like a terrible distraction. He should have been getting on with writing poetry or thinking about science, and certainly should not have spent his days worrying about roads and fire brigades. One can imagine Flaubert expressing such an opinion.

At other times, it has seemed as if the role of the intellectual should be to challenge government: to point out the inadequacies of the powerful, to be in moral and imaginative opposition. For an intellectual to be involved in running the state, living with and being complicit in its imperfections, is regarded as 'selling out'.

However, Goethe has drawn nearer to us – and we to Goethe. Goethe's example seems more interesting and valuable than either the pure artist or the critical intellectual. He is a new kind of hero. The real task is not merely to criticize power, but to exercise it well; on the other side, the task is not merely to make 'pure art' or conduct 'pure research', but to bring art and knowledge into fruitful engagement with experience. Goethe's example is powerful because he undertakes these tasks as a creative artist of the highest order. So, the integration of art and life doesn't – when we fix our attention on Goethe – look like a grubby compromise. *Tasso*, for example, would have been a much less fine play if Goethe had simply been on Tasso's side – if he had hated and mocked Antonio. Goethe's greatest achievements, *Wilhelm Meister* and *Faust*, owe much to his experience of worldly matters.

The name of a hero is shorthand for an approach to life we find helpful. If we have a habit of flinging ourselves on the sofa, sighing about the impossible burden of finding the right word, we might be very pleased to remember that Flaubert often did this; our lassitude can be experienced as noble suffering rather than incompetence. Which suggests that we need to be careful in our choice of heroes – since we may be led to be proud only of our weaknesses. Goethe's role is that of integrating two demands, creative and administrative; he invites those of us who lament such dual lives to follow him in seeing this as a great opportunity (although obviously difficult as well).

8

Egmont: The Psychology of Power

Goethe never wrote an explicit or systematic political philosophy; we have to reconstruct his views from his literary works. In the period prior to the French Revolution – which in 1789 was to permanently alter the political landscape – the most revealing expression of Goethe's political instincts and ideas is to be found in his play *Egmont*. Initially sketched in Frankfurt in the months following the publication of *Werther*, Goethe worked fitfully on the drama through the first ten years in Weimar, completing it only while in Italy – the year and a half he spent mostly in Rome between 1786 and 1788 being the decisive break between his first period in Weimar (late 1775–mid 1786) and his residence there from 1788 until his death in 1832.

Egmont was published in 1788 as part of Goethe's first authorized *Collected Works* (there had been pirate editions going under that title). Hence the dates of the writing and publication of *Egmont* are very similar to those of *Tasso* and the two plays do in fact have a deep relation – they are almost companion pieces – despite the obvious differences in the overt actions with which they deal. While *Tasso* plays upon a personal, private history with few repercussions for anyone except the principal character himself, *Egmont* draws upon and dramatically intensifies one of the great political narratives of early modernity: the rise of Holland as an independent and highly sophisticated state.

The play is set in Brussels in the second half of the sixteenth century. Although, of course, Brussels is today in Belgium, this territory was – at the time of the play – included in the Netherlands. Margaret of

Parma, sister of Philip II of Spain, is regent on behalf of her brother. She exercises legitimate feudal rights. Their father, the Holy Roman Emperor Charles V, had divided his world-encompassing domains, passing Spain and the Netherlands to his son Philip. Thus despite being King of Spain, Philip is actually a Hapsburg; and his feudal overlordship in the Netherlands is not very different from the Holy Roman Emperor's authority over Weimar; the Netherlands had passed to the Hapsburgs by marriage and inheritance, as had many other dominions.

At the start of the play Margaret's rule is light; she has no army and much of the real power in the Netherlands lies in the hands of two local aristocratic magnates: Egmont and Oranien (in English, the Prince of Orange). There has been some civil unrest provoked by supporters of the newly reformed protesting churches, particularly the followers of Calvin, and those who violently resent them. Margaret, like all the Hapsburgs, is a firm Catholic. She has dealt mildly but effectively with the disturbances. But the quiet assuredness of her rule has not impressed her brother: 'The good I have done' – she bitterly reflects – 'looks like nothing, precisely because it is good.'

Philip resolves to send an army under a fearsome general, the Duke of Alba, ostensibly to 'help' Margaret, but really – as she knows – to replace her. Backed by the rigours of the Inquisition, Alba is to stamp out the new religion and generally bring the Netherlands to heel.

Goethe sets the scene with the citizens in the streets lamenting the disordered times and calling for 'Security and peace, order and freedom.' Very probably no crowd has ever chanted such a slogan, but Goethe clearly intends these words to articulate the deepest political needs of all societies. These are the things all people want from government – the rest of life is private. More specific demands on the government of the day are always the more or less appropriate means by which they might be achieved. And the end of political wisdom, the goal of government, is to attain 'security and peace, order and freedom' for a whole society – when these are obtained people can themselves pursue the natural human goal of individual happiness.

When public unrest threatens to turn violent, the sudden appearance of Egmont restores calm. Egmont is the popular hero, for his dashing ways, liberal style and military valour. His authority is essentially intimate: individual citizens trust and like Egmont and obey him because they trust and like him.

The character of Egmont is rounded out in Act II, in which we see him dealing with administrative business; in his judgements he seeks to render justice to the person, rather than abide by any prior legal formulation. A woman has been badly treated – roughly seduced – by two of his men. They are to be flogged on three successive days and then they must pass over a significant portion of their property to her. A Calvinist preacher has been apprehended; he claims to be on his way to France; under the Spanish regime he could be executed; this time, says Egmont, have him escorted quietly to the border, but make it clear that if he comes back there will be no pardon.

Egmont is short of funds and his bailiff complains that no more money is to be had. Egmont will not listen to this: money is necessary: it is to be procured, by whatever means (presumably selling assets or borrowing). An old friend has written to advise Egmont to moderate his habits – he is living without regard to the future. But Egmont refuses to be lectured, even by this kindest and wisest of voices. What he is advocating, in the end, is only this, says Egmont: 'I ought to live, in a way in which I cannot live. That I am joyful, that I take things lightly, that I am lively and impetuous – that is my happiness . . . Do I live merely to *think* about living? Am I not to seize the joys of the present, just so that I can be sure about the future; am I supposed to consume my life in care and melancholy?'

This phrase about 'consuming life in care' is a direct biblical reference: when Adam is expelled from the Garden of Eden – when he loses his innocence – God proclaims that Adam and his descendants shall live a life of toil, winning their bread by the sweat of their brow. Egmont is an aspect of Goethe – the lively, dashing, charming, irresistible man who so delighted Wieland. But Egmont is also 'Adam before the Fall': a man as he should be: radiantly at ease with himself and his God: a man undamaged by the human condition. He is, like

Christ, the second Adam. The point of all this is not that Goethe wants to present Egmont – or indeed himself – as the saviour of humanity. It's crucial, here, that Egmont isn't a self-portrait; no more than Tasso is a self-portrait. Adam before the Fall, and the second, restored, Adam are part of Goethe – just as (potentially) they are part of everyone. The difference of course – which must have been overwhelmingly obvious to Goethe as he wrote snatches of the play between ministerial meetings and administrative duties in Weimar – was that Goethe really did care about tomorrow, really did worry about where the money was going to come from, really was subject to self-criticism and anxiety.

Tasso is a wonderful poet, but his life is tragic because he cannot really befriend Antonio, the man of experience and practical wisdom. Egmont is a magnificent human being, but his life is cut short – he can succeed only through his own death – but why? Because, he cannot marry himself to the prudence and cunning of his co-leader, Oranien, the Prince of Orange, who – after Egmont's death – leads the successful revolt against Spanish dominion.

There is a secondary plot in *Egmont*, which follows the hero's love for a local woman – Clärchen, a plain citizen rather than a woman of his own noble status. Their love is intensely mutual; we see them together in the third of five acts.

The scene midway through the play is also the symbolic centre of the drama. But the action it contains is at first sight deeply puzzling. One of the first reviewers of the play was Schiller, not yet a close friend of Goethe. Schiller is critical of the fact that *Egmont*'s central scene – the scene in which we are primed to discover Egmont as a hero – doesn't take place on the battlefield, although we have heard that he is a great warrior; nor does it show a diplomatic triumph – in fact we later see Egmont being diplomatically outwitted. The core of the drama takes place in the home of Egmont's lover – Clärchen. Egmont enters wrapped in his long riding cloak; he hesitates and then he throws wide his arms revealing the most splendid costume adorned with the insignia of the most august chivalric order: the Golden Fleece. Egmont's spiritual beauty is made manifest. But this is not a scene of pomp and majesty – it takes place in the quietest, most serene domestic interlude. For Egmont's splendour, like that of the Christ, is not terrifying or humiliating – it is adorable, and Clärchen embraces him.

9

Egmont: The Education
of Authority

Alba arrives and parades his troops through the city, imposing a curfew. He summons Egmont and Oranien, ostensibly requesting their advice and assistance. The astute Oranien suspects a trap and declines – encouraging Egmont to do likewise – even though he recognizes that refusal will be taken as revolt and will lead to war. Egmont, however, attends partly because it is not in his nature to ponder consequences; partly because he is genuinely loyal to Philip, whom he acknowledges as his rightful feudal lord; partly because he has a sort of buoyant fatalism, a spirit that has made him such a formidable leader of cavalry charges, when death is faced down moment after moment.

At the duke's palace, Alba and Egmont trade philosophical attitudes, debating the nature of freedom and the principles of government. When Alba and Egmont discuss the nature of freedom in Act IV Alba asserts – rightly – that we often feel free only when we are in a position to do things we shouldn't. Licence is knowing that you can do something even if it's not actually a very good idea to do it – in short, you can do whatever you want: that's one of the most obvious ideas of freedom we have. And, as Alba says, this makes freedom seem an abuse. Surely it is the proper task of government to curb our freedom, in this sense?

Egmont's reply is a brilliant intervention in political theory. This kind of authority is incompatible with human nature. Such control breaks the human spirit. Of course, that makes the task of government much simpler – it is easier to rule a broken population. But this is no longer genuine power. In other words, the problem of power is that to be powerful in life one has to accommodate the reality of human character. And that requires giving up a certain amount of authority and handing it over, however difficult that may be. Egmont is rehearsing arguments that, in the end, are inescapable for parents of adolescent children. It might be tempting to keep your teenagers under lock and key but to be a genuine parent requires allowing some degree of autonomy, and that is painful because it might be used badly; but it is not open to us to ensure that this cannot happen.

The key thing about Egmont, then, is that he is able to cede some power to others while retaining a sense of his own responsibility and dignity. And he is able to do this because of his inner security – his inner Golden Fleece. Egmont isn't trying to compensate for an inner emptiness by dominion over others. He holds dominion over others because of his inner richness – because he is loveable, rather than because he is terrifying.

But Alba is not really listening; while Egmont discourses on power and freedom, Alba's guards – led by his natural son, Ferdinand – file into the adjoining galleries and chambers. As Egmont turns to leave, he is arrested, disarmed and escorted to a prison cell. He is immediately condemned to death as a traitor and preparations are made to have him beheaded the following morning.

Searching for Egmont, Clärchen hears of his arrest and of the erection of a black platform in the square where he will be executed. Hopelessly she attempts to rouse the citizens, but they are incapable of such heroics without much stronger leadership than she can provide. Unable to face a future without Egmont, Clärchen poisons herself and dies.

In his cell, Egmont hopes that the people will rise to save him, or that Margaret will intervene to secure his release, or even that an angel will descend from Heaven and miraculously fling open the prison gates – in the same way, as we are told in the Acts of the Apostles, that St Peter was rescued from a Roman cell. Finally, Egmont falls asleep. He dreams of Clärchen, now enthroned as a goddess of peace and victory, smiling down on him and placing a laurel wreath upon his brow. This dream sequence is enacted as a *tableau vivant* behind the sleeping Egmont with incidental music, later supplied by Beethoven – in fact his music for the play is probably now better known than the original drama it was intended to support. The peace and victory represented by the wreath are the final consequences of Egmont's death; his execution will be the catalyst for revolt and the eventual independence of the northern part of the Netherlands – a narrative trajectory beyond the limits of the play, but one that would have required no explaining to Goethe's contemporaries.

Early in the morning, Ferdinand comes to the cell to read the death sentence. After doing so he reveals that he has been since childhood a fervent admirer of Egmont. Finally accepting death, Egmont bequeaths his last responsibilities to Ferdinand, gives him his horse – the symbol of his authority – and steps calmly towards the place of execution.

In the last lines of the play Egmont gives himself as an example to Ferdinand: 'be like me'. Although here he is referring explicitly to his manner of facing death, the real point is much broader. Like Christ, Egmont is an example in death, but, also like Christ, it's not the death so much as the way of living that is being recommended. This is right, since it is Egmont's mode of being – rather than any particular rules that we can formulate – which is admirable.

The final act brings psychology and politics together. Why is Alba so keen to get rid of Egmont? Well, officially, it's because Egmont is a traitor; pragmatically, it's because Egmont is a barrier to royal authority – since Egmont stands as an intermediary, as local power. But, finally, Egmont suggests it is to do with envy. Once he and Alba had been at a gambling party where Egmont was in the middle of a lucky run. Alba himself was not losing money but was enraged by Egmont's success. The gambling image is apt because what Alba hates here is luck: Egmont's good fortune.

Ferdinand is the illegitimate son of Alba. Alba has – he says – great hopes for the boy and is – in his own fashion – deeply devoted to him. But Alba knows of Ferdinand's natural liking for the dashing, charismatic Egmont. So Ferdinand is the one appointed to read Egmont his death sentence; a move designed to crush him, to destroy his humanity. This is the most intimate exercise of power that we are shown and it fails. Ferdinand is ever more impressed by Egmont.

Instead of being a continuation of Alba – the one moment of tenderness given to Alba is when he gazes fondly at his son – Ferdinand becomes Egmont's spiritual heir. This is the clearest case in which a certain kind of power meets its limitations. Ferdinand's love cannot be coerced. It is only by killing Egmont – killing his inner life and crushing him – that Alba hopes to 'win' his son; but this is not to win a son at all, only to create an obedient instrument; and even then it fails. Egmont, however, has real power over Ferdinand – he wins Ferdinand's devotion, he moulds Ferdinand's aspirations and character.

The play can be read as a charged and painful dialogue between two kinds of power. On the one hand there is mechanical power – which is exercised completely but over inert material. This is often referred to (in the play) as the power to crush because it operates by deadening the object of control – an individual, a population. Thus when the Spanish troops under Alba enter Brussels the city becomes a ghost town, the life goes out of it. Of course now there is order and quiet and peace – but it is the absence of individual and civic life which brings these things.

The contrastive power is that of power over life – not power to remove life but to guide and enhance it. Egmont compares it to riding a horse; the horse is mastered, certainly, but with a good rider the horse is not deadened, but brought to its highest performance. So the sign of this power is abundance of life; not chaotic abundance, but secure, peaceful vitality.

The play is a tragedy, in that the central character is executed. But, what is the nature of this tragedy? The minor, personal tragedy is that of Egmont himself, in that he is unable to live, because – being as he is – he cannot accommodate the good advice of Oranien or of his old friend. But a deeper, larger, tragedy comes into view if we regard the play as showing the human condition as one in which Egmont simply could not have his grace and nobility but for his weakness. Is his glorious 'I am what I am' attitude both the essence of loveliness and bound for disaster? Is the very most desirable thing also fatal? The play does nothing to resolve this question. As with Tasso so with Egmont: we cannot tell whether we are concerned with a study of one person's flaws that could, in principle, be healed without damage to their good qualities, or – by contrast – whether we are concerned with the delineation of a flaw in the human condition as such: in which the remedy could only cause a general weakening of the individual. Are we seeing a Greek tragedy – in which life itself is tragic; or a Christian tragedy – in which only human frailty, not the cosmic order, can be catastrophic?

At one point Egmont says: 'I stand high, and I can and must stand higher; I feel in myself hope, courage and power. I haven't yet attained my full stature, nor reached the summit of my life.' Here, Egmont is not talking only about political power or authority. He has no inclination to lead a national revolt. In his eyes Philip II of Spain is his legitimate feudal overlord, rather as Götz was deeply loyal to his lord, the Emperor. Philip is the grandson of the Duke of Burgundy, whose dominion Egmont's grandfather would have recognized. What Egmont wants is for his own legitimate lordship – below Philip – to be secured.

But the growth in his being is, rather, in his love for Clärchen and – doubtless – for his own, their own, future children: the Egmonts-to-be.

In his sustained analysis of the psychology of power – and especially in this admission of ambition in the voice of Egmont – Goethe is writing a genuine 'Fürstenspiegel'. And it is here that we see the deeper character of Goethe's political philosophy. We search in vain in Egmont and elsewhere for an obvious political philosophy in Goethe – do we know what he considers to be wise laws, what kind of constitution he favours?

In Goethe's view, the epicentre of politics is the spirit – the minds or souls – of those who stand high and drive themselves to stand higher. Nothing is more important than the spirit of their ambition, the spirit in which their ambition is conducted. Alba is a tyrant; Egmont is a gracious, merciful and just lord, and what makes the difference? It's not to do with political systems, but with people. And this is a point that applies in democratic societies too – although with slightly less urgency than it did in the societies Goethe knew.

10

Disillusion

The meaning of Weimar, for Goethe, can be understood in terms of a 'solution' to the problem of personal development. Goethe had absorbed, and enriched, the prevailing idea of self-improvement. He had traced both the impetus to this and the dangers it seemed to bring with it. Self-cultivation is good – but it often results in excessive introspection and over-dependence on the flow of mood. On the other hand, he is concerned with political or social development and improvement.

These two ideas can be placed under the terms 'Bildung' and 'Kultur': personal culture and civilization. The opportunity of Weimar is to integrate these. Goethe's personal development can proceed through the widening of his experience – through contact with new kinds of people (aristocrats and the common people over whom he holds administrative power). But civilization is the attempt to 'express' that personal culture in a more concrete and lasting way – to give it external form.

One minor but telling example of this was the setting up of a drawing academy in Weimar. Goethe had been a keen amateur draughtsman for years and had taken lessons from the distinguished teacher Oeser while a student at Leipzig. There were others who shared this recreation, Anna Amalia among them. In addition there was a continual need for artistic advice and work in the normal running of the court (designing a new table, decorating a ceiling).

This enthusiasm was focused and developed through the establishment of the Drawing Academy – which came into being in 1776. By establishing an institution, with a properly paid professor and regular lectures and classes, an unstructured enthusiasm was given a permanent basis. Professional expertise got the chance to develop – and to influence the efforts of amateurs. And other interests were able to accumulate around this.

For example, as Goethe got more and more excited by comparative anatomy, he took up a systematic study of skulls, and gave lectures at the academy, following the traditional and sensible view that figure drawing benefits from an understanding of anatomy. As part of these researches, Goethe set his heart on procuring an elephant's skull – on the natural assumption that the standard elements of the skull would there be reproduced on a larger scale and could be more easily detected. While he was staying in Erfurt in 1784 he wrote to Charlotte von Stein about the awkwardness some of his investigations were causing: 'the elephant's skull has arrived from Kassel and what I'm looking for is clear beyond my expectations. I'm keeping it hidden in a cupboard so they won't think I'm mad. My landlady is sure that there's porcelain in the huge packing case.'

Early on in his Weimar days, Goethe commented to Merck that now he was actually involved in the realities of power he could see the 'absolute shittiness of all that passes for earthly glory'. This is just bravado; Goethe is absolutely thrilled to be on the inside of things and the tone of disgust is an insider's joke. The premise is that this is worldly glory and he's got it.

But the bravado was to wear off rather quickly. And it is clear that he was approaching some kind of crisis – a crisis to do with the point or meaning of his life. Whatever his original fascination with administration, the reality of the burdens, the intractability and difficulty, must have been extremely obvious as he clambered down the mine shafts and made his way through the muddy countryside.

He felt confused about what he was doing – he had been in Weimar for two years – what, if anything, had he achieved? Certainly nothing along the lines of his work in the years before – like *Werther* or *Götz*.

Without telling anyone what he was doing, Goethe slipped away in early December – heading over to the Brocken – the highest mountain in the region. Going up mountains in winter was not a recognized sane activity; we get some idea of what it meant to Goethe in the biblical language he uses to describe his journey. The archetypal story of mountain climbing – in Goethe's imagination – comes from the New Testament. During the forty days spent in the wilderness, before the start of his public ministry, Christ climbs a mountain and there is tempted by the Devil. Looking down on the kingdoms of the earth he is tempted by the possibility of worldly power: a kingdom of this world.

Goethe, too, is in the wilderness, not only the literal wilderness of the Harz Mountains, but also the wilderness of uncertainty: what is he doing with his life? He too recognizes the possible divergence of the spiritual and temporal realms. For Christ the temptation is to abandon his real mission and replace it with worldly success. But Goethe's relation to 'the Devil' is not like this. Worldly power or riches are not opposed to his spiritual aims – in fact he is precisely trying to integrate these. The temptation is to abandon the material world – to flee from Weimar – and dedicate himself exclusively to art.

Goethe came down from the Brocken in a much more cheerful frame of mind. For the next few years he was an assiduous member of the duke's council – meetings were twice a week and Goethe attended some five hundred sittings. As a well-trained lawyer he accepted, and saw the point of, the complex legal formulation of the decisions. The duke heartily despised all this and wanted everything stated in simple, clear German. To a large degree Goethe accepted these burdens – and their frustrations – as a species of education. 'He who wishes to rule others must learn to rule himself. That is, must undertake tasks not because they are pleasant or interesting but because they contribute in some small but necessary way to the proper and wise exercise of power.'

However, the conflict did not go away. The demands placed upon him gradually increased. In 1779 Goethe had to take over the role of treasurer – the inefficiency of von Kalb, whom he liked, having finally become insupportable. The frustrating thing was that governing was really just endless management, rather than real improvement. Goethe's original hope had been to govern in the sense of shaping and forming a small state. But the reality was rather different; he was forced continually to try to merely get by, to keep disaster at bay.

What seemed, eventually, to turn Goethe away from this was what he called the 'Sisyphean' character of the task. The work he was doing was not – in the end – actually making things much better; at best he was maintaining the status quo; at worst (and this was often the case with the finances) he was managing a permanent crisis, with no reasonable prospect of positive constructive results. The activity seemed 'aimless' beyond the mere fact of keeping going – and this was something he found completely intolerable. And, indeed, the whole character of Goethe's private life is that of little aims, little projects, which are seen through.

For example, he would form a plan for upgrading a road and start transporting the necessary stones. But since the road was in such a bad condition the materials would be used for temporary piecemeal repairs. And so the improved road would never get built. Instead of constructing proper foundations with good drainage, they would be forever replacing the surface of the road only to see it rapidly deteriorate – because there were no proper foundations.

'Chronic lack of funds makes it impossible to plan ahead and to accomplish with economy the task undertaken' – doing things bit by bit is actually more expensive. 'Compelled as he is to leave so many defects unremedied, the person in charge of these activities loses all interest, a thing that would never happen if he could work on a proper basis and feel his efforts were producing some results.'

He valued the experience of government – and especially the contact it brought him with the actual condition of society. Later this was to underwrite his negative reactions to the French Revolution – not because he thought that the poor were getting fair treatment, or that the aristocracy were doing a great job, but because he recognized (as almost no other German intellectuals did) that the business of government is not achieved by decrees or legislation – and that implementing actual improvements is astonishingly difficult.

He prided himself on learning through the demands of responsibility to see things as they are; not in relation to his own fancies or preferences; not in terms of their private significance to him; but 'as they are' – as they need to be seen to be judged from a practical point of view. It made him feel 'clean'; his experience was purged of 'false echoes': those private resonances which seem, at first, so charming, but which prevent contact with reality. To see things this way is not only a relief, not only practically advantageous, but also – in Goethe's eyes – philosophically and aesthetically satisfactory. For, in such a condition, you can properly trace the connections between things (between action and consequence); the world comes to seem less arbitrary, less capricious.

But the process of self-education was not pleasant: 'It seems as if this mighty hammer' – the cares and demands of administration – 'was needed to free my nature of all its slag and make my heart clean. And yet how many defects manage to hide in it still.'

Perhaps the final disillusionment came, for Goethe, when Carl August himself decided to leave the state. There was, of course, no actual requirement for him to live in Weimar or to take any effective interest in running the state. His great passion was the army and the possibility of satisfying that in Weimar itself was more remote than ever. In 1786 Carl August joined the Prussian army as a colonel.

Goethe's political views were centred on the responsibility of the prince: he admired hierarchical government; but the basis for such a state was the devotion of the prince to his people. It was surely the quasi-abdication of Carl August, the duke's decision to put his private needs (such as they were) before devotion to the state, that emboldened Goethe to take the next great step in his own life.

Goethe's decision to leave adds a further – and important – step to the discussion of his integration of administrative and creative undertakings. Goethe saw the importance of his 'civil service' career in terms of its contribution to personal growth, to the way it could balance his character and help him grow up and face reality. So, there could come a point where this had been achieved. Goethe had absorbed what he could from his decade of public responsibility; there was no need to keep on learning the same lesson for the rest of his life.

PART FOUR

Art

I shall never rest until I know that all my ideas are derived, not from hearsay or tradition, but from my real living contact with the things themselves. From my earliest youth this has been my ambition and my torment.

Goethe, *Italian Journey* (1816–17), entry for 27 June 1787

I

Into Italy

On 3 September 1786 – a Sunday – at three in the morning, with the minimum of luggage and no servant, Goethe boarded the mail coach out of Carlsbad. He had been taking the waters at the famous spa with a party from Weimar and had just celebrated his thirty-seventh birthday in fine style with a grand dinner. The night before he left he had written to Charlotte saying, vaguely, that he was going away for a little trip; and to Carl August – now preoccupied with his duties as a colonel in the Prussian army – asking for leave. He was heading south; heading, in fact, for Italy and Rome, and had no idea how long he would be away. The risks were obvious – would his friends ever forgive him for abandoning them? Would he ever be welcome in Weimar again? Could Italy really do for his soul what the waters of Carlsbad had done for his body?

Although furtive and – to his companions – unexpected, Goethe's 'flight' to Italy was the most premeditated step of his life. Along with training as a lawyer it was central to his father's expectations: Goethe was born to go to Italy; he had learned Italian, he was intimately acquainted with the works of Ariosto and Tasso as well as, of course, the Latin classics.

As if to take his mind off the anxieties of abandoning his friends, and perhaps as a way of fixing in his mind the detail of this thing he had so longed to do, Goethe paid the utmost attention to the geology of the districts the coach passed through, as though he were on another of his scientific trips. In Bavaria, though, snacking on some nice pears, he lets slip a more open-ended desire: 'I am longing for grapes and figs'; but his real longing was for what he might become in a sunny climate; who he might be if he could feast on southern fruit. At last he crossed the Brenner Pass and arrived in Italy, or, more accurately – since Italian unification was more than a hundred years in the future – in the lands belonging to the Republic of Venice.

'At present I am preoccupied with sense impressions; the truth is that in putting my powers of observation to the test I have found a new interest in life. Can I learn to look at things with clear, fresh eyes? How much can I take in at a single glance? Can the grooves of old mental habits be effaced?'

In Strasbourg, Goethe had deliberately set out to overcome his fear of heights – and he conquered by a sustained effort his natural propensity to vertigo. Now we see this same 'will to power' – will to self-mastery – being exercised in a more complex way: Goethe was trying to make himself more attentive and more receptive. The notes on different kinds of soil, different atmospheric effects and new plants are not ends in themselves. He is determined to train himself to see what is there; he wants to overcome the tendency to see only what one expects to see: the tendency of the eye to be governed by habit. This active, even authoritarian, attitude towards himself is one of the most conspicuous features of Goethe's personality. He takes the idea of self-improvement very seriously and systematically. He was afraid of heights – very well, that hindrance must be overcome. He had a tendency to flit from object to object: very well, he would discipline his mind. He would force himself to notice, compare and remember.

There was another side to this exploration: for the first time since his student days Goethe had only himself to rely upon; in Weimar he was at the centre of a social and administrative system – there were secretaries and servants always on hand. Now, on the road, he is not only his own master but also his own servant. 'The fact that I have to look after myself keeps me mentally alert . . . I find that I am developing a new elasticity of mind.'

The further he got from Weimar, the more at home he felt. He had the strange feeling that he had been born in Italy but had passed most of his life 'on a whaling expedition to Greenland'. 'Someone familiar with all this would think my enthusiasm very childish. I have the pleasure of experiencing this happiness as an exception which by rights we ought to be able to enjoy as a rule of our nature.' If Italy was 'home' then what was Goethe to make of the rest of his life – has it all been some terrible mistake, a mere exile in the Arctic?

After more than a week travelling, on 12 September Goethe arrived at Lake Garda. The inn where he stayed had only the most basic provisions for his comfort: on inquiring where he could perform his ablutions, Goethe was robustly directed to the courtyard and in-structed to relieve himself there – just like everyone else. But this could not dampen his delight. For the first time, as he noted, he was able to see with his own eyes a place memorialized by Virgil, who had described the waves on the lake. A small thing, no doubt, but of symbolic importance to Goethe because a central aim of his journey, as he keeps on reminding himself, was to transform knowledge by description into knowledge by acquaintance.

The following day, as he was sketching the remains of a nearby medi-eval fortress, the whole project nearly came to ruin. He found a convenient nook and started drawing a crumbling tower. Some locals came by and their curiosity was aroused: what could he be up to? This was not a place tourists ever visited. Goethe refused to be disturbed by their presence. Eventually, one of the locals came over, brusquely stated that drawing was not allowed and proceeded to tear up the sketch. Then the podestà, a sort of local magistrate, arrived; he was deeply suspicious: why draw some stupid old tower? The only signifi-cance of the place was that as a frontier post between the territories of Venice and Austria. Goethe must be a spy selecting targets for the Imperial artillery.

Goethe could not brush this off by explaining who he really was, for that would have looked even worse. There he was, an Imperial baron, minister of war (among other things) in the State of Weimar, recently arrived – at maximum speed – from Carlsbad, a well-known centre of international intrigue and plotting; a man known to undertake diplomatic missions; and now at the Venetian frontier, under an assumed name, pretending to be an artist. Such conduct could only look extremely suspicious.

Goethe went on the offensive and tried to convey the allure of the place – look at the ivy climbing the ruins – and generally went into raptures over the beauty of the spot. The podestà was not impressed by aesthetics. So Goethe tried another tactic: 'I'm not an Austrian, I'm from Frankfurt.' They sent for one Gregorio who had been in service with a mercantile family back in Frankfurt and the matter was resolved – Goethe knew the family. And in any case his effusions about the scenery had inspired an innkeeper with visions of streams of German sightseers passing through.

Goethe was always immensely proud of his ability to deal with people and get himself out of scrapes.

2

The Imaginary Friend

Goethe's next stop was Verona, where he wanted to inspect the Roman arena. The great, empty oval amphitheatre struck him as a bit desolate. But in a little local museum he saw some late Roman sepulchral monuments that, at last, really spoke to him. These small-scale carved reliefs honouring the dead show modest scenes from daily life: 'A husband and wife look out from a niche as from a window'; 'a father and mother and son look at each other with indescribable tenderness; a married couple join hands; a father reclines on a couch and appears to be chatting with his family'. They are simple, natural and expressive – and, to Goethe, deeply moving. They contrast very favourably, he thinks, with the Christian tombs he knows from home. He's touched by the fact that there's no intimation here of a future life – no claim that this life is only a prelude to another, more important, existence. If life is to be redeemed – these carved stones seem to say – it must be on the basis of the ordinary realities of human beings. And it's hard to resist the thought that Goethe is lonely – where is domestic tenderness and emotional security for him? 'My natural disposition,' he comments, 'is to revere the good and the beautiful: to be able to cultivate this tendency in the presence of noble objects makes me very happy.'

With all this in his mind it's not surprising that Goethe is so annoyed by some of the motifs in the religious paintings that he goes to look at the next day. He particularly dislikes an image drawn from the story of Moses showing the starving Israelites receiving the miraculous rain of manna in the desert. What could be more idiotic, he thinks, than all these people grubbing about for bits of bread that have fallen out of the sky? The evident technical skill of the artist is wasted on such subjects; what have they to say to someone trying to live an interesting and purposeful life today? Wait for a miracle? Goethe's whole life was an attempt to feed himself – as it were – by his own efforts.

One of the most fruitful and revealing episodes of Goethe's time in Italy occurred in Vicenza, his last stopping place as he made his way towards Venice which was to be his first major halt. In Vicenza and the surrounding countryside he visited some buildings by Palladio; he had long been familiar with these from descriptions and prints, but 'you have to see them with your own eyes to realize how good they are'. Seeing them was a revelation. In fact Palladio became the single most important role model for Goethe; it is this sixteenth-century architect of villas and churches who represents most vividly some of Goethe's deepest ambitions for his own art.

The terms in which Goethe comments on Palladio are intimately related to those that he was to employ when he came – decades later – to the task of conveying the meaning of his own life in his autobiography, *Poetry and Truth*. 'There is something divine about Palladio's talent, something comparable to the power of a great poet who, out of the worlds of truth and deception, creates a third whose borrowed existence enchants us.' He wanted to do with his life what Palladio had done with stone.

Goethe is deeply attracted to what he sees as the 'nobility' of Palladio's buildings. But he is upset to see how badly they are treated: people were using the serene porticos as public latrines. 'How little these precious monuments, designed by a superior mind, are in accord with the life of ordinary people. It's the same with everything. You get small thanks when you try to refine people's sense of what they need, give them a greater sense of what they can be or try to get them to respond to what's really noble. But flatter them, tell them lies, cater to their weaknesses – you're their man.'

And then he adds an extraordinary comment: 'I don't say all this to do down my friends.' In other words, the 'ordinary people' who are so misguided in their distribution of praise and resentment, who turn away from what is precious to what is banal, are not the nameless multitudes: they are Goethe's friends, people he lives with and generally likes. 'I only say' – he says to himself – 'that is what people are like: don't be shocked that things are as they are.'

It is a reminder – if we need one – that the people we like, the people we are friends with, may be unable to grasp certain things that are deeply important to us. In which case we have to turn elsewhere for companionship. But where? Goethe immediately seeks a solution.

As he wandered around some of Palladio's buildings, Goethe fantasized that he was in conversation with the great architect. He would pick out some detail of the construction which he thought rather imperfect, and – in imagination – turn to Palladio with a quizzical look, saying: what happened there? Well, says Palladio, certain things I had to do against my will; I did it because in the circumstances it was the closest I could get to my ideal.

Goethe imagines the 'extraordinary' man's working practice: he's commissioned to add a new façade to an old building, and – of course – the existing structure limits what he can do. 'He must have said to himself: "How can you give this building the noblest form possible? Because of contradictory demands, I'm going to mess up some of it; there are going to be a few points that won't look quite right. But the building as a whole will be in a noble style and I'm going to enjoy working on it." It was in this way he could bring forth the great idea he had within him, even though it couldn't be done perfectly.'

Such thoughts were painfully, joyfully, appropriate to Goethe's own condition; he was carrying around with him various manuscripts that needed new façades; building on what was there was going to require some compromise – the only alternative being to abandon them; a course already ruled out by his contract with his publisher Göschen, which committed him to completing a lot of work that had been begun years before: *Egmont* and *Tasso* were awaiting major revisions. The last, desperate, alternative – breaking the contract – was out of the question because he was already spending the money.

The endearing imaginary friendship with Palladio is a kind of professional memorandum to himself: it's possible to compromise and still hold on to your ideals; and compromise needn't spoil the fun. That's the hope; at any rate, it's necessary to live as if this were true.

The identification with Palladio went much deeper than a shared experience of the vicissitudes of artistic ambition. Goethe saw his own style – his private literary, artistic and political ideology – as being fundamentally similar to Palladio's architecture. Palladio used comparatively simple elements, his work is free of bombast or pretension; it addresses real needs and provides perfect dwelling places for serious and active lives. It's true that the buildings embody an ideal; but it's an ideal derived from knowledge of life. The fear is that in avoiding excitement, in their restraint and serenity, they will leave out the very things that – unfortunately – attract people. There's a paradox here: the qualities that make something valuable to people are the very ones that make people think it is boring.

There is a Palladian aspect to Goethe's vision of what his own work should be – and, by extension, what he considered of worth in any work of art or literature. The work should constitute a kind of habitat: something we can live in. Palladio's buildings are not particularly individual, they don't seek to capture and express the specific inner life of individuals. They encourage us to gracious moderation.

'Palladio was strongly imbued with the spirit of the ancients and felt acutely the petty narrow-mindedness of the times, like a great man who does not wish to conform to the world but to transform it in accordance with his own high ideals.' It's the nobility of Palladio's aims – not their eccentricity – that sets him apart from his time. The great architect's aim was to give his ideals reality, to give his noble vision of simple grandeur concrete expression as houses and churches. 'Palladio has opened for me the way to the glorious days of antiquity – and the way to all art and life as well . . . How different from our saints, squatting on their pillars. Thank God I'm done with all that junk once and for all.'

And visiting one of Palladio's fragments – quite a few of his largest projects were only partly constructed – Goethe cannot but think of his own unfinished manuscripts. He reflects painfully on the fact that so many lesser buildings get built; so many lesser plays and novels get completed: 'Oh kindly Fates, who favour and perpetuate so many stupidities, why did You not allow this work to be completed?'

On his last evening in Vicenza Goethe attended a meeting of the grandly titled Academy of the Olympians – a semi-learned discussion society. They debated the question 'Which has been of greater importance to the Arts – Invention or Imitation?' 'Not a bad idea: if you treat the alternative as exclusive you can go on and on about it for centuries' – not bad, that is, if your aim is to chatter away for eternity. He got quite irritated by the behaviour of 'the common herd' who applauded even the crudest arguments in favour of whatever they already believed and were deaf to any intelligent points made on the other side. But the sociability of the occasion leads him to a morose thought about himself: 'If only I could stand up like this in front of my own countrymen and entertain them in person instead of having to confine my best thoughts to the printed page of some book which a solitary reader then nibbles on, hunched up in a corner.'

Then the next morning he's off, heading for Venice with only a brief pause to make a note on the local girls: 'have seen some very pretty creatures; the dark ones particularly exciting; also some blondes – less arousing'.

3

Venice

'It was written, then, on my page in the Book of Destiny that at five in the afternoon on the 28th day of September in the year 1786 I should see, for the first time, the beautiful islands of Venice – a kind of Republic of Beavers. Thank God "Venice" is no longer just an empty place name: I really hate mere words.'

He found comfortable lodgings near Piazza San Marco; the view was modest rather than grand – but characteristic of the place: his windows looked out over a narrow canal lined with tall, rather plain houses; one of the typical low single-span bridges was immediately below. In Venice he could be inconspicuous in a way that was not possible in the smaller towns he had been through.

Goethe spent much of his time in Venice working quietly on his manuscripts, particularly *Iphigenia* (about which more will be said later). On the evening of 7 October, a week into his stay in the city, Goethe was moved to tears. The moon came out and he took a gondola with two singers. They sang some old songs – verses from Tasso and Ariosto set to an intimate, flowing melody 'as if someone were idly singing to himself, adapting the tune to poems he knows by heart'. Then the boatmen tethered the gondola on the shore of the Giudecca and walked far along the *fondamenta* in opposite directions, still singing in turns. 'The sound of their voices far away was extraordinary, a lament without sadness.' The voices carry clearly over the still mirror of water; each is the echo of the other; each voice 'is the cry of some lonely human being – sent out into the wide world till it reaches the ears of another lonely human being who is moved to answer it'. This vision of art is, perhaps, the counterpart to the poise and maturity of Palladio. There is a loneliness in Goethe which his art is trying to overcome; if only he can make his voice carry far enough perhaps it will reach the ear of someone like him; someone who will understand – who will love him.

Towards the end of his time in Venice – he was there almost six weeks – Goethe struck up an acquaintance with a French tourist whose behaviour intrigued him. If the vision of Palladio was his search for a soulmate, this new encounter sharpened Goethe's sense of what his own journey was about by providing its negative image. The Frenchman was some years older, rather dignified with gracious manners: educated, decent and brave – the perfect incarnation of a Versailles courtier. He had been travelling around Italy at great speed and in high luxury – yet had noticed nothing; he was completely at sea. The impression Goethe got was of a man who has no genuine interest in anything, for whom nothing outside himself has any real importance.

But if this sophisticated French tourist seems to have missed a great deal, we might be tempted to come to the same conclusion about Goethe himself. He visited the law courts – where he was entranced by a little egg-timer used to limit the speeches of the advocates; but he has nothing much to say about San Marco. In fact, he seemed to miss all the things that people, or at least men, usually came to Venice for. At the end of the eighteenth century Venice was a tourist magnet not so much for its architecture as for sex, music and gambling. Cards were never very interesting to Goethe and he says nothing of the sexual enticements that were everywhere on offer – and about which other travellers of the period, including Rousseau, write with candour and delight. Goethe merely notes: 'It was impossible to walk across the Piazza San Marco without being offered a liaison with any number of noblewomen.' When Goethe returned to Venice in 1790 it was another story entirely – *then* sex seemed to be the only thing that interested him.

As if to explain his present primness, Goethe mentions his anxiety about sexually transmitted diseases – a very reasonable worry. And this has sometimes been taken to suggest that he avoided sexual contact through the whole of his youth and early manhood – in fact, until well into his stay in Rome. But it would be naive to suppose that this put all sexual experience out of bounds for Goethe. It is inconceivable that a man of Goethe's curiosity, intense visual imagination, freedom from self-reproach and prudery, great sensual responsiveness and appetite, could have passed his life without allowing himself a great deal of sexual activity, taken in whatever ways appealed.

In the considerable later evidence of Goethe's sexual enthusiasm, he exhibits the interesting and rather normal quality of 'polymorphous perversity'. As we discover in *Wilhelm Meister*, Goethe was a connoisseur of rather masculine women; and women dressed as men have a special charm. Wilhelm spends a blissful night in the company of the high-heeled shoes belonging to a woman whose direct offer of sex he has recently refused. Goethe produced quite a few erotic drawings. In other words, the fact that Goethe was anxious about infection through genital intercourse leaves open lush erotic territory that he was clearly eager to explore.

When the six weeks in Venice were up, Goethe aimed as directly as he could for Rome. On the way, jolting along in the stagecoach, he thought of Albrecht Dürer – the most celebrated of German artists – some of whose works he had admired in Munich. Around the turn of the sixteenth century Dürer made two prolonged trips to Venice, which had a profound effect upon his style and on his conception of himself as an artist. Dürer, whose father was a goldsmith, had grown up in a world that saw painting as a craft, as the activity of a skilled artisan. He was the first northern painter to see himself, and his work, as belonging to a learned, humanist tradition – a conception of the artist that had emerged in the Renaissance courts of Italy. In this respect, at least, Dürer was an important point of reference for Goethe. For Goethe, too, was trying to work out what kind of artist he was; indeed he was more ambitious. Goethe was in search of a new cultural conception in which he could recognize himself. Dürer found such a concept ready-made – the individual, sophisticated artist; Goethe had to initiate his project.

One of the most important legacies of Goethe lies, precisely, in this area. He introduced a shift as radical and important as that from artisan to artist. We get a hint of the direction of Goethe's view in the comment he makes on Dürer: 'When he was travelling in the Netherlands he bartered the supreme works of art with which he hoped to make his fortune for parrots; he made portraits of the servants, who had brought him a plate of fruit, to save himself tips. The thought of such a poor fool of an artist is especially moving to me because, at bottom, my fate is the same as his; the only difference is that I know better how to look after myself.'

What was Goethe's idea of 'looking after himself'? Goethe, certainly, was a man of the world; he knew what sort of tips to give. But there is a broader significance to the point. What he is getting at is that in some sense Dürer didn't know how to judge his artistic merit – his works of 'inestimable value' – in relation to the practicalities of life. Dürer didn't grasp – Goethe is saying – just how important his works were. By contrast, Goethe had come to think that the royal pension, which was still being paid to him in Italy, was not just a kindly favour from the duke; it was, in fact, the best decision – the best investment – Carl August had ever made. Goethe realized, as he suspected Dürer did not, that the balance of need was ultimately in favour of the artist, assuming the artist to be of the stature of Dürer – or indeed of Goethe. Carl August needed his poet more than Goethe needed the duke. And in retrospect we can easily see this. The only reason anyone, other than specialist historians of minor German states, has heard of Carl August is because Goethe was his man. And to a very large extent the cultural prestige of the State of Weimar depended upon Goethe's presence. This did not, of course, mean that it was a straightforward matter to turn this cultural capital into the means of a dignified life and public respect.

4

Iphigenia

Anxiety about status – and about how to look after himself – were pressing in on Goethe because during this period, in Venice and on the last stages of the journey to Rome, he had been revising one of his sketches for a play. *Iphigenia in Tauris* was Goethe's reworking of Euripides' drama of the same name. His earlier, much less accomplished, version of this play had been in existence for some time and had been performed in Weimar, with Goethe himself playing Orestes, the brother of Iphigenia. The revisions would be completed during the tranquil Roman mornings of the coming months. But on the way to Rome Goethe already had a clear conception of the kind of rewriting he was engaged upon and had well-founded worries about how the new version would be received. He was intent on reducing the dramatic tension of the play; he was aiming at a more serene, more noble – and less exciting – kind of dramatic art. The day after his reveries about Dürer, Goethe saw a painting by Raphael that he especially admired: 'I found a female Saint, an exquisite picture; Raphael has made her healthy, secure, youthful; but she's not frigid or unsophisticated. I'm going to read my *Iphigenia* to her.'

Iphigenia was the daughter of Agamemnon, King of Mycenae and leader of the Greek forces against Troy. When Agamemnon neglects his long-standing promise to the goddess Artemis to sacrifice to her honour the most beautiful thing he possesses, his thousand-strong fleet is held up at Aulis by stormy weather, and Artemis demands Iphigenia's sacrifice in return for a favourable wind for the ships.

Agamemnon summons his wife, Clytemnestra, and their daughter to the military camp, under the pretext of marrying Iphigenia to

Goethe's ideal reader

Achilles, the greatest of heroes. But at the moment when Iphigenia believes she is going forward to her marriage ceremony she is surrounded by fire and approached with the knife. At the last moment the goddess takes pity on Iphigenia and transports her to a shrine in far-off Tauris and installs the girl there as her priestess. Artemis substitutes a deer for the human sacrifice, but the Greeks know nothing of this and believe Iphigenia dead.

The ships sail to Troy; eventually the city falls and Agamemnon returns to Mycenae. While he has been at war, Clytemnestra – who cannot forgive him for sacrificing their daughter – has taken up with Aegisthus, a cousin and bitter enemy of Agamemnon. Together Aegisthus and Clytemnestra kill the great king upon his return. But then Agamemnon's son, Orestes, avenges his father's death by killing his mother. And, although he is required to revenge his father's death, matricide is unforgivable; and so Orestes is caught in one of the most horrific situations of Greek tragedy.

Because he has killed his mother, the avenging Furies attack and

torment Orestes. He pleads his case before the gods and Apollo promises
to release him from the Furies if he undertakes a special task. Orestes
is required to go to Tauris and bring back the statue of Artemis from
the temple. This is especially dangerous since a religious cult in Tauris
requires the sacrifice of all strangers. Orestes does not know that it is
his own long-lost sister, Iphigenia, now the priestess at Tauris, whose
duty it is to oversee these sacrificial rites.

The play by Euripides takes up the story at this point. Orestes
comes to Tauris, accompanied by Pylades – who is his cousin and
comrade-in-arms. Technically, this play is not a tragedy – it takes the
hero through danger to a benign ending. Its drama is that of recognition – Orestes and Iphigenia have not seen one another since childhood; each, in fact, believes the other dead. But their identities are
revealed through their sympathy. Iphigenia questions the strangers
about what has been happening in Troy – having been cut off in Tauris
she knows nothing. The pathos she feels and the anguish of Orestes'
telling of the story soon make their close connection to the events, and
to one another, evident.

That Goethe should have chosen this, of all the extant Greek plays,
to reinterpret for a modern German audience is not too surprising. It
marks the end of the appalling sequence of events which have devas-
tated two generations of a family. As it opens, Orestes is haunted by
the Furies and is facing almost certain death – in ritual sacrifice to
Artemis (or, as Goethe adapts it, to Diana – the Roman approxi-
mation). Through recognizing one another Orestes and Iphigenia re-
unite the remaining family and the sister suggests a plan for escaping
from Tauris with the sacred statue. In the version by Euripides, Iphigenia
tricks the guards and the King of Tauris by insisting that the statue
and the sacrificial victims, Orestes and Pylades, need to be purified of
the taint of matricide in the open sea before the ceremony can take
place; and since this is a mysterious rite no one else is allowed to
observe. So, in Euripides, the simple superstition and piety of the
guards and the King of Tauris leaves an opportunity for escape. Of
course, once in the water, the three Greeks jump into the ship Orestes
has left waiting and set off for home.

But they are not yet safe. The swell of the ocean – provoked by

Poseidon – pushes them back to the now vengeful Taurideans. At this moment – when tragedy might occur – the goddess Athena appears and orders the king to let the Greeks go; she foretells that the Greeks will arrive home safely, that a new shrine to Artemis-Diana will be established. Orestes is now free from the avenging Furies and has expiated the crime of killing his mother. The horrific cycle of murder and retribution is finally over.

The appeal in all this for Goethe is that the terrible things are in the past – the question is how to deal with the fact that they have occurred – and that Orestes, of course, has been an agent within the sequence of family killings. It is, for Goethe, the classic post-Werther problem. What do you do if you don't kill yourself? How can you recover? And recover from what? The actual story of the family of Agamemnon is too horrific for us to draw any sane conclusions; on a practical level one would not ask the insane question – what do you do after you've killed your mother because she killed your father because he (apparently) killed your sister because the gods (who are real and vengeful) ordered him to? In Euripides we begin to hear concerns about the nature of the gods – Iphigenia asks if it could ever actually be the will of the gods that strangers are sacrificed; could the goddess really have ordered her father to kill her so that the ships could sail? Goethe takes this up and has Iphigenia shift the focus from sacrifice to devotion – what the gods really want is human reverence; but we have mistakenly seen this under the guise of sacrifice.

The horrors of the past – and the Furies that hunt down Orestes – become more internal, more imaginative, in Goethe's treatment. It is memory and remorse, and the fact that he could have acted otherwise but did not, that is destroying Orestes. It is not stealing a statue that will heal him, but an encounter with his sister, and the realization that she has survived. And, of course, the horrors of the past need not be actual killing – just things we deeply regret, and the sense of being enmeshed in a sequence of ghastliness not of our own making but through which we were made: the family tragedy of psychology rather than an actual bloodbath. The risk that Goethe is taking can be put like this – he enriches the humanity of the play at the expense of its drama. As the presentation gets more serious and sensible it also becomes less exciting. Goethe was additionally on dangerous territory not only because he was meddling with a Greek classic, which runs the risk of hubris, but also because he was returning to such explicitly classical models at a point when just about everyone else was going in divergent opposite directions; either towards the realistic bourgeois plays of Lessing or the overtly dramatic and impassioned plays of Schiller.

A central role to which Goethe assigns Iphigenia is that of 'making mild'. In his version Iphigenia has, since her arrival, persuaded Thoas – King of Tauris – to abandon human sacrifice; and indeed his state has prospered in this time. Thoas in fact wants to marry Iphigenia. Her task is one which clearly mattered to Goethe; it is the task of women, he says, to make men less wild and rough – and he may have been thinking of his mother's influence on his father, or that of Charlotte von Stein upon him; but perhaps the most obvious parallel is with himself. For in Weimar his job was to make mild the duke.

A fundamental change that Goethe makes in the story is the avoidance of trickery. In his version, the Greeks do not escape from Tauris by deception, by exploiting the credulous king. Instead Iphigenia persuades Thoas to let them go, drawing upon his genuine affection for her – so that he finally accepts because he recognizes that it will be best for her to leave and he, in loving her, wants what is best for her. This is the healthy reversal of escape by deception. If Goethe had feared that by going to Weimar he was imaginatively killing off his mother, he now presents the precious, and reasonable, alternative: that in loving him his mother doesn't have merely a possessive relationship to him, but also a benign interest in what is in his best interests, even extending to the possibility that those might override her longing to hold on to him.

The first rougher version of the Iphigenia story had been written in Weimar and the task that occupied Goethe in Italy was that of transcribing it into verse. The verse version does not change the story in any essential way; it aims at a kind of calm grandeur, a noble simplicity – the essential characteristics of classic art as Johann Joachim Winkelmann had seen them. It offers less and less, therefore, to the common and popular taste; it gives fewer points of entry to those who are on the lookout for excitement, passion, wit, a racy story.

It is clear from the way Goethe writes about his efforts at revision that he loves his play and that he is happy in the quiet hours of effort. But he is also facing two fears: one is the fear of competition – in making a play by Euripides his own he is setting himself up for comparison at the highest level; the second is the fear of loneliness – no one will love what he has done. Hence the imaginative friendships with Dürer – to whom he has an elder brother's words of advice – and with Palladio and Raphael's St Catherine. Goethe is trying to lighten his burden by sharing it with some of the greatest figures in the history of civilization: he may be troubled by anxiety and loneliness, but they are precisely the ones who would most understand – and be closest to him. His suffering gains in stature: it becomes understandable as part of the condition of high creative ambition.

5

Rome

The last stage of his journey to Rome was not at all pleasant. The inns were wretched, his chance travelling companion – a papal diplomat – was a bore. He gave Goethe some particularly unhelpful advice: 'Why do you think so much? A man should never think. Thinking only makes him grow old.' Goethe passed through Assisi and did something that, to the modern traveller, seems almost sinful. He 'turned away in distaste' from the enormous Franciscan church now famous for Giotto's frescos of the life of St Francis. His lack of interest offended some rough locals who could not conceive of a traveller indifferent to the celebrated shrine. Goethe much preferred the little Roman temple of Minerva: 'I cannot describe the sensations this work aroused in me, but I know they are going to bear fruit for ever.' Perhaps 'for ever' was just an optimistic way of thinking about his own future; or maybe Goethe really did hope that the motions of his soul in those minutes really were going to have some kind of eternal life.

Goethe arrived in Rome on 29 October 1786. Rome, he says, is the hub of the world. Less than three years before the opening events of the French Revolution it was in a personal and artistic sense only that Rome – rather than Paris, London or Vienna – could be considered the centre of the human universe. Although Goethe was clearly interested in administration – when visiting other Italian cities he often makes remarks about street lighting, rubbish collection, the functioning of law courts – he makes no reference to the general political situation of his times.

The city was, in some respects, deeply familiar to Goethe. The beloved images from his childhood – the engravings of Rome his father had hung in the hallways of the Frankfurt house – were now being given reality. His acquaintance with classical architecture and sculpture from images in books and plaster casts was the source of deep satisfaction. He had the sense of already being intimate with – of already being at home in – the very place that seemed to him the centre of the human world.

It is testimony to the richness of the education Goethe acquired naturally and at home that it prepared him so intimately to meet the needs of his adult mind. Goethe didn't have to slough off his background in order to be an independent adult. And this isn't because Goethe was somehow unquestioning or meek – the opposite is true. It's just that he was extremely fortunate: the culture he was introduced to in his childhood was highly sophisticated and serious. Someone like Carl Moritz – with whom he spent some time in Rome – had to remake himself as an adult because the culture of his childhood was manifestly unhelpful: extremist, philistine, ignorant, parochial. The encounter with Rome reveals the integrity of Goethe's personality. 'I have not had a single idea which was new or surprising, but my old ideas have become so much more firm, lively and coherent that they could be called new.'

During the first few days Goethe rushed around the city seeing all the major monuments. Primarily he was interested in the ancient remains. His companion from the start was the German painter Johann Heinrich Tischbein. Tischbein, who was two years younger than Goethe, came from an extended family of artists and had lived in Rome since 1782. There was a 'colony' of German artists in the city – as there were from England, Scotland and France. Rome was certainly by that point on the periphery of politics, but it was the artistic capital of the world – in the way that Paris was to be a century later. But it was not the work of Roman or Italian artists which gave the city this importance. It was, rather, the history of the place (both with respect to antiquity and to the tradition which derived from Poussin and Claude).

Tischbein had been in Rome before – between 1779 and 1781 – supported by a stipend from the art academy at Kassel, of which his uncle was the director. But his money had run out and Tischbein had been forced to return to Germany. He wrote to Merck – Goethe's old friend – who worked in the Darmstadt government, asking for help. Merck arranged to have Tischbein's letter published in the *Teutscher Merkur* (edited by Wieland) and also sent Goethe some of the artist's drawings. Goethe admired the drawings and was instrumental in procuring further support for Tischbein from the Duke of Sachsen-Gotha – a cousin of Carl August. With a one-hundred-thaler stipend Tischbein was able to continue a modest, productive and very pleasant life in Rome from 1782 onwards. By the time Goethe arrived at the end of 1786 Tischbein was living in a house in the Via del Corso, near the Piazza del Popolo, sharing with two other German artists: Friedrich Bury and Johann Georg Schutz. The day after meeting Tischbein, Goethe joined the household, renting a small and simple room and living communally with the artists, cared for by the elderly owners who treated the artists as favoured children.

6

The Life of the Artist

In Rome Goethe registered himself under the assumed name of Filippo Müller; while he was about it he claimed a semi-assumed profession: painter; and a purely wishful age: thirty-two (lopping off five years). Goethe spent his time with younger people, mainly German artists; he did not get involved at all in the high society life his fame and connections to Weimar would have opened to him. Later on, when his presence in the city was widely known, Goethe had to decline many invitations in order to preserve his time for the things he really wanted to do. Broadly, he had three major interests. The first – which occupied him early in the mornings – was to complete the literary tasks he had set himself: the revisions of the plays for the *Collected Works*. Later in the day he would go and study the great works of antiquity – forcing himself to look carefully. Thirdly, he was deeply interested in drawing; he practised a great deal and took lessons from the artists he knew.

Goethe's daily life in this first period in Rome was recorded by Tischbein in some of the most charming images we have of Goethe – images which, if they were better known, would do much to change the broader image of the man.

The chair is as simple as can be; the floor tiled, the window plain, the walls unadorned; Goethe has his feet drawn up, he leans back swinging the chair against the wall; he cradles a book between his knees; he is casually dressed, his shirt open, his sleeves up. It is a simple sketch – a sketch of a body, of posture – rather than of the details of the face; Goethe is concentrating, his head inclining a little to the book. In a way, it could be anyone who reads and finds an intense

What was he thinking?

relationship to the written word. It is a drawing of Müller – the Filippo Müller in Goethe.

Another image of the same period shows Goethe from behind – he is looking out of the window, leaning over the sill.

Perhaps because we cannot see his face – which is so much part of the mythology of Goethe (the huge eyes, the noble forehead) – this is one of the most endearing and attractive images of Goethe that we have. His weight is partly on his elbows as he leans over to look down into the street; his shoulders are slightly hunched, his weight more on his left leg than on his right, which gives a delicate lift to one hip, and allows the slipper to drop from his right foot; again he's in his shirtsleeves. The window is simple, but with attractive shutters; the room is fairly dark: we sense the bright light of the day; the room is plain, although there is a trace of modest, subdued patterns on the upper portions of the wall. The spontaneity of the image allows us to feel that we are sitting with Tischbein just a few feet away from Goethe; it has that sense of intimacy in which there is no need to be

Goethe in his Roman slippers

talking to or looking at the other person in the room. There is a sense of adequate time, there is no haste or rush; Goethe is not wasting his time, he isn't distracting himself as he gazes out of the window (otherwise almost a cliché for inattention).

Among the drawings Tischbein made of their common life, the most private is also the least artistically refined.

Goethe is stretching over the bed to do something to 'the damned second pillow' – place it there, take it away? Will it be needed tonight? Must he sleep alone; or has he committed himself to sleeping with someone when – now – he'd rather be on his own? Again his slipper falls from his foot – a favourite motif; we see the simple table with a vase of flowers and the burning oil lamp, so it must be evening; the drawings on the wall above the bed are unframed; a pile of heavy books, evidently not required for reading, support a shelf on which

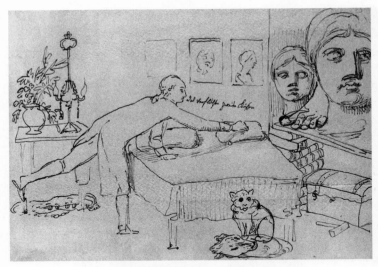

'The cursed second pillow'

stand two colossal ancient heads and a massive foot: casts of fragments. Below the shelf is a trunk and a hammer probably used for
getting rock samples – as Goethe tells us he did around the ancient
ruins. For once Goethe is in his coat; the house cat has come into his
room, which, he tells us, it often did.

Goethe spent a lot of his time looking at marble statues – much
influenced by Winkelmann, who had raised these mainly Roman
copies of Greek originals to the highest possible status among human
artefacts: about one hundred and fifty – mainly broken – statues
constituted an attractively limited, and hopefully permanent, visual
canon. Extremely widespread admiration had led to a flourishing
industry in plaster casts – providing copies for enthusiasts across
Europe. Goethe, like everyone else, preferred the originals, but typically much enjoyed visiting the works where the casts were made. He
had a keen appreciation of technical processes, ever since as a child
he had watched the goldsmiths and builders and etchers at work in
Frankfurt. But the plaster works offered something more. The originals
were scattered in many different collections; in the workshop it was

possible to see the whole classical corpus together and that greatly facilitated comparison and classification – always dear to Goethe's heart.

Goethe himself bought a cast of a colossal head of Jupiter – he was later to purchase many more casts, and they were at length installed in his house in Weimar. This head he placed in his room in the Via del Corso and – half-serious, half-joking – would say his prayers to 'the King of the Gods'.

Not long after this acquisition, the old landlady was tidying up his room while Goethe sat in the hallway; suddenly the old lady flung open the door, terribly excited, insisting that Goethe come in immediately to witness a miracle. Her cat, who always accompanied her, was worshipping 'God the Father', as she innocently called the bust of Jupiter. And indeed there was the little creature stretched upon the pedestal licking the divine beard. Goethe found her excitement charming and didn't trouble her with the real explanation: a kind of fat was used to grease the moulds from which the casts were taken, and a little of this savoury goo would always be left behind in the deepest grooves – such as one would find in the stylized beard.

The artists' landlady was not the only local Roman to have imaginative ideas about the appeal of ancient sculpture. Goethe often went to the Palazzo Gustianini to admire a statue of Athena – or Minerva, as the Romans called her. His repeated visits intrigued the wife of the custodian, who came to the conclusion that Goethe must have a faraway girlfriend who looked just like that, and that – lovesick – he was consoling himself with the presence of the statue. This same woman also had a theory that the English visitors who were so keen on that particular statue belonged to a pagan religious cult. Goethe comments gently: 'religious worship and romantic passion were the only things the good woman understood; disinterested admiration for a noble work of art, brotherly reverence for another human spirit, were utterly beyond her ken.'

'When I indulge in self-reflection, which I like to do occasionally, I discover in myself a feeling which gives me great joy. I'm going to risk putting it like this: in this place, whoever looks seriously about him and has eyes to see must become *solid*: his idea of *solidity* must become vivid.

'The soul is moulded to healthy strength; one becomes serious, but not dry; one attains the capacity for measured, rational joy. At the very least I feel as if I have never before been so properly appreciative of the things of this world as I am here. The blessed consequences will, I love to think, affect my whole future life.' (The added emphasis marks Goethe's employment of the German word 'solid' – a self-consciously classical term deriving from 'solum' meaning 'soil' or 'ground' – rather than the more usual 'fest'.)

We get some insight into what Goethe means by 'healthy strength' from his repeated use – around the same time – of the word 'noble'. 'I am not here simply to have a good time, but to devote myself to noble objects.' The idea of nobility is partly to do with being free from what is trivial, from what is petty and what passes for fashion or excitement. The impact of the objects he sees, the way they work their effect on his inner life, is that they make Goethe much more determined to abide by the values he finds in them; to confirm himself in the way of life they articulate. He wants, as it were, to become what they represent; and for this influence to spread through all his actions and every detail of his mode of life.

Nobility carries many resonances: it is a spiritual adjective, indicating a lofty conception of life, and freedom from fear. It is a stylistic term, suggesting restrained grandeur; and, as the name of a social rank, it connotes security, prestige and independence.

7

In the Campagna

It was Tischbein who painted the central icon of Goethe's time in Rome – indeed the classic image of Goethe: the celebrated picture of *Goethe in the Campagna*, the countryside around Rome.

The creation of a new kind of hero

We see Goethe sitting upon some massive weathered blocks strewn on the ground; leaning on one elbow, one leg stretched before him, his position is halfway between sitting and lying; far off we see the somewhat bald landscape of the Roman countryside, the hills softened to a blue-grey, their forms slightly misty; the light is moderate – far from the harsh glare of summer – and the ruins in the distance are touched with a pale golden light. The long mantle that covers most of the wanderer's body is loosely reminiscent of the classical toga, allowing a few characteristic folds of drapery to be included – a rather imperfect evocation of Goethe's relation to the past.

The broad hat, with the brim turned up at the side, is a starkly modern element, but the outline of the brim frames Goethe's head like a nimbus; the darker shadow it affords is a necessary relief to heighten the effect of the face, allowing the light on the forehead to come to our attention more powerfully, to give a setting to the eyes and nose. In another sketch of this pose, the hat is raised slightly and we see a wisp of hair above the forehead, which lessens the impressiveness of the face; and in that sketch the right eye is in deeper shadow, giving Goethe's face a more intent, dramatic aspect. In the finished painting, Goethe's face conveys a more self-possessed condition. It is the face of a man who has full control of his faculties, who is ripe for action, or thought; it is an image of a man in his prime – the point of perfect ripeness. He is among the lovely remains of the classical world, a world of which he has taken inner possession; he is at ease and yet he is completely in earnest.

Goethe's posture has some affinity with the image – very dear to the late eighteenth-century imagination – of a man reclining in the countryside; an action with definite literary associations. And, in fact, in an early sketch for this picture, Goethe is shown in a rather more recumbent position, his weight thrown further back. In the fifth of his *Reveries of a Solitary Walker* Rousseau describes how he had once gone down to the banks of a lake and lay there listening to the sound of the water lapping on the shore – and how this had been, for him, a moment of great happiness when he felt at one with nature and free of his troubles. Goethe himself had beautifully evoked just such a moment in *Werther* – when Werther lies down on the grass and is overwhelmed by his thoughts about nature.

The pose is also related to an image with which Goethe and Tischbein would have been familiar from their visits to the Sistine Chapel: that of the recumbent Adam in the panel showing the Creation of Man. Adam is magnificent, but he is nothing without God; he stretches out gracefully to the hand of divine power which will animate and complete him and give him a world in which to live. Goethe, as it were, is Adam made mature; Goethe isn't reaching out to his maker; he has assimilated his own religion: his God is everywhere – in the plants, in the landscape, in the remains of antiquity, in Goethe himself.

Although not terribly explicit, the reformulation of a religious image as a secular one – but with no sense of mockery or denigration – is consistent with Goethe's central statement of his experience of Rome. As he noted during those first winter months: 'The entire history of the world is linked up with this city, and I reckoned my second life, a very rebirth, from the day when I entered Rome.' The language is biblical: being 'born again of the spirit' was an important notion in the Christian conception of a life. Here, Goethe is applying it, with great seriousness and yet without its specifically Christian connotations, to himself. That is, he accords the moral seriousness of baptism – when it is taken as assurance of the salvation of the soul and the moment of entry into God's family – to a purely secular experience: immersion in the classical art of Rome.

Although this is an amazingly self-assured image it is not particularly heroic or presumptuous; Goethe was adept at finding space between humility and vain pride; he was self-conscious of his capacities and his powers – he wasn't at all a humble man, and yet it would be misleading to describe him as vain; 'he knew his worth' is perhaps as close as one can get.

Goethe was particularly indebted to Tischbein for instruction in drawing; in Rome he made a serious attempt to improve his drawing and made rapid progress under Tischbein's direction. It is hard to know what Goethe's intentions really were in this direction. Although his work is sometimes quite attractive, he never produced any pictorial work of really high merit – nothing which would set him even at the level of a skilful professional. And there is no reason to doubt that Goethe recognized this. In the other fields of his diverse efforts, Goethe usually operated with large ambitions of making a fundamental contribution to the relevant field. He did not study optics or physiognomy just to grasp what others had discovered. He was driven by a deep need to see himself as making an original contribution – and one which he could make because of his general character. Thus, in physiognomy, he was very proud of his original work identifying the residual intermaxillary bone; and what had led to that discovery was his general commitment to clear observation and to the 'gradualist' position in science to which he had a kind of moral attachment. It was because of this commitment that he felt there must be some evidence of such a bone in the human skeleton because it was apparent in other mammals.

However, in drawing he never expressed such high ambitions. One of the standard concerns of art theory in the late eighteenth century was to demarcate the relative competencies of the different arts – a project in which Lessing's *Laocoön* held the leading position and of which Hegel was to make a great deal. The basic idea is that particular art forms are limited in what they can express and in what can be done in each. Thus Virgil's description of the death of Laocoön can describe the agony of the priest (and still succeed as a poem) while the late classical sculptor of the famous group had to avoid presenting agony and concentrate on stoicism.

So, perhaps, we are witnessing something not too surprising: Goethe's attempt to convey his visual experience, not by words, not by describing them, but by showing them. And showing them not only to other people but also to himself.

8

Paradise

After three months in Rome, and more than six months away from Weimar, Goethe made up his mind to head south to Naples. He didn't, in principle, want to leave Rome, but news had reached him that Vesuvius was active. This volcano, close to Naples, was itself part of classical culture: its eruptions had buried the ancient towns of Pompeii and Herculaneum, the excavations of which were among the great cultural undertakings of the epoch.

When he arrived in Naples at the end of February 1787, with Tischbein rather reluctantly in tow, Goethe was deeply impressed by the beauty of its coastal setting between the mountains and the famous bay. He'd never before stayed in such a magnificent place, nor indeed in such a large city. With a population of around four hundred thousand, Naples was far larger than Rome, over ten times the size of Frankfurt or Strasbourg, and – of course – vastly bigger than Weimar.

Naples was – he thought, and repeatedly said – 'the happy city', 'an earthly paradise'. Goethe wasn't just referring to the obvious delights: the superb views, the abundant countryside. He extended this 'Garden of Eden' image to the lives of the local people, particularly the poor; and this was radically unorthodox. Naples was known to educated Europe for its collections of antiquities, its Enlightenment intellectuals, and the poverty and squalor in which the majority of its inhabitants apparently lived.

Even the poverty enchants him – but no, it is not really poverty at all. For, Goethe tells himself, these people are carefree and happy, even though they lack the amenities and resources considered indispensable in the north. They have no fireplaces – what does that matter?

It is usually hot here. And even when it is cold (as it was when Goethe first arrived in the city) they will extract the maximum benefit from every possible source of heat. After a blacksmith has shod a horse, the street urchins will sit around on the warm stones where the shoe was heated.

Goethe himself never for a moment wanted to live like that, but he found in the poor of Naples a political lesson. The fundamental point was that they were content. What could political reform possibly mean here? Any well-intentioned scheme of improvement would be likely to leave them less satisfied with life – and surely such satisfaction is the only proper aim of government?

13 March – Naples: 'Tischbein has a great gift for sketching in pen and ink the figures of gods and heroes, large as life or larger. He dashes them off with a few strokes and then puts in the shadows with a broad brush, so that the head stands out in relief. The company were amazed at the ease with which he did this and expressed their enthusiastic delight. Then their fingers began itching to try it themselves. They picked up the brushes and began daubing beards on each other's faces.

'This happened in a cultured circle and in the house of a man who is himself a sound painter and draughtsman. Is not such behaviour an expression of some primitive trait in the human race?'

This is a quick statement of a failure of development. At first, people are amazed by technical facility; they love skill – rather than artistic merit. Second, there is the longing to repeat and to try for oneself. Thirdly, there is the reduction of something fine – if only in a modest way – to an absurdity. And this brings the destruction of the very thing that was originally admired.

This little anecdote is characteristic of Goethe's literary manner. He loves observing people's behaviour and always tries to draw from it a larger implication – what does this little episode show of the human condition? He is not over-concerned to draw such remarks together into a coherent order, so what we encounter is a style rather than a system of thought.

In Naples Goethe was a visitor at the villa of the British ambassador Sir William Hamilton. There, Goethe was present at one of the most picturesque moments in art history. The ambassador's mistress, Emma Hart – real name Amy Lyon, later Lady Hamilton, later Nelson's mistress – fused nature and artifice by climbing into a large gold frame and striking what she called 'attitudes'. It was also Hamilton whose example encouraged Goethe to climb Vesuvius – which he did three times.

From Naples Goethe took a boat to Sicily, which he regarded as the 'key' to Italy. Sicily was – in his eyes – a more intense and more pure version of Italy. Sicily had been an Athenian colony and it was there he saw the Greek temples at Agrigenti which lay behind the architecture of ancient Rome.

24 April: 'I swear that I have never in my whole life enjoyed such a vision of spring as I did at sunrise this morning. The new Girgenti stands on the site of the ancient citadel. From our windows we looked down over a wide, gentle slope, now entirely covered with gardens and vineyards . . . All one can see is the Temple of Concord rising out of this green and flowering area.'

The voyage from Sicily back to Naples was all too exciting. In the treacherous waters around Capri it looked as if the boat would surely be dashed against the rocks; the wind had dropped and the current was drawing the boat gradually towards destruction: it was agonizingly inevitable and slow – the passengers became desperate and started shouting for the captain and sailors to do something. Goethe tried to keep them calm: what good would come of panic? As if the crew weren't already doing everything they possibly could to save themselves and their passengers. At almost the last moment the wind rose and the boat was able to pull away from the rocks. As always, Goethe had his eye on the symbolic character of the moment. This isn't just one more near miss – it's also an image of life itself. Life is a very slow shipwreck; but it's the only life we have. Goethe tried to communicate a cheerful pessimism: to see life as it is and yet to enjoy it as it is.

The account of the near miss can be seen as a sketch of the human condition, which also offers a suggestion about the role of art and thinking. There are forces beyond our control: we cannot ensure that our own ship will not strike the rocks; we cannot prevent our own death. However, there is much that can sensibly be done to make the best of our chances. That is the role of the captain: all he can do is organize the resources he has so as to stave off disaster for as long as possible and then to be ready to take advantage of any little opportunity which comes along. However, because good captaincy does not guarantee survival (it only gives the best chances of pulling through) there is a tendency to panic – to scream: 'Do something!' While understandable, this reaction actually distracts us from making the best of things. Finally, there is Goethe: the artist-intellectual. What is his role? He sets himself to control unhelpful anxiety.

Much of the time – Goethe is suggesting – we are already doing pretty much all that can be done to make life satisfactory. Apart from the real dangers – the rocks – we have an additional problem: the clamouring voices shouting: 'Do more, do something, we're all going to die, it's your fault!' These wails and complaints do nothing to help matters and may make things worse. Goethe – in his more irate moments – thought that this is generally what 'modern' artists and intellectuals do: they stir up panic and shout that we are all doomed.

Goethe imagines our problems in a way strikingly different from that of a great many current writers on art and intellectual life. In general, the modern assumption is that we are sleepwalking to disaster and need to be roused from our complacency by angry, disturbing voices that tell us how bad things really are. Goethe's assumption is that – as individuals – we are, at least quite often, not complacent but the opposite: hysterical. Therefore a significant task for art and culture might be to calm us down, to bring order and harmony – so that we can do what we need to do.

Goethe spent his last day in Naples – 2 June 1787 – taking leave of his acquaintances. Although the people he saw – aristocrats, diplomats and intellectuals – were admirable enough it was a dreary business, since he was obliged to concentrate on them and their concerns, breaking the communion with himself, the storing up of his own thoughts and impressions. Steeling himself for an equally 'lost' evening he made his way to the royal palace to visit the Duchess of Giovene on whom he had promised to call. Goethe was shown up many flights of stairs and along many corridors, finally arriving at a large chamber made rather gloomy by the fact that all the window shutters were firmly closed. The duchess was young and gracious and clever. They discussed the work of his German contemporaries – not exactly Goethe's favourite topic of conversation. At last it grew really dark and Goethe was put out that the duchess did not order candles to be brought in. As she paced up and down the room the duchess suddenly stopped and flung open a pair of shutters: 'the sight was such as one sees only once in a lifetime. The window at which we were standing was on the top floor directly facing Vesuvius. The sun had set some time before and the glow of the lava, which lit up its accompanying cloud of smoke, was clearly visible. The mountain roared, and at each eruption, the enormous pillar of smoke above it was rent asunder as if by lightning, and in the glare, the separate clouds of vapour stood out in sculptured relief. From the summit to the sea ran a streak of molten lava and glowing vapour, but everywhere else sea, earth, rock and vegetation lay peaceful in the enchanting stillness of a fine evening, while the full moon rose from behind the mountain ridge.'

A table was set before the open window, an exquisite supper served, the candles placed well to the sides so as not to reduce the overwhelming effect of the view. It was the perfect evening, but finally Goethe had to tear himself away to be ready to head back to Rome the following morning.

9

Second Period in Rome

Back in Rome, Goethe continued with his quiet routine: writing (he was polishing *Egmont*), drawing and looking again at statues, paintings and buildings. The gentle, meditative character of this time is captured in a description of his evening walks with his friend Moritz. 'We take a walk every evening; and he tells me what he has thought for himself during the day [Moritz was writing on the works of antiquity with the hope of making them accessible to non-specialist readers] and what he has read in other authors. Through him a gap in my knowledge is being filled, for other occupations have forced me to neglect these matters, and if I were left to myself it would have taken me much time and effort to make up for my neglect. While we talk I look at buildings, streets, landscapes, monuments, etc.; then when we come home in the evening and sit chatting and joking, I draw some view which struck me particularly.'

One of the few members of high society Goethe did visit in Rome was the famous painter Angelica Kauffmann. She was extremely prosperous, and was living in Rome with her second husband, the decorative painter Antonio Zucchi. Her first marriage had been farcical: she wedded a footman posing as a Swedish count. Her work is distinguished by an extraordinarily graceful presentation of noble themes – especially intellectual and artistic friendships between women.

She painted a portrait of Goethe at this time which is an interesting counterpoint to the heroic, mature image that Tischbein created.

Goethe is shown here as younger than he really was – and despite his own attempts to pass himself off as younger he wasn't very pleased about this. Angelica has painted the portrait of the author of *Werther*,

Goethe as Werther

even (following the persistent line of interpretation that so irritated Goethe), the author *as* Werther. She has concentrated on his tenderness – there is a fragile delicacy behind the eyes, a sweetness in the mouth. It would do, in fact, as an image for one of Balzac's heroes – one of the men who conquered Paris by having love affairs with the right older and powerful women. Angelica specialized in presenting men, especially heroic and famous men, in the light of her own fantasies – they become infinitely genteel, sweet and effeminate. Michelangelo famously used male models for the women in his frescos; it certainly looks as if Kauffmann must have used women as models for some of her male figures, especially the younger men. She projected her private fantasy of noble, intelligent femininity (as the ideal human condition) on to all her material: her classical and Shakespearian heroes, as well as the intellectual heroes of her own epoch. It is not, one might think, Goethe as Angelica saw him – but Goethe as she would have liked him to be; her ideal author.

During his second period in Rome it became Goethe's habit to spend every Sunday with her. In the morning he would drive out to look at paintings with her – which he greatly enjoyed: 'She has a trained eye and knows a great deal about the technical side of painting. Moreover, she is sensitive to all that is true and beautiful, and incredibly modest.'

Angelica was not the only modest person in Rome. Goethe himself was going through a period of self-criticism that left him with a rather deflated view of his own merits. As he noted in his journal on 20 July, a month or so before his thirty-eighth birthday: 'I have plenty of time here to discover two of my capital faults, which have pursued and tormented me all of my life. One thing is that I could never be bothered to learn the mechanical part of anything I wanted to work on or should have worked on. That is why, though I have plenty of natural ability, I have accomplished so little. Either I tried to master it by sheer force of intellect, in which case my success or failure was a matter of chance, or, if I wanted to do something really well and with proper deliberation, I had misgivings and could not finish it. My other fault, which is closely related to the first, is that I have never been prepared to devote as much time to any piece of work as it required. I possess the fortunate gift of being able to think of many things and see their connections in a short time, but, in consequence, the detailed execution of a work, step by step, irritates and bores me. Now it is high time for me to mend my ways.'

Goethe stayed in Rome this time for almost nine months. The order of his life was irritatingly disturbed in the early days of 1788 by the eruption of the carnival in the week before Lent. The street below his windows was unfortunately a principal thoroughfare for the parades and general cavorting.

Nevertheless Goethe wrote out a detailed 'report' on the carnival – listing and describing all its phases, its stock characters and traditional symbolism. 'Essentially, all that happens is this: a few days before the start of Lent, at midday the bell on the Capitol is rung; this is the signal – now everyone has leave to be as mad and as foolish as he likes.' The proprieties of everyday life are abandoned: coachmen dress up as women (some of them very alluring); the ladies put on male clothes; distinctions of social rank are temporarily forgotten – everyone is equal; people wear masks; they pelt each other with confetti; wild horses are sent careering down the packed street; respectable people pose as beggars, gangs of young women carrying brooms assault men; people shout obscenities and insults at their family and friends.

By Ash Wednesday the Saturnalia had run its course. The whole thing deeply disturbed Goethe because it struck him at once as repulsive and oddly serious. The carnival, he thinks, is a representation of the mysteries of life: we are born in obscenity and destined for death. The narrow, crowded and very long Corso is the course of each individual life. In disguise or out of it we try to make our way through the crowd and reach a better position, only to be jostled out of it; we are carried by the surging masses against our free will. And we are reminded too that: 'the most intense and finest satisfactions are like the horses racing by. They appear before us only for a moment, and leave hardly a trace in the soul of the spectator when they have passed.' In other words, in the excited moment we feel that 'this is it' – as we gaze at the Apollo Belvedere or read the works of Tasso (or of Goethe) – and yet what of substance gets lodged in our inner life? Perhaps almost nothing.

And he continues in this vein: 'Liberty and Equality' – the targets of political longing – 'can be enjoyed only in the tumult of madness.' 'Pleasure strives towards maximum intensity only by mixing pain, danger and sensuality.' And he concludes: 'Life taken as a whole is like the Roman Carnival: unpredictable, unsatisfactory and problematic.' And yet the Romans are not unhappy: they are – like Egmont – carefree and able to enjoy the pleasing moments as they pass.

Such sentiments, such a perception of life, perhaps allow us to make sense of some comments Goethe made while he was in Naples and Sicily. When he was about to get on the boat from Naples to Palermo Goethe jotted down a note asking himself – 'Can I ever learn to be happy? Those who I see with a talent for happiness seem so different in temperament and cast of mind from the way I am.' It seems that Goethe experienced a tension between the grandeur of the big view – 'life, viewed as a whole' – and the needful thing for happiness: carelessness, seizing the moment.

Goethe's question 'Can I ever learn to be happy?' is one that, after a fashion, we are all asking all the time. He makes a useful distinction between learning and temperament. Some people have 'a talent' for happiness: they have a buoyant, sunny nature. Goethe himself is not like that, so if he is to be happy it will be an achievement, not a lucky gift of nature. Goethe was very keen on the biblical line: 'By their fruits ye shall know them' – an idea is only as good as the results it brings. He would have been the first to mock a gloomy character who claimed to know the secrets of a good life, or someone unhappy in their relationships who advised others on this issue. So, it might seem alarming to hear Goethe – who clearly did want people to take him seriously as a 'guide to life' – confessing his anxiety: 'Can I ever learn to be happy?'

Of course, just asking this question is not the equivalent of leading an unhappy life. In fact it is clear that Goethe had – taken as a whole – a wonderful life and he knew it. But he would be inhuman, and useless as a guide, if he did not know and experience the normal range of anxieties and pains. What was remarkable about Goethe was not that he was immune to distress but that he found in himself the resources for making the best of himself.

10

Exile

'I am now so remote from the world that it gives me a curious feeling to read a newspaper. "The fashion of this world passeth away" and my only desire is to follow Spinoza's teaching and concern myself with what is everlasting so as to win eternity for my soul.'

This reflection is perhaps one of the most illuminating clues to what Rome meant for Goethe – Rome was the physical home of 'what is everlasting'. The language could hardly be more religious – and yet the Rome he is interested in is not the centre of the Catholic Church, but the Rome of antiquity and the Renaissance; the eternity is not personal everlasting life in the next world, not even eternal fame. Rather, the longing is that what is eternal in art should become the current possession of his soul.

Goethe's departure from Rome was painful. At the end of each sad day, which had been occupied with the mechanics of departure, he would take a walk with some friends. On one evening he went out alone, wandering along the Corso and up to the Capitol, a kind of terrestrial Olympus – thinking that this would be the very last time he would walk there; the Capitol was like an enchanted palace and one from which he was about to depart.

In the growing dusk, the central statue of Marcus Aurelius seemed to him like the ghost of the commendatore in Mozart's *Don Giovanni*, who, in one of the grandest and most dramatic moments of Western art, summons don Giovanni, the libertine, to hell. Goethe went down the steep steps to the ancient forum, lying behind and below the Capitol. The shadows in the moonlight were intensely dark; the

familiar ruins of the triumphal arch of Septimus Severus were solemn and awe-inspiring. But it is as if, on the point of departure, the full weight of what he was leaving behind – so longed for over many years, now so familiar – hit him. Staring at the gigantic mass of the Colosseum the whole of his encounter with Rome flashed before his eyes (as life is said to do on the point of death); his departure from Rome seemed at that moment a kind of death: the north, Germany, Weimar, all seemed like the shadowy underworld – a place of exile from life, a hell.

But why did Goethe have to leave Rome? What was forcing him? A clue is to be found in a comment Goethe made while he was in Naples – on a journey, as it were, within his journey. He says, in effect, either this is a dream or the rest of my life has been a dream. In Italy, the first thirty-seven years of Goethe's life counted for little. They were the 'whaling expedition to Greenland', as he put it in his first days on the road after striking out from Carlsbad some eighteen months before. The real point of Italy was to be an episode within his life as a whole; what he wanted was to redeem the rest of his northern existence in the light of what had been happening to him in the south. So although it was a terrible wrench to depart he had to leave if he was to make sense of his life as a whole. The hope was that, just as he had internalized his parents and so could break from them physically without losing the security and inspiration they had given him, so – perhaps – now he had internalized Rome to such a degree that he could take it back, that it could live on – fruitful and whole – in his imagination.

PART FIVE

War

Do you know the land of lemon blossom,
Where oranges glow among the dark leaves;
A soft wind turns in the blue sky;
Still and tall grow the myrtle and the bay trees;
Do you already know this place?

Do you know the house with the lovely colonnade?
Do you know its beautiful rooms?
Where household gods would watch over me and ask:
How have people hurt you, my precious child?
                    Goethe, *Song from Wilhelm Meister's*
                                        Apprenticeship (1796)

I

A German Italy

One of the most attractive – and standard – consequences of a visit to Italy was the attempt to recreate, at home in the north, some of the charms of the south. Many artists depicted their local landscape with the warmer light and softer distances of Italy. Others, like Wilhelm von Humboldt, who had been Prussian ambassador in Rome, used the works and casts they had acquired there to decorate their homes in a manner reminiscent of a grand Roman palazzo. Goethe was attached to both of these strategies – these attempts to give a journey to Italy a permanent position in later life. But Goethe also undertook a Roman revolution in his private life.

On 11 July 1788, not long after his return to Weimar, Goethe took a walk along the river Ilm, near his garden-house. His stroll was interrupted by the approach of a young woman of twenty-three, Christiane Vulpius. Christiane bravely – or perhaps naively – asked the great man if he could do anything for her older brother, Christian August; he had just completed his university studies and the recent death of their father had now laid the burden of supporting the family on his shoulders.

Goethe found the girl immensely appealing. She had a fresh, round face, dark hair and dark eyes; she was very good-natured, easily moved to laughter – which showed off her neat white teeth and pouting, well-rouged lips. Christiane was not especially pretty, but she was good-looking in a homely, plump way. Almost immediately they became lovers. Probably the next day, since in later years they used to mark 12 July as a special day.

One day, not long afterwards, Goethe was longing to see Christiane;

but he was afraid to call on her openly, since the gossips of Weimar were already on the alert. That evening, under cover of darkness – since there was no street lighting – Goethe made his way to her house, unable to keep away from her a moment longer. Pausing beneath her window he heard voices talking in the room and didn't dare go in. Retreating along the dark streets he roamed about for an hour, in a state of desperate yearning and longing. At last he went to her window again but now her room was unlit – since it was not yet late, he assumed she must have gone out.

In a frenzied state he wandered madly around the streets hoping against hope that he would somehow bump into her as she came back from wherever she had been. In the black night he kept on imagining he could see her approaching; he approached several shadowy figures before realizing each time he had been mistaken. At last, going down a narrow lane, he passed a dimly lit window; in its glow he thought he could just make out a woman coming towards him. Not wanting to run the risk of another mistake, or of being recognized, he held back. The street was so narrow that as the woman passed, her arm touched his: 'Is it you?' came a whisper, and he heard the voice of Christiane. 'I thought you had forgotten me,' she said, 'but I was so desperate to see you this evening; two female friends came to visit me – I just could not get them to leave although I was longing for them to go. When they finally went I rushed out into the night, I hardly knew where I was going, hoping and hoping that – somehow – I might find you.' As she said this she clasped his hand and led him back to her house, pulling him up the stairs to her bedroom – and (as he says) to indescribable happiness.

The Vulpius family – though comparatively poor – were not at all un-known in court circles; a couple of generations earlier the family had been prosperous lawyers. The Latinization of their name – 'Vulpius' being the learned version of 'Wolff', that is, 'wolf' – points to an earlier period of dignity. Christiane's father, however, had only ever occupied the lowest paid of court positions: archivist in the ducal lib-rary. Following complaints that he was continually drunk, old Vulpius had been removed from even that minor post and had gone into rapid decline. Her brother had been educated at Heidelberg but was now having extreme difficulty in establishing himself in a career.

Christiane herself had received little education and could not possibly have held her own in the circle of cultivated and intellectually sophisticated women of Weimar: the likes of Anna Amalia, Frau von Stein and Caroline Herder. Christiane worked in a little factory making artificial flowers: genteel industry, admittedly, but inconceivable for a woman of the upper class. Goethe did try to help her brother, recommending the young man – who in fact merited the recommendation and was eventually to become a very successful novelist – to various friends who might be able to help with employment, but without immediate success.

This relationship need not in itself have caused much of a scandal – the duke, after all, had many liaisons with women of the lower classes. If Goethe had simply invited Christiane to his garden-house from time to time few people would have been upset, although they would certainly have been interested. But early the following year Goethe did the unthinkable: he installed Christiane in the fine apartment he rented in the town, together with her stepsister and her aunt.

Christiane may not have been socially acceptable, but she had many virtues – in addition to her appealing face – which drew Goethe to her and enabled the relationship to last until her death in 1816. She had a practical and straightforward turn of mind and loved organizing the domestic side of life; more than anything, perhaps, it was her frankness and her sensual ease that appealed to Goethe. Everything we know about her bears witness to her pronounced sensuality: her fondness for wine, for lively company and louche jokes. She was erotically adventurous and Goethe talks of their mutual exploration of 'all twelve books' of sexual experience. Meaning, presumably, she was keen to do pretty much anything and everything with him.

Probably the single most important factor holding the relationship together was simply that Christiane could not believe her luck. Goethe was a god from another world. He was rich, funny, handsome, generous, famous, passionate, keen on drinking and by turns quietly domestic and outrageously dirty. And somehow this magnificent creature

Goethe made many drawings of Christiane in the early years

had latched on to her. He was deeply in love with her, and spent hours sketching her face, trying to find just what it was about the way she looked that he found so moving.

2

Roman Elegies

It was in this period – the early days with Christiane – that Goethe wrote his poetic memoirs of Rome: a sequence of poems known initially as *Erotica Romana* and later (when they came to be published in 1795) furnished with the less inflammatory title *Roman Elegies*.

The *Elegies* open with an evocation of the sense of frustration that many visitors to famous places feel. The writer senses that something wonderful is on offer – and yet he cannot grasp quite what it is. The spirit of Rome refuses to speak to Goethe; and he calls out to the places and the streets – say something, speak to me. He is frustrated at being merely a well-behaved typical tourist – seeing the sights. He wants more than this; he wants to enter into some intimate and personal relationship with these objects. The 'spirit' or 'soul' of eternal Rome is all around him, and yet – to him – it has nothing to say. (Proust was a connoisseur of such moments – at which one is unable to identify the 'message' that everything seems to be trying to send.)

Goethe feels like an outsider at the temple; he can admire, but he cannot participate. If the stones are silent, there is still hope – who did he notice at a window? Some woman, whose enticing appearance has, as it were, whispered to him an exciting promise: 'Without love, the world is not the world, and without love, Rome is not Rome.'

The movement of ideas here is almost too dense – yet elucidation risks making it all seem plodding and coarse. We get a clue to what is going on here by recalling Goethe's first, happy reaction to the image of Frau von Stein. Then – some thirteen years before – Goethe had attributed to her a striking capacity: 'She sees the world as it is, and yet through the medium of love.' Now in Rome he needs love to see

Rome as it is – something has to awaken in him before he can really grasp what these stones have to offer. This joins up with another, initially puzzling, idea, which intrigued Goethe. Plato had once suggested – in one of his more obscure passages – that perception requires an object to actually be in us; the eye must be a kind of sun, because it can see the sun.

Of course, as a theory of how vision works, this is about as mad as can be. But a more important point is being articulated, or at least hinted at: recognition is built around sympathy – I can recognize states of mind in others because I know them in myself. So, if Goethe can make nothing, as yet, of Rome, it is because the required sympathetic love is not, as yet, alive in him. The self that Rome can speak to – the self that is responsive to what Rome has to offer – is currently dormant. The coded and veiled discourse of the buildings cannot be grasped by him – except in an external, 'well behaved' and sterile manner.

This impasse – and Goethe's sense of how he overcame it – is noteworthy, if only because Goethe had clearly done everything right in terms of the official view of how to see Rome. He had his guide books, he had been training himself to be perceptive, he spoke Italian and was conducted by learned and well-respected guides.

Goethe feels like a conquering barbarian who can stride into Rome, his pockets full of money – a representative of the Gauls, the military masters who eventually overran the city. But, in turn, Rome conquers the conquerors; she takes their money, making herself rich again; she isn't afraid of them, she learns from them – and cares for them. And here, we can trace a decisive, enticing, confusion of reference: from the persona of Rome – an abstract representation of the city – to the specific person of a particular Roman woman, one who will eventually be named as Faustina. Rome – in the person of this woman – will love him; and in loving her, Goethe will come to love the city; and in loving it, it will speak to him.

The *Elegies* can be a bit confusing because they bring together two registers of thought which are generally kept distinct: homely, intimate conversation and elaborate classical reference. For Goethe it is no accident that these come together.

In the third of the *Elegies* Faustina is lamenting that she has given herself too quickly to him: surely he can't respect her if she's so ready to jump into bed with him? 'Don't be upset, darling, that you gave yourself so quickly to me,' says Goethe. He tries to get her to see how noble and fine her sexual eagerness is: isn't classical mythology full of stories of the gods and goddesses acting at once on their sexual desire? Did Venus – the goddess of love – hold back when she was attracted to the beautiful Anchises? And their child was Aeneas, the Ur-father of the Roman people, according to Virgil. Hero, priestess to Venus, gave herself at once to Leander, who swam the Hellespont each night to be with her. They did not wait for a marriage ceremony, or think ill of themselves after the act.

The poet invokes a world-view, derived from classical antiquity, in which it is right and proper that desire is aroused at first sight and acted upon at once. It is an attitude to life that finds its symbolic home in the city of Rome. It is touching that Goethe – the northern barbarian – should be the one to preach this consoling lesson to his Roman lover. Although she is a part of Rome, a representative of the essence of Rome, it is the outsider, the lover, who tells her about who she is. Rome needs Goethe as much as Goethe needs Rome.

This is one of the points in the *Elegies* at which we can sense that they refer both to a relationship with 'Faustina' in Rome and his relationship with Christiane in Weimar. The third elegy contains a message for Christiane; it is the Good News brought from Rome – sexual spontaneity is natural and admirable; it is sanctioned by the gods. And one might also think that there is a message to Goethe himself: Christiane or Faustina is telling Goethe that they don't think he has been impetuous; he isn't less impressive in their eyes just because they've been cavorting around on a bed with him.

The sixth elegy describes the way in which, through his relationship with Faustina, Goethe is learning to appreciate classical sculpture more fully; spending time with her takes him away from his overt education – reading, visiting museums, drawing and writing. But it is with her that he comes to appreciate the shape and texture of the body; he learns to 'see with eyes that touch; touch with hands that see'. His intimate sensitivity to her body allows him to recognize the sensitivity displayed in classical sculpture. And so he is not only close to Faustina, but close to the great artists of the classical world.

When, after making love, she falls asleep he lies awake 'thinking of many things'. In her arms, he touches her lightly, moving his fingers to the rhythm of classical poetry – bringing her, by hexameters, to another climax. In his imagination, he is doing as the Roman love poets would have done; with Faustina he is reliving the classical experience of love. Amor, the god of love, looks after the lamps, and recalls the times when he looked after his 'Triumvirate' (the Latin poets Catullus, Propertius and Tibullus). Goethe is constructing for himself a private history of culture in which his actions now (lying in bed with his mistress) can be grasped as absolutely the right thing to do. Think of the questions in the background: why are you living like this, running off to Rome, when you should be at home in Weimar helping run the state like a responsible adult? Taking an uncultivated woman into your house and bed, when you should be marrying into the aristocracy? And Goethe can say, I am being true to the classical ideal, I am doing what the great Latin poets did, I am following their example, I am right to do as I do.

The poems include several little touches of delicate evocation: a happy, mutual contentment in bed. He watches her breathing as she sleeps so peacefully; they hold each other close and listen to the rain and the wind outside their snug bedroom. He describes loosening her dress; it falls to the ground, he lifts her easily and carries her, laughing, to the bed; the room is uncluttered and spacious; the simple bed is large and comfortable. Could any man have a happier experience? Both naked, delighting in each other, the bed creaking sweetly. This is Eros at its most wholesome; here, sex is innocent and deeply loving.

But can we really believe that this is the whole story of Goethe and sex? Goethe's sexual passions were, in fact, more diverse, more complicated – perhaps more disturbing to him – than the happy episode in the bedroom with Faustina (or Christiane) considered in isolation would suggest. Among the many antique gems that Goethe purchased in Rome were several with a phallic motif. In this genre of erotic carving, the erect penis is presented as an independent creature, as a being in its own right, occasionally endowed with little legs and a tail. It is an image of completely undomesticated male sexuality – an invocation of energy and excitement with no attention paid to the object of desire. If mutuality was the keynote of the erotic encounter with Faustina, these priapic images convey pride in the fact of arousal, but no curiosity about who or what is doing the arousing.

Goethe was particularly interested in a kind of statue called a Herm; this is a sort of obelisk with a bust of Hermes at the top. From the middle of the obelisk emerges the erect penis of the god.

There is a drawing by Goethe, probably done around the time he was writing the *Elegies*, of an infinitely more lewd character, of the same classical conception.

What kind of sexuality is on display? On the one hand the image of Hermes, and the closely related picture of Pan by Poussin, suggest a protean potency; sexuality is everywhere, unrestrained by social convention or moral anxiety; it is part of the abounding fruitfulness of nature. On the other hand, there is something solitary and static in

Goethe's drawing; this may be the unintended effect of his hesitant graphic technique, but it may have a deeper significance.

In *Lotte in Weimar* Thomas Mann fantasizes about Goethe lying in bed in the early morning, mixing his thoughts about poetry, politics and his own past, with erotic images ('my unquenchable friend here'). Goethe's sexuality is presented as intimately interwoven with his poetic imagination:

'Ah! If only one lived in a free, intellectual society, what powerful, extraordinary things one could write for it! Art's natural ruthlessness is shackled and limited by all sorts of petty considerations. But it may be good for her; maybe she is all the more feared and loved, mysterious and powerful, wearing a veil instead of going naked, and only now and then giving a startling and rapturous glimpse of her native brazenness! Cruelty is one of the chief ingredients of love, and divided about equally between the sexes: cruelty of lust, ingratitude, callousness, maltreatment, domination. The same is true of the passive qualities, patience under suffering, even pleasure in ill-usage. And five or six other perversities – if they are perversities – that may be a moral judgement – which, without adding anything else, are the chemical components of love.'

Goethe was, however, no rebel in such matters. He clearly felt that people were wrong to be shocked by the manifold objects of sexual desire. But, at the same time, he didn't hate people for being what they were: respectable, unadventurous and superficial. He was still going on about this late in life. On Wednesday 25 February 1824, he tried to explain this position to his good friend Eckermann, who carefully recorded the conversation – as he did on so many other occasions:

'Today, Goethe showed me two remarkable poems; both highly moral in their tendency, but in their several motifs so unreservedly natural and true, that they are of the kind which the world styles immoral. On this account he keeps them to himself and does not intend to publish them.

' "Could intellect and high cultivation," he said, "become the property of all, the poet would have fair play; he could be always thoroughly true, and would not be compelled to fear uttering his best thoughts. But as it is, he must always keep on a certain level; must remember that his works will fall into the hands of all sorts of people and must therefore take care lest by over-great openness he may give offence to the majority of Good men." '

The *Roman Elegies* had a Prologue that Goethe, perhaps rather wisely at the time, suppressed, presumably for fear of offending just such 'Good men'. In this he addresses Priapus, whose duty it is to stand guard over Goethe's garden of erotic delights. 'Everyone is welcome here,' he says – but if anyone turns their nose up in disgust, then Priapus should punish them by 'shafting them up the backside with his big red tool'.

The *Elegies* read as if written in Rome; he keeps on saying how happy he is in the city. But Goethe's Rome should perhaps be thought of as a way of life as well as an actual place. He made a shorter trip to Italy in 1790, accompanying the duke's mother, the Dowager Duchess Anna Amalia; they spent most of their time in Venice. Goethe was much less enthusiastic on this second trip and made various cutting remarks about the tourists who clogged up the place. His *Venetian Epigrams*, which originated in this visit, are much more revealing about Goethe's erotic life than his high cultural ambitions.

There's one extremely explicit – and very short – poem (the eighth in the sequence) in which he's pushing his way through the narrow alleys of the city. He meets a charming young woman – one of the band of prostitutes who populate the *Venetian Epigrams*. Well, he says, I decided to explore; but what's this – she's as wide as a river. In Venice there are as many prostitutes as there are canals, but they've got it all wrong; they need to model their c***s on the tight little lanes, not on the Grand Canal.

In many other poems from this sequence we encounter a breezy, obscene and very witty, erotic philosophy. Jesus, he notes, would have liked it here; the place is full of the sinners and whores with whom the Good Lord liked to pass the time. So, Goethe reflects, perhaps I'm a decent Christian after all – since I love that kind of company too.

We learn more about the kind of company he liked when he gives – as in all areas of life Goethe was so keen to do – some advice about sexual satisfaction. Learn from me: I've tried it with boys; interesting, but not as much fun as it is with girls. However, should you find you're getting bored of sex with your woman, just turn her over and try her backside for a change. There are plenty of useful tips on the argot of the Venetian prostitutes: 'coffee' means she'll masturbate you. And on the topic of masturbation, how could God have made such a mistake? If He was so keen on us having children and getting married and all that why did God make it so easy to enjoy yourself on your own? And, on top of that, to make masturbation a sin! No, really we need a new religion: couldn't Jesus come back to earth and found one – a sex-creed in which wanking would be a moral obligation. I'd join that Church, he says; in fact, I'd be an apostle; I'd be the first martyr.

In the early twentieth century – following the publication of the more explicit verses – there was a good deal of anxious scholarly debate about their significance. In terms of creative trajectory all this frank – and lascivious – discussion of sex followed on from the writing of *Iphigenia*, a classical temple of nobility; and precedes *Hermann and*

Dorothea, a hymn to the comfort and security of respectable, married middle-class life. A bizarre – and unsuccessful – attempt was made to show that all the wicked bits in the *Elegies* and *Epigrams* were simply translations from scattered lines of standard classical authors. Goethe was merely a sophisticated philologist; no personal enthusiasm need be imputed. Perhaps he was like someone writing the history of the Punic wars – who could hardly be motivated by a personal desire to wipe Carthage from the map. From the mere fact that Goethe *writes* 'I'd like to be a martyr to masturbation' we should draw no personal conclusions whatever; he is merely quoting a classical source.

It would have been helpful to have invoked the standard praise of Goethe as 'many-sided' at this point. The attraction of the noble works and the sensitive praise of domestic peace and quiet is enhanced – not destroyed – by the fact that Goethe also wrote the *Elegies* and the *Epigrams*. We trust Goethe's love of ideal beauty and cosy evenings all the more because we know that he wasn't using them to hide from or deny – or whitewash – the earthy and transgressive parts of himself.

3

The French Revolution

Goethe and Napoleon both regarded the opening scenes of the French Revolution as occurring in August 1785. It was the symbolic power of what became known as 'the Diamond Necklace Affair' – rather than any real causal significance – which appealed to the dramatist in such observers. In that month the Cardinal-Duke de Rohan was arrested. He had guaranteed payment for and taken possession of a necklace of almost unbelievable value (about five times the annual state revenue of the Duchy of Weimar), which he intended to pass on to the queen, Marie-Antoinette, having been duped into believing that she would pay for it herself, despite the monarchy being badly short of funds. Apparently the queen knew nothing of this, but a prostitute posing as her in the gardens of Versailles under cover of darkness promised the cardinal the highest possible favours in return for this service.

The affair came to light when the jewellers sued for payment; the cardinal believed that the queen had been meeting subsequent instalments. The resulting 'celebrity' court case represented the queen and the high aristocracy as corrupt and incredibly greedy. When Alexandre Dumas wrote his entertaining novel about this episode, *The Queen's Necklace* (1848), he suggested that the master conspirator was Cagliostro. The great swindler was supposed to have set up the whole thing in order to bring the monarchy into disrepute and foster rebellion. In his own dramatized version – *The Grand Kophta*, published in 1792, long before Dumas got to it – Goethe had, in fact, taken a similar line.

In that play, the Cagliostro figure sets up a cult which is devoted to the moral wisdom of 'The Grand Kophta' – who turns out to be (of course) Cagliostro himself. Goethe shows himself acutely aware of the follies and incompetence of the ruling French aristocracy. But at the same time as 'Count' Cagliostro's antics reveal this decadence, the illusory cult of the Kophta comes to stand for the psychology of revolution as well. Goethe's view was that the ambitions of the revolutionaries – even in the early phase of the Declaration of the Rights of Man, and increasingly as the Revolution became more radical – were essentially delusional. To preach 'equality' was to worship an imagined, unreal divinity – like the Kophta. Equality for Goethe was unreal in the sense that it wasn't a possible basis for a good society. The aristocrats might be doing a bad job but putting 'the people' in charge wouldn't make things better and would merely introduce a new ruling class, not equality.

From the early days of 1790, French aristocrats began leaving the country, heading particularly for the neighbouring German states. The émigrés expected sympathy from the absolutist rulers of the German states as well as from the Austrians. Whatever the earlier animosity that had resulted in so many wars and shifting alliances, Austria, Prussia and the French monarchy were all on the same side now.

The first phase of the Revolution was relatively moderate. The National Assembly developed from the Three Estates and was dominated by the liberal aristocracy, lower clergy and lawyers. It aimed at a constitutional monarchy. It sought to move away from the absolutism of Versailles to a system more like that of Great Britain; one in which the monarchy played a significant part but where real power lay in the hands of a competent and prosperous elite. The idea that lawyers and bankers might have a greater share in running the state would have seemed quite straightforward to the ruling class in Frankfurt or Hamburg, for example – since that was exactly the arrangement they had enjoyed for generations. Such oligarchic government in fact existed in many parts of France. Perhaps the clearest way of seeing the movement of 1789 was simply as the assertion of an already powerful oligarchy fighting off a king who needed more and more of its money.

The Versailles model – with the king as the sole source of authority, and the court entourage also being the executive power – had a strong appeal for many German rulers. But it had not been fully realized in

France; symbolically Louis XVI was absolute, the owner of the country; but in fact his power was drastically limited – it was his inability to raise taxes from the nobility and the Church that precipitated the crisis of 1789. In other words, it was not initially clear to the German states what lessons, if any, to draw from this situation – or what action to take concerning it.

The danger came not so much from the National Assembly and its constitutional meditations as from the public disorder that accompanied them. The new government was not in any better position to manage the economy than the king had been. One measure – taken to stave off national bankruptcy – was to 'nationalize' Church lands; 'assignats' were issued: paper money supposedly guaranteed against Church land. But this guarantee was insubstantial and the value of the notes fell, causing inflation.

The apparent weakness of the government seems to have emboldened Louis and his advisers. At this stage they had little reason to think that the population as a whole were particularly enamoured with the new regime. In June 1791, Louis attempted to leave France with the aim of recruiting foreign support and returning forcibly to power – willing to make some concessions, but as concessions, not as recognition of rights. But this plan miscarried. The king was stopped on his way to the border and returned to Paris, with whatever moral authority he had previously had much reduced.

A 'war' party gained the upper hand in the Assembly; seeing such a course as a way of escaping financial difficulties (on the assumption that a war would be successful) and predicting that it would galvanize public support for the government. The hope was that in making war the government would be seen to govern and complex questions about the nature and form of political authority would become irrelevant. And in April 1792 this strategy was put into effect; the Assembly declared war on Austria – or rather the House of Austria, since they didn't aim at Vienna, but at part of the Netherlands belonging to the Emperor, although not part of the Empire. However, Austria was not entirely unprepared, having negotiated an alliance with Prussia earlier in the year. The anticipated aggression of France had brought together the two countries that had been at odds for thirty-five years.

The initial French action in the Netherlands was ineffectual. Prussia and Austria joined forces to counter-attack in the late summer, marshalling their forces on the Rhine under the command of the Duke of Brunswick. Brunswick was the most experienced general in Europe, and also the brother of Anna Amalia, hence uncle of Carl August. Carl August was keen to participate in the campaign and held the rank of general in the Prussian part of the army. He was also keen to have the company and assistance of Goethe during the campaign – which, like everyone on the German side, he assumed would be brilliantly successful, ending, no doubt quickly, in entry to Paris, the restoration of Louis, and eternal glory for the victorious generals.

4

The Campaign in France

Goethe was not enthusiastic. He was certainly not a supporter of the Revolution, and he didn't dislike the army – in fact he got on well with many senior officers and was highly appreciated by them. But there were several reasons why the present campaign did not attract him; not so much reasons against the campaign per se, but against his involvement in it. He did not approve of the sovereign of Weimar, whose duty it should be to rule his own territory as well as possible, going off to fight in the Prussian forces. Goethe's son, August, was only two and a half and much loved. A portrait by Meyer from that time, though slightly clumsy, shows a charming little boy; Christiane had in October the year before given birth to a dead child.

Goethe had also just taken possession of the Frauenplan house (although he had rented part of it for many years). He had been living with Christiane and August at the Jager house, but the duke needed that to accommodate guests. He had offered to relocate Goethe in another of his properties – but one that was currently being occupied by Wieland and his family, so the domino effect was going to push them out too. Fortunately, the Frauenplan house came up for sale and – using the duke's money – Goethe got possession of the whole thing and was further provided with funds to undertake substantial improvements. In June the whole family had moved into the rear portion of the large house while work was undertaken at the front. Goethe was always a keen supervisor, and cared enormously about the arrangements of his house. Despite his domestic preoccupations, Goethe's immense personal gratitude and loyalty to Carl August made it impossible for him to refuse to accompany him on the campaign. And in August he set off to join his sovereign.

In the last days of July, Brunswick issued two severe 'manifestos', much influenced by émigré sentiments. Their core assertion was that the German troops were not so much invading France as acting as the army of the legitimate French authority; that is, that they were soldiers for Louis XVI. The French people, therefore, could not be treated as an enemy; so any action against the troops would not constitute war, but would be merely criminal action. Brunswick and his generals seemed to have assumed that the Revolution was more of a coup, lacking popular support; and that his army would be welcomed as restoring rightful authority. Opposition was expected to melt away.

The effect of the manifestos, when they became known in Paris, was quite the contrary. On 10 August, the National Guard, supported by many sans-culottes, attacked the Tuileries – the palace where Louis was lodged in Paris. The king took refuge in the Assembly, where some six hundred Swiss Guards, acting on the orders of the Assembly, were supposed to protect him. This event marked a considerably more extreme phase of the Revolution – or perhaps more accurately a second Revolution.

This humiliation of the palace enraged the émigrés. Although regarded as barbaric, the event didn't in itself indicate military strength, but merely illustrated the wild behaviour of the 'rabble', who (the émigrés concluded) would be no match for the Prussian and Austrian troops.

The early events of the campaign certainly pointed to French weakness. The frontier fortress of Longwy was easily persuaded to surrender. And it was near there that Goethe joined the army on 27 August, having delayed his departure as long as possible.

His first sight of the military operation was not at all reassuring. 'It was raining heavily and the sentries had hidden themselves away to escape the deluge. The ground had been turned to mud by the passage of so many horses. A nearby ditch had been turned into a receptacle for all the camp's refuse; it had become stopped up; then in the night violent torrents of rain broke through the dyke and brought the most disgusting calamity down upon the tents. Entrails, bones and every-thing else the butchers had discarded had been carried down into the already damp and unhealthy sleeping quarters.' Goethe preferred to spend the night in the large sleeping carriage – and though this was only thirty yards from the tents he had to be carried there at night and back in the morning.

This passage – describing Goethe's first day and night with the army – rehearses two of the continuous themes of the campaign. One is the appalling weather – which really caused immense difficulties for the allies. Such things are always a matter of chance, or hazard, in great political affairs. The other theme, however, is human folly or careless-ness, which makes things much worse than they need be. The pos-itioning of the camp left it open to just this kind of revolting inundation; and a better way of disposing of rubbish should have been found. This was important because of the threat of dysentery – a permanent threat to any army and which in fact ravaged the allies. Goethe's hint here is that there is some connection between the future success or failure of the campaign and the 'household economy' of the army.

Goethe was moved to similar reflections when he witnessed requi-sitioning and procurement in operation. Some shepherds had tried to hide their flocks, but they were found by the German patrols. There was a semblance of due process; the sheep were counted, their owners ascertained. Then worthless coupons drawn in the name of Louis XVI were distributed as compensation, and the sheep were immediately slaughtered. 'My eyes and soul have never witnessed a crueller scene or a more profound sorrow,' commented Goethe.

Goethe's political instincts are revealed in this statement. The aim of good government is that people should be allowed to tend their flocks. This image of a simple but satisfying life is one that has been revered since Theocritus – and is at the heart of Virgil's *Georgics*. It's not so hard to live well, to provide for yourself and your family 'good beer, good bread and good soup', which is how, Goethe tells us, some peasant boys define the good life a few days after this incident. A flock can be built up over a few years; a house which is well built last for several generations; so long as people are not disturbed in their accumulation of sufficient resources it isn't too much of a challenge to secure a happy existence. The 'delusion' of freedom and preoccupation with rights and constitutions has nothing to contribute directly to the attainment of human happiness – as it has been understood for millennia.

5

Verdun

The army proceeded to Verdun, the last major fortress on the road to Paris and fated to be for generations the site of terrible conflict. Because of his high position at the Weimar court and his cultural éclat, Goethe was often privy to the inner workings of the campaign. He was just waking up on the morning of 30 August – in the sleeping carriage – when he heard a noise outside. It was Carl August bringing a certain Herr Grothaus to say good morning. Grothaus was an old acquaintance of Goethe, and he had been delegated to conduct negotiations for the surrender of the city. But to do this he needed a trumpeter to accompany him – and the duke was to supply a man from his regiment. But nothing came of the negotiations and a bombardment of the city began at midnight, keeping Goethe, and everyone else, awake.

Unable to sleep, Goethe went out to inspect the batteries pounding away at the town. The appalling noise was too much for him and the situation was becoming dangerous as the French guns returned fire. Goethe sought some relief and security in a nearby vineyard protected by high walls. There he bumped into Prince Reuss, an Austrian diplomat with whom he was well acquainted; the two men passed the night pacing up and down along the rows of vines. The prince wanted to know what Goethe was working on, expecting to hear of some new novel or drama. He was very much surprised when Goethe broke into an impassioned lecture on colour. In a state of high excitement, Goethe told Reuss all about an observation he had made the previous day at a neighbouring village. He'd noticed a group of soldiers sitting round a little pond, fishing in the exceptionally clear water. Goethe amused himself by watching the fish, noticing that their colours appeared to change as they swam about. Why did this occur? Was it that the colour of the skins was itself affected by the movement? Then Goethe noticed something else. A piece of pottery had fallen into the pool; it appeared to be red on the near side and blue on the side further from him. As Goethe walked round the pool he saw that the colours from this bit of pottery didn't change position. The blue still seemed to be on the far side. So the colour effect couldn't be due to the colour of the pottery itself but must be brought about by the water acting as a kind of huge prism. Hence, the changing colours of the fish would be due to their movement altering the angle from which they were observed, rather than from any change in the skin itself.

Many people since then have been – like the patient prince – puzzled by Goethe's intense reaction to such things. Instead of finding this mildly curious, Goethe was completely fascinated. He was especially pleased since he was observing this phenomenon in the midst of life, rather than under the special conditions of the laboratory.

Two days later Verdun capitulated. The fall of Longwy and Verdun seemed, to the German forces, to indicate that all was over with the French. In Paris, it caused panic and desperate measures. The enemy were almost at the gates. The nation must now be mobilized in self-defence. However, the aim of getting all available manpower to the front left a gap in the rear – at home. The prisons were full of enemies of the state. How could they be guarded? How could they be prevented from taking advantage of the military crisis? An extreme solution was urged by the supporters of Robespierre – the enemies within must be killed. And they were, in what became known as 'the September massacres'. Of course, when this became known to the émigrés and to the allies their sense of righteous indignation was only heightened.

Another consequence was the defection of the leading French general, Lafayette. Following the mob violence – which seemed to indicate that the government had lost control – Lafayette defected to the allies, although few of his soldiers followed him in this step. In his place a minister of no military experience, Dumouriez, was appointed. Dumouriez turned out to be a highly competent general; but the defection of Lafayette introduced a complicating factor into the allied war aims. The émigrés had always insisted that support for the

Revolution was weak in France; and the allied leaders always considered it a real possibility that the French generals in the field would defect and lead their armies against Paris.

6

Valmy

This hope led to considerable difficulties when the allies finally came up against the French forces at Valmy. Marching in terrible weather, with inadequate supplies and ravaged by dysentery, the Prussian and Austrian armies were confronted by French troops occupying a strong position on a group of hills that formed a wide, natural amphitheatre. Brunswick recognized that an attack would hardly be feasible in the circumstances. And after an exchange of cannon-fire, a truce was declared for negotiations. Discussions lasted for several days, during which the allied forces were encamped on a plain, continually drenched and without shelter. Brunswick was hoping that Dumouriez would change sides. Goethe, together with senior officers in Carl August's regiment, slept in a shallow ditch. Goethe saw his role as that of keeping up good cheer among the officers and as providing a philosophical perspective upon events.

In the neighbouring village, he meets an old acquaintance who (like Goethe) is hungry and thirsty – but everything seems to have been taken already by the troops. Goethe decides that this is the moment to display all his practical good sense. They approach a village where a great crowd of soldiers are already foraging, but in their haste they are ransacking the nearest houses, so Goethe and his friend head on to the far side of the village. At almost the last house they see a soldier coming out cursing the fact that there's nothing left. Goethe's suspicions are aroused and entering the hut he finds two more soldiers loudly complaining that they can't find anything to eat – but all the same staying put. Applying his ready charm and frank friendliness Goethe soon gets them to admit that, actually, the cellar of the house is filled with excellent provisions; they had concealed the door but now clear everything away and Goethe clambers down. He and his friend gather as many bottles of good wine as they can carry and head back to the camp.

Sitting himself down near a big campfire Goethe quietly opens the bottles and hides them behind him. He takes out one and showily starts swigging from it. Of course this attracts attention and soon he's offering the bottle to several soldiers. Every so often he puts the bottle down behind him and – unknown to the others – picks up a new one. No one minds a second round and so the 'miracle' continues: 'by the third bottle they were cheering the magician loudly, and in such miserable circumstances the merriment was extremely welcome'.

This whole episode is absolutely Goethe. He's proud of his practical turn – he can forage well; and he knows how to use this ability to comfort himself and to cheer others up too. And Goethe takes this task very seriously – both in literature and in everyday life. He works on the assumption that people already know how bad things are. The task of the intelligent man is to make life more bearable – not to rub people's noses in their misery. This is Goethe's personal version of Christ's miraculous feeding of the five thousand with only a few loaves and fishes. The miracle here isn't supernatural: it's just a little trick – but the effect is as good as a miracle. The men who were worn out and miserable are made merry and given new hope.

Among those in the company Goethe provided for was a French marquis – a man Goethe had met in Venice, where the marquis had been French envoy, when he had been there in 1790 with Anna Amalia. Goethe thought to please him by recollecting the beauty and pleasure of former days on the Grand Canal. The marquis, however, cannot bear to hear of these things – he has been too cast down by what has happened in France, and dread of it, he says, had poisoned his last years – including the period when he knew Goethe and had passed himself off as light-hearted.

The juxtaposition here – Goethe gets the lads a drink, the marquis remains glum – shows up the underlying art in Goethe's apparently simple narrative of his own experience. No doubt these events did happen side by side, but Goethe turns them into a study: the task is to be cheerful; the marquis is spreading gloom, and even plumes himself on this, upbraiding Goethe for having been too much at ease in the past – why wasn't he more upset about what was about to take place in France? Goethe does not record his answer – and needn't because he has already demonstrated it. What good would it have done? Were the French going to alter their course because a famous German writer was, privately, anxious about what they might do? What matters is dealing with what lies to hand – if something is outside your power then you are entitled not to worry about it – even if, in principle, you think it horrible. And if cheering up others and yourself is simply not possible then you should aim at diversion – at least take your mind off the problems that there is nothing you can actually do to alleviate.

The allies remained camped on the plain at Valmy for a week – enduring the most appalling weather – constant heavy rain – with provisions in extremely short supply. On 28 September the truce was finally called off and the allies were obliged to retreat, returning along the route by which they had advanced into France. Although not technically defeated, the allies could not afford to remain where they were or to attempt an assault on the French position. The conditions of the retreat were terrible – illness, bad weather, impassable roads, the sense of failure. The French, in fact, followed the retreating allies and were soon to push over the Rhine into the German states. The pursuing French, however, did not launch an attack on the bedraggled troops – an agreement had been reached whereby the allies would hand over the fortresses they had taken (Verdun and Longwy) in exchange for an unmolested passage.

Goethe was appalled at the activities of the foraging soldiers – he especially hated their carelessness. As if it was not enough to just take what they could the men stupidly ruined much more; in one episode some soldiers start robbing – taking tools only to have to abandon them soon after. Their senseless actions, making even worse a terrible situation, seem to Goethe to be history in miniature. Things are bad – of course – but greed and folly compound the evil.

7

Separation

At last, at the end of October, Goethe was able to free himself from the horrors of the general retreat and to take off on his own. While he was lodging in the ancient city of Trier a letter was forwarded to him from his mother. His uncle – his mother's brother – had died. During the life of this Textor uncle the rules of the Frankfurt administration had prevented Goethe from himself being a city councillor. Now such a path was open to him. If he decided to follow it, it was highly probable that he would be able to take up an important post on the council – in view of both his technical seniority (as a doctor of law) and his obvious practical experience of government.

For a moment Goethe is transported back into his childhood. He thinks of his grandfather, head of the Frankfurt administration, whose career he was supposed to emulate – something which is now within his sights. He fondly remembers the old patriarch in his garden, tending his fruit trees; he thinks of the family continuity – might he now take possession of the garden? He recalls too how this ambition had not been thrust upon him but had been his own – how as a boy he had longed to occupy a leading role in the city. And now all of this is open to him – and he no longer wants it.

For one thing, Frankfurt was not what it had been in his youth; French forces were already reputed to have taken the city; dangerously located as it was, near the border with France, Goethe had no wish to be – in some indefinite future – the governor of a garrison town or a city under siege.

But his strongest objection to a Frankfurt career was simply that in the twelve years of his connection to Weimar he had found a better setting for his particular capacities and interests. 'I had enjoyed a rare good fortune, the confidence and indulgence of the duke.' In other words he wasn't dependent on political factions or popular good will. 'This sovereign, who was not only endowed with natural talents, but also highly cultivated, took some pleasure in my well-meaning, yet often inadequate, services to him, and gave me opportunity for my own development, something which would not have been possible anywhere else in Germany.'

His motives were partly to do with personal comfort and opportunity; but in addition Goethe judged the specific kind of contribution he could make to a state (that he could make some kind of contribution he never doubted). The government of Frankfurt was more in the manner of a permanent civil service – more specialized, dependent upon continuous application and skill in management – and in dealing with collective government. Although Goethe had some experience in the right direction, at the very least since his departure for Italy, now five years back, he had moved away from this kind of rigorous collective application. In short he didn't have the required temperament.

Finally, desperate to get further away from the army, Goethe hired a little boat to head north to visit his old friend Fritz Jacobi at Pempelfort, his fine country house near Düsseldorf. Floating down the Rhine Goethe reflected further on his current state of being: 'In Italy I felt myself raised above petty thoughts, lifted beyond the level of false wishes, and in place of longing for the land of the arts, I experienced a longing for art itself.' This, he thinks, has alienated him from others. What makes someone attractive is the way they share their longing, the way in which some good passion (as yet unfulfilled) draws them to others in the hope of finding another who shares this wish. While Italy was merely a dream, Goethe was searching for something and this made him eager to engage with other people. By going there and sating his longing, he has taken that urgency out of his life and – he now thinks – removed the engine of his social life.

The sequence is this: it is dissatisfied longing which draws us to others – we are seeking something from them. The more content and secure we become in ourselves – the more we satisfy our longings – the less we need others. 'The study of art, like the study of ancient writers, gives us a certain steadfastness, an inner satisfaction; while it fills us inwardly with great objects and sentiments, it takes control of all those desires that strive for external expression . . . It becomes ever less necessary to communicate with others . . . the artist (and the genuine art lover) strives for pleasures which he hardly ever has occasion to share with others.' His passion for science has only increased this. He enjoys solitude: working alone in his darkened room, considering plants in his garden. His domestic life with Christiane and his young son, August, has provided human refreshment – so he has had little deep need for outside contact.

8

Boredom

Long before, in the days of *Werther*, Fritz Jacobi had been a close friend of Goethe. He was a man of considerable talent – a good poet and later president of the Munich Academy. However, he and Goethe disagreed about how to interpret Spinoza – a rather recherché dispute, it has to be said. Goethe later summed up their differences by saying that Jacobi's whole cast of mind required him to distance himself from the world, while Goethe wanted to engage ever more closely with the external world. At first sight this seems completely wrong-headed. Goethe has just been describing his deep solitude; while at Pempelfort he was immediately drawn into the highly sociable and cultivated Jacobi circle.

In its way, Jacobi's cultivated, prosperous family life was perfect; he and his family occupied a fine, substantial house surrounded by delightful gardens. They ate well and always had interesting guests around. An almost permanent fixture at the house was the writer Heinse, who had translated one of the most overtly obscene of the classics – the *Satyricon* of Petronius. He greatly admired Goethe and had written a novel called *Ardinghello* – which in its mixture of sensuality and reflection on art was broadly Goethean in inspiration; Goethe hated it. Heinse, however, was a great wit and there would be evenings when the whole company could hardly stop laughing. Whether sitting in the gardens or in the gracious interiors the conversation was always spirited and cheerful.

But by 'the world', Goethe did not mean a social circle; he meant rather an engagement with the material world – an embrace of science, a desire to follow things rather than ideas. And the effect of a fine and cultivated social circle is, he felt, often to push one in the opposite direction; ideas become fixed and only those that support the doctrine of the clique can get a hearing. In reality Goethe must have been a difficult guest – famous and admired, certainly not ill-mannered, but preoccupied. He tried a few optical experiments – which he loved demonstrating – but his interpretation, departing from Newton, was regarded as merely eccentric. 'I had no talent for true conversation or for dialectics – for the give and take of argument. I must confess however, that often a bad habit came to the fore: since I found ordinary conversation quite boring, because nothing is expressed there except limited, particular modes of representation, I was in the habit of making outrageously paradoxical statements in order to provoke the narrow-minded disagreements that people normally get themselves into, and to force them to extreme conclusions. This was, of course, usually offensive to the company and annoying on more than one count. For often, to attain my end, I had to play Devil's advocate, and since everyone wanted to be on the side of good and wanted me to be good as well, they would not let me do that.'

To be 'good' in conversation is to be on the side of well-intentioned people. The problem that was affecting Goethe, here, isn't hard to sympathize with. There are lots of topics on which a kind heart and disposition to believe what's morally appealing (what we call 'political correctness') inhibits investigation and the mutual pursuit of the truth. Goethe was in a painful position because he was not content with that sort of superficial approach yet far too decent to deny that these were good people. It would be a simpler world if superficiality were the prerogative only of the malicious or the dim. Goethe's isolation comes from the fact that these people are interesting, cultivated, kind and witty. So he can't launch a moral crusade; he can't argue that the longing to understand things is a necessary condition of being a decent person. The Jacobi circle shows it isn't.

9

Plessing

Goethe couldn't really have hated being at Pempelfort since he stayed a month. Then he set off to stay with another old acquaintance – the Princess Gallitzin. But on the way he dropped in to see Professor Plessing; and this little visit is extraordinarily revealing about Goethe's view of life. He had known – or at least known of – Plessing since his early days. When *Werther* came out, Goethe became a cult figure for sensitive young men who felt that the world did not appreciate their talents. They felt that *Werther* dignified their own self-torment and showed depression to be an exalted state of being – practically a proof of genius. 'Everyone felt entitled to think the best of himself as a separate and complete being, and, thoroughly validated in his separateness, considered himself to have the right to weave eccentricities, follies and mistakes into the complex of his beloved existence.' Yet many such people were genuinely very unhappy and wrote to Goethe as one from whom they could expect both admiration and sympathy.

Goethe had struggled to free himself from this 'evil' depression and sought – as was his native cast of mind – to guide others in the same task. He believed that the real solution lay in 'assistance from the external world, whether in the form of knowledge, instruction, an absorbing occupation or the favour of others'. Goethe realized, however, that this advice could not be followed by the disturbed individuals who wrote to him, since such things would be seen through the lens of subjectivity and transformed into irritants. One young man who wrote at great length was a certain Plessing. Goethe did not reply – feeling there was nothing he could usefully say. Then he got a second letter in which Plessing pleaded for a response. Still Goethe did not write back – but the despairing and insistent writer stayed in his mind.

Some time later, when Goethe had moved to Weimar, Carl August decided to set off on a wild boar hunt in the vicinity of Eisenach. Goethe was naturally asked along and got leave to make a brief detour to go and see this Plessing and satisfy his curiosity.

Goethe made his way to the little town of Wernigerode where Plessing lived and stopped at the inn. He rather liked the waiter and started asking about the local intellectuals. The waiter told him that he should call on young Mr Plessing, the son of a church dignitary; he had the reputation of being very clever, although people complained of his gloomy temperament, his aloofness and unfriendly manners. So, Goethe paid a call.

He told Plessing he was an artist with some vague connections to Weimar. Plessing was curious to hear how things were going in that famous place. Teasingly, Goethe started talking about all the intellectual figures there – omitting only himself. Until Plessing insisted he describe the great writer.

Goethe describes the scene: 'He gripped my arm tightly and exclaimed: "You really must pardon my strange behaviour! But you have inspired so much confidence in me that I must tell you everything. This man, as you have described him to me, should have answered me; I wrote him a long and heartfelt letter, described my situation and my sufferings, begged him to take pity on me, to give me counsel, to aid me, and now months have gone by and I have heard nothing from him; I should have deserved at least a negative response to the boundless confidence I placed in him."'

Goethe had engineered a situation in which he, the beloved object, can see the unrequited lover. He had entered into the private space in which he can hear what the young man would never say directly; and in which his resentment and indignation can be given full rein – in which we get to see how the other person misunderstands us.

'I replied to this that I could neither explain nor condone such behaviour, but I did know for a fact that this young man, who was otherwise quite well-intentioned, benevolent and ready to lend assistance, suffered so much from the demands made on his emotional as well as on his physical constitution that there were times when he was totally unable to move, much less to have any effect on others.'

What was wrong with Plessing – why was his life so bad? 'It was simply that he had never taken note of the outside world, although educating himself widely in books: but he had turned all his energies and inclinations inwards and as good as destroyed himself in this way, since he found no productive talent in the depths of his life.'

Goethe then undertook a little bit of psychological research. He'd recently visited some caves in the vicinity which, though interesting, had struck him as a bit gloomy. Plessing said he had been there and found them disappointing – they had not matched his expectations. How had he imagined them? 'He gave me a description such as the most audacious scenery painter would not have dared to paint as the yard of Hell.'

In other words, Plessing's imagination is morbid; he projects his dismal, horrible fantasies on to the world – which is really not so grim as he imagines it. But then, when he actually goes to see it he's not relieved. He's actually annoyed that things aren't so ghastly as he had imagined them to be. And this is why he is unhappy. The point about the caves is crucial in understanding Goethe's perspective on this unhappy man. Goethe knows that the caves – like many bits of life – are far from agreeable. The fact that life is not a bed of roses does not prove that it is a cesspit.

Plessing is, for Goethe, the 'perfect' modern intellectual. He displays the spiritual sickness of modernity with special clarity: the perverse pride in misery, clinging to distress in the mistaken belief that tormenting oneself is somehow a fine and intelligent thing to do; regarding unhappiness as the perverse proof of excellence. This is clearly a selective caricature but Goethe does have a point: surely the value of intelligence lies in its contribution to life? Yet people like Plessing seem determined to employ their considerable mental ability in finding new ways of being distressed.

Goethe's recollections of the social life he led after the campaign in France (Jacobi, Plessing, Princess Gallitzin) reveal something of his sense of isolation. And this is more poignant because of his evident regard for these people. They are not fools or mean – but they do not have anything to offer him; and they are not particularly interested in what he can offer them. Like Plessing, they all want him to conform to some image of their own that they have created of him, a partial truth, but a distortion. Jacobi wanted Goethe to be a classic poet, Princess Gallitzin wanted him to be on the verge of conversion to Catholicism; Plessing wanted him to be a saviour.

Eventually Goethe made it back to Weimar; the small satisfactions of domestic life – with Christine and August – meant a great deal to him. Work progressed on the Frauenplan house, which gradually developed into a highly distinctive setting for Goethe's life.

10

The Siege of Mainz

The recoil of the allied troops from Valmy had been accompanied by the advance of French forces into German territory. Frankfurt had been taken, as had the city of Mainz – seat of one of the richest and most powerful clerical rulers. But early in the following spring (of 1793) the allies recovered, retook Frankfurt and encircled Mainz in a blockading manoeuvre. Towards the end of May Goethe rejoined the duke and the army.

The French occupation of Mainz – and the project for its recapture – was of considerable symbolic significance. A major concern of the French Assembly was to give its military activities a moral or ideological character – quite different from the dynastic-territorial concerns which had motivated so many of the European conflicts of the previous hundred years. In fact Mainz was home to a number of people who deeply sympathized with the aims of the Revolution – at the level of ideas. They had formed a Jacobin Club and were known as the 'Clubbists' (in reference to this society rather than to any preferred weaponry). When the French forces, under General Custine, took the city, they were in a position to think of themselves as liberators – as coming on the invitation of the people, or at least of a few self-selected 'representatives' of the popular will, rather than as traditional invaders.

At the same time, on the last day of May and into early June 1793, the French Revolution entered a new phase. There was a violent shift in power away from the relatively moderate Girondins, who held the majority in the National Assembly and believed the Revolution was over and had achieved all that could realistically be achieved (and perhaps had even gone further than really desirable), to the Jacobins – under the leadership of Robespierre – who held that the real Revolution had hardly begun. The Jacobins aimed not merely to transform such things as the constitution or introducing a limited form of democracy; they hoped to institute a reign of reason and virtue – to reform human nature as well as the fabric of the state.

The Jacobins were associated with the sans-culottes – on whom they relied for brawny support in the streets but whose interests they only partly reflected. Robespierre shared some of the sans-culottes' conceptions of a 'good society' – and curiously so did Goethe, although he had completely different ideas about how to go about getting it and a much more sophisticated sense of who the enemies were. The sans-culottes really wanted to see the world remade in their own image – everyone an artisan – rather than thinking through a more complex image of what a state might look like in which they could live well.

Goethe joined the besieging army around Mainz in July 1793. Conditions were infinitely superior to those of the campaign in France the year before. The duke was now in a fine house – although it was rather messy, and Goethe made it his first duty to have this put right. 'In accordance with my usual concern for order and cleanliness I had the nice plaza in front of the house swept and washed. It was littered with straw and shavings and all kinds of refuse.'

The bombardment continued; on 22 July a truce was finally declared – a sign that the French were about to surrender. The French forces agreed to depart without the city actually being stormed, and safe passage was accorded to the leading French figures who were – as it happened – keen to return to Paris, in order to secure their places there.

As the French troops and their politically oriented leaders departed, the local populace, who had not supported the French and whose lives had been severely disrupted and property damaged, gathered to watch them go. They were immensely angry about what had happened – and also about what was happening now. Some of the retreating French were taking the opportunity of their safe passage to carry off whatever they could from the city.

Watching this closely from the upper balcony of the duke's quarters, together with an Englishman by the name of Gore, who was a good friend of Carl August, Goethe noticed a very beautiful woman dressed as a man leaving the city together with her handsome male partner: they had no military escort and were followed by several large wagons packed with crates. 'The quiet was ominous. Suddenly there was a murmur in the crowd: "Stop him! Kill him! That's the scoundrel who plundered the cathedral chapter and then set fire to it!"'

Fearing that the crowd would rush forward and murder the couple, and smash up whatever treasures the man was taking from the cathedral, Goethe rushed out – not quite knowing what he was doing – and shouted 'Halt!' as loudly and authoritatively as he could. The enraged crowd was blocking the path of the carriages and Goethe started haranguing them – hoping somehow to distract them or, if only for a moment, to break their mood of vengeance. He told them they were not allowed to make a disturbance in front of the head-quarters of the Duke of Weimar, that the King of Prussia had guaran-teed the safety of those leaving the city – that it was a military decision which should be left to those in charge.

'The crowd was astounded and fell silent for a moment, then there was another surge of grumbling and curses; a few individuals became furious, some men pushed forward to grab the reins of the horses . . . I said whatever I could think of that was brief and to the point, loudly and with conviction.' Finally the mob drew back just enough to let the procession through. 'The man rode up and said he would never forget the service I had done him; the woman expressed her deep gratitude. I told them I had only done my duty and maintained the security and sanctity of the place. The crowd was still eager for ven-geance but the moment of crisis was passed.' Goethe knew perfectly well that they would face many other dangers. 'But that is the way of the world: whoever has managed to get past one obstacle can get past a thousand. Chi scampa d'un punto, scampa di mille.'

Goethe then went back upstairs to rejoin Gore, who clearly thought Goethe had been extremely foolish to confront the crowd in that way.

' "I wasn't afraid of that," I answered, "and don't you find it nicer that I kept the plaza clean in front of the house? What would it look

like if it were all full of little bits and pieces of smashed-up things?"
But my good Gore could not get over his unhappiness at having seen
me, at some danger to myself, venture so much for the sake of a
stranger who was quite possibly a criminal. I kept pointing out to him
in jest the clean plaza in front of the house and finally I said impatiently,
"It is simply in my nature, I prefer to commit an injustice rather than
endure disorder." '

How much better for Goethe's reputation if his persistent friend
had not provoked him to such a remark – and even more so if Goethe
hadn't bothered to record it in this section of his autobiography. It
seems to give encouragement and solace to extremely unattractive
attitudes. But the real meaning of Goethe's remark is more sophisticated – and doesn't lie too deep under the surface. All it means here
is: I don't want to see a man lynched by a mob for a crime against
public property when this violence will – in addition – destroy the
very things he is said to have stolen.

PART SIX

Friendship

Life lies before us, like a huge quarry lies before the architect; he doesn't deserve the name of architect except when, out of this fortuitous mass, he can combine with the greatest economy and fitness and durability some form – the pattern of which originated in his spirit.
Goethe, *Wilhelm Meister's Apprenticeship* (1796), Book 8

I

Schiller

The most fruitful – and the most intense – relationship Goethe ever had with a male friend was with the poet and dramatist Friedrich Schiller. The friendship had a slow start. Schiller first came to live in Weimar for two years in 1787; he was just past his mid-twenties – ten years younger than Goethe. Goethe was still in Italy but his intimate connection to Weimar – together with the presence of Wieland and Herder – was certainly relevant to Schiller's decision to move there. Yet Schiller's admiration for Goethe the writer was complicated by considerable hostility to Goethe the man.

It was partly a problem of envy: Goethe appeared to have things easy and hence to be a living summary of what Schiller himself lacked. Goethe had financial security, social prestige, freedom to travel; his literary achievements seemed to be effortless – in any case he had combined writing celebrated works with ministerial duties. He was also physically robust, whereas Schiller was frequently ill and in order to make himself write he performed all kinds of strange rituals: he generally worked in the middle of the night; to stimulate his brain he sniffed rotten apples which he kept in a drawer of his desk, drank too much wine, smoked a great deal and took a lot of snuff. In other words he had to force himself; while Goethe's life appeared regular, elegant, natural. As Schiller wrote to a close friend: 'This man, this Goethe, is completely in my way; he constantly reminds me of my hard lot. How easy it's been for his genius to flower – while I've had to struggle right up to this moment.'

In order to support himself, Schiller had resorted to writing popular histories. His series on violent rebellions was successful but, as so often in the period, the income from writing never matched public popularity; any popular work was simply reprinted by other publishers with no fee going to the author.

When Goethe returned from Italy the following year, 1788, he could hardly help bumping into Schiller in the small arena of Weimar. They had several mutual friends who occasionally tried to bring the two great men together. Schiller's aristocratic wife, Caroline – endearingly known as 'Lollo' – suggested many little schemes, but these gambits led to nothing. To Schiller, Goethe seemed aloof and preoccupied with thoughts of Italy. In fact the situation was embarrassing and awkward; eventually arrangements were made with Carl August to have Schiller appointed to the chair of history at Jena – on a very low salary – basically to get him out of Goethe's sight. It was a compromised, pragmatic appointment; Schiller was not a serious historian but he was a 'name'.

Jena – the capital of a tiny neighbouring dukedom – was home to a long-standing, but small, university. The town lay only twenty kilometres to the east of Weimar and Carl August was the feudal protector and patron of the university. After his return from Italy, Goethe was appointed 'overseer' – akin to a modern-day chancellor – of the university. This was part of his wider role as a kind of arts-culture-education minister: a more congenial governmental position that Carl August had created for him, replacing his earlier portfolios – roads, armed forces and finance. Jena was on the cusp of a renaissance, at least with respect to its leading academic appointments. Immanuel Fichte, Friedrich Schelling and Georg Wilhelm Hegel were to hold appointments; the Schlegel brothers were to live in the town. Although there were multiple tensions among these figures, they are the great names of German intellectual culture of the generation following that of Goethe.

In fantasy, Schiller likened Goethe to Julius Caesar – the undoubted leader, but a tyrant – while he himself was Brutus, who might have to kill such a man in the name of freedom. Or, again, Goethe was imagined as an older brother – an intimate relation but potentially humiliating for the younger sibling.

*

Schiller was known to the public – and to Goethe – primarily as the author of an intense and wild drama called *The Robbers*, written while he was still at school (published in 1781). *The Robbers* presents the story of a good young man, Carl von Moor, who is disinherited from his rich family estate by the machinations of his evil older brother, Franz. Franz is motivated partly by financial greed, partly by resentment at his father's preference for Carl, and partly by envy: he covets Carl's beautiful fiancée. But there is also some elemental malice, some radical evil, at work – the desire to see all good and beautiful things destroyed.

The unjust disinheritance leads Carl to turn outlaw. At first his band of followers behave in a vaguely Robin Hood fashion; they are not within the letter of the law, but their actions are not contrary to natural justice. Nevertheless the impetus of their actions drives them to more extreme measures and the play ends in carnage for which Carl is, ultimately, responsible. The play has a manic, rebellious and rather irrational feel to it. Carl's behaviour could seem heroic only to people who feel trapped in overwhelming frustration – whose every attempt at a decent life is mocked by an infernal contrary force. Similar themes were pursued, in more perceptive and more moderate – and more realistic – scenarios in the next couple of plays Schiller wrote.

Even in the virulence of *The Robbers* there are passages of great beauty. The third act opens with Amalie, Carl's beloved, thinking of him. The poem in which she expresses her longing, in very physical terms, was beautifully set by Schubert – and the resulting composite work of art is a magical praise of the power of kissing: a musical and literary equivalent of Rodin's famous statue; one which has a timeless validity.

Such a poem reveals that there was always more to Schiller than bombast and hysteria. The more contemplative and philosophical aspect of his mind gradually became dominant; it found memorable expression in *The Gods of Greece* – a poem again wonderfully set by Schubert, who brings out the yearning and loss concentrated in the iconic opening line of nostalgia and longing: 'Schöne Welt, wo bist du?' ('Where are you, beautiful world?')

Goethe very much liked this poem, which perhaps captured something of his own painful separation from Italy: the Italy he had loved and left. Yet Schiller had not only moved to a more serious conception of art than anything that might have been suspected from *The Robbers*. He had at the same time developed a highly theoretic and intellectual interest in the fundamental questions of the nature and value of art. He was excited by the logical, rigorous – and intensely abstract – system of thought being developed by Kant. As far as Goethe was concerned this was a case of jumping from the frying pan into the fire. If Schiller had been manic and wild in the past, this over-intellectual discipline would ruin whatever talent he might still have.

Physically, Schiller was tall and lean; his long red hair flowed freely; his nose was finely shaped, but very prominent; his eyes noble and distant. Although not rich he was famous – as well known to the educated German public as Goethe; when in 1789 the National Assembly in Paris sought to demonstrate the cosmopolitan character of the Rights of Man by declaring suitable foreigners French citizens, Schiller was included in the list – a kind of contemporary who's who of celebrity progressives. By then it brought Schiller no satisfaction.

Schiller's sympathy for those who felt frustrated by the existing order had not disappeared, but he no longer thought that a violent sweeping away of that order would make things better; he had become much more pessimistic about the relationship between political action and social improvement. He now held that the good society depended upon the maturity of its citizens, and that political revolution could do nothing to make people less greedy or corrupt.

Contrary to expectations, Schiller had become the darling of courtly society – an aristocrat of beauty and truth. He was more at ease in polished society than Goethe. Much later – long after Schiller's death – Goethe's memory latched on to an episode involving a golden tea-spoon. Schiller and Goethe were having tea in some very grand place, and – to Goethe's quiet dismay – the teaspoons were made of gold rather than of the customary silver. Such an ostentatious sign of wealth and status (and all that would go along with it: etiquette, court gossip) made Goethe clam up. But Schiller, he recalled, was unaffected by such things. At the plutocratic tea table Schiller remained himself – completely in possession of his great ideas, unafraid to assert them, to

expand upon them – he was free, unintimidated. And it worked; rather than being thought a bore or a pedant, Schiller managed to impart such grace and charm along with the dignity of his ideas that he was very popular in Weimar and Jena.

It might seem trivial – but anyone who has felt paralysed by the fear that high-flown ideas and noble ambitions will meet with incredulity, or with embarrassed silence, at the tables of the well-to-do will understand just how impressive Schiller must have been, how securely he must have felt the worth and dignity of his own ideas.

But this was far in the future. The stand-off continued for an amazingly long time: Goethe in Weimar, and then off on campaign to Valmy and Mainz; Schiller in Jena doing his best to lecture on history and poring over the intricate rigours of Kant's philosophy. For six years, they lived in the same milieu, with many friends and acquaintances in common; and during those six years they had almost nothing to do with each other.

In 1793, after the relief of Mainz, Goethe had some time, at last, to devote himself to his Frauenplan house. The large garden at the back of the house was particularly important to Goethe and he gave much time and energy to cultivating it. It was laid out along the lines of an English cottage garden – deriving its basic character from the charming but utilitarian model of a kitchen garden – with plants selected for use and arranged according to type. Working in the garden stimulated Goethe's enthusiasm for the more scientific aspects of botany and he quickly decided that what the state needed was a proper botanical garden.

Jena was the ideal place: since the study of plants was to be undertaken on a scientific basis, the botanical garden should be attached to the university. A modest donation was extracted from Carl August and a garden in Jena belonging to the duke was handed over to the fledgling institute. To oversee matters Goethe had to spend some time there and entered into renewed, more frequent, contact with the leading figures of the university town. And it was this greater exposure to Jena – and closer involvement with plants – that was finally to bring him close to Schiller and to open the way to the deepest relationship of his life.

*

It was, in fact, a conversation about plants that broke the ice between the two men. Years before, in Sicily, Goethe had had a kind of epiphany – he had seen (or thought he could envisage) what he called 'the primal plant'. After a public lecture about botany in Jena, Goethe was making for the door when he almost literally ran into Schiller – a gaucherie orchestrated by friends making one more attempt to bring the two together. Forced to say something, Goethe tried to tell Schiller about the primal plant.

As they left the room, Schiller very naturally suggested that what Goethe surely meant was that he had an idea of the 'essence' of plants. That is, from his observation of actual plants Goethe had constructed a concept or idea of what a plant fundamentally is. A very interesting project – indeed a central scientific task – but this is an idea of what a plant is, not a physical object.

Goethe was immensely irritated – this was just what he expected of Schiller: impertinence in philosophical fancy dress. Somehow Goethe mastered his annoyance and told Schiller that he wasn't talking about an idea but about a visual experience: he had seen the primal plant. As they walked towards Schiller's house, the younger man made a determined effort to get the dispute on to more fruitful territory – to make it a real conversation. Schiller tactfully proposed that Goethe wanted to start with visual experience and find in it richer and more general significance. Certainly he was looking at an actual plant, but he saw in it the essence of plants. To make sense of this, forget about plants and think about art. A Greek statue is a single piece of shaped stone; yet in it we see an ideal of humanity. The ideal isn't merely added in thought; it's as if we actually perceive it with our eyes. The idea is embodied. This was something Schiller could get excited by.

Indeed he could hear in Goethe's irate words his own longings presented in reverse. Schiller's ambition as a poet and dramatist was to clothe his ideas in convincing individual characters: he started with ideas and wanted to create objects that would embody them. Goethe seemed to start with individual objects and find ideas in them.

Thus it seemed to Schiller that they were both engaged – from opposing directions – in the same basic task: the marriage of the general and the individual. And thus, through an awkward but intense conversation, Schiller found a point of common interest – one that allowed them to be interested in the same thing but in different, and perhaps complementary, ways. It transformed rivalry into collaboration and envy into mutual regard.

Behind the intellectual discussion, there is something unusual – the romance of male friendship; after years of distrust and anxiety, there is movement towards one another; they were on the brink, just about to fall into each other's life. It is a universal story of the transformation of envy and fear into mutual love.

Schiller's situation might have some similarity to our own: we, like him, might initially feel threatened by Goethe's achievements and character. In comparison with him we feel uncomfortably small. This is a kind of suffering to which good people are necessarily exposed. It is good to be able to admire people for being better than oneself – but it is also painful. Schiller's advice to us is, firstly: try to discover common ground. Instead of asking: how am I different from Goethe? one might inquire: in what way am I involved in broadly the same project? Schiller found a way of making the project broad enough that both he and Goethe could have a share in it. In other words, he was able to see that if Goethe was concerned about important things, those things could not belong just to him. The issue must be bigger than the man, and therefore there must be room for other people.

Secondly, although Schiller saw Goethe as a hero, he came to see that Goethe was also a human being: he at last grasped that Goethe might have needs and anxieties of his own – despite his success and public status. Because Goethe protected his time and emotional energy, he did not quickly launch himself into new friendships; and this invited the mistaken view that he didn't need other people. Once he had matured enough to have something valuable to offer, Schiller could become Goethe's friend. Goethe did not need Schiller's adulation; but when a meeting of true minds was possible Goethe was quickly responsive. This is painful, for we often want friendship beyond our current means: the hard lesson is that we may have to wait, may have to develop and refine our own capacities before we are genuinely capable of intimacy with people we admire.

2

The Birthday Letter

There was a practical side to Schiller's determination to get on with Goethe and to cultivate the possibility of friendship. At the time when he was talking to Goethe about plants he was also engaged in negotiations with the enterprising publisher Cotta for a new periodical to be called *Die Horen*. The name derives from the classical 'horae', 'the hours'. They were the goddesses of the order of nature and of the seasons and were stationed at the doors of Olympus. Like the goddesses, the new magazine would protect the realm of high culture from desecration while greeting and helping those who sincerely wished to ascend the holy mountain. Schiller's aims for this journal were not exclusively on such a lofty plane. At the crudest – but for him highly relevant – level of discussion, he wanted to make money.

There were many small and financially precarious journals scattered across Germany. Schiller's hope was that rather than merely add to their number he would take over their readership. His economic concern dovetailed with his cultural ambition – for he was precisely aiming at an authoritative, national publication; one that would raise the tone and guide the ambitions of educated people across the German states. And a journal attaining such a position would also be extremely profitable. At this stage in his life, at least, Schiller was in the grip of one of the most fundamental hopes of culture – that quality can be made authoritative, that authority can be loveable, that excellence shall be profitable, that those who devote their lives to noble tasks should be able to make a comfortable living from doing so. The way to achieve all this, he thought, would be to get all the best writers of the nation – and only the best writers – to contribute to the magazine.

He already had offers of support from the leading lights in Jena – including Wilhelm von Humboldt and Fichte. But Schiller – and Cotta – knew that Goethe's support was an essential requirement. Following up the primal-plant discussion, Schiller wrote to Goethe soliciting his involvement. When Goethe replied that he was interested in the venture, Schiller took a daring step. He didn't just want Goethe's good will – although that was something. He was aiming much higher – at bringing Goethe's whole mind and energy into the project. In a sense, this was only logical. The journal and its aims were Goethean in character. And Schiller was determined to make Goethe see this.

It was Goethean in the sense that it hoped to bring together impressive work in a range of different disciplines, and yet present such work in a way that could be assimilated by a non-specialist. The imagined reader was assumed to be interested in philosophy and history, science and the classics – but these were all interests for the sake of personal culture and development; thus they had to be communicated in an elegant and lucid manner.

Schiller timed his follow-up beautifully: he wrote a long, deeply meditated letter to Goethe from Jena at the end of August 1794, so that it became a kind of massively superior greetings card for Goethe's forty-fifth birthday, which fell on the 28th.

The birthday letter builds upon the foundation laid down in the discussion. His key point was to stress their need for one another – each one supports, balances and corrects the other. For all its philosophical clothing this is one of the world's greatest love letters. Not in the sense of it being an outpouring of passion, but as an attempt to understand why two people need each other – why they will each be better together than either of them would be on their own. 'Your observant gaze, which rests so still and pure on things, never leads you to the errors to which speculation – guided by capricious imagination, and merely obeying its own rules – so easily falls prey.' In effect Schiller is saying: my mind has a tendency to run away with itself, to fancy all kinds of possible arrangements of things – but these are unhelpful and untrue. I need to be restrained and guided by a careful observation of life. Your 'still and pure' gaze is the thing I need.

Goethe unites, Schiller analyses. Schiller later expanded upon this point: 'The philosopher can only discover how things are combined by analysing them, only lay bare the workings of spontaneous nature by subjecting them to the torment of his own techniques. In order to lay hold of the fleeting phenomenon, he must first bind it in fetters of rule, tear its fair body to pieces, and preserve its living spirit in a sorry skeleton of words. Is it any wonder that natural feeling cannot find itself again in such an image . . . ?'

Again and again 'the philosopher' is the name Schiller calls himself – he needs Goethe to save him from himself. But Schiller was too mature to think that Goethe could be won over simply because Schiller needed him. The whole point was mutuality.

Having depicted his own needs, Schiller goes on, in that wonderful birthday letter, to evoke in the most delicate terms something of Goethe's loneliness. You are a Greek soul, living in Germany. That is, your compatriots do not really understand you – and to say this, of course, is also to whisper: but I do.

He accords Goethe the highest term of contemporary praise – Goethe is a 'Genius'. In the hands of Schiller this is much more than a routine compliment; he intends by it that Goethe has a deep natural instinct, that his creative capacity is spontaneous and an expression of himself, rather than something learned or acquired. And although it is clear that Goethe was deeply devoted to self-cultivation and self-improvement, that he learned a lot from others and was an intellectually studious man – still, Schiller has a point.

The point he wishes to draw out is that genius is by its nature not self-knowing. 'Genius is a secret to itself' and in this Schiller is holding out the promise that he will be the mirror in which Goethe can – for the first time – see his own reflection. But Schiller doesn't raise this allusion until he's made it clear just how appealing the image will be. While of course there is a touch of flattery here, it would be uncharitable to Schiller to see the letter only in those terms. The undertow here is that Goethe's isolation is somehow connected to his not having a full picture of himself.

Perhaps the real recipient of this letter is Schiller himself – he needs to show himself that the relationship he is trying to forge with Goethe is not just opportunistic; and that his earlier antagonism to Goethe – his deep ambivalence – wasn't stupid, but could be redeemed as an attitude which picked up (though too simply) on the real differences between them; there was an opposition, but now he was coming to understand it properly and could see that it wasn't strictly competitive. Perhaps his need to have Goethe as a friend was of deep psychological urgency for a man of such ambition as Schiller. The ambition of *Die Horen* was, after all, to dominate the intellectual life of a whole nation. Schiller was setting himself up as the leading spirit of the time, and Goethe was his main rival. But if he could be an ally instead, the historical place Goethe occupied would no longer strike Schiller as a reproach to himself – as something to be envied and despaired of – but as part of Schiller's own success.

Goethe was deeply moved by this letter and not surprisingly. After this, he and Schiller were bound together. Goethe spoke of their attachment as permanent: they must go through life together. And, in fact, they did, for ten years until Schiller died and Goethe lost, as he put it, half of his life.

3

The Ideal Person

Schiller's love – like all genuine loves – revealed something wonderful about his friend. In an incredibly bold move, Schiller took his profound encounter with Goethe as the basis of a view of life – he built an account of human culture and history around the most important experience of his life. Schiller projected Goethe's personality into two books that have shaped the Western educated vision of what it means to be a human being. His *Letters on the Aesthetic Education of Humanity* (first published serially in *Die Horen* in 1795) and his long essay *On Naive and Sentimental Poetry* (also 1795) are meditations on the meaning of Goethe. And though they may not now be particularly celebrated, their influence has been much greater than their current relative obscurity suggests.

Everyone knew, of course, that Goethe did a lot of things, that he was busy and productive across a large range of fields. In a sense he was a 'Renaissance man' – able to shift from government business to art criticism, to writing poetry, to science, to flirtation, to healthy exercise. It is no doubt impressive to have varied skills; but is there more to Goethe than that? Is this merely unusual, or is there something more fundamental we are witnessing here?

Schiller thought there was. He brilliantly shifted attention from Goethe's 'many-sided' personality to its seeming opposite: wholeness. It wasn't so much that Goethe could do a lot of different things, but that all of these things were natural to him – he was merely expressing the same personality, just being himself. Schiller's thought is that the multiplicity we see in Goethe strikes us as unusual – as special – only because we have given up on the original wholeness of our own personalities. It's not that by nature we are specialists – that by nature we are good only at accounting but mediocre when it comes to love affairs or art, or good only at athletics but useless off the track. Far from this being natural, it is in fact profoundly unnatural: we know only too well the pressures that lead people to live as 'fragments' – to develop only a tiny portion of their potential. It is, however, a situation that we have come to accept. We define ourselves by those things we are best at, and neglect other parts of ourselves.

The centrality of Goethe – Schiller is saying – arises because he reminds us, shows us, what we ought to be like. We ought not to be specialized fragments of competence – we ought to be whole, rounded people. Thus Goethe lives out – constitutes in himself – the goal of proper development. Not, of course, that other people should replicate his life (live in Weimar, dash off to Italy, fall in love with someone called Charlotte Buff and write a novel about it, wear a yellow waistcoat). Rather the ideal is that we should live our own lives and become whole and balanced versions of ourselves.

Just one instance of the unacknowledged influence of these thoughts: in *Brideshead Revisited*, when Evelyn Waugh's heroine Julia is trying to pin down what it is she hates so much about her husband, she frames her disgust – without knowing it – in Schiller's terms: 'He was a fragment, a tiny little bit of man pretending he was whole'. When we talk nowadays of needing a balanced life, or of wanting our children to develop as rounded individuals, we are, unconsciously, following in the footsteps of Schiller and shaping our hopes and aspirations in the light of what he loved in Goethe.

To draw attention to another aspect of Goethe that he deeply admired, Schiller coined a rather unfortunate term: 'naive'. The misfortune came with the subsequent colouring of the word in German as well as English; 'naive' now implies inadequacy: one is too simple, too trusting, too open for the usages of this world. Hence it names a failing. Schiller's use doesn't carry this implication of excessive artlessness or failure. Goethe's naivety consists in his simplicity, his trust, his naturalness – which, far from making him unable to function in the adult world, are sources of great strength and productivity. It's not that Goethe doesn't know how to look after himself or will fall into the hands of swindlers and rogues: he has his wits about him.

A more modern way of rendering 'naive' might be to say that – in Schiller's eyes – Goethe has nothing to prove. He's not trying to justify or excuse himself before an imagined hostile audience – he's not preparing the case for his own defence. Goethe is not made awkward by the obvious or the simple – he is the antitype of modern intellectual celebrity. What Schiller is picking up on is, in part, the combined result of Goethe's fortunate experience with his parents and his own robust personality. Goethe's entire oeuvre – his works, his conversation, his letters – is remarkably free from any attempt to blame other people for his own problems (except as we shall see in the strange case of Goethe contra Newton).

But Goethe's naive character would be closed to us if it were nothing but the consequence of early good fortune. For it would be a character we could not come to share if we did not also happen to start with his advantages. The centre of naivety – in this special sense – is devotion to what we love, as opposed to preoccupation with what we hate. And that is an attitude we can cultivate in ourselves: it is not merely a gift of nature.

Schiller was also responsible for one of the most controversial – and most easily misunderstood – perspectives upon his friend. As an artist, Schiller saw Goethe as essentially apolitical: as above politics, rather than as indifferent to the current state of society. The apparent paradox goes like this: since politics is the arena in which the biggest social issues get played out, how can art be important if it isn't political? Together Goethe and Schiller advanced a view of things that came to be called 'Weimar Classicism'; a conception of art, of the role of artists, which – if we take it seriously – dissolves the paradox. Political progress can occur only if there is a transformation of people's inner lives. Otherwise, factions are merely the voices of human fragments, seeking dominance over society. The aim of art is to ennoble us, to make us whole and balanced; then we can engage maturely and sensibly in political processes. The aim of their 'classical art' is to promote a kind of lucid inner stillness and equilibrium: it aims to heal us, to soothe our agitation and focus our strength. Their approach was 'classical' not so much because it sometimes drew upon Greek or Roman prototypes – as does Goethe's *Iphigenia in Tauris* – but rather in the sense of 'classical' meaning centred and calm, vital but poised: like an ideal Greek athlete. The ambition of art should be directed to spreading energetic sanity – and the more of that there is around the better the body politic is likely to perform. What is crass and destructive is agitating people and spurring immature zeal. Politics, however important, is a secondary activity – the mark of the good state is that it nurtures and multiplies the virtues of its citizens; but it is classic art which is the true home of those qualities.

4

Together against the World

Schiller, however, wasn't merely a fine reflecting surface, he was a genuine and warm friend to Goethe. Their closeness can be seen in their joint need to distance themselves – as a couple – from the rest of the world. There are many touching hints of the more intimate aspects of their relationship. When Schiller got into a bit of difficulty with Fichte, having been critical of an essay by this brilliant but awkward Jena professor, he wrote to Goethe about it with the sure sense that Goethe was on his side. They call Fichte – whom they both otherwise rather liked and certainly took seriously – 'the Big I': a joke version of Fichte's theory of subjectivity, which made the ego the focus of the world. They are doing one of the core things that friends do – which is create little emotional gaps between themselves, as a pair, and all possible rivals.

This theme of their relationship – the need to join themselves together by jointly attacking others – developed into a private ritual. Their ire was stimulated by the less than enthusiastic reception of *Die Horen* and some philistine criticisms. Because Goethe's *Roman Elegies*, which appeared in the opening numbers, were occasionally of a mildly erotic nature it became customary to call the journal *Die Hören* – 'The Whores'. And naturally they were enraged by this wilful distortion of the poems.

Goethe and Schiller amused each other by inventing damning little poems about other writers, many of whom they knew personally, some with whom one or other had been friends. This after-dinner game got out of hand when they decided to make these squibs public under the title of 'Xenien' – 'Gifts', although mostly of a poisonous kind. Appearing as a joint production, they amounted to – Goethe cheerfully admitted – 'a declaration of war against shallowness of all kinds'.

The Xenien are by their nature ephemeral – they were attacks on particular individuals who played a part in the literary world of the day but who are not now much remembered. The fact that the targets were not named – together with some really vicious thrusts – ensured considerable success, from a commercial point of view at least.

By castigating so many, Goethe and Schiller were united in the public imagination – they were not only declaring war, but also declaring their unity. Eventually – having alienated practically every living writer in Germany – Goethe decided he had had enough and that such street fighting should never be their real business. At the end of 1796 he called a halt in a letter to Schiller: 'After the mad risk of the Xenien, we must work only on great and worthy works of art and transform our protean nature – to the confusion of our enemies – into noble and good characters.'

One can easily form the impression that their friendship was purely intellectual – and of course it was deeply intellectual. But there was more to it than that. The primary record of their relationship is the thousand letters they exchanged, but they did in fact quite often stay with each other – and later, at the end of 1799, Schiller moved to Weimar permanently, at which point their correspondence becomes, unsurprisingly, thinner. There's a terribly poignant moment in this record when the deeper terms of their relationship become apparent.

In October of 1794, when Schiller and Goethe had been close friends for rather more than a year, Christiane was in the last stages of pregnancy. Schiller writes hoping that Goethe and Christiane will have a daughter, in the wild but lovely hope that maybe one day his own son, Carl, could marry her. When in fact a son was born, Goethe joins in the tender joke and writes that now it's up to Schiller to have a daughter. There is something infinitely simple and sweet about these wishes – irrespective of their plausibility; they are not plans for the future, they are expressions of yearning – for a closeness that cannot be made real in wise letters or intelligent conversation alone, but seeks a living, permanent object – a joint family: their grandchildren. This touching idea was short-lived: Goethe's second son died after only a few days.

There is a reverberation of these sorrows – and these needs – in a comment Goethe makes when someone mixes up their works: 'I like the fact that people confuse the two of us in our work. It shows that, more and more, we are leaving our mannerisms behind and proceeding rather towards the general good. We must also consider the fact that we can cover a good deal more ground if we grasp each other with one hand and stretch out the other as far as nature will allow.'

It is their need to grasp one another – the support, the physical reassurance – that is also exhibited in a famous posthumous statue of Goethe and Schiller, outside the present-day German National Theatre in Weimar – and the pose is developed from an earlier prototype.

The visual core of the composition is Goethe's hand on Schiller's arm – it is their closeness, their need of one another, which is embodied. And this intimacy is all the more striking because the images are so easily misread, so easily seen as cold and distant or aloof – just because they are statues of a traditional type.

Even while Goethe and Schiller were separating themselves off from others, they wanted to share what they had found. As writers and thinkers they could genuinely learn from each other – they could trust each other's judgements, and take seriously the criticisms they occasionally made of each other's work. For writers there is a horribly fine line between learning from criticism and being crushed by it; or, on the other hand, being made stronger by admiration, rather than corrupted by it. In finding one another, Goethe and Schiller contributed to each other's work. They were conscious of how rare this is.

By contrast, Goethe saw the lesser figures of the German literary scene as struggling artisans – the cultural equivalent of the sans-culottes of revolutionary Paris. These writers have to learn everything by themselves; when they do get reviewed they are not assessed by highly competent and constructive critics – instead they are pointlessly trashed or stupidly celebrated. Facing an unsophisticated readership and subject to petty infighting in their peer group it is exceptionally hard for an individual writer to attain artistic maturity and stature. Weimar, Goethe hoped, could be the spiritual capital of the West – a cultural Bethlehem – that would overcome this universal provincialism. If readers were more discerning, fine writers would have an easier time of it and would write better books, thus raising the level of society a notch higher.

In an almost fantastical – and deeply moving – ambition, Goethe and Schiller hoped, in effect, to spread their love across the world; their joint authority and glamour would be the focus for cultural leadership – people would take their cue from them; their serious nobility of mind would be the yardstick of acclaim.

Goethe to Schiller from Carlsbad (8 July 1795): 'Being a famous author I'm well received – although not without the occasional humiliation. For example, a certain woman says she's been reading my recent work with the greatest of pleasure, especially the *Gifar der Barmecide* – "indescribably interesting". You can imagine that I very eagerly put on the Arabian disguise of old Klinger – so as to appear to this goddess of a girl in the most appealing light.' Anton Klinger, whom they both knew well and rather looked down on, was the author of this piece – although it had appeared anonymously. Schiller wrote back quickly, advising Goethe to take advantage of the confusion and pursue the adventure.

5

Wilhelm Meister

Schiller had hoped that Goethe might wish to complete and publish some of his long-standing projects in *Die Horen*. Unfortunately Goethe had only recently agreed to a very generous contract with the Berlin publisher Unger for a four-volume novel to be entitled *Wilhelm Meister's Apprenticeship*, which Goethe was developing from a highly elaborate, but unfinished, earlier version, now accorded autonomous standing as *Wilhelm Meister's Theatrical Mission*. When he agreed to the contract, the rewrite was far from finished; and Goethe created an obligation in order to force himself towards finality.

Goethe's most famous works are *Faust* and *Werther*; *Wilhelm Meister* is, however, his most characteristic and most revealing; it is the centre of his oeuvre. It is a great pity that Goethe's public persona – limited as that now is – has not been connected more powerfully with this novel, since it is much more accessible and entertaining than the story of Faust and much broader and richer than the story of Werther.

The novel opens with Mariane, an actress, returning home from the theatre still dressed in the hussar's uniform in which she has been performing. Her elderly maid, Barbara, shows off the expensive gifts that have just arrived from Mariane's protector, Norberg, a local businessman, currently away. But Mariane has no interest in them and announces that she has a new lover – Wilhelm. Since Wilhelm has no money, and since Mariane is dependent on the patronage of a man, she is not free to follow her love – and Barbara reminds her of this with a forceful combination of pragmatism and malice. Mariane bows to this logic, but clings to the brief opportunity that the presence of Wilhelm and the absence of Norberg affords: 'When Norberg returns, I'll be yours, I'll be his; do with me what you will. But till then I will be mine, and if you had a thousand tongues you wouldn't be able to talk me out of it. And I'll give this whole "me" to the one who loves me and whom I love.'

The striking expression 'Ich will mein sein' – 'I will be/want to be mine' – contains within it the project of a whole life. What is it to belong to oneself? It is, in fact, the question that Wilhelm faces throughout the novel. But already the question is framed within two complicating issues: that of material dependence – Mariane needs someone to pay the bills; and that of emotional dependence – love. Mariane states this problem as if it were merely a pragmatic, or external, difficulty.

What is the hope or ambition enshrined in the phrase: 'I will be mine'? It aims at integrity and independence. Mariane can give a part of herself to Norberg or Barbara; she longs for a relationship in which the whole of her nature will count and be appreciated. Because she needs money – which she gets from Norberg – Mariane cannot 'afford' integrity. But this is to identify only one difficulty. Material independence might facilitate integrity, but it does not guarantee it.

The central character, Wilhelm, picks up this great theme from Mariane. He wants to be his own person – and the question, then, is: who is he really? The novel traces the many phases of his self-imagining – the many provisional answers he gives to the question: 'Who am I?'

A couple of pages later, Wilhelm is having breakfast with his mother. She tells him that his father is cross with him; he is always asking: what's so good about the theatre? What good can possibly come of Wilhelm devoting all his time and energy to it? Wilhelm's father is a prosperous businessman; on the death of his own father (Wilhelm's grandfather) the capital available for the family business was significantly augmented by the sale of the works of art that the grandfather had collected – and of which Wilhelm retains a distant, enticing memory. The father's attitude – liquidating artistic assets to enhance business – is one of the opening shots in a battle that runs throughout the book: between the relative claims of commerce and art.

Even at this early stage, Wilhelm can recognize a problem in his father's outlook. 'Is everything useless, then, unless it puts gold straight into our pockets?' After all, the older man has spent a great deal of money buying fashionable new English furniture. And, of course, carpets and looking-glasses and side tables – however elegant – don't bring in any income. So there is an incoherence in the father's presentation of his own concerns.

Wilhelm's position – as he sees it – is radically different. He considers himself something of a poet; an early poem of which he is rather proud compares and contrasts 'the two goddesses', the guiding spirits of art and business. The goddess of poetry and art is youthful, charming and beautiful; the spirit of business is ugly, aged and dull. All that is good is on one side; all that is horrible is on the other. But Wilhelm, of course, is not really in a good position to make such a judgement – since he doesn't actually have much knowledge or experience of either of these undertakings.

His friend Werner, who soon marries Wilhelm's sister and is already involved in the joint business undertakings of the two families, tries to change Wilhelm's views. It is part of the fineness of Goethe's imagination that a minor – and otherwise rather unappealing figure – is both tactful and insightful. Werner seeks to convert Wilhelm not by disabusing him of his love of poetry, but by recruiting his love of poetry to an appreciation of business. Werner paints a prose portrait of a couple of great trading cities and their ports: 'the smallest, most inconspicuous, item is profoundly related to the whole trade; indeed because of that it isn't small or trivial; everything increases the intercourse and, hence, the life, of the cities'. Trade is connected to the satisfaction of human desire, to progress and to government. The care and attention that successful business enterprise requires is a good discipline for the soul; and the reward of such care and attention is security, respect and a sense of achievement. Business is a spiritual exercise and a path to spiritual growth.

And in an elegant aside, Goethe suggests that it is precisely through his friendship with Wilhelm that Werner has come to have such a 'poetic' and noble conception of his own work.

*

The novel is divided into eight books and towards the end of the first one another theme – which again runs right through the whole of the novel – is introduced. Whiling away a few hours before a rendezvous with Mariane, Wilhelm is accosted by a stranger who asks for directions. There's something uncannily familiar about this character and Wilhelm suggests they have a drink together. It turns out that, when Wilhelm was a child, it was this man who had organized the sale of the grandfather's art collection. He recalls Wilhelm as a bright little boy showing him round the house and commenting on the pictures – very much, in fact, the kind of child Goethe himself had been, although he never had to perform such a sad office. Their conversation ranges widely, and Wilhelm confides his view (stimulated by this chance encounter) that there is a fate which guides each life, leading us to what is good for us – even though at the time we cannot understand the significance of the very events which set us upon the right path. Wilhelm is thinking, here, of his early enthusiasm for the theatre, which has brought him to a happy loving relationship with an actress in whose arms he can now, as it were, finally possess that magical realm.

Fate is one of the ideas we might turn to when we try to make sense of life – is there a way my life is supposed to be: a life that fate has designated as mine? Is my path through life directed in some way?

The stranger is unimpressed, rather worried even, by this kind of talk. It's not so much – he says – that such a view of life is entirely wrong. It's just that it's so unhelpful. The trouble with terms such as 'fate' is that as events unfold there are no rules that allow us to be sure where the hand of fate is pointing. We can perfectly well understand what is meant by fate – it's a pattern we discern retrospectively – but we don't have any sure grounds for assigning this or that event in the present to the workings of fate. And it seems to be just this point that is bothering the stranger. What he objects to is that a young man should try to apply this term; it might have some use in old age – when we can look back over the connections and see (once we know how things actually did turn out) how this or that event provided the right stepping stone (unrecognized as such at the time) to a later destination. But to believe in fate before the outcome is known is dangerous. It undermines our sense of freedom and responsibility.

Goethe, we might readily guess, is priming Wilhelm for a harsh lesson.

6

Learning from Experience

Wilhelm plans to elope with Mariane – a scheme she encourages; they will run away and join an acting troupe. On the last evening before their planned escape, Wilhelm turns up early at Mariane's house; she puts him off for a few hours, pleading a headache; as she closes the door he grabs her scarf and keeps it. He waits near by in the gathering dusk, filled with happy presentiments about their future life. Then, finally, the door opens again – and a man slips out and disappears into the night. Desperately Wilhelm hugs the scarf, and a note falls to the ground: it is from Norberg, arranging to see Mariane; and it is Norberg he has just seen departing.

Wilhelm is completely crushed; and as his love for Mariane has been disenchanted, so all the dreams and longings that were linked in his mind to her lose their magic. This is the point at which Werther would have borrowed some pistols and blown out his brains. The rest of the story can be seen as the investigation of what to do if you don't die when your love is unrequited.

Slowly Wilhelm recovers, makes his peace with the practical, responsible world of business and devotes himself to the family firm. He burns his poetry – despite the protests of Werner. But Wilhelm has now reversed his earlier prejudice: poetry is dreamy nonsense, only business and hard work are real. And so a couple of years pass. Wilhelm is sent off on a business trip: to collect some debts; to scout for new trade. After a few conscientious days trailing from village to village in the mountains, he arrives in a pleasant town and decides to take a couple of days off. Wilhelm puts up at an inn on the market square.

The inn is in turmoil since a group of unemployed actors – whose company has just gone bankrupt – are holing up there. Out in the square, Wilhelm notices a handsome young woman looking out of a window across the square; he's just bought some flowers and a young servant runs up to him asking if he wants to offer a flower to his mistress – the lady at the window. Of course Wilhelm is thrilled by this approach. And so he comes to meet the most charming character in the novel, an actress called Philine.

From the start Philine is predatory and manipulative – she flirts with Wilhelm and with all the other men in the book. She seems to be careless of the future – assuming that her winning ways and her power over men will always see her through – and in this she is quite justified. One of her favourite resources is to talk about her high-heeled shoes. They are always dangling from her pretty feet right in the line of vision of the nearest attractive man. She asks coy questions: do you prefer the sound or the sight of them? Are you more interested in the heels or in the soles of shoes? – holding the sole up to her cheek as she inquires. One evening she places her shoes below the curtain in Wilhelm's bedroom. At first he supposes that the rest of her is there too. Eventually he discovers that they are there on their own, as though acting as her ambassadors. He places them on the table by his bed, picks them up and eventually, Goethe relates, passes a happy night most of which is spent toying with the heels.

Gradually Wilhelm gets mixed up in the affairs of the theatre troupe and – having plenty of money to hand since he has been collecting sums owed to the business – puts up the funds to re-establish the company, buying back all the old props, sets and costumes that have been taken into receivership. Wilhelm feels that his past is being redeemed – he is rediscovering his vocation for the theatre; but as the owner-manager this involvement isn't directly opposed to business, in fact it is a form of business.

This is a central pattern of the book. We start with a black-and-white opposition. Poetry (or the theatre) is good; commerce is bad. Then there is a reversal: poetry is bad and commerce good. Finally there is a development towards integration: perhaps theatre and commerce are not directly in competition – since running an acting troupe is a business venture.

As soon as the company is re-formed, they get an invitation to perform at a not-too-distant schloss, or castle, where the count and countess are about to play host to a prince and the army high command. A play would be an appropriate entertainment – and perhaps they can put on a welcoming pageant, symbolizing the heroic virtues of the military leader. This is Wilhelm's introduction to the upper world of the aristocracy – and he is entranced. An aristocrat is the only thing to be: prosperous townspeople, like himself, always have to act, because they have to please in order to make a profit. Wilhelm's fantasy of the ideal aristocrat is enchanting – someone who can be natural, who can let his personality shine forth because he has developed under the influence of beauty in an expansive, healthy and secure environment. The noble does not fear ridicule; does not have to bow or scrape before his superiors – because he hasn't any.

As it turns out, life at the schloss doesn't quite run along these lines. The count is a timid, bumbling, superstitious and distracted man; he has no interest in Wilhelm's creative energies or ideas. He hasn't hired the troupe (whom he treats as servants) for their ideas – they are there to do exactly as they are told and to perform exactly as he sees fit.

The countess is altogether more alluring – in fact extremely so to Wilhelm; and she is rather taken with him in return. Still, her interest doesn't extend to his writings – she invites him to read something he has written but gets distracted by trifles. Wilhelm eventually kisses her and she reacts very badly to his assertion of desire. Fortunately the prince and the army are now moving on and the services of the actors are no longer required.

Wilhelm has rapidly traversed another key sequence of experiences: idealization followed by recognition of a less impressive reality. Still, by encountering the aristocratic world first hand his view of the world is now broader than it was before. There certainly is something admirable in his imagined ideal aristocrat; but those good qualities are not automatically possessed by every count and countess. The genuinely good qualities of frankness, self-possession and elegant style were first grasped by Wilhelm in an exaggerated and simplistic manner. And perhaps that is how our ideas generally do progress. But now Wilhelm can absorb these good qualities – or at least the desire to be like that – into his own ambitions.

When Wilhelm says that he wants to be himself – that his goal in life is not specifically to be in business nor in the theatre but to be himself through doing both these things – he is inventing a new kind of vocation. In a sense the problem with the middle-class ambitions he's had up to now is that they take your career as the full expression of you – you are a business manager or a theatre director. His aristocratically inspired aim is now bigger than either of these; it doesn't exclude doing such work: it means that neither role could define him.

The story of Wilhelm Meister belongs to the genre of the 'Bildungs-roman', the novel of education and development of an individual – and in fact is the central work of this type. Historically speaking, Wilhelm is faced with a relatively new set of questions – a new set of problems which he has to try to resolve through experience. What should he do with his life? What kind of career to have? We can see the novelty of the question through an examination of other characters for whom such questions do not arise. Werner, for example, is a traditional character in that the general outline of his course through life is not something he has to work out for himself. He simply follows in the family business. For Werner, the question 'Who am I?' is already answered in that respect, and does not extend into a larger field. He already has an answer deriving from the past. But the answer is so secure that, in fact, the question itself does not arise; whereas Wilhelm cannot answer the question 'Who am I really?' just by reference to his family, his place of origin, his father's occupation and his social rank.

Wilhelm, in other words, is the representative of a new kind of person – one who is socially and culturally mobile; who might find himself in a completely different kind of occupation, might change social status, might live in another place. Instead of inheriting a culture – and a life – he has to invent one.

*

Philine is an important foil because she does not undertake any of the serious developmental struggles that are central to Wilhelm's life; she isn't trying to raise the pyramid of her existence or 'become' who she is or form a national theatre or discover some special destiny. For her, existence is easy and light.

One reading of this could be that, as a woman, Philine is cut off from the process of 'Bildung'; and since it is this developmental course which is essential to maturity and to becoming fully oneself, Philine might be regarded as a lesser creature, a kind of gracious animal. But she plays a more interesting role than this. What she does is indicate that Wilhelm's development is not a universal path to a happy existence. 'Bildung' is not a requirement of everyone. Wilhelm's path to maturity is complex because he isn't, at the start of his life, a coherent being. He is drawn to the theatre and the arts, but he is born into a family in which such a way of life is regarded as not possible. Wilhelm has to make a life for himself because he has been unfortunate in that he is not at ease in the life that he is born to. So, Philine can be seen – in the coherence and happiness of her existence – as indicating the goal to which Wilhelm aspires. She is at one with herself, and that is how he wants to be.

7

Hamlet

Wilhelm and his group of actors pass from one adventure to another – including being attacked by bandits. Wilhelm is severely injured, and is aided by a mysterious and beautiful woman called 'the Amazon', who at once departs. Wilhelm spends a great deal of time trying to find her again. He is held responsible by the troupe for this disaster since it was on his passionate urging that they had collectively decided to follow the particular route through the wild hills where they fell prey to the robbers.

Wilhelm doesn't abandon the theatre but instead heads off to offer his services to the most professional and substantial company in the country – operated in a large town by a highly accomplished, but flawed, actor-manager called Serlo. Wilhelm persuades the company to put on *Hamlet* – now his favourite play. The play is discussed at great length, and Wilhelm suggests very radical revisions, claiming they improve the work.

In Wilhelm's interpretation, the key to the whole play is to be found in the lines Hamlet speaks near the beginning: 'The time is out of joint O cursed spite, that ever I was born to set it right.' Hamlet, he thinks, has been brought up with the expectation of one day succeeding his father on the throne of Denmark. But the early death of his father – in fact old Hamlet's murder – leaves the son too immature to play the required role. For Wilhelm – and here he surely is the mouthpiece of Goethe – the basic human problem in Hamlet is immaturity; a burden of leadership is placed upon the shoulders of Hamlet, but he is unable to bear that responsibility.

Within the play the way in which the times are out of joint – and the task of putting them to rights – is relatively clear. The problem is just that the old king has been murdered. It might be beyond Hamlet to do anything about that, but it's not hard to see what the problem is. But the power of the phrase, in Wilhelm's imagination, lies in the way it extends to the modern condition of the world. The problem for Wilhelm isn't how to avenge his father, but how to educate his own society – and the difficulty he has is that to do so he has to educate himself first. But, like Hamlet, he feels he is alone in this – how can he educate himself? He needs someone to do that for him; he needs a spiritual father to get him through his immaturity so that he can become – so far as possible – equal to the task.

There is a terrible conflict, for Hamlet, between his capacity to grasp what he is required to do, and his inability to carry it out. He must remove the usurper and become king; but he isn't capable of doing this. Immaturity is not cast as silliness – it records the gap between the tasks we set ourselves, the ambitions we embrace, and the internal resources and capacities we have. Hence, the period we call adolescence is just one conspicuous point at which immaturity is evident. For the serious person, life is a sequence of immaturities since we repeatedly develop ambitions and longings that we are not yet internally equipped to fulfil. When the aspiration is noble in its aims the self-cultivation that moves us towards being able to achieve it is a genuine and good process of development.

Hamlet's problem – according to Wilhelm – is thus intimately linked to his father. The father's ghost imposes a great task but is then no help in carrying it out. To put it crudely: Hamlet needs a father because his father is dead. But it's not just the fact of a father – the mere fact of a father being alive – which is at issue. Rather it is the role of a father – the paternal care and support. *Wilhelm Meister*, with its twin and conflicting themes of independence and vulnerability, is a novel about adolescence. Wilhelm has to separate from the world of his father but to do so he needs a father's support.

The solution within the novel is equally double-headed. Wilhelm encounters substitute fathers. His real father dies but Wilhelm is drawn into a circle of older men who seek to play a paternal role towards him. At the same time he discovers that he is a father. Mariane had actually borne his child, Felix – now about three years old. When Mariane died she handed over the child to the care of an actress now playing alongside Wilhelm as Ophelia to his Hamlet.

The tale of Wilhelm Meister, then, is, in short, a study of fathers and how to get them, so that a degree of maturity can be learned in order to carry out the burden of one's destiny. There are implications here for writers – and, more broadly, for culture.

In fact Wilhelm's pursuit of the Amazon leads him to a secluded castle where he is gradually brought under the guidance of a secret society of cultivated, practically minded men. At the moment of induction Wilhelm is led into a tower room which contains the stories of all the members – specifically the stories of their formative experiences, of their own struggles towards maturity, the history of their difficulties, failings, confusions and weaknesses as well as the way in which – eventually – they have become competent though far from perfect adults.

This moment is the centre of Goethe's entire cultural vision; the emotional heart of his world and his life. For what is revealed here is the meaning – for Goethe – of culture: the fundamental task of literature and art in relation to life. The ideal of culture is the same as that of the ideal parent with respect to the continued 'adolescence' – the repeated immaturity – of anyone who takes life seriously. Culture is the collective wisdom of humanity: it is collected, held and revealed in 'the tower'. In the Preface to *Werther* Goethe had written: 'Let this little book be your friend.' Now it is as though he is saying: let this big book be your parent. The role of parenthood here is collective – there isn't a single person who occupied this position for Wilhelm. What these parents do is write their lives: that is, transmit their experience. They have faced what we face.

It turns out that the members of the society of the tower (the 'adults') have been watching Wilhelm all along. In terms of plot this is cumbersome – it is now revealed that apparently minor figures who had crossed Wilhelm's path in seemingly inconsequential ways were in fact emissaries from the tower. Psychologically, however, the point is well made. For loving parents really are always watching the growing child and adolescent; although the nature of their care cannot always be understood by its recipient. Wilhelm asks: if you were watching, why did you not intervene to prevent my blunders? Why did you not help me more directly? The answer is painful but realistic: human nature is such that we have to learn by experience; it is only through our errors that we come to knowledge. Wisdom falls flat – appears to be merely a set of truisms or platitudes – unless grounded in experience. What we learn is not a set of beliefs; we acquire a set of capacities. You cannot simply tell someone how to cope with life, how to bear responsibility or disappointment, how to love another person, and expect that will equip them to deal with such things.

The tower places Goethe's work in perspective. We are invited to see *Wilhelm Meister* as Wilhelm's own record, as the account of his passage to maturity recorded by him. More broadly, 'the great confession', of which Goethe claimed all his works were fragments, is Goethe's own record for the tower. The point – and value – of culture is that it helps us face life successfully. By this standard we can identify some of the problems of our own collective culture. If, in effect, the tower contains the record of fake adults we will be given a false view of life. What we today call 'celebrity culture' is just such a thing: it is the amassing of records of existences from which we cannot learn anything, through which we cannot properly grow. Goethe's tower avoids flattery: it does not say to Wilhelm – or to any serious person – you are just fine as you are; instead it says: to become the best possible version of yourself is a long and difficult undertaking, but we will be at your side. The message of mass culture in effect is to say: there is nothing you don't know that is worth knowing; there are no interests or capacities you need to acquire: you are fine as you are. And this, in other words, amounts to a systematic denial of adulthood.

8

Domestic Economy

Once he is drawn into the cultivated, practical circle of the tower, Wilhelm withdraws entirely from the theatre. He has moved on; he has acquired certain competences and has learned from his experience – especially from his mistakes. He now knows that he has no special vocation for the theatre or for poetry.

Recall Plato's point that it is better to become a good general than to write about generals: it is better to do the real thing than to create images of good things. Instead of acting out the drama of life on a stage, Wilhelm should become the director of an actual life – his own; instead of writing poetry about art and graceful goddesses, Wilhelm should make a fine life for himself and his son and find a partner with whom to do this. The move, always, is from representation to reality.

This condition is most fully realized by a woman Wilhelm meets – a good friend of Lothario, the leading figure in the society of the tower. She is the perfect director of her own existence. Wilhelm spends a few days with her; one morning they take a walk through her small farm, across the fields, round the orchards and meadows, giving instructions to her staff: 'Everywhere Theresa kept instructing the steward; nothing so minute but she could give an account of it; and Wilhelm had reason to wonder at her knowledge, her precision, the prompt dexterity with which she suggested means for ends. She loitered nowhere; always hastened to the leading points; and thus her tasks were quickly over.'

Theresa is not covetous – a rich marriage with an elderly neighbour is on offer. However, she is content with the modest plenty that she already has. In fact she holds that she has no business with greater possessions; she knows her own limitations: what would she do if she

275

had great estates and huge resources at her command? To make good use of them she would require talents she knows she does not possess; she would need to take into account much larger considerations – political dangers, great alliances, the welfare of many people. What grounds does she have for thinking that she would exercise those duties with any great skill? Theresa thus sums up one of the key claims of Goethe's political creed – and also of his view of human contentment. We are envious of more than we can use: we want more, but don't have the skill to use it well. And hence we don't rest content with the good things we have.

Returning to her small, neat and very comfortable house, Theresa excuses herself and suggests Wilhelm look round her little garden. 'Here he could scarcely turn himself, so narrow were the walks, so thickly was it sown and planted. On looking over to the courtyard he could not help smiling: the firewood was lying there, as accurately sawed, split and piled as if it had been part of the building and had been intended to continue permanently there. The tubs and implements, all clean, were standing in their places: the house was painted white and red; it was really pleasant to behold. Whatever can be done by handicraft, which knows not beautiful proportions, but labours for convenience, cheerfulness and durability, appeared united in this spot.'

Although he does not love Theresa in any intense Romantic sense, Wilhelm decides that he should marry Theresa, and she accepts. He has been chasing after his remembered Amazon for months and hasn't found her. He now thinks that his love for her is no basis for his life; he should abandon that – resigning himself to the probabilities that he'll never see her again; that she's already married, or if not married, wouldn't be interested in marrying him. All these vague hopes seem to threaten his real chances of happy and productive life.

Theresa is the embodiment of one kind of adulthood, one 'solution' to the question of how to live well. But not long after Theresa has accepted Wilhelm's proposal of marriage, he finally meets his Amazon. She is a woman called Natalie and her life is quite different from that of Theresa. She embodies another vision of the good adult existence.

As with Theresa, Goethe conveys her life through the description of the fine house in which she lives.

Natalie's house is a small schloss – although 'castle' is misleading since this is a purely classical environment which should be imagined along the lines of a Palladian villa. It was built by Natalie's great-uncle: the man, it turns out, who purchased the art collection which had once belonged to Wilhelm's grandfather. We first learn of the house from the memoirs of Natalie's aunt – a woman referred to as 'the beautiful soul'. Natalie had heard of this celebrated house through these memoirs, but – like many people – had imagined it as a pompous and highly decorated confection. She had, that is, assumed that great architecture could only be an affair of outward show, and could have nothing of value to offer a person like her. But on seeing the house she finds something completely unexpected: the fineness of the building has nothing to do with pomp or the splendid assertion of wealth and status. Instead the building concentrates and reinforces her own inward, reflective nature: it is serene and gracious. This building has a personality. 'As the aspect of a well-formed person pleases us, so also does a fine house, by means of which the presence of a rational intelligent mind is manifested. We feel a joy in entering even a clean house, though it may be tasteless in its structure and its decorations; because it shows us the presence of a person cultivated in at least one sense. Doubly pleasing is it, therefore, when from a human dwelling, the spirit of a higher though still sensual culture speaks to us.'

Natalie thus represents a higher culture than Theresa. Theresa releases Wilhelm from their engagement and he is left to choose between the women. Their worlds are not opposed and the two women – it turns out – are friends. The question is only: where does Wilhelm belong? Is it in the wisely limited sphere of Theresa, or in the more intellectual and cultivated and powerful environment of Natalie? He would be welcome in either.

This returns us to one of Goethe's original problems: a man having to choose between two loves. In the early stages of his writing career, Goethe had placed three characters in a related situation, in his play *Stella*. In that play, recall, Goethe suggested two endings: either the three all live together or they kill themselves. Now, in *Wilhelm Meister*, we can see just how far Goethe's conception of life had developed. Clearly it would now make no sense for Theresa and Natalie to 'share' Wilhelm. Although the women are friends, their lives are different – there could be no common place that would be home to both Theresa and Natalie. And while Wilhelm has to choose one or the other – or neither – there is not the slightest fear that anyone is going to turn to suicide. For their lives – the lives of all three – already have a solid, real, continuing character. A loving marriage would be a wonderful addition, but life would not be worthless without that.

At the close, it looks as if Wilhelm will marry Natalie and be drawn into her aristocratic environment of great resources and noble ideals. And yet it remains open, even then, that he might not marry her. But whatever happens he is – for the present – happy and will not have to lose his friendship with either of the women he so much admires.

9

Meaning and Meaninglessness

Goethe used to like to say that people were always trying to pin a particular 'theory' of life on *Wilhelm Meister*. They wanted to see it as the elaborate assertion of a single view of what life is really about. A generous reading might see it as saying that through the travails of experience we come to a stable and secure sense of identity. But really this is Wilhelm's hope, rather than a conclusion the novel reaches. In fact, Wilhelm's dreams of maturity are always being controverted; his expectations of a clear and contented view of himself are not met.

A harsh reading might suggest – as it did to one contemporary critic – that the goal of life, as articulated by the novel, is the possession of a country estate. This interpretation is given some plausibility by the weight that is clearly given to comfortable domestic order in the later stages of the book. But this way of dismissing the book is immature – it is precisely the kind of objection that the young Wilhelm would have made. He too would have seen any concern with worldly things to be a betrayal of the spiritual ambitions which ought to guide a noble life.

The criticism is, in any case, far too general. The point isn't that everyone or anyone should aim at worldly prosperity ('an estate'). It's rather that it's good and proper that Wilhelm should have such an ambition. This accords perfectly with Goethe's general political philosophy and is acutely relevant today. There never has been an equal distribution of goods and power and there never will be; whoever holds the larger possession of goods and power greatly influences the life of everyone else; therefore it is extremely important that wise and fine people gain control of as much of the material resources of the world as possible. As a character in one of Trollope's novels puts it: if good men won't struggle and fight to take possession of the resources of the world, the bad men will get the lot. It is, Goethe is saying, vitally important that people of Wilhelm's calibre – people with his intelligence, sensitivity, capacity to learn from experience, warmth and curiosity about life – should prosper. But the very complexity and refinement of Wilhelm's nature is such that he comes close to floundering in his early engagements with the real world. The political message of *Wilhelm Meister* is that youthful good people need to be helped so that they can go into life armed and fired with ambition. Otherwise the coarse philistines will 'get the lot'.

The problem with both of these ways of seeing the book – in Goethe's eyes – is that they try to draw from it a lesson which is too obvious. Each picks out a theme that is of some weight and then suggests that it is Goethe's attempt to pin down the meaning of life.

A better view of what is going on is suggested by some of Goethe's short stories, one of which appears in the sequel to *Wilhelm Meister's Apprenticeship*: a more diffuse and complex book, in which the narrative thread gradually unravels – *The Years of Wandering*. This sequel contains a story called 'The New Messalina'.

It is a tale that Goethe had been interested in for many years. It has a dreamlike quality to it; a youth finds a magical gate in a wall and enters an enclosed garden filled with fantastical, symbolic objects. Eventually he meets a fairy who turns him into a pygmy, marries him and lives with him in a tiny house. At last the youth escapes and returns to his real size by filing through his wedding ring. At one level this is a cautionary tale about marriage – don't get married, it will make you small. But the story appears to be much richer than this: everything in it is symbolic and laden with significance. Only – as in a dream – we can't quite grasp what the overall meaning is. Every item is meaningful – but can't be brought into a coherent interpretation along with everything else.

This story is a microcosm of the *Wilhelm Meister* sequence. Wilhelm's life is not lacking in meaning when we consider it episode by episode. It's just that when we try to draw a single clear conclusion either we give up or we fall back on banal formulations: don't get married; try to gain possession of a country house. And while these may be – in the right cases – appropriate bits of advice they cannot even begin to be impressive as general understandings of how to live a good life or how to make sense of your own existence.

The question of the meaningfulness of life – or of its opposite, the sense of life being pointless – had long been understood as a 'transcendent' question. That is, if life has a meaning it would have to be located outside (hopefully after) our present worldly existence. If God has set this mortal life as a kind of preparatory ground for our future being, then the meaning of life here and now is entirely determined by that further concern.

When this came to seem less plausible it looked as if life might, therefore, have no meaning or purpose at all; clearly life wasn't for anything, because normally when we want to know what something is for we are asking about some use it has relative to something else – the corkscrew is for opening wine bottles. The day there are no more corks to be drawn the corkscrew will be pointless, it will have no meaning.

Wilhelm's task is to find meaning in his own life. His 'apprenticeship' is not to do with gaining a skill so much as gaining a view of life. One reference, here, is to the traditional guild system of apprenticeship, in which a young man is assigned to a master (for seven years) in order to learn his trade. The same terms had been absorbed by the Masonic Order, to indicate grades of initiation and enlightenment. It's not hard to see what Goethe is getting at – he wants to trace a young man's apprenticeship in life. But both resonances are misleading and even unhelpful. For, in each case, a clear account can be given of exactly what it is the apprentice has to learn, and what constitutes mastery in a given field. But the human process of maturation is much less clear than this – and Goethe is quick to make this apparent. So while Wilhelm certainly does develop and undoubtedly gains in maturity across the course of the novel, it is extremely hard to pin down quite what it is he now knows. And this is at odds with the craft tradition in which the master can be relied upon to get it right and to be able to explain how things should be done.

Goethe is continually warring between two conceptions of the human condition. On the one hand he has great affection for the 'technical' view – one which his mother supported. We can overcome the problems of existence by learning how to do things – we need to internalize a few rules (get the unpleasant tasks out of the way first, don't let them fester; concentrate on what is within your grasp).

'Man is intended for a limited condition; objects that are simple, near, determinate, he comprehends and he becomes accustomed to dealing with such means as are at hand. But on entering a wider field, he knows not either what he would nor what he should; and it amounts to quite the same whether his attention is distracted by the multitude of objects, or is overpowered by their magnitude and dignity. It is always a misfortune to him when he is induced to struggle after anything with which he cannot connect himself by some regular exertion of his powers.'

Goethe didn't just admire this approach – he sought very actively, and with considerable success, to apply it in his own life. This is the view of the meaning of life embodied in the character of Theresa.

IO

Home

As we might expect from reading *Wilhelm Meister* the place where Goethe lived and the kind of life he led there are central to who he was. It's clear that in his writing and ideas Goethe had a high regard for domestic life and saw this as a major source of happiness.

From his early forties to the end of his days, Goethe's home was the Frauenplan. A dignified staircase with broad, shallow steps was inserted – taking up rather too much room – providing an easy ascent to the upper floor where Goethe had his rooms.

The new staircase provided a most august prelude to the formal rooms but Goethe sometimes regretted the amount of space it took up

The long house looks directly on to the street; but behind there is a large garden and the back part of the house looks out on to this pleasant space. The street building and the garden building are separated by two internal courtyards. Goethe made use of this division in arranging the use of the house – something that was clearly very important to him. There were quite separate quarters occupied by Christiane and little August.

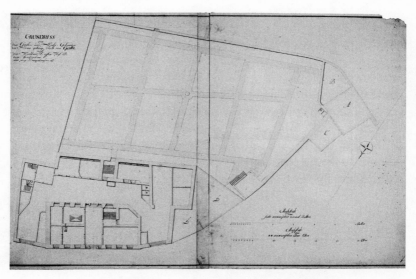

The formal rooms are at the front, the working and family
accommodation at the back

On the upper floor the front rooms were designed for social life – and also to house Goethe's collections. These rooms are meant to have a symbolic meaning and to reflect Goethe's life. In the Yellow Room, which was the formal dining room, there were copies of paintings by Titian (*Sacred and Profane Love*) and Raphael.

The use of copies of classical statues and busts had been widely accepted; but Goethe's admission of copies of paintings is quite striking – and revealing about his attitude to art. It's not that he was unable to see the difference between an original Titian and a copy, or that he couldn't recognize the superior merits dependent upon the touch of the master. It was, rather, that he could get much of what he wanted from a copy. The copy could preserve the symbolic power of Titian's conception; the structure or form of the work could still be grasped and appreciated.

A neo-classical spirit is particularly evident in the little vaulted chamber that joins the front and back portions of the house at the upper level. Visitors often said that the place looked like a museum – and it's easy to see why.

In fact the Frauenplan house was to develop into a kind of insti-tution; not so much a museum as a state department of the realm of literature and the arts. The first recruit to the 'institute' was the painter and art historian Johann Heinrich Meyer, who lived in the house and who was to collaborate with Goethe over many years.

Meyer painted a watercolour portrait of Goethe at around this time.

This image is radically different from the better-known pictures of Goethe. His hair has continued to recede, and he has not yet found an effective way of arranging it. He was later to try a longer style and eventually to hit upon a happy technique of brushing it backwards,

Goethe at the time when his friendship with Schiller began

giving greater animation to his appearance. Folds of fat are starting to accumulate below his chin and we sense the spread of his stomach below his heavy coat. All this was only to get worse over the next few years.

The workroom and the bedroom overlook the garden. They are plain to an almost severe degree, with wide uncarpeted boards, no curtains (just green blinds), very functional furniture, with no attempt at grace or elegance: 'Splendid edifices and apartments are for princes and kingdoms. Those who live in them feel at ease and contented and desire nothing further. To me this is quite repugnant. In a splendid abode like that I am instantly lazy and inactive. On the contrary a small residence where a sort of disorderly order . . . prevails, suits me exactly. It allows my inner nature full liberty to act, and to create from itself alone.'

The house isn't just an impressive or dignified setting for Goethe; it wasn't just a way of conveying his dignity as a member of the duke's council and a minister of state, or as a successful writer. It's quite clear that Goethe had only limited interests in such matters – he lived for quite a long time in the garden-house across the river, which was extremely modest, and did not feel that his dignity was compromised. Rather, the move to the Frauenplan and the investment of his personality in the property is an effort of self-extension, a way (as it were) of translating his inner life into outer objects; an attempt to embody his personality in physical arrangements of stone and furniture. When we seek to impress others, our primary question is: what will they think? If you want to show off you have to second-guess what will awe others. That wasn't at all Goethe's concern; he was infinitely more interested in how it struck him.

Sadly there were drawbacks to the house. Soon after Goethe took possession of the Frauenplan house, a smaller house next door came up for sale. Goethe was away at the time – this was in 1793 during the siege of Mainz – and instructed a couple of his friends to bid for it on his behalf. Unfortunately they did not succeed in securing the property and it was purchased by the proprietor of a weaving business who proceeded to install several pieces of machinery. The noise of the looms was to disturb Goethe for the rest of his life.

During these years life in the big house was, in the main, very happy. While he was away on campaign, Goethe would write tenderly to Christiane saying how much he longed to be with her and August; he sent sweets and little presents. Goethe very much wanted a larger family – his own memories of childhood were particularly happy – but this was cruelly frustrated.

At the end of 1793 – on 21 November – Christiane gave birth to a daughter, who was at once christened Caroline. Goethe was 'dreadfully pleased about it', Charlotte von Stein noted. A sister for August would have brought back his own happy childhood with Cornelia. But within two weeks Caroline was dead of pneumonia. Goethe wept and lay kicking the floor in an agony of loss.

PART SEVEN

Nature

The world contains riddles enough as it is: why turn the simplest phenomena into riddles as well?

Goethe, *Art and Antiquity*, Volume III, issue 1 (1821)

I

Sentiment

Throughout his long life, Goethe was interested in the study of nature. In this respect he was a man of his time. The cultural divorce of the arts and sciences – which reached its bitterest point in the middle years of the twentieth century – had not yet occurred. Continuity of interests was greatly facilitated by the comparatively rudimentary character of scientific knowledge. A well-educated person could hope to master much of the relevant material and even make modest but genuine contributions to scientific knowledge, without having undertaken specialist training. Goethe grew up in the age of the amateur, and universal, scientist.

It is particularly in relation to science that the image of Goethe as 'the last man' has grown up. That is, the last man who grasped everything thought to be significant in the realm of knowledge: the several arts and their histories, medicine, law, literature, classical culture, the sciences, philosophy. After Goethe it all becomes too complex, there is too much for a single person to absorb and organize. A certain image of completeness – an attractive image of the essential comprehensibility and containment of the world – dies with Goethe, and he becomes the hero of nostalgia for that lost world.

But this nostalgia is misplaced. Goethe did not know all there was to be known in many of the areas in which he made contributions. He was not universally intelligent in the way this image suggests. Rather, Goethe identified the kinds of specific contribution he could make in various fields by drawing upon his own distinctive style of thought.

*

Goethe's interest in nature – and his conception of how we might engage with nature – changed considerably over his life. Briefly, he grew out of a 'sentimentalist' attachment to the countryside and grew into an obsession with natural science. The sentimental approach was primarily concerned with the individual's felt response to the natural world. This is given expression in a poem, called 'On the Lake', that Goethe wrote while travelling in Switzerland in 1775 – at the time when he was engaged to Lili.

> I suck fresh food and new blood
> From the open world:
> Nature is so kind and good,
> Keeping me at her breast.

He goes on to say that here, on the lake, in the middle of the open world, is where pleasure and vitality are to be found: implying – and not in the gilded salons of Lili's family home. By the time Goethe wrote these lines, Rousseau had long been preaching the idea that the uncultivated countryside is the true home of humanity: it is only in forests and by the sides of lakes that people can be happy and good. Goethe never lost this grateful, rapturous enjoyment of natural scenery. But even as he compared nature to his mother's breasts he had already become aware of the limitations of this emotional and instinctive attachment to nature.

There are several passages early on in *Werther* – written a year or so before the lake poem – in which Werther is entranced by the natural world. He goes into ecstasies about the loveliness of the spring. He lies on the grass, looks at the insects and thinks of the infinite variety of creation. This feeling of benign immersion is beautifully evoked, but it is the record of a happy moment. Here, communion with the appearance of the physical world is dependent upon the emotional condition of the beholder. The view of nature is an expression – or a projection – of a state of satisfaction. The image of nature as benign, as a mother, records but does not cause the satisfaction. Nature is experienced as nourishing because one feels well fed already.

If our view of nature as supportive and kindly depends upon sensation it is left vulnerable to changes in mood. Later on in the novel

Werther has a completely different experience. A few weeks before he shoots himself Werther contrasts his previous experience – of the paradisal spring – with his experience now: in his depressed state nature has nothing consoling or helpful to say to him. The morning sun breaking through the mist leaves him unmoved. His response is governed only by what he is presently feeling; so when he was joyous nature was joyful; now he is miserable nature is dreary and cold. The sentimental attitude serves always to reinforce the current mood. So at the time of crisis contemplation of nature provides no sustenance or relief. It is as if he were trying to lean upon his own shadow for support.

At this point Werther encounters a madman – who, also, had once been in love with Lotte. The madman is searching for summer flowers in the woods, although it is now winter. He cannot accept that they are not there, because he 'loves' flowers. This is the lowest point to which a sentimental attitude to nature leads. He is trying to get the material world to play the sentimental game and meet his present needs.

In his later work Goethe undertakes a revolution in perspective. His approach to nature becomes 'objective'. The word is perhaps misleading. By 'objective' he is signalling an approach that is not governed by projection – it is not the attempt to read into nature some correlate of present emotional needs. Rather, it is the attempt to understand and see the natural order as it actually is. But this is not, in the end, emotionally neutral. On the contrary, Goethe holds that when viewed objectively the material world becomes more important and powerful in our lives.

This change is really to do with adding in an additional step. Goethe's view is that when we study the processes of nature carefully, when we understand them, we discover a more profound connection with life. The solace we find in the objective encounter with the natural world is stable. It is liberated from mood.

It is also broadened in range. The focus is no longer upon those parts of nature – such as a beautifully wooded Swiss lake – that are obviously attractive and where nature seems most suited to please the

senses. To the 'objective' eye the process of nature – and the consolation of nature – may be revealed in apparently much less promising
encounters. Goethe had a vivid revelation of this one afternoon in
Venice when he watched hordes of crabs scuttling about by the sea
defences. Such a sight could easily strike one as revolting. It is the
addition of natural science that is crucial here. For science breaks
the immediate connection between nature and the projection of our
emotions.

2

The Metamorphosis of Plants

If Goethe's interest in science was normal – and to be expected of an educated man of his era – the place he gave science in his life is, at first sight, frankly shocking.

At the end of a long day's conversation about colour – on Wednesday 18 February 1829 – Goethe's friend Eckermann made some notes: 'His feeling for the theory of colours was like that of a mother who all the more loves an excellent child the less it is esteemed by others. "As for what I have done as a poet," he would repeatedly say, "I take no pride whatever in it. Excellent poets have lived at the same time with myself; poets more excellent have lived before me, and others will come after me. But that in my century I am the only person who knows the truth in the difficult science of colours – of that, I say, I am not a little proud, and here I have a consciousness of superiority to many."'

One of the reasons what he called 'science' appealed so strongly to Goethe was its grounding in close and persistent observation of external things. Goethe saw it as counteracting one of the prevailing spiritual sicknesses of the times – one from which he himself had suffered.

There's a passage in *Wilhelm Meister* that addresses exactly this issue: Wilhelm is talking to an actress who is most impressed by his interpretation of *Hamlet*; but she goes on to comment – 'I've never met anyone who so completely misunderstands the people with whom he actually lives, as you, who misconceive them from the ground up.' It's a candid self-portrait that Goethe gets one of his characters to draw. And she dwells on the most painful point: when it comes to art Wilhelm-Goethe speaks like a god – when it comes to art, to characters in plays or novels or paintings, then he is superb, he seems to be able to reach into the inner recesses, to identify the subtlest movements of imagination and feeling. But when it comes to seeing his effect on others, or seeing what is going on around him in the lives of others, he is hopeless. In order to live well – or, in the case of Werther, in order to live at all – you have to become perceptive of what is 'not you'; you have to break the circle of your own emotions, your preoccupation with what is going on inside your own head or within your own heart, and see what is also going on outside of you. This is the necessary escape route from self-obsession and the threat of insanity.

Attention to detail and the lucid ordering and recording of observations is the keynote of Goethe's first serious bit of independent scientific research. Around 1784 – while he was still deeply involved in governmental duties in Weimar – Goethe set himself to resolve a tricky anatomical question: do human beings have an intermaxillary bone? This bone – which introduces a degree of movement and flexibility in the jaws of many mammals – was well known in animals. But the human jaw does not obviously have such a bone in it; and this had been regarded as an interesting and significant point of difference, one that demonstrated at a physiological level the separateness of humanity from the rest of creation. Goethe, having examined various skulls, human and animal, showed conclusively that such a bone is residually present in the human jaw. This little avenue for demonstrating the uniqueness of the human condition was now closed.

The appeal of the discovery, for Goethe, was that it suggested the opposite: humanity was indeed continuous with the rest of the mammals, and hence with nature in general. At the crudest level, Goethe's sense of his own dignity did not require validation in a scientific 'break' between his own body and that of animals. On the contrary, Goethe thought that there were great advantages to be won from demonstrating the connection between human life and that of the rest of nature. Being part of nature was not some kind of demotion – not a way of drawing us down from a privileged status one grade below the angels and perversely glorying in an 'animal' identity.

*

No one had disputed that human beings were – in part at least – animals. But this had often been given a negative interpretation. Our bodies are similar in principle to the bodies of animals. But that reveals only the unhappiness of the human lot; for our inner lives – our souls – have an entirely different mode of being. The two are joined – at least temporarily – in a most unsatisfactory marriage.

The discovery of a tiny residual bone in the jaw is, in itself, not all that significant. It reinforces the view that the human body has a structure which is very intimately connected to the structure of lesser creatures. Suppose it weren't there – what difference would that have made? Well, one might have seen this tiny differentiation of humans from the normal organization of mammals as a token – at the physical level – of a spiritual gulf. But really nothing very much could hang upon the presence or absence of this tiny bit of gristle. Its presence doesn't show that there is no essential distinction between human beings and other mammals – in terms of the mind or soul. And its absence would not confirm any substantial distinction – since there are plenty of little physical ways in which human beings differ from other creatures.

Goethe's little bone is only an opening shot in a larger investigation; and that is to see the ways in which human life – and not just the structure of the body – adheres to patterns of growth and development that can be found in the realm of nature. Goethe's exploration of this idea led him not further into anatomy but towards the study of plants. The result was 'The Metamorphosis of Plants', an essay written in early 1790, when Goethe was forty, in the weeks following the birth of his son, August, on Christmas Day 1789. (Confusingly, Goethe also wrote a poem with the same title some eight years later.)

In the essay Goethe considers the growth of a plant from the first stirrings of the seed through maturity and reproduction to eventual decay. Such concerns gain a pertinent poignancy when we think of Goethe formulating his thoughts about the earliest moments of a plant's growth – and contemplating the whole of its life cycle – with his own child only days old.

Goethe regards growth as essentially self-reproduction. The living power of the plant is expressed by repetition: the stem is pushed from node to node; leaf is added to leaf. The same power is displayed in the comparatively concentrated appearance of blossom and fruit and in the full reproduction of another living organism. Goethe insists that these are closely connected, are expressions of the same power: 'the power shown in gradual vegetative growth is closely related to the power suddenly displayed in major reproduction'.

It is hard to miss the psychology here – we can almost hear Goethe explaining his own creative life to himself: don't, he says, make too big a distinction between the bursts of productivity and the periods of apparent vegetating. For vegetation is a form of growth and is closely connected to the 'sudden' reproduction. When I write a book, like *Werther*, in three weeks, that is the 'flower and the fruit' but I must not condemn myself for not always working that way.

Those plants termed 'annuals' are particularly exciting – for Goethe – because they go through the whole life cycle in one year and display in the most lucid fashion the connection between the developmental stages – seed, first tender shoots, development of leaves (for taking in light, oxygen), development of roots (water and nutrients), the gradual extension in scale (from node to node); then the bursting into flower, the gradual ripening of the fruit and finally death. If only the phases of human life were as clear as this.

In fact Goethe thinks that human life has essentially the same pattern of development that we can trace in the growth of plants – although the human case is more complex and harder to observe. The continuity is asserted in Goethe's choice of vocabulary. He speaks repeatedly of the 'Bildung' of plants: that is, of their development or cultivation. But the same term 'Bildung' was also the master term employed by Wilhelm von Humboldt in his educational theory and practice. The aim of education is the development, or cultivation, of the human individual. It was this concept which came to dominate the whole idea of Western culture, and which is still absolutely central to it. It is no coincidence that Goethe had first come into close contact with von Humboldt only in December 1789, in the period immediately before he wrote the metamorphosis essay. (In fact Goethe had been introduced to Wilhelm von Humboldt by the aristocratic von Lengefelds, whose daughter Charlotte was shortly to marry Schiller. But at this point rapprochement with Schiller was still some five years into the future.)

This notion of 'Bildung' provides a clue to Goethe's view of the continuity of art and science. A central scientific task is to trace the pattern of development and growth of the living organism. And what has Goethe been doing in his novels? *Wilhelm Meister*, which is the original and best Bildungsroman, pursues this scientific enterprise in its most difficult and yet most important form: the attempt to trace the general principles of growth and development of an individual human life.

3

A Novel: The Universe

The connection that Goethe wants to make between human life and the developmental process of plants runs the risk of seeming to be merely a 'projection'. It's not all that difficult to find analogies between the two realms. But Goethe clearly wants to make a much bigger and more controversial claim – that there really are profound connections. It's not hard to take elements of human experience and project them on to plants – to say, for example, that leaves love the sun or that plants desire water; but – in a simple sense – we know that they cannot really have such emotions. It helps create a fiction of closeness that is harmless and quite charming – but can hardly be said to amount to an insight into botany. And it is similar the other way round. We can happily call a novel the 'fruit' of experience, but again it is just a nice metaphor – hardly a contribution to the study of creativity. Or is it? Goethe is trying to get us to take seriously the idea that there is much more at stake here than a metaphor or an analogy.

Goethe had already made an attempt to address this subject in a few remarkable pages written in Weimar on 18 January 1784. These paragraphs were envisaged as part of a work to be called 'A Novel: The Universe', of which unfortunately only this fragment, dealing with granite, was completed. The title, however, would be highly apposite for *Faust*, were the play to be recast as a narrative fiction.

Goethe explicitly addresses the objection that he expects to meet from his friends: what on earth are you doing writing about stones when you could be writing about people? 'I do not fear the accusation,' he says – implying: I expect it will be made – 'that a contrary spirit has led me away from my consideration and depiction of the human heart: the youngest, most diverse, most fluid, most changeable, most vulnerable part of creation, and has brought me to the observation of the oldest, firmest, deepest' – and literally – 'most unshakeable son of nature.'

The way he puts the imagined objection already contains the answer. The human heart and granite are both products of nature. But that does not mean that they are the same. On the contrary, Goethe is suggesting that it is not only individual organisms that develop: nature as a whole undergoes a process of growth. There is a Bildungsroman of the history of nature to be written; the fragments we possess were to have been an early chapter. This anticipation of evolution – lacking Darwin's insights (which came over seventy years later) into the role of competition for survival as the motor of change – provides the necessary distance that allows us to see ourselves as part of nature. Human nature is not just the same as the nature of granite or the nature of a tree. To say that we are part of nature isn't to say that – in the end – we are the same as plants or rocks or even apes. According to this vision of things, an ape is like the seed from which human beings have grown. A seed grows into a mature plant – but it would be quite wrong to say that the seed is a mature plant.

The gradual unfolding of nature as a whole proceeds from the simple to the complex, from the inert to the more and more responsive, from static to dynamic. Therefore whatever lessons we learn from contemplating plants – lessons about the necessary sequence of life, about the stages of growth – cannot be taken to apply directly and simply to human experience. But nor are they irrelevant. They are simple versions of us – hence illuminating, because the pattern is clearer, and moving, because they are free of the kind of complexity which is the source of both our dignity and our suffering.

Thus Goethe goes on to describe the consoling power of nature. 'I have suffered and continue to suffer much through the inconstancy of human opinion, through its sudden changes in me and others, and I may be forgiven my desire for that sublime tranquillity which surrounds us in the solitude and silence of nature, vast and eloquent with its still voice.' Of course the heart that had most disturbed Goethe's tranquillity was his own. The lesson of the rocks is not 'be like us' but rather, 'know that you cannot be like us'. The enviable steadfastness of a granite mountain is necessarily closed to Goethe, just as the innocence of a child cannot be regained as an adult.

It is deeply characteristic of Goethe that he moves between careful analysis and observation of external nature itself and then close examination and description of its significance for him: his emotional and spiritual reaction to the ancient mountain. And that reaction, while loving and excited, is not stable. The man who cultivates a lonely eternal truth doesn't necessarily feel secure and happy. The volatility of the heart – our complexity – means that we cannot live by granite alone, as it were. 'But soon the burning sun will bring back thirst and hunger, the human necessities . . . I envy the dwellers in those more abundant and plentifully watered plains, the inhabitants who have built their happy homes on the debris and ruin of error and opinion, who scratch in the dust of their ancestors and quietly meet the modest needs of their daily existence within those narrow confines. With these thoughts as an overture his soul will make its way into centuries past and recall all that was noted by careful observers, all that was imagined by fiery spirits.'

In other words, the full range of the individual personality is a mirror of nature in its entirety. We have our granite aspect but also our 'burning sun'. The key phrase here is this: 'his soul will make its way into centuries past'. What Goethe is asserting here is not antiquarianism – not the curiosity about times and places radically different from those in which we can and do live. Rather, we can find ourselves at home in earlier times, because in earlier centuries a part of human nature came to fruition and flowered. At no stage is the whole on display; therefore we need the whole history of humanity and the whole history of nature as our imaginative dwelling place if we are to be complete.

To see clearly what is going on here we need to contrast this essay on 'The Universe' – sketched when Goethe was thirty-five – with his very first attempt to understand the position of the individual in history and society: the essay on Strasbourg Cathedral, which was written in

1771 when Goethe was twenty-two. What change in outlook has occurred in thirteen years?

In the Strasbourg essay, Goethe had tried to isolate a particular kind of object which would provide the 'true home' for the good individual; and that individual was seen as essentially, irreducibly Germanic. One kind of architecture – Gothic architecture – could exclusively and adequately nourish the soul. 'The Universe' sketch massively broadens the horizons, extending them – as the name indicates – to the whole of creation and the whole of human history. The good individual can no longer be seen as exclusively ethnic. True, there may be a part of a person that responds with a particular thrill to the style of Strasbourg; but the same person may also need Paris and Rome. The ethnic focus now looks like a mistake: it sought to make a fragment of a person into a model for life. What was good about the earlier version was that it recognized the strength of attachment an individual might feel to a work from the past. Where it went wrong was in the zealous aim of prescribing a single period, a single style, as sufficient for human satisfaction.

4

God and Spinoza

Why does science matter to us? One important element in the human significance of science is that it contributes to our sense of who we are. The human predicament is framed by our grasp of the order of nature and our position within that order. That is why people had been excited by the supposed absence of the intermaxillary bone in the human jaw, since this appeared to support the view that human beings were fundamentally different from other animals. It is this, too, which explains the controversy – later in the nineteenth century – around the work of Charles Darwin.

The link between our account of nature and our view of life was not a new topic. In the *Nicomachean Ethics* Aristotle tried to integrate his views on how we should live with his study of biology. A human being is to be understood as an animal with distinctive needs and specific capacities. In the modern era, the philosopher who most impressed Goethe was the seventeenth-century philosopher Spinoza. Spinoza produced highly technical philosophical arguments, but it was not the detail so much as his general outlook – his world-view, as it might be called – that attracted Goethe to him. Briefly, Spinoza was arguing against Descartes. For entirely logical reasons, Descartes had constructed a 'dualist' account of reality. Fundamentally there are two kinds of thing that exist: physical objects and minds, of which by far the most comprehensive is what we call God. But this left a deep puzzle about the interaction of these two modes of being: how could non-physical, purely mental entities interact with completely physical bodies? No one doubted that there was some kind of connection – our ideas and thoughts seem to translate into actions and physical events;

you think about going on holiday (mental event) and then you go out and buy a ticket (physical event). But if the two kinds of events are on totally different planes of being, how can the thought make the action happen? In a way it's merely an extension of the observation that just thinking about an object moving doesn't make it move.

One way past this problem is the theory of 'monism' – it asserts that instead of there being two kinds of thing, there is really only one. Of course this does away with the problem of interaction, but introduces a new and equally resistant problem – what on earth is the one thing? How can it be one, while seeming to have such divergent properties? Thoughts and objects seem to be so different.

One lens through which the problem can be viewed is that of the relationship between God and nature. For Descartes, an immaterial God created a physical order that we call nature – an assemblage of purely material objects that interact with each other according to causal laws. Thus to approach God we have to detach ourselves from nature – nearness to God is a wholly mental phenomenon. By contrast, Spinoza denied the existence of a 'transcendent' God and equated God with nature. God, he thought, is immanent in nature. That is to say, God isn't to be identified with some special and privileged bit of nature – perhaps the wind or the sun. Instead, God should be seen as existing in the totality of nature, and to grasp God – to find God – the required approach is to grasp nature as a whole.

A further consequence of this is that it elevates and reanimates our conception of nature. On the one hand Spinoza is bringing the transcendent down to earth, but at the same time he is suggesting that nature is more than an assemblage of pure matter.

Thus Spinoza drew together his views on nature, his views of God and his ethics – his views on the meaning of life, his sense of the human condition, are intimately and explicitly linked to his account of the order of nature.

Goethe first came across the work of Spinoza as an adolescent through a highly critical, even dismissive, article in Pierre Bayle's celebrated *Historical and Critical Dictionary*, first published in 1696 and a key text of the early Enlightenment. Goethe didn't like the judgemental tone of the piece, since – really – he wanted to make up his own mind about everything. He was also struck by what he considered a paradox: he was being lectured on how misguided and confused the philosophical work of Spinoza was. But at the same time it was stated that Spinoza 'was a calmly reflective and very studious man, a good citizen, a communicative person, a quiet individual not involved in public affairs. And so the Bible verse "By their fruits ye shall know them" seemed to have been completely forgotten. For how can pernicious principles result in a life pleasing to God and men? I devoted myself to this reading and felt, as I looked into my inner self, that I had never viewed the world so clearly.'

Spinoza's refined approach to the relationship between creator and creation, which has important implications for the relationship between a writer and his writings, led to him being charged with atheism; a charge which was taken up again in the 1780s. Irritatingly for Goethe it was his friend Jacobi – with whom he was later to stay at Pempelfort in the weeks following the campaign in France – who led this attack. In fact, by the standards of Christianity, Spinoza may as well be an atheist. Technically he allows that there is a God; but he claims that this God is identical with the created world. And this is certainly not the kind of God that Christians were interested in; they wanted a personal God – a God who had a particular and individual concern with human life. There's no place for this in Spinoza, who draws the austere conclusion that if there is a God there certainly isn't much reason to believe that God loves individual people. Jacobi's book attacking Spinoza appeared in 1785 and not long afterwards Goethe assembled some notes and aphorisms seeking to convey his own interest in the philosopher. In fact the record we have of these thoughts – which were not published during Goethe's lifetime – comes in the form of some notes written out by Charlotte von Stein, although the expression and the content is very much Goethe's. He frequently relied upon secretaries to write at his dictation, and it is highly probable that these notes were dictated by him.

A big theme in the notes is holism: the theory that what we call the parts of a living being are actually inseparable from the whole – they can be understood only in and with the whole. To achieve holism we must try to connect up all the fragments of our different thoughts and draw them into a living whole, and in so doing we enrich the meaning of each individual element. 'We are aware of a huge crowd of things; the soul can grasp extraordinarily diverse links between these things. Souls that have the inner strength to open up to the world begin to organize these links, so as to think more easily; and they begin to take pleasure in putting two and two together and establishing connections between diverse elements of their world.' Here, Goethe isn't much concerned about the truth of what we believe; he's drawing attention to the need to join up different parts of our mental life – to draw together the things of which we are aware.

Goethe might have usefully published these notes under the title: 'What is thinking?' The essence of thinking is this: we are trying to give ourselves – limited and imperfect as we are – a vision of the whole of experience, indeed of the whole order of things. And such a task is necessarily impossible. We cannot possibly grasp all the relationships there are between things – the nature of life and of the universe necessarily eludes us. The soul grasps some harmonious connections between things; and this is like a seed which, if it were to fully mature, would constitute a harmony that we are incapable of understanding or perceiving. Yet certain things point us powerfully in that direction and these are the great experiences of our lives.

But Goethe goes on to confront a deep problem with this 'connectivist' vision of thinking. We strive to join up different parts of our experience and make sense of them collectively, but where and when does this process end? Within the limits of our ability and our experience we 'close the circle': if we can do this we feel sure that we have understood life – everything hangs together. Thinking of this kind brings peace and security. And in a way this must be the proper goal of thinking. After all, could we seriously assert that the goal of thinking is to make us unhappy? However, what we may fail to see is that this is an individual project: how one person 'closes the circle' is determined by the character of their experience and the quality of their mind or soul. What brings peace and security to one person may not be sufficient for another. Hence the danger is smugness and condescending pity. Such a person says: my way of thinking makes me happy, therefore you should think this way too. They seem kind; they want us to be happy. But they haven't seen that what makes them content is the particular suitability of those beliefs to them, to their own character and engagement with the world. Therefore they are offering the wrong gift. What we need isn't their way of seeing things, but our own way.

What's wrong with this person isn't that they feel comfortable and secure in their beliefs – Goethe admires that, in principle. It's rather that asserting that you are secure and comfortable doesn't help others to find their own good and satisfactory view of things.

This helps explain what Goethe was trying to do in his later autobiographical projects. He was attempting to connect up the principal experiences of his life and trace the mutual relations among them, which would allow them to add up to a coherent, and whole, life. In other words, wholeness is a product of a 'connectivist' style of attention, and, Goethe hints, crucial to happiness. This was a view shared by Proust, whose great work as a novelist is essentially an application, to his own life, of Goethe's vision of thinking.

5

Influence

The terms in which Goethe describes his relation to Spinoza are deeply revealing of his own personality. It was an imaginary relationship, of course, since Spinoza died over seventy years before Goethe was born. Goethe speaks of the happiness he felt: 'I still remember the feeling of calm and clarity that had come over me when I once had paged through the posthumous works of that remarkable man. While I could not recall individual details, the impression was still quite distinct whenever I reread those works to which I owed so much: the peaceful breeze wafted towards me once more.'

It was the effect of reading, it was the calm and clarity in himself, that Goethe enjoyed rather than the particular content of Spinoza's writings. Indeed Goethe hastens to say that he never read Spinoza carefully. As he puts it: 'I didn't want to subscribe to his writings and literally profess a faith in them,' and 'I had already very clearly recognized that no one understands anyone else.' He isn't interested in taking the ideas he finds in the work of others literally – Goethe wants to work out what the words of another suggest to him. And this, he surmises, is the only non-delusional thing to do.

It's a delusion – and a waste of one's life – to be devoted to understanding another person's ideas. This attitude is asserted and explained in Book 16 of Goethe's autobiographical account of his earlier years, *Poetry and Truth*, so it is hard not to read it as a fairly blunt message to future biographers. He is not saying: please don't write my life. What it comes to is something more interesting: obviously you can't understand my life and that's just how it is; but please do as I would do: try to make something of me, as I made something of Spinoza.

Don't 'subscribe', but try to hold on to the effect I make on you, if it is an attractive one. He is throwing out a question: can I come to live productively in your life, the way Spinoza did in mine?

There was a particular attitude to life, which he discovered as he flicked through the pages of Spinoza's *Ethics*, that deeply impressed Goethe. He saw Spinoza as a kind of hero of resignation. People like Spinoza, Goethe thought, fix their view of life quite early on. They attempt to see the core of life, to see fundamentally how life goes, and then try to live in the light of those beliefs. Spinoza thought that all efforts to make life pleasant and comfortable were, ultimately, doomed.

Goethe sums it up as follows. 'Our physical as well as social life, our manners, habits, worldly wisdom, philosophy, religion, indeed many a chance occurrence, all proclaim to us that we must *renounce*. Many an inward, very personal quality is not destined to be developed for outward use; we are deprived of what we require from without to supplement our existence; and on the other hand a great deal is thrust upon us that we find alien and burdensome. We are robbed of hard-won gains, or privileges graciously bestowed, and before we really know what is happening we find ourselves compelled to abandon our personality, at first bit by bit, and then altogether. At the same time, however, it is customary not to have regard for someone who rebels at this: instead, the bitterer the cup, the sweeter the expression one is supposed to assume, so that the tranquil spectator may not be offended by any grimace.'

The core idea, here, is that expressed in the famous opening lines of Ecclesiastes: 'Vanity of vanities, saith the Preacher, vanity of vanities! All is vanity.' Most people, Goethe thinks, come to a conclusion rather like this by the end of their lives: the things we strive for turn out to be less rewarding than we had hoped; our best efforts and ideas are without influence; 'the forts of folly' (as Matthew Arnold calls the ordinary range of common thought) never fall: if you sacrifice your life assaulting them you are not a hero, only a fool.

It is not that Goethe endorsed or believed such an extremely gloomy account of the human condition. What impressed him was the way in which Spinoza – who did believe this – faced up to it and tried to accept it. Having come to this conclusion Spinoza attempted to live his life accordingly. He didn't publish his major work during his lifetime, he worked as a lens grinder: quite a sophisticated trade, but still a trade, an occupation with no glamour or power or worldly rewards.

Goethe regards such an approach to life as heroic. Someone who seeks to go through life without illusions, without hope and without ambition is not exactly human. It is not that they are subhuman or degraded, but they are attempting, as it were, to stand above the human condition, to escape from what it is to be human. They are, as Goethe puts it, 'Übermenschliches' – 'superhuman' – a term which was to play such an enigmatic role in Nietzsche's later philosophy.

'Nature has equipped human beings with adequate strength, energy and toughness to accomplish the task of renunciation. We are aided especially by the indestructible light-mindedness that has been bestowed upon us. Thanks to this we are capable of renouncing an individual thing at any moment, so long as we can still reach for something else.' Nothing will console you so much for the loss of a lover as the start of a new affair. 'And so, unconsciously, we are always recreating our whole life. We replace one passion with another. Occupations, inclinations, favourite pursuits, whims, we try them all out only to exclaim at the last that all is vanity. No one is horrified by this false, in fact blasphemous, expression; indeed it is thought to express something wise and irrefutable. There are only a few persons who have a premonition about this intolerable feeling that life is in vain and they have avoided all these partial resignations by resigning themselves totally, once and for all.'

In thinking about Spinoza's view of life Goethe is mixing awed admiration with horror; it is true that life is vain, that it's all pointless, that we will all end up as dust, and that this is completely appalling. And yet it is also appalling to believe this, to go through life thinking this. And here, Goethe thinks, our natural weakness comes to the rescue. While we can go around saying that 'life is vain' and praising this biblical line as wise and deep, we generally are quite incapable of living as if it were true.

Think again of the passage in which Werther talks of the vanity of life and the enviable condition of children who cannot grasp this. It is thinking, he says, which messes up life. Or, more accurately: thinking alone cannot get us out of our troubles. The way we can live, Goethe now suggests, is not by being more intelligent, by seeing our condition more sharply and with fewer illusions – but rather by being 'light-minded'. We have to respect this as part of the natural order.

6

The Suffering of Light

Of all his scientific undertakings, Goethe's engagement with colour caused him the greatest trouble. It wasn't directly that his own research was particularly anxiety provoking – in fact he clearly enjoyed it a great deal and was always encouraging others to undertake the same kinds of experiments. The difficulty arose because optics was a much more highly developed branch of science than botany or physiology. It was therefore more difficult for Goethe to enter the field as an outsider and convince the existing scientific community of the value of his contributions.

This difficulty was massively compounded by the fact that Goethe came into violent disagreement with the legacy of the most revered figure of modern science: Sir Isaac Newton. Goethe's intense opposition to Newton seems – at first sight – bizarre. Why hate Newton, who seems to us in his scientific work a model of rigour, clarity, accuracy and originality?

It came about like this: Goethe had borrowed some prisms from an academic friend in Jena, but had done nothing with them. His friend's servant called to collect the pieces of glass and just when he was handing them back Goethe decided to have a quick glance at them. He'd heard about the claim that when light passes through the prism it will project the spectrum on to a white wall – like an artificial rainbow. So, Goethe held up the prism in the broad daylight and looked at the white wall – nothing – the wall was blank. Therefore Newton is wrong.

Goethe was not quite as stupid as he sounds in this anecdote. He was, in fact, acutely aware that Newton had specified very precise and restricting conditions for the appearance of the spectrum. It is only when a very narrow ray of light is directed on the prism in a darkened room, and the prism is correctly positioned in relation to the light source and the wall that the phenomenon can be observed. The whole point of the experiment is to control the circumstances under which the phenomenon is produced. Goethe did not overlook this difference – between the special circumstances of Newton's experiments and his own broad daylight efforts. In fact he was to make this central to his position.

Goethe went on to produce his own very detailed and elaborate account of colour, published in 1810, when he was in his early sixties, as *Towards a Doctrine of Colours*. Apart from the careful detailing of visual experience, the book contains a good deal of bitter – and rather crude – abuse of Newton and his followers. Right at the start, in the Preface, Goethe attempts to explain the character of his battle with Newton.

'In reality, any attempt to express the inner nature of a thing is fruitless. What we perceive are effects, and a complete record of these effects ought to encompass this inner nature. We labour in vain to describe a person's character but when we draw together all his actions, his deeds, a picture of his character will emerge.'

Clearly, Goethe is on to something here, but unfortunately it doesn't really capture what is at stake in the dispute about the nature of light. Goethe is suspicious of the move from perceived effects to an understanding of the 'secret character' of a thing. What, we might ask, explains how light can produce so many diverse visual effects? The best answer – for a very long time – was that provided by Newton. Equally, the best explanation of the perceptual properties of gold lies in statements about its atomic structure. The whole point about Newton's experiment with the prism – the whole point of setting up an unusual situation – was to produce an extremely unusual phenomenon which would lead one to a better understanding of the secret inner nature of light: namely, that it can be separated into different colours. And this can be shown to be consistent with – and have explanatory power in relation to – many other diverse phenomena. And, clearly, that is not a misguided project.

However, Goethe could have put the issue another way which would have more clearly revealed what he was up to. He wanted to understand our experience of light, and to be able to set forth the major characteristics of that experience. With such a project in view, it is obviously important to concentrate on common experience, rather than experience under special circumstances. The less usual the phenomenon, the less important it is. Since we almost never experience a narrow beam of light striking a prism in a darkened room, this simply isn't an important feature of light as we interact with it.

Consider a parallel case. Suppose we wanted to understand the experience of love. We might be able to devise extremely unusual and restricted circumstances in which special phenomena would appear: we might see what happens if a pair of lovers is kept isolated from each other, and everyone else, and allowed to communicate only by Morse code. Will their love become more intense, or will it fade? Everyone would admit that however intriguing such a scenario might be as the plot of a novel (Stendhal would certainly be the person to write it) the 'results' of the experiment wouldn't really tell us anything important about love. For what we want to know isn't what happens to love under unusual circumstances. Instead we want to know about what happens to lovers in ordinary circumstances – when they move in together or get married, that sort of thing.

Following Goethe's 'describing a person's character' analogy, we could dream up very odd situations and trace an individual's behaviour in those predicaments, but it is precisely the oddness of the situation that reduces its significance. In the realm of experience experiments are indeed misleading. And so it should have been obvious to Goethe that what he really wanted to know about – and indeed what he studied – was the human experience of light. In respect of that, the spectrum experiments really are not all that significant, whereas gazing at the sky on a clear day, or the moving effects of the blue haze over distant hills, clearly do matter.

In fact, the two projects – Newton's and Goethe's – are intimately compatible. In principle, there is nothing about the study of the secret nature of light, the study of its intimate structure as waves or corpuscles, which in any way prejudices the careful observation of normal experiences: the sensitive study of visual effects as we encounter them. And this is what makes Goethe's attacks on Newton sound so strange, since it's not really as if Newton's approach is in opposition to Goethe's. So Goethe can at times sound like someone studying the social prestige of gold – why this substance has played such a powerful role in human history – getting immensely worked up about the fact that natural scientists have also discovered quite a lot about the inner nature of this metal.

When Goethe claims that we cannot get behind the veil of appearances to study the secret nature of things, he sounds as if he is giving a moral warning. It is a shame he didn't explore this idea and elaborate on the dangers of such inquiries. For the world-view of the natural sciences is one that cannot privilege human experience or human life. Ultimately the universe really is constituted by the play of impersonal forces – or 'atoms and the void', as it was once expressed. And this is a universe in which human beings have no home; the fundamental organization of things is alien to us. Moreover it is a way of thinking that we cannot possibly import into daily life – we cannot experience ourselves or others or our own lives in such terms (except, perhaps, at the lowest moments of depression and despair). There is, in such a case, a gulf between two worlds: the world as the natural sciences describe it, and the world as we experience it.

But this fascinating tragedy goes sadly unremarked by Goethe, whose only concern is to prove Newton wrong, rather than exploring the idea that certain kinds of knowledge might be dangerous.

7

Storming the Bastille

One outstanding problem Goethe identifies is the dependence we come to have on 'theory' – and here he might well be talking not about science but about literature or political history or moral philosophy. When we get excited too quickly, too early, by a theory it stops being merely that – a provisional attempt to codify and explain experience. Instead it becomes a substitute for – and ultimately a bar to – experience. So that someone in the grip of a theory cannot really recognize what is before their eyes.

This isn't ultimately to say that there is no place for theory – and, in any case, Goethe has plenty of theories of his own. The distinction he is trying to draw – and it is a highly pertinent one – is to do with the stage at which you apply the theory, and what role it plays in your experience. Anyone who has taught theoretically minded undergraduates will be well aware of the degree to which devotion to a theory can blind a student to an actual case in hand. Evidence is no longer considered with an open mind – but only in so far as it supports the intellectual basis of the theory; and any apparent counter-instance can, by ingenious manoeuvres, be forced to fit the original thesis.

So even if Goethe turned out to be mistaken about certain features of Newton's scientific project, he did identify a very large issue within academic culture, although it is one which plays a bigger role in social, moral, historical and political thought than it does in the natural sciences. And now the basis of Goethe's charge comes through. Such a person loves the theory more than the phenomenon, and, as he puts it, this is a moral problem – it is a problem to do with the character, the life, of the person. And we can understand the degree of their attachment to the theory only by understanding them.

However, Goethe did not really put his finger on the issue in quite this way. He wanted to believe that he was in fact doing the same science as the Newtonians, only doing it better. But as can be seen from the reference to 'inner nature', Goethe certainly wasn't doing the same science as Newton. His whole conception of the enterprise was different. This was doubly unfortunate because it meant that Goethe's most interesting question – 'Why is it good to know that?' – tends to fall into the background in his work.

Goethe described his attack on Newton as an attempt to 'storm the Bastille'. He thought of Newton's followers as imprisoned in a crumbling castle, energetically insisting that everyone else must come and join them inside. Goethe was immensely disappointed when his scientific work did not receive very much recognition from others working in the same fields. His literary works were not always enthusiastically greeted by the reading public: *Iphigenia*, for example, was generally regarded as rather dull. But this did not distress Goethe too much because he had had overwhelming recognition for *Werther* and some of his later works – the first part of his autobiography and *Faust* (Part One) – were very successful. Goethe could cope with periods of relative indifference on the literary front because that was his doing; he knew that some works would not be very popular: he was not seeking, but failing, to win an audience.

For his scientific works, however, Goethe had a very particular audience in mind: what he called 'the guild' – the prisoners in the Bastille – the university-based professional scientists: by this audience Goethe was regarded with a mixture of scepticism and polite embarrassment. His immense cultural prestige counted for nothing. Goethe found this extremely difficult to cope with.

Goethe hoped that the pursuit of science would make us more perceptive of the world around us. This goes a long way to explaining his hatred of Newton, who focused on the inner nature at the expense, as

Goethe saw it, of the outer. It also explains his admiration for the English scientist Luke Howard, who studied clouds, and in 1803 categorized them and gave them their present names. His work, which was very well known to Goethe, represented Goethe's ideal of scientific activity.

Howard classified clouds according to their visual characteristics. His terms, such as 'cirrus' and 'stratus', are applied on the basis of visual experience – how high the cloud is; what density and texture it has. It doesn't seek to differentiate clouds on the basis of some 'hidden' or 'secret' characteristic that is veiled from our eyes. In learning and deploying Howard's terms, we become better observers of the sky; we become more aware of the character and quality of individual clouds. Our visual engagement is finer, more stable and more acute than it would otherwise have been.

And from these observations we can also improve our understanding of the workings of the world: certain types of cloud are more likely to bring rain; others might show that there will be rain tomorrow, but not today. So we can extend the scope of our observations, refining our grasp of the connections between things. Here, the work of a scientist has made visual experience richer and more useful.

8

Yellow and Blue

Goethe's own account of colour has at its core two of the most central visual experiences: sunlight, which usually looks yellow; and the appearance of the clear blue sky. Why do they have the colours they do?

'The most energetic light is blinding and colourless like pure sunlight.' But pure sunlight lies at the limit of visual experience since, precisely, we are unable to look directly at it. However, when viewed through a medium that is slightly 'turbid' – it looks yellow. By 'turbid', Goethe means that it has minute particles in it – like water droplets or dust. And as this haze gets thicker, sunlight passing through it deepens in colour, until we reach the red of sunset. Thus Goethe understands colour as the effect of light 'seen through darkness'.

'On the other hand, darkness viewed through a cloudy medium filled with light will appear a blue colour, which grows lighter or paler as the medium becomes more turbid, but darker and deeper blue as the medium becomes more transparent. With the minimal degree of the most rarefied turbidity this colour will appear to the eye a beautiful violet.' This explains why the sky looks blue in the daytime: 'The darkness of infinite space viewed through atmospheric particles illuminated by sunlight will produce blue.'

Thus blue stands together with yellow as the most basic of colours. One thing Goethe likes about this explanation is its link to variation in the colour of the sky. Why is it that the sky appears a different colour when seen from the top of a mountain than it does when viewed from down in the valley? 'On high mountains the heavens are seen as royal blue because only a few thin layers of brightly illuminated haze float before the dark infinity of space. When we descend to the valleys, this blue will become lighter until in certain regions, and with increasing haze, it finally changes completely to a whitish blue.' So here, Goethe is doing science out in the open, and trying – with his explanations – to help us look more attentively at the sky, to see it not as mysterious but as explicable. As Goethe is keenly aware sunlight and the sky are among the most resonant and emotive natural aspects for us. The core of his account, then, starts with the very things – precisely the colour experiences – that are most meaningful to us. Rather than trying to produce a highly unusual situation in a laboratory, Goethe wants to work from our most common colour experiences and make these the centre of his account.

He then turns his attention indoors and thinks about the second major encounter we have with light – flame. 'If we hold the flame against a white background, we will find no trace of blue. But the colour will appear immediately when we hold the flame against a dark background.'

His book on colour includes many accounts of phenomena that the sensitive reader can personally observe, and he often gives a personal narrative of the experience. For example, one evening, on 19 June 1799, Goethe was walking round his garden with his good friend Meyer – the painter and art historian who had rooms in the large Frauenplan house. It was twilight and there was not a cloud in the sky. 'We distinctly saw something flamelike appear close to some oriental poppies, a flower redder than any other. We stood in front of the plants and observed them closely but were unable to see anything more; at last we succeeded in repeating the effect at will by walking to and fro while looking at them sideways.' Goethe thought that the flamelike effect was produced by the particularly strong 'after effect' of the bright red flower. Glancing at it and away and back again produced a rapid transition between the red and its after-image (which was a bluish green), and this alteration was experienced as being like the movement of a flame.

This leads into much more discussion of after-images – Goethe wants us to stare at a red patch on the wall for a few minutes then close our eyes and observe the colour which seems to swim before us in the darkness. How does it compare with the colour we were looking at before? How long does the after-image last? Does it last longer if you practise? Goethe was keen to make the reader a participant in his experience, rather than just the recipient of abstract information or technical understanding.

We cannot control what colour the after-image will be – so he calls it the 'required' counterpart to the original colour that stimulated the response. So this provides one model of colour harmony – an explanation of why certain colours look well together. The Werther costume of blue and yellow looks so good because yellow requires blue and blue requires yellow.

Such knowledge might prove useful to painters. If you stare intently at a scarlet bodice (Goethe's example) and then look away at a dimly lit wall (the wall of an inn parlour at twilight – the sort of place Goethe collected his data) then you will see a lovely patch of sea-green. Thus, he says, the eye calls forth sea-green in response to scarlet. Imagine you are painting the portrait of a woman wearing just such a scarlet bodice and you are wondering what colour you should make a curtain that you intend to drape in the background. Goethe has supplied the answer. Sea-green might be a good choice because this will seem subconsciously to the beholder to be the 'required' foil for the bodice and so the picture will appear whole and natural.

This discussion of colour originates in our natural experience of sunlight and the sky. But the home of colour is art. And, as the bodice example shows, Goethe is always keen to connect up his understanding of colour with guidance for practising artists. Again we see the contrast with Newton. Newton, we might say, merely wanted to know the truth about colour. Goethe wants to know how we can use colour to best effect.

His discussion of the perception of dark marks against a lighter background culminates in a point about chiaroscuro – the balance of light and dark in a painting: Rembrandt is an outstanding exponent. There had been many intense discussions about how artists should carry this out in practice. Goethe's view is that a careful examination of the way the eye works can give artists useful guidance in these matters. At the simplest level he notes – as artists had of course long been aware – that a dark background makes lighter tones stand out more strongly; hence they appear lighter than they would in other visual contexts; and the same is true in reverse. These are little practical hints that help us understand visual effects achieved in the art of pictures.

Goethe came up with some ideas that were only much later exploited by painters. He writes at length about coloured shadows – the standard idea had been that shadows are, essentially, a grey overlay (simply a dimming). Therefore the shadow itself is essentially colourless. Goethe noted that there are many cases in which the shadow itself carries a tint (which then interacts with the 'physical' colour of whatever it happens to fall upon).

This is worth pointing out because it has been a long-standing misconception that it was only when the Impressionists came along that people – guided by the painters' close observation of natural effects – first noticed this phenomenon. But Goethe had documented it and provided guidance on how to set up intense phenomena of this kind in the early years of the nineteenth century.

At every turn Goethe is trying to teach us, not so much about an abstract theory of colour, but about how to be more perceptive – how to be more receptive to the colour effects which are all around us all the time. His preferred method of doing this is to note an unusual natural instance, then to set up a special situation (a kind of 'home experiment' – most of which really can be done at home). In the special instance we see more intently what we were first alerted to in ordinary experience. We then return to 'normal perception' with a more alert eye – and with a clear sense of how to relate that phenomenon to others. It is not only our intellects that are educated but our eyes – and our curiosity.

9

Ur-Experience

Goethe tried to register the centrality and importance of certain experiences by giving them a special name. Our primary experiences of colour – as he argues – are of the blue sky and brilliant yellow sunlight. And he labels these with the striking technical name: 'Ur-phenomena'.

The prefix 'ur', meaning 'original' or 'primary', is like the name of what was believed to be the world's first city – the town of Ur, located on the banks of the Euphrates and going back to somewhere around 3500 BC.

Goethe is not saying that blue and yellow are our first colour experiences, but rather that they come first in an explanatory sequence. If you want to understand colour, it is to the phenomena of sunlight and the sky – and the colours yellow and blue – that we must turn. In grasping these we grasp the cardinal points by which many other things can be explained.

The task of science, Goethe believes is to direct us to the most lucid and central experiences – the Ur-experiences. When we see these clearly we are on solid ground and we can extend our understanding to more complex and more obscure cases.

But the point of calling sunlight and sky Ur-phenomena is also to mark a boundary. Goethe hopes that we will not want to cross that boundary and pursue the question: what is sunlight made of? The reason is this: with the Ur-phenomena we have reached a point of simplicity and ease. To pursue inquiry further is to disturb that simplicity and start making things complicated once more.

This general point holds not only for science but also for life. If we have reached a point where things seem clear and simple, that might be a very good place to rest. There is an image of insanity in which the mad person will not rest content with simple explanations. How do I know there is a desk in front of me? Well, I can see it. But how do I know that I'm not having an hallucination, or dreaming, or being manipulated by demons or evil scientists? If those questions were raised not as languid, undergraduate games but in full earnestness, with an urgent need to find answers, the questioner would be destined for psychiatric treatment or a professorship in philosophy. For we cannot give ourselves usable answers to those questions, although we can become immensely sophisticated in pursuing solutions to them.

Wittgenstein, who studied Goethe's work on colour very carefully, suggested that the proper ambition of philosophy is 'to let the fly out of the fly bottle': to allow us to stop worrying about questions to which we cannot provide good answers. This liberatory ambition is at stake in Goethe's idea of the Ur-phenomenon. It is his attempt to mark out the limit of intellectual sanity and, as it were, the neck of the bottle. We can ask for further explanations; but the answers we get will be like the frantic efforts of trapped flies.

In a sense Newton is, in Goethe's view, the Werther character in the novel of the universe. Of course, in some sense it might be possible to penetrate the inner nature of things – just as it is possible for Werther to dwell endlessly on the real meaning of his life. It is only in connection with psychology that we can make sense of the request that we leave Ur-Phenomena undisturbed. It goes without saying that we can inquire further even about such things. The Werther analogy, however, reminds us that certain strategies of inquiry are destructive – even though the questions are intellectually legitimate.

Later, somewhere around 1816, Goethe drew the notion of Ur-phenomenon that he developed in connection with science into the larger web of lived experience. He sought to identify, within the pattern of an individual life, similarly basic ideas or experiences. And he called the words that named those experiences 'Ur-words'.

In a poem called 'Ur-words' he identifies five terms that he thinks structure human experience – and are fundamental in revealing the human condition. They are – in one sense – very simple: we really do grasp what it is they name; but in another, when we ask what they 'really' are, we end up baffled and find no aid to living our lives.

DAEMON: This Greek word, for the 'intermediaries between gods and men', picks up on the way we experience ourselves. It is Goethe's broad term for the spiritual dimension of life. Irrespective of what we may believe about our material condition (that we are just flesh and bones) we cannot help experiencing a sacred or transcendent aspect to life.

CHANCE: Things happen in life which are unaccountable. We cannot escape being haunted by the possibility that 'things could have been otherwise'. Chance is the flip side of calculation, prudence, planning and foresight.

LOVE: This is the clearest and most complete form of attachment.

NECESSITY: When we consider our lives as a whole we are often struck by the inevitability of the great structures of existence. Everyone we love will die. All that we have worked for will sooner or later be forgotten.

HOPE: Hope concerns our orientation towards time, it is the condition of projecting our ideas forward with the sense that we may get what we long for. Goethe's point isn't that this is somehow justified, or reasonable (or even unreasonable). It is just an unavoidable aspect of what it is to live. To give up on hope is to die, even if one's body keeps on going. We don't hope because it is reasonable to do so, although we do try to adjust what we hope for to what it is reasonable to expect. Whether someone has a hopeful disposition or not isn't usually connected to how rational they are, but reflects something quite fundamental – and private – about the kind of person they are.

It is of decisive importance that these terms do not cohere neatly with each other. There is an obvious tension between seeing the centrality of chance in one's life and seeing the centrality of necessity. The implication is that the human condition cannot be presented in a completely neat and coherent way – it exists in the tense spaces in which we are fundamentally committed to these divergent perspectives. We not only can, but also need to, see and live our lives within these incompatible perspectives.

10

Science and the Meaning of Life

When we think about the meaning of life – and particularly the meaning of our own lives – we have the sense of approaching something profound and, at the same time, of not being sure what we are asking. Hence, asking about 'the meaning of life' sounds like both the biggest kind of question and also the most stupid, most meaningless, kind of question.

The reason is that the question itself – posed in terms of meaning – is too compacted: it doesn't help us see what it is we want to know or understand or think about. It is, in fact, several loosely related questions squashed into one.

Aristotle thought that when we want to understand anything, there are basically four questions we need to ask:

(a) What is it made of?
(b) How is it structured?
(c) How does it work? (How do I use it?)
(d) What is it for? (What does it aim at?)

We can see how this would work in relation to a banal object – like a kettle:

(a) It's made of metal.
(b) It's got a curved, hollow main part, with a little protrusion at the top of this (the protrusion is round and has a large hole in it; it is fitted with a cap).
(c) You fill it with water – not too much – plug it in, and press the red

switch at the base; wait for about three minutes and then lift it, tilting it so that the base rises while the protruding bit goes down a little – the water should come out.

(d) It's for heating up water – however, you will really only understand what a kettle is for if you understand what we use hot water for. The 'meaning of a kettle' is 'transcendent' in the sense that it lies beyond itself. We don't admire kettles or hot water for their own sake – however, hot water plays an important role in our strategies of hydration, which are interestingly interwoven with social rituals.

We can – and should – ask these questions about life (most importantly our own life) and one of the main things that serious authors offer us is their responses to these questions, together with their sense of the evidence which leads them to reply as they do.

Our answers to these questions add up to a view of the meaning of life.

(a) The material question: what kind of thing are we – an immortal soul trapped in a perishable body? An ape with extra neurones?

(b) The structural question: what is the structure of life? Does a life have a meaningful structure? Freud thought it did: adulthood is the after-effect and fallout of childhood trauma.

(c) The 'use' question: how should we act – what should we do? Can we change ourselves, or are we stuck as we are? Do we need to be plugged in; what do we need to operate properly? Some people think that we need to renounce worldly goods, others that we need to acquire as many as possible as quickly as we can.

(d) The final question: what are we trying to achieve (what do we want from life)? What makes us happy? What is life for? Is there some purpose bigger than ourselves?

We can plot in outline the philosophy of life of various writers and thinkers according to how they answer such questions – 'the meaning of life' questionnaire that, ideally, one would send out to the people one is most impressed by. My list: Jane Austen, Henry James, Proust, Tolstoy, Goethe.

We can sketch Goethe's answers:

(a) Human nature is continuous with animal nature – we are animals; and our later answers must always bear this in mind. However, unlike other animals, we also think: we seek satisfaction in ideas and relationships as well as in sensations.

(b) The structure of life is given by the trajectory of growth and decay – just as in the case of a flowering plant. Like plants we have many external needs and face many external dangers – if the soil isn't rich enough we won't yield good fruit, although we might have done had we been planted elsewhere.

(c) The use we make of life is, essentially, to learn from experience. This is not by any means just a matter of intellectual learning. It couldn't be – since we are not exclusively intellectual creatures. We don't control our environment and need to adapt to it – while not abandoning our individuality. It is a waste of one's life to fight only battles one is likely to lose. We should take material possessions seriously – since we need them to make life physically comfortable and efficient; therefore – so far as this is reasonable – we need to adapt ourselves to 'get on' in the world as it happens to be. But we should 'get on' only as far as is required to live a comfortable and productive life.

(d) The purpose of life is to be happy: this means being fully ourselves. The core problem is that 'being fully ourselves' isn't a matter of doing whatever we happen to like. It lies, rather, in fully developing the capacities we have – which must be physical as well as mental. However, this generally requires quite a lot of self-control and courage. Self-control because development may be slow and painful, or (due to social pressure) we may have a false vision of who we are. Courage, because 'being oneself' may require us to give up certain bits of social prestige or to confront the ideas others have of who we should be. Hence Goethe is at odds with both conformism and eccentricity. Conformism is the desire to be like other people, just because we want to fit in. Eccentricity is the condition of wanting to be different from other people, because one fears being like others. What's wrong in each case is that the focus is on other people. Being oneself is an independent project.

The striking thing about Goethe's view of life is how sane and normal it is. Like most people before and since Goethe takes an undramatic view of life. It really is important to have a decent house; having relationships which are stable and loving and comfortable is a key aspect of happiness; having an interesting career is important too – although he's fully alive to the sacrifices to drudgery this often entails. Where possible you should focus on the things that keep you cheerful – intelligent people are prone to thinking themselves into despair or misery. It's important to eat well, keep regular hours; don't spend more than your income. Take lots of exercise; spend plenty of time in your garden. Dress appropriately in public – but in private concentrate on comfort.

In a way this is scandalous: surely the writer of *The Sorrows of Young Werther*, the 'central point of European culture' (as Milan Kundera calls Goethe), must have a mystifying, strange – even incomprehensible – account of life? Surely he must want to tell us that life is awful, that our daily life is a sham, that we are wicked or shallow? We think this because we've come to assume that the task of really serious writing is to tell us how bad things are – a task which the newspapers aren't quite up to. Goethe takes it for granted that many terrible things happen. His aim isn't to force us to see that; rather, it is to see how we might live well given the circumstances.

Basically, Goethe's work involves fitting the largest themes of human culture into this sane and workable vision. We can see the centrality of Goethe for our time by observing the battles he fought in pursuit of this project. On the one hand, Goethe was resistant – although with some underlying sympathy – to Romanticism. He saw Romanticism as rightly seeking to endow life with a degree of grandeur and nobility. It recognizes the lofty and ideal longings that we have; we want searing love, intense loyalties; we want to escape from banality and constraint; we want life to have an air of mystery and drama. His problem with this is that such a view of life isn't viable: it's a flight. It recognizes our spiritual dignity but is uncompromising – and therefore you can't sustain it. It leaves the meaning of life – all the things that give life value – in opposition to the basic condition of existence. Hence the valorization of suicide and despair: the contraries of normal ambition. How are you going to buy a house, have a stable domestic life, run the economy?

On the other hand, Goethe is the enemy of the philistines who see life merely in terms of the house, the economy, social status, what you can leave to your children. These concerns aren't silly – indeed they are completely sensible. What they miss is any conception of growth or development – any higher view of what these material goods are for.

Goethe thus occupies a position whose time has never come, but whose time is always. Idealists, progressivists and socialists have never liked Goethe's acknowledgement of the conservative, material basis of happiness – which the majority of people have always taken seriously. But Goethe is, at the same time, intensely rich in his awareness of the complexities of the human heart ('What is the heart of man?' is a question he keeps on asking himself) – our desperate longing for love, our folly and confusion, our sexual depths, our craving to make sense of life. Thus he is unsettling to complacent, conventional or reactionary readers.

What Goethe achieved in his life – even more than in his literary and intellectual work – is the closest we have yet seen to a solution to the problem of modern life. The question can be posed in various ways – one is 'How do you combine art and sanity?' Another: 'Can you be both comfortable and high-minded?' Or, to put it in its oldest form: 'How can our spiritual and material needs be allies rather than enemies?'

PART EIGHT

Peace

I

You come to me from above
And quieten both my ecstasy and anguish:
Distress is twofold; you heal both kinds.
I'm sick of my impulsive drives:
Am I always going to swing
From the desperate pursuit of pleasure
To wretched misery?
Mild, gentle peace,
Come, please come, into my heart.

II

It looks so peaceful
Over there on the hills
And here, even in the tree-tops, it is perfectly still;
The woodland birds are quiet now.
If only you stay here a while
You will find stillness and peace as well.

Goethe, Two Night Songs, 1776 and 1780

I

Germaine de Staël

After 1793 and the relief of Mainz tension between the Germanic territories and France lessened for a while. Prussia and other northern states took the reasonable view that, for them, restoration of the Bourbon monarchy in France was not a high priority. In 1795 they agreed to a treaty of neutrality with France. This set Prussia at odds with the Hapsburgs in Vienna, who were still extremely hostile to the Revolution. This diplomatic fissure was to undo the Holy Roman Empire, which having survived for eight centuries was now entering its final decade.

These developments were being played out during the years of Goethe's friendship with Schiller but their correspondence barely touches on the great dramatic theme of the era – the rise of Napoleon. Napoleon became First Consul, the leader of the French Republic, at the end of 1799 – three weeks after Schiller finally moved to Weimar and came into much more regular personal contact with Goethe. In 1800 Napoleon led his troops over the St Bernard Pass and into the north Italian state of Piedmont, inspiring the wonderful equestrian portrait by Jacques-Louis David – and menacing Austrian interests in Italy.

One person who was not at all inspired by Napoleon was Germaine de Staël. Germaine was one of the most arresting characters of the era: fabulously rich, sexually voracious, highly intellectual and an accomplished essayist and novelist; she was also a devoted tormentor of Napoleon. In 1804 Madame de Staël made a tour of the German states, gathering material for a book about the country and hoping to spread her hatred of Napoleon. She was among the first to proclaim Goethe's importance to the wider world. She placed him on a par with Rousseau – who was probably the most influential European writer of the preceding half-century.

When it appeared in 1810 her three-volume work, *On Germany*, was described to Napoleon as unobjectionable; there was nothing hostile in it: in fact nothing about him at all. 'A three-volume work in which I am not mentioned,' Napoleon is reported to have said, 'is to be banned immediately.'

While she was actually in Weimar in January 1804 Germaine did not receive much encouragement from Goethe. He was not indifferent to her; in fact he admired and even translated an essay she had written on the nature of fiction. Perhaps he was spurred on in this endeavour by the praise of *Werther* it contains – concluding that this is the best book ever written in German.

However much he may have liked her attitude to his work, Goethe was not sympathetic to her view of Napoleon. He saw Napoleon as guided by a grand ambition: the ending of hostility between nations by the instigation of rational government. Goethe – like Napoleon – assumed that conflict between nations, and conflict within nations, was the consequence of foolish authority. Well-governed nations would be unlikely to go to war with one another.

Germaine de Staël's intense dislike of Napoleon would not be welcome in Goethe's house. Besides, she was a great talker – she was endlessly curious and demanding, she consumed people; she got on well with Schiller, who was diplomatic and able to hold in check any need to dominate discussion himself. Goethe was more easily bored, or less adept at hiding it.

Goethe did his best to avoid Germaine but, eventually, allowed her a little of his time. 'If,' as she bravely puts it, 'if Goethe can be made to talk he is admirable' – 'he is incredibly witty', although she stresses the 'drawbacks of his character: bad temper, awkwardness, constraint', meaning, in part, he did not receive me with open arms as I deserved. She did not notice the force of her own demands: Goethe didn't particularly want to be made to talk, like a superior parrot. In his conversation, Germaine says, Goethe was rather like Diderot –

drawing the most flattering comparison; the advantage that Goethe has, however, is that he does not write the way he speaks. Diderot 'is a slave to his wit': he cannot resist being charming.

The problem with Germaine's analysis was that she tended to see writers as expressive of national characteristics – this was rather appealing to some German readers, since in their minds Germany was far from being a nation; to have a distinctive national character seemed exciting. In her own efforts she fed the nascent German ideas of a specific and privileged national identity: one which was at odds with the spirit of France and which had something crucial to offer the modern world. Polemically stated, Germany was the corrective of France: the French were obsessed with superficial wit and wanted to appear knowing – which they demonstrated by being indifferent or cynical; French vanity led to mockery – since to mock is to present yourself as superior to that which you ridicule. By contrast, the Germans (Germaine argued) displayed seriousness, sincerity and depth: Goethe was a chief representative of this national spirit. The Germans are passionate about ideas; Napoleon and modern France are obsessed by action.

This view of German culture – and of Goethe's position as the centre of that culture – was seductive and influential. In its broad outline it was still being invoked in the early twentieth century even by such a sophisticated thinker as Thomas Mann. In 1918 Mann wrote a tortured essay in which he presents the German soul as the necessary point of resistance to France and 'the Roman West'.

Whatever else it might be, this is not a statement of Goethe's position. The fact is that Goethe was decidedly cosmopolitan in outlook. He lived, for the greater part of his life, in the small town of Weimar – and for the rest of it in other small towns. He was loyal to Weimar but not in a blind, partisan way. He didn't think that Weimar was the best place in the world, just the place where he could live best, mainly because it was the place where he could make most money, have most power and most control over the conditions of his existence.

Goethe had returned from Italy to Weimar in the spirit of a man making the best of things in an imperfect world – not in the guise of one returning to his true home. His ideals had nothing particularly to do with Germany; his favourite architect was Palladio, his favourite authors were the classical poets. He was interested in Spanish and English writing, and deeply indebted – as we shall see – to Islamic poetry; his interests in botany, geology and the rest were without national focus; he agreed or disagreed with particular thinkers (he hated Newton, admired Spinoza) but without there being a national rationale for these attitudes. He was deeply impressed by Benjamin Franklin and always had an enthusiastic, hopeful attitude towards the new United States.

The identification of Goethe with the German soul, an identification that Germaine de Staël encouraged, was to have unfortunate consequences for Goethe's reputation in the twentieth century. If people know only one thing about Goethe it's always that his works were read by Nazi guards in the death camps. And the horrible conclusion is assumed to follow – that there was something in Goethe's work that fitted it to such an audience. If Goethe was the German spirit, and if the German spirit was – in its most perverse aspect – enacted in the camps, then Goethe is complicit.

This view of Goethe seeks support in occasional remarks that can be found in his writing. For example, Faust ends up directing the development of wasteland: barren areas are to be populated and made productive. Is this to encourage and endorse the Lebensraum policy of the Third Reich? Not really: Goethe was probably thinking of the Dutch polders or the draining of the Pontine Marshes near Rome.

A more sophisticated criticism admits that Goethe absolutely did not encourage people to be nationalist zealots. The problem isn't Faust and his property development schemes but the lyrical poetry. People might spend their time rhapsodizing over such gentle lines as 'It looks so peaceful/Over there on the hills . . .' and absorbing its hazy love of tranquillity. You can cocoon yourself in such comfortable sentiments while the ethical fabric of the world is being ripped apart. Perhaps if Goethe hadn't scribbled those lines but had written something like: ignore anyone preaching a doctrine of Strength and Joy and please, please don't believe all that nonsense about being a master race –

things would have been better. But this is a misplaced objection. For it comes to the view that no writer has any business with emotions other than those of eagle-eyed political wariness. But if writers stuck to that forlorn repertoire they would certainly never gain a broad hearing and their warnings would be ineffectual.

The facts about the guards do not tell us anything about Goethe; where does the fascination come from? The anecdote offers to humble the proud: you like *Faust*, you admire Goethe, I don't condemn you but I'm not going to admire you either; let me remind you: some of the worst people have felt as you do. (And one might be saying this to oneself.) Here, the greatest imagined danger is the pride of the admirer of Goethe. The fact is no writer can prevent horrible people from reading his work, or admiring it for their own misplaced reasons.

2

The Battle of Jena

Not long after Germaine had swept through Weimar a French plot aiming to overthrow Napoleon and restore the monarchy was discovered and averted. Blame for the attempted coup was directed – incorrectly – at the young Duc d'Enghien, a member of the deposed royal family. On Napoleon's orders d'Enghien was seized from Baden – a small state on the German side of the Rhine – and executed. At the high-society party that opens *War and Peace* (1863–9), Tolstoy has one of his characters speculate on Napoleon's motive for the state assassination of d'Enghien. The duke had gone secretly to Paris for a rendezvous with a famous actress; and while with her encountered Napoleon, another of her lovers. Napoleon is supposed to have fainted at the sight of this rival – who might have taken the opportunity to assassinate him, but did not. Humiliated by the magnanimity of his enemy, Napoleon was thereafter determined to eliminate the young duke.

The execution of d'Enghien roused the fears and indignations of other governments: a secret alliance was formed between Britain, Russia and Austria dedicated to containing Napoleon. Napoleon raised a large army for a projected invasion of Britain; but then changed direction and ordered his troops to deal with Austria first. In October 1805 the Austrian forces under General Mack were surrounded and captured at Ulm; Napoleon entered Vienna; the allies did not yield and a large combined Russian and Austrian force assembled at Austerlitz only to be 'Macked' in their turn, as an elegant Russian diplomat puts it in *War and Peace*.

Napoleon now exercised his overwhelming authority to reorganize the western parts of Germany into the Confederation of the Rhine. This grand attitude was deeply threatening to Prussia, whose position as the leading German state and the supposed beneficiary of Austrian weakness was being dramatically disregarded. Despite her large army, in which the Duke of Weimar was now serving as a colonel, Prussia could not possibly face France alone; but in September 1806 Napoleon learned that Russia was now allied with Prussia – although technically Prussia was still bound by a treaty of neutrality towards France. Napoleon's response was ferocious; he advanced his large army rapidly towards Berlin encountering half the Prussian forces at Jena on 14 October and defeating them decisively. Simultaneously the other part of the Prussian army attempted to retreat to the north but was met at Auerstädt by French troops under Davout, who won a remarkable victory. The Prussians fled through Weimar pursued by the French.

For a few anxious hours Goethe's house was prey to marauding troops – although stoutly defended by Christiane. Eventually, the house was occupied by one of Napoleon's generals and Goethe's personal safety was secured. Napoleon installed himself in Carl August's palace and set about berating the duchess for her husband's traitorous behaviour.

In the immediate aftermath of the battle, Goethe decided to marry Christiane. Perhaps he was touched by her loyalty; perhaps he wanted to give her the security of a legal tie; perhaps he wanted a less awkward social position for his son. The marriage was conducted privately, but the fact of it changed Christiane's position in Weimar. She might not be liked, and she certainly wasn't respected by Weimar society; but the excuse for ignoring her – that Goethe treated her as a creature with no life beyond the back part of his house – had disappeared. The first person to invite her to a party was Joanna Schopenhauer – mother of the philosopher Arthur and a great supporter of Goethe. 'If Goethe has given her his name, the least I can do is give her a cup of tea.'

When his friends were sitting around lamenting the disasters of war, Goethe struck an odd note. His calm demeanour had attracted attention – how could he feel calm at a time like this? He tried to explain himself: 'I've nothing to complain about. Something like a man who, from a high cliff, looks down to the raging sea, not being able to offer any help to those shipwrecked below but is also himself safe from the pounding surf – and according to some ancient authority that is supposed to be a consoling feeling.'

One thought which is operative here – and which is being used to draw some comfort from the difficult situation – goes like this: we wouldn't normally feel all that pleased about the mere fact of sitting on a bit of stone. We would not appreciate how fortunate we were until the sight of the suffering of others makes this obvious: they would give anything to be out of the raging sea and sitting on a stone. The comment is not quite as callous or cold-blooded as it might at first appear. The idea isn't that we should be glad that others are suffering while we are safe; rather, that recognition of their suffering helps us appreciate our own security. To sit shivering on a cliff in the teeth of a gale would – on first thought – seem highly unattractive. But we need to hold on to the very major goods that we have: being alive, on solid ground. And while those can – in principle – be grasped and valued independently, it may take the shock of seeing how badly off others are to get us to see how fortunate we are.

It's not that Goethe was glad that Weimar had been occupied by the French or was pleased that the Prussians had been defeated at Jena and Auerstädt. He was simply attempting to use those horrors to make himself see that things he had taken for granted – the presence and loyalty of Christiane, the security of his home, being alive and physically unharmed – were actually of great importance.

There is another aspect to this philosophy that was also much on Goethe's mind. And that is the idea of acceptance or acquiescence in the face of things we cannot change and over which we have no control. Goethe and his friends obviously could not get Napoleon or his troops out of Weimar. So, they should accept the fact and not struggle against it. The struggle, here, is imaginative rather than physical. For even if one accepts defeat, the ensuing mental struggle is one of continually being frustrated, disappointed, humiliated, filled with regret and resentment; but to what constructive purpose? If you really cannot do anything, then you should try to accept the situation and get on with other things. And it is this strategy that Goethe is trying to work with and which lies behind his words: 'I've nothing to complain about.'

The discussion after the occupation of Weimar illuminates the whole of the latter part of Goethe's life. The core theme is that of concentration. Goethe was obviously a man easily touched by the experiences of others, deeply responsive to changes in his environment. But these strengths carry with them an obvious weakness – being sucked into the lives of others to such an extent that it becomes impossible to lead one's own; being so affected by the outer world that one is unable to concentrate and get on with one's own work. Goethe could have been so disturbed by the incursion of Napoleon and his troops that his own projects – his own life – might have been derailed for a long time. The idea of putting up with what cannot be changed is not merely fatalism. It is a strategy of concentration and of insulation for the sake of something else. Goethe did not 'put up with' the occupation because he did not mind it; rather, he did so in order to preserve his ability to work. Someone who is temperamentally tender hearted may have to steel themselves to say 'no', may have to force themselves to be in-different, if they are to get on and do what they have to do.

The core of Goethe's maturity was self-discipline. And the cost of this was that he appeared – to some people – to be indifferent or numb to the things that are supposed to be affecting.

3

A Life 'According to Nature'

Like many people, Goethe thought that the goal of individual life was happiness and that happiness is intimately related to pleasure. If we take this seriously as part of the meaning of life – as a statement of what life is for – our attention cannot help but focus on some difficult questions: how are we to be happy? What sort of pleasure should we seek?

Goethe's vision of happiness – and of pleasure – gives an important role to renunciation and resignation. This is perhaps puzzling at first, until we recall that pretty much everyone seeks pleasure, but many people are unhappy. An obvious cause of unhappiness is the excessive pursuit of pleasure, summed up in the word 'dissipation'. We intensify our sensuous pleasures and devote so much time and so much of our mental resources to them that we are unable to pursue anything else. How was Goethe able to achieve so much? In a painfully accurate note, he provides one bit of the explanation.

'People are always saying that life is short; but you can do a great deal if you use your time properly. I've never smoked tobacco; I don't play chess; in short, I haven't given myself up to the things that steal time. I've always regretted that few people know how to gain time – or how to use it.' The problem, of course, isn't that smoking or playing chess are generally unpleasant (for those who engage in these activities); it is that they are all too absorbing, all too pleasant. The grip of these pleasures is such that they rob us of our time; we end up feeling: life is so short, I haven't been able to do the things I should have done.

Such examples, however, are only the simplest cases. As it happened

Goethe wasn't tempted to smoke, and chess wasn't the sort of thing to attract him. The painful logic is simple – certain things we are attracted to, or certain sources of pleasure, get in the way of doing other more important and more ultimately rewarding things. And this logic doesn't just apply to those activities that rob us of our time. The problem for Werther is that he can't 'renounce' or give up Charlotte: he can't resign himself to living without her and, ultimately, that inability costs him his life. Werther has a fantasy of the immense happiness, of the great pleasure, he could have if only he could always be with Charlotte; it is the compelling power of this fantasy – of this longed-for pleasure – which, in reality, prevents him from enjoying anything. Werther lacks a certain kind of courage – the courage that enables a person to face suffering; he isn't sufficiently tough on himself. He can lament his 'fate' and curse his misfortune and life and feel terrible; but he will not face the one terror that would actually free him: the admission that he could survive without Lotte.

Because Goethe lived a fairly comfortable life, and because of the different habits of the era, he can come across as a rather self-indulgent character. He often drank a glass of wine in the morning, and always had plenty of wine with his long lunch (which was his main meal of the day); he drank luxury drinks – hot chocolate and coffee. He lived, in the second half of his life, in a fine house surrounded by his art collection and cared for and assisted by a substantial household. These facts tend to disguise – but do not really controvert – the reality of Goethe's devotion to self-control. Because he had quite a lot of money, Goethe could afford these things without getting into debt; but he didn't overspend. He was in fact exceptionally self-controlled in his economic life. There are many meticulous records of expenditure, in which he precisely reckons up how much he has spent on a particular trip or on certain household expenses.

The ideal of living 'according to nature' had been taken seriously in antiquity – it is a central concern in the work of Epicurus and in that of his follower Lucretius; it had been taken up, and given a fresh and seductive appeal, in the work of Rousseau. However, the very strong contrast that Rousseau made between nature and culture – with goodness entirely on the side of nature – was problematic. Rousseau was willing to accord the evaluative status of 'natural' only to those longings and actions that could exist without any complex society. His vision of a life 'according to nature' was that of a primitive life: dwelling in the forest, gathering nuts and berries.

This is not at all what Goethe has in mind. The central difference is that Goethe's view of 'nature' is more complex: a Palladian villa is not 'unnatural', since the desire to find intelligent order in one's environment – a desire which the building acknowledges and satisfies – is not somehow imposed upon us by society; it's not the result of corruption. In other words, Goethe is happy to accept that the natural longings we have may require techniques and artistry for their fulfilment. In the absence of society, in the absence of technology and art, we are not more natural, but less ourselves.

Goethe's idea was that 'being ourselves' is a project – rather than something that comes easily. One difficulty lies in finding out what it is we really want to do. We might imagine that to be true to ourselves requires only that we do what we want. Apart from this being faced with all sorts of practical restrictions (not enough money or time) it assumes that we already know what it is we want to do – that we already know what is important to us. The story of Wilhelm Meister is the story of a man gradually discovering – through many mistakes and exaggerations – an increasingly solid and serious vision of what is important to him.

Probably the hardest thing for Goethe – as he got older – was paying the price for his devotion to his own vision. When he started out as a writer, Goethe benefited not only from serious critical acclaim but also from the tide of fashion. *Werther* was not only a classic – in the sense of being a book for all time – it was also, and this is an extremely rare conjunction, an immense popular and fashionable hit. That is the secret meaning of all the fashionable spin-offs from the book – the teacups illustrating scenes from the book, the 'eau de Werther' cologne, the adoption of the Werther costume. A few serious writers happen to coincide for a short time with fashion. But such an alignment cannot last. Goethe never lost his high standing – but he did fall from fashion.

In the middle years of his life (roughly from forty-five to fifty-five) he was shored up by his deep friendship with Schiller. However unsuccessfully he and Schiller may have battled against the popular tide, they had each other and a strong sense of historical destiny – which was largely Schiller's creation. At this stage Goethe seemed to believe that together they might actually be able to abolish fashion – and establish a permanent and constant artistic and intellectual model. What Goethe discovered – to his dismay – is that serious younger writers were coming along who not only did not copy or absorb his ideals but were also actively opposed to what he stood for.

4

The Olympians

In September 1808, Goethe was presented to Napoleon at the Congress of Erfurt, not far from Weimar. The congress marked the high point in Napoleon's fortunes. He was the master of continental Europe. After the battle of Jena two years before, Napoleon had made a triumphal entry into Berlin, but Prussian resistance – encouraged by an alliance with Russia – continued in the eastern part of the country. Eventually, in the summer of 1807, Napoleon had confronted and defeated the Russians at the battle of Friedland. The Russians decided that peace was preferable to more defeats and abandoned Prussia, leaving the Prussians no option but formal surrender. At this stage, Napoleon was keen to sustain peaceful, even friendly, relations with Russia and the Congress of Erfurt was designed to impress – and flatter – the Russian Tsar, Alexander. Napoleon demonstrated his potency by the line-up of kings and princes who had to wait upon him and whose overlord he was; and he turned this into diplomatic capital by treating Alexander as the sole exception: the two Emperors were together, above the rest.

The summoning of Goethe to an interview was, of course, a side event in this majestic display. When Goethe was shown in, Napoleon presented himself in the guise of the ideal administrator. He was enjoying breakfast while – between mouthfuls – directing his Empire: receiving reports from his adjutants; a few generals in an antechamber waiting to be told where to direct their forces; his minister Prince Talleyrand flitting in and out for instructions. A really great leader can combine breakfast, vast administration and lofty, poetical conceptions.

Like every educated person in Europe, Napoleon knew of *Werther* and professed to have read it several times. This might well have been true; Napoleon had made a serious attempt at writing a novel, working on it as late as 1800 when he was already First Consul and had a string of military campaigns behind him. That such a heroic figure should have bothered penning a really very competent romantic story – *Clisson and Eugénie* – tells us something about the age and about the influence of Goethe himself. It would have been inconceivable for any of the Bourbon kings to have written a novel. Napoleon was on the cusp of the era in which it would be possible for Disraeli to be a leading novelist and then prime minister; for Balzac's Lucien de Rubempré to rise quickly from poet to minister of state. As author to author Napoleon made some remarks about a 'defect' in the plot of *Werther*.

Somehow the legend grew up that Napoleon had discovered a secret flaw that no one else had been able to detect; thus revealing his 'genius' of discernment in romantic fiction as well as on the battlefield. But novels are not like battles; a 'defect' in a novel which only one person can detect cannot be regarded as a real flaw. And, in fact, Napoleon merely pointed out that there is a double motive for Werther's suicide: he is losing Charlotte and he has been unsuccessful in his career. But this is only a defect against a doctrinaire, and irrational, assertion that actions in novels should only ever have a single motive.

Nevertheless, Napoleon's attempt to engage Goethe in critical discussion – his willingness to receive Goethe among his generals and diplomats – is admirable and was connected to an interesting ambition. Napoleon wanted to organize the whole of Europe into a harmonious, consistent political federation. In other words, he saw Europe as a potentially coherent entity; and he hoped to symbolize this in the creation of an Imperial court of unsurpassed – unsurpassable – artistic greatness. Parallel with the aim of making the Louvre the home of great art, he hoped to bring Goethe and Beethoven to Paris and to enlist them in the intellectual and artistic creation of Europe.

Unfortunately, Napoleon didn't sell the project to Goethe in a sufficiently intelligent manner. He proposed that Goethe should write dramatic plays glorifying French arms – under the guise of classical prototypes. Might Julius Caesar be a suitable topic? It was an opportunity missed: Goethe didn't write plays of that kind. Had he been thirty, rather than, as he now was, a few days past sixty, it would have been perfect; perhaps from Paris he could have done for Europe what he did for Weimar. But by now Goethe was not the man to subordinate his life, even to the Emperor.

The fruitless and even tedious encounter between these two men did have one memorable moment. Speaking loudly so that his courtiers can hear, Napoleon looks at Goethe and says, 'Voilà un homme!': rather than praise Goethe for this or that particular accomplishment he seizes on the whole person: it is the sum total of Goethe that is most impressive.

Madame de Staël's well-intentioned portrayal of Goethe as the soul of Germany turned out to be a millstone; another well-meaning characterization of Goethe also became a liability. It became habitual to refer to Goethe as an 'Olympian' – a god and an immortal, but one surveying the human condition from above. There are many images of attractive life on Olympus – the Greek gods were human in their appetites and not all were callous or cold. If one is thinking of the loves of the gods as depicted by Raphael or by the Carraci then there is something to be gained from this otherwise overblown term. Goethe was – at times – Olympian in this sense: enjoying the pleasures and respect the world has to offer, in an endless prime, a man of many loves but free of the reproaches which would attach to an ordinary individual; one who is strong and happy and healthy.

Unfortunately, the term became attached to manifestations of coldness – an Olympian in the sense of a statue: forbidding, distant and inhuman. This image has some basis in fact – Goethe did sometimes behave in an offhand manner; he made some aloof pronouncements and could be stiff and cold when receiving visits. But the allure of this image is surely to do with the way it secretly aggrandizes the critic. To call Goethe Olympian at once acknowledges his merits – and at the same time makes them irrelevant. Goethe is 'up there' but so high 'up there' as to be disconnected from human life as we (who are down-to-earth) know it. This kind of backhanded compliment has its place in relation to science – after all, a scientist might be producing wonderful work which we mortals cannot comprehend. But in connection with the arts it is incoherent – although expressive of a real problem. What makes a work of art genuinely great is that it can speak deeply and powerfully and beautifully to us about the human condition (and hence about our own condition). But if a work is aloof or incomprehensible it simply cannot be great in that way. The idea that a writer might be too great to be readable is an appalling confusion.

The supposed consolation is that it doesn't matter if you find Goethe a bore or intimidating – the problem does not lie in you; it lies in him.

5

The Science of Love

In the middle of 1808, a couple of months before his encounter with Napoleon, Goethe started writing a story called 'The Renouncers'. Taking it up again early the following year, the tale ballooned into a novel. Uncharacteristically, the work progressed quickly and before the end of the year it was in print under the enigmatic title *Elective Affinities*. Goethe was now sixty. He had been with Christiane for over twenty years, and legally married to her for three, but the habit of falling in love never left him. The list of women Goethe had relationships with, however, is not an especially long one – excluding casual affairs (about which we know very little) and flirtations (which would go on for pages).

Elective Affinities is a study of the conflict between marriage and love. However, it does not address the conflict between a loveless marriage and a passionate new relationship. It isn't a study of the crisis of duty versus pleasure. Instead it looks at the richer – and more unusual – case of a loving marriage and the emergence of a new and additional love. Such situations were central to Goethe's imagination and experience. One of Goethe's assistants noted – at about this time – that the great man was contemplating a novel in which the hero is simultaneously in love with four women: 'each in her way is loveable; whichever one he is drawn to in the mood of the moment, she alone is loveable'. The fantasized solution is polygamy. And Goethe didn't experience this ideal of multiple marriages as a uniquely male privilege. It is a fantasy of interlocking groupings: men with several wives, and wives with several husbands – a situation of erotic charm, perhaps, and of emotional chaos and wreckage, certainly.

In *Elective Affinities* Goethe studies another attempt to square the romantic circle. If polygamy won't work, what about serial monogamy? But now he is not exploring the possibility as something which he thinks might work for him; instead the proposed 'solution' is tested on his central character, Eduard – and the tragic fate of this character is something Goethe himself was determined to avoid.

The novel opens with a little evocation of paradise. Eduard ('the baron') and Charlotte have been married for a year or so. They live very pleasantly on Eduard's estate – there is a fine mansion, splendid gardens set among hills, woodland and lakes. They live alone like Adam and Eve – except, obviously, for their servants. They spend their time improving the grounds: Charlotte has just had a little pavilion constructed on one of the hills, commanding a delightful view. Eduard plays the flute, Charlotte the piano. Together they are slowly editing the journals of his travels in Italy.

But this is an artificial paradise – it is not the place where life starts but an intelligent and deliberate refuge from the storms of earlier years. Eduard and Charlotte are no longer young: each has been married before. Long ago they had been in love but pragmatic considerations had kept them apart. Each made a rich marriage to a partner they liked and respected but did not love. The course of events – a death and a divorce – has left them both free. They have finally married and so, by chance, have been able to achieve what they had once longed for but which had seemed impossible.

Elective Affinities recounts the break-up of this 'perfect' marriage. It is Goethe's secular version of 'the Fall': the exile of the first humans from the perfect garden. In the Book of Genesis, the downfall of Adam and Eve comes about through the acquisition of illicit knowledge, specifically the knowledge of good and evil. Once you know or understand too much a simple, contented and sweet life becomes impossible. Genesis can be read as the tragedy of growing up. We eat the apples from the tree of life not because we are somehow bad or wicked, but because gaining knowledge is an inescapable part of living.

Knowledge, which is in principle a good thing, is also the cause of a new kind of suffering. Knowledge stands for a perspective upon oneself – the capacity to judge one's own actions, to have regrets, to have hopes for the future (and hence fears for the future), the power to imagine a better world than this (and hence feel dissatisfied with our present condition). Genuine development, which enriches and strengthens the mind, introduces new arenas of distress, new ways of being unhappy.

The paradisal seclusion of Eduard and Charlotte is compromised not by illicit knowledge, but by love. Just as we may have naively assumed that the gaining of knowledge is an unalloyed good, we might equally imagine that love is always and necessarily a benign force in our lives. The painful 'moral' of *Elective Affinities* is that love can be a hugely destructive force in human relationships.

Eduard is troubled by the difficult circumstances of his close friend, 'the captain', as he is called. The captain is a man of considerable talent and expertise in estate management, but without private wealth. Following his retirement from the army (presumably in the wake of the first phase of the Napoleonic Wars, which culminated in the collapse of Prussia) he has been unable to find an adequate position. Eduard's friendship towards him, and more general moral conviction that a good man should not be left idle, inclines him to invite the captain to come and live in a wing of the mansion and use his abilities in the service of the estate. Charlotte is alive to the dangers of introducing a third party into a happy situation that seems to depend upon the absence of others.

Charlotte also has a tie to the wider world. She is the guardian of a young woman called Ottilie – currently at boarding school, and unhappy there. The school is clearly not helping with Ottilie's develop-ment – which would be far better undertaken by Charlotte at home. And yet Ottilie was sent away precisely so that Eduard and Charlotte could be alone. In fact not so long before Charlotte had considered that Ottilie would make an ideal partner for Eduard – and had even encouraged this relationship. But by that time Eduard was exclusively interested in Charlotte, so nothing had come of her plan. The underlying point here is that Charlotte has perceived a deep compatibility between her ward and the man who is now her husband.

With some misgivings the captain and Ottilie are both invited to come and live in the mansion. And so the step is taken which will result – inevitably it seems – in tragedy. It would be wrong to call this step a mistake. Eduard and Charlotte are in a situation in which whatever they do will be the wrong thing – and their situation is not unusual. Goethe set it up as a picture (in aristocratic dress, admittedly) of the human condition at large. Eduard and Charlotte – Adam and Eve, everyman and everywoman – seek their happiness in each other. But this happiness depends upon an exclusive mutual regard. They care about each other, and that care is not intruded upon or diverted by outside concerns. And yet no loveable person could really be like this. Any person capable of love will necessarily have other concerns and attachments – other loves. These further moral and emotional links cannot be and should not be sacrificed; at the same time, they are incompatible with the stable union of the loving pair. The source of 'the Fall', the cause of the breakdown of the loving relationship and the exit from the garden, does not lie outside of us, but is something within human nature. But it is not a perverse force; it is not that there is something in us urging us against our better judgement to do the catastrophic deeds that will undermine our happiness. It's an inescapable feature of the human condition: not all the good things that we rightly desire, and rightly esteem, are actually compatible. So whatever we do something bad will result.

6

Elective Affinities

The title of the novel derives from a chemical theory, which studies the breakdown of physical compounds. One evening when the four are together after dinner, Eduard reads aloud, as he likes to do. He's reading a scientific book when he suddenly realizes that his wife is looking over his shoulder at the book. This infuriates him. Charlotte excuses herself. She had not been attending closely to the reading and on hearing the word 'affinity' she had assumed that the book must be concerned with human relationships. But as the reading had progressed she realized that inanimate things were being spoken of. This had confused her: she had lost the thread of the discourse and had read over Eduard's shoulder to find it again.

Eduard comments: 'It is a metaphor which has misled and confused you. Here to be sure it is only a question of soil and minerals; but man is a true Narcissus: he makes the whole world his mirror.' This is Goethe at his best. Here is a comment that arises naturally from the mouth of an educated, polished man; it sits simply and naturally within the domestic, intimate scene – reading, a moment's irritation, a slight confusion. And yet this is the topic that is at the centre of Goethe's entire life as a writer and a thinker. The world is the mirror of man. It is a metaphor; but is there a truth being presented metaphorically here?

Charlotte asks for further explanation – what is meant by 'affinity'? Eduard offers an example: 'If you think of water, or oil, or quicksilver, you will find a unity and coherence to their parts' – they are stable and don't change, they stay just as they are. 'They will not relinquish this unified state except through the action or force of some other

356

agent. If this other agent is then removed, they immediately revert to their former state.' Each thing remains what it is, until something else interacts with it. And the consequences of the interaction depend on the nature of the two things brought into contact.

'Sometimes,' says Eduard, 'they will meet as old friends and acquaintances who hasten together and unite without changing one another in any way, as when water mixes with wine' – the water remains water and the wine remains wine, only the droplets of each distribute themselves evenly in the glass; the intrinsic nature of each is unaffected. 'There are others who will remain obdurate strangers and refuse to unite in any way – no matter how hard you try to unite them – as oil and water shaken together will a moment later separate again.'

'Nevertheless, these obdurate strangers can be combined by the introduction of a third agent. Water and oil can be combined by the addition of "alkaline salt",' the captain informs Charlotte – and us. And now we are ready to learn what is meant by an 'affinity'. 'Those natures which, when they meet, quickly lay hold on and mutually affect one another we call affined. The affinity is striking in the case of alkalis and acids which, though they are mutually antithetical, and perhaps precisely because they are so, most decidedly seek and embrace one another, modify one another and together form a new substance.'

So what is an 'elective affinity'? The picturesque chemistry continues: put a piece of limestone (calcium carbonate) into some sulphuric acid. The acid attacks the stone, extracting what it wants, and together they form a new compound – gypsum. A gas is also released – the lonely residue, now divorced from the calcium. Why 'elective'? Well, it looks as if the calcium preferred the new relationship with the acid over the old tie to the gas. Charlotte feels sorry for the gas but the captain consoles her: 'All it has to do is join up with water to make some tonic,' and together they can set up a profitable spa resort.

'Feeling sorry for the gas' is perhaps the key emotional point in the book. Because Edouard still actually loves Charlotte he cannot pursue his new love until he believes that Charlotte will be happy – will have a new love of her own. This is 'squaring the circle'. The hope of the seraglio was that all one's loves could coexist happily. In this new scheme all loves can coexist only if there is a perfectly orchestrated sequence of partnerships.

By now the human implications are only too apparent. Marriage, divorce and remarriage may be understood not merely by analogy to chemistry but as phenomena of the same kind. Human interaction is not free, but is determined by factors that we do not control. What we regard as choices are really only the working out of natural forces which are not at our command. Morality, the idea of doing something because it is good or avoiding it because it is evil, has no purchase, no point of application within this scheme. The term 'elective' makes it sound as if chemical interactions are a matter of choice for the elements involved. Hydrogen 'loves' oxygen and 'chooses' or 'elects' marriage with it, thus forming water. But when an acid is introduced the oxygen discovers that it 'prefers' a new partner and 'decides' to divorce the hydrogen.

Of course in such cases we know perfectly well that what appears to be a choice isn't one at all. The elements have to act as they do. And this is where the shock of the analogy comes in. Rather than suggesting that chemical reactions are theatres of choice, the implication is that relationships are governed by natural forces over which we have no control. We cannot choose who we fall in love with, nor how long our love will last; if a new person comes along who has an 'affinity' with us we have no choice – we simply are compelled to break away from our existing relationship (however stable that may have seemed up to this point) and form a new compound.

This disconcerting theme encouraged some of Goethe's contemporaries (including his good friend von Knebel) to see it as an 'immoral' work – that is, as a book propounding a seductive but wicked view of life.

It was, perhaps, because just such an attack was anticipated and feared that the publisher, Cotta, took such a strange line in his advertising campaign. The advert in the *Morgenblatt* of 4 September 1809 claimed that 'elective affinity' is a metaphor in chemistry with a 'spiritual origin'. In other words: the novel seeks to show not that love is merely chemistry in disguise but that chemistry maps the erotic relations of acids and salts. Far from there being no love in the world, it turns out – in Cotta's blurb – that there's nothing but love. But this is a hopeless stratagem of interpretation. If chemicals 'love' one another they do so in a terrifying way: they have no control over their relationships and are moved to new relationships by the mere presence of another compound of an appropriate sort. If chemicals love they do so blindly, promiscuously and without regret.

7

Marriage

Woven into the fabric of *Elective Affinities* is a discussion of the status and value of marriage. At one point Eduard and Charlotte have among their guests at the mansion an infamous pair of lovers: the count and the baroness. Each is married to another but they contrive to spend a great deal of time together on the estates of their noble friends where it is the established custom to provide them with interconnecting suites. The merest surface of decorum is maintained (anything risqué or controversial is spoken in French so as not to scandalize or excite the servants) while everyone understands – and accommodates – what is going on.

The count and the baroness are charming people, excellent company, witty, urbane, intelligent. 'Their easy manner of accepting and dealing with life's circumstances, their cheerfulness, their apparent unaffectedness communicated themselves right away . . .' While the party are at dinner, Charlotte asks how things are going with a mutual friend and is surprised to learn that this woman is about to get divorced. It's always disagreeable, she comments, when someone who you thought was safe and secure is in a precarious position.

This precipitates a general discussion about divorce. The count seeks to correct Charlotte's surprise. 'We do so like to imagine that earthly things are so very permanent, and especially the marriage tie. And as to that we are misled by all those comedies we see so much of into imaginings which are quite contrary to the way of the world. In a comedy we see a marriage as the final fulfilment of a desire that has been thwarted by the obstacles of several acts. The moment this desire is fulfilled the curtain falls and this momentary satisfaction goes on echoing in our minds. Things are different in the real world. In the real world the play continues after the curtain has fallen, and when it is raised again there is not much pleasure to be gained on seeing what is going on.'

He goes on to describe a more appealing arrangement. 'Marriages ought to be contracted for only five years ... this would suffice to get to know one another, produce a few children, separate and then be reconciled. What a happy time you would have at first. Two or three years at least would be spent in contentment. Then one of the parties would be interested in seeing the relationship protracted and would grow more attentive as the end drew closer. The indifferent or even discontented party would be propitiated and won over by this behaviour.'

The count is presenting the view that marriage as a permanent, unbreakable union is unnatural. The solution he advocates is more natural – more in line with the dynamics of human nature.

While this couple are in the house, an enigmatic character called Mittler – the name suggests something like 'mediator' – drops by. Mittler plays the role of confidant and helper to couples in distress, and his aim is always to reconcile differences and preserve marriage as a permanent union. On learning that the count and the baroness are guests, Mittler is furious: 'I will not stay under one roof with that pair. And you watch out for yourselves too: they bring nothing but harm.'

They try to appease him, but Mittler only becomes more irate. 'Whoever attacks marriage,' he cries, 'whoever undermines the basis of moral society – because that's what it is – by word or deed, has me to reckon with. Marriage is the beginning and the pinnacle of all culture. It makes the savage gentle, and it gives the most cultivated the best occasion for demonstrating his gentleness. It has to be indissoluble: it brings so much happiness that individual instances of unhappiness do not come into account. And why speak of unhappiness at all? Impatience is what it really is, ever and again people are overcome by impatience, and then they like to think themselves unhappy. Let the moment pass, and you will count yourself happy that what has so long stood firm still stands. As for separation, there can be no adequate grounds for it. The human condition is compounded of so much joy and so much sorrow that it is impossible to reckon how much a husband owes a wife or a wife a husband. It is an infinite debt, it can be paid only in eternity. Marriage may sometimes be an uncomfortable state, I can well believe that, and that is as it should be. Are we not also married to our conscience, and would we not often like to be rid of it because it is more uncomfortable than a husband or a wife could ever be?'

Thus there is a tension in the book between the advocacy of marriage as a permanent and exclusive bond – as a special and important arrangement for securing human happiness – and an account of the passions – of erotic and amorous attachment – which stresses their unstable, changeable nature. The unchosen 'elective affinities' that govern our longings can, obviously, come into conflict with marriage. It is only through divorce – through the negation of marriage – that we can live in accordance with our passions.

Until near the end of the book it looks as if things are going to work out well for the four main characters. Ottilie agrees to marry Eduard, providing Charlotte will marry the captain – thus avoiding being left as 'the lonely gas'. And it looks certain that a painless divorce, followed by two quick marriages, will leave everyone contented. The very day it looks as if all this will be settled, Ottilie takes the baby daughter of Eduard and Charlotte for a walk in the home park. As dusk falls she heads back for the mansion, taking a short cut by rowing across the lake. There is an accident; the child falls in the water and drowns.

This horrific event is seen by Ottilie and Charlotte as dictated by 'fate'. The proposed dissolution of Eduard's and Charlotte's marriage has 'tempted fate' and now they are being punished. The theme of fate – which occurs throughout the novel – stands in direct contrast to the 'affinity' view of life. For the idea of fate is that the universe as a whole behaves like a person: if we act badly we will be punished by the universe; if a cup is thrown in the air but does not smash upon landing this 'means' something. Far from human drama actually being governed by the impersonal laws of chemistry, the idea of fate projects personal life into the universe as a whole, which is regarded as a kind of judgemental parent or stern theatre director.

Because of the accident – which isn't seen as an accident but as caused by the intended divorce – both women renounce the possibility of new relationships. Ottilie grows pale, weak and detached. One day entering the salon she overhears Mittler condemning adultery. His words, which she applies to herself – although she has only ever kissed Eduard once – cause her unbearable distress and she dies that evening. Soon, Eduard too is dead.

As a formal defence of marriage the plot is clearly inadequate. The 'lesson' one might be expected to draw from the book is this: if you try to get divorced your child will have an accident. But the sequence of events in this particular story can hardly be taken as a necessary – or even likely – outcome.

The real problem of divorce – and more broadly the instability of adult relationships – isn't that it courts death but that it risks damaging the life of a living child. This was all too apparent to Goethe. He and Christiane had lost four newborn children – a high but not uncommon rate of infant mortality. But the child who survived – the first-born, August – was, by the time *Elective Affinities* was being written, causing his father considerable distress.

August had been born on Christmas Day 1789 and was approaching twenty when *Elective Affinities* was published; he had just finished his secondary schooling at the Weimar Gymnasium and would soon enrol at the University of Heidelberg as a law student. The first few years of August's childhood had been delightful.

There had of course been periods of separation in the early years – Goethe had been required to join the Dowager Duchess Anna Amalia in Venice in 1790; had been ordered to attend Carl August on military manoeuvres with the Prussian army in Poland in 1791; and then on active campaign in 1792 and 1793. Goethe had also spent time in Jena in 1794 to set up the Botanical Garden attached to the university. But all through this period there is considerable evidence of Goethe's very warm devotion to August and to Christiane. He and Christiane wrote to one another during his absences, and the letters are filled with the

details of domestic life: how the crop of cucumbers has been spoiled, but thankfully the asparagus is doing well; what has happened to August's pet squirrel? How is the boy's reading progressing? Will Goethe bring August a toy sword? And Goethe says how he is longing to be home again so he can take August on his knee and feel again the security and peace of family happiness.

But as August got older the problems began. Goethe somehow persuaded himself that August should grow up as a young Greek sailor might have in classical times: living the communal life of the ship, taking part in raids and battles and joining in the rough entertainments of the crew. This was radically different from the childhood he himself had enjoyed in Frankfurt. The sensuous indulgences of Christiane, the drinking bouts, dancing and singing with the wild Jena students, formed August's character, and from a young age he was drinking heavily. August of course was growing up as an illegitimate son, and growing up in the courtly aristocratic circles in which legitimacy was a great principle of status. The boy was granted official legitimacy in

1802 when he was twelve – at around the time of his confirmation (performed by Herder). After one painful incident, when the adolescent August was reported to have drunk dozens of glasses of champagne, Goethe broke down in tears. If he had any sense, the meaning of the tears could not simply be horror at how August was turning out, but rather horror at what he, as the father, had allowed to happen. In 1806, with August now sixteen, Goethe and Christiane finally married. But to the small world of Weimar he would forever be 'the love child' and the son not only of Goethe but also of 'Mademoiselle' Vulpius – the outsider, the woman who had no business living with Goethe, the uneducated, unrefined woman; someone who was an embarrassment in polite circles, someone who could not be invited to tea, whom one could not meet socially.

Thus, when Goethe was writing about the centrality of marriage, in *Elective Affinities*, and when fate punishes the characters by drowning the baby, the death of an infant stands for the relationship between a stable home and the life of a child. The instability of the Goethe household didn't kill August – but it may well have seemed to his father that he had damaged his son. The extraordinary stability of his own childhood – the deep psychological security Goethe drew from his parents – was unavailable to his own son.

Despite his frequent amorous attachments to other women, Goethe's respect for marriage was not a sham. His most eloquent and interesting – and admittedly unusual – account of marriage was written a year after *Elective Affinities*. It is a longish poem of almost two hundred lines called *The Diary*. It describes the experience of a married man, on the return leg of a long journey. He puts up at a pleasant inn and is immediately attracted to the nubile young serving girl. She flirts with him as she serves him supper in his room, but explains that they can't do anything just then – her aunt is downstairs checking up on how long she is with him. 'I'll come at midnight,' she promises. And she does. She's really delightful and very keen. But his body just won't respond: 'The "master" was playing hot, then he shrunk back and went cold.' The 'master' – in German 'Meister' – was one name he and Christiane used for his penis. Of course it was also the surname of Wilhelm Meister, about whose doings Goethe wrote for over fifty years, from the first sketches in 1775 to the final additions in 1829. His other name for it was 'Iste', which in Latin indicates approximately 'this thing of yours'; significantly not 'this thing of mine'. In other words, his penis doesn't belong to him but to someone else. And that is just what is at stake in the little episode in the bedroom of the inn. He wants to have sex with the young woman, but his penis does not agree.

Then he remembers how different it was when he first got together with the woman he later married. Then there had been no problems; he recalls too that when they got married – years after they first met – standing with her at the altar, Iste had responded magnificently. As he thinks of his wife, his erection returns. But now he no longer wants to have sex with the serving girl. So, in the end the night passes chastely. He gets out of bed and writes to his wife, and intimates that he'll show her his diary: which, we must suppose, will include the poem in which this episode is recounted. He still finds the young woman very sexy but he's glad to be going home to his wife.

A poem must have a moral, Goethe jokes at the end, so let's see if we can find one here. 'We're fools; we blunder our way around the world, but two things help our earthy nature: duty, and something that's infinitely greater: sexual love.'

8

Life into Art

In 1811, at the age of sixty-two, Goethe started publishing his principal autobiographical work: *Poetry and Truth*. It clearly does not attempt to be a straightforward retelling of his early years. Instead it offers a symbolic account of his existence. It is Goethe's attempt to impose an artistic order upon his life – and he saw this attempt as more important, more valuable, than historical fidelity.

If we want historical fidelity it is easy to find; modern scholars undoubtedly know much more about what Goethe did day by day than he did. What, for example, was he up to on 25 November 1812? It was a Wednesday and Goethe wasn't feeling very well; not exactly ill, just a bit weak. So he lay late in bed and read a biography – about one of Luther's friends. Then he wrote a letter to Frau von Wolzogen – an in-law of Schiller. He had lunch alone then read more of the biography. He arranged some bits of his mineral collection and in the evening read more of the book. He had some conversation with Meyer, who reports that Goethe was lively – in spirit if not in body.

The next day, Thursday 26 November, he wrote to Carl Körner – who had been a close friend of Schiller; also a letter of condolence to a certain Frau von Eskels; he looked at a chemistry textbook (Parts Two and Three in particular); had lunch at home; spent some time with his son, August. In the evening he chatted with his assistant Riemer about Greece, Greek history and morals.

And so on for decades – we can trace where he was, where he had lunch, who he wrote to – and of course what he wrote about since a great deal of the correspondence survives – what was on at the theatre in the evenings, who visited, what he read.

Such a work as that which traces Goethe's life day by day has a potentially addictive quality: we can't help feeling that if only we knew a little bit more (what he had for lunch that day, what he was feeling when he wrote those letters) we would somehow get closer to Goethe – and that his value for us would be revealed. Of course, it also teaches the useful lesson that much of Goethe's life was normal and banal.

This approach stands in the greatest possible contrast to a biographical technique which Goethe employs repeatedly in his own writing. He very often sketches in the personal history of a character. There's a typical example in *Wilhelm Meister*. The production of *Hamlet* is put on by a professional company, led by a man named Serlo. His attitude to the theatre combines highly developed technique and an eye for the box-office returns; he appreciates artistic merit but is devoid of idealism.

Goethe gives us a brief history of the man: he was literally born to the stage – his first words were spoken before an audience – both parents being actors. He was roughly treated by his father: every mistake was severely punished. With a natural aptitude for mimicry he rapidly developed into an accomplished performer. As soon as he could he ran away, finding succour in a monastery where he earned his keep by performing in religious plays; taking flight again he sustained himself by acting out whole plays in solo performance at the various town fairs. These performances were taxing and he learned to economize on his efforts. Always dependent upon public response, he sought the simplest, most straightforward ways of holding his audience. Necessity taught him not to exaggerate, not to shout – in short to become a natural actor.

This biographical narrative is obviously short on detail. What did Serlo have for lunch? On what precise day did he run off from his parents? What was the weather like that afternoon? The account is governed by a simple and very normal purpose: we want to understand this person – we want to know how he ended up being a successful theatrical manager. More importantly – within the novel – Wilhelm wants to know this because he is trying to work out what he can learn from Serlo and whether he could successfully follow such a career.

*

Goethe's own explicitly autobiographical works are very extensive. There is the 'fragment' *From My Life: Poetry and Truth*, which starts with the moment of his birth and ends with his departure for Weimar in 1775 at the age of twenty-six. Then there is the *Italian Journey*, dealing with the years 1786 to 1788; *The Campaign in France* covers 1792 and *The Siege of Mainz* 1793. *Letters from Switzerland* describes his travels of 1797 and there is also a long description of his journeys to Frankfurt and other cities in the western part of Germany undertaken in 1814 and 1815 – latterly while Napoleon's last army was rampaging around Belgium until it was defeated in June 1815 at Waterloo. In addition Goethe wrote year-by-year memoirs, called 'the Day and Year Books', covering the four decades from 1780 to 1822. As if all this were insufficient Goethe also took care to organize and have edited and (eventually) published his collected correspondence with Schiller (which took place between 1794 and 1805) and with his Berlin-based musical friend Zelter (which ran from 1799 to Goethe's death in 1832).

These many writings belong to different genres and do not add up to a single continuous narrative account of Goethe's life. Despite the lack of a unifying narrative it is clear that Goethe was hugely concerned with keeping together this vast record of his existence.

To round out the information about Goethe's life, Eckermann – his devoted assistant during the last ten years of his life – left a detailed record not only of his own conversations with the elderly, but often sprightly, Goethe but also noted down his own impressions of the great man's day-to-day existence. All this was clearly done with Goethe's careful cooperation and as a self-conscious addition to his huge autobiographical enterprise.

All of this raises the obvious question: what did Goethe think he was doing – or, to put it another way, why did he do it? Why did he record his own existence at such extraordinary length?

One motive was economic. By the end of Goethe's life publishing conditions had improved. In 1815, for example, Goethe had signed a contract with Cotta for a new edition of his works (which appeared over the next four years) for the very substantial sum of sixty thousand thalers. We get some idea of the scale of this payment when it is compared with the highest-paid salaries of the Weimar administrators – three thousand thalers a year, which was certainly sufficient for a comfortable existence. Goethe was now receiving twenty times that amount – and for works that had been published, and paid for, before. So in the later years of his life Goethe knew that his *Collected Letters* would be of considerable commercial value – and he took care in the various wills he drew up at different times to assign half of the proceeds to the descendants of his correspondents.

We get a clue to Goethe's deeper autobiographical ambitions in the initiation scene at the end of Book 5 of *Wilhelm Meister*. Wilhelm is being received into the adult community of mature and successful men. And as soon as the formal words of welcome have been said, he is invited to look around him. The room in which the ceremony occurs is filled with scrolls, each one recording the autobiography of a mature man, and specifically telling the story of his path to maturity – however convoluted or painful or unlikely (and yet real) that might have been.

9

Beethoven's Hat

From 1785 onwards, Goethe made many long summer trips to the spa towns of Bohemia, now in the Czech Republic but then in the territories belonging to Hapsburg emperors. In the years from 1807 to 1813 he made six extended stays at various spas – although always spending much time at Carlsbad. In these years his trips were regularly three months in duration – generally leaving Weimar in May and returning in September; thus, in these seven years alone he spent about a year and a half in these environments.

Carlsbad owed its prominence, in the first place, to the curative waters and this was important to Goethe who found that such cures really did improve his health. But the spas had another significance – in a fragmented Empire, with many small states, summer trips to the spas provided a meeting point for fashionable people and courtiers from across the Empire – and beyond. They might be likened to Bath in Jane Austen's contemporary England. Hence Goethe's spending so much time there was significant socially as well as medically. Goethe had been raised to the nobility in April 1782, he was a celebrity and prominently attached to the Duke of Weimar – which certainly gave him a respectable position among the glittering international aristocrats of the spas. Goethe always claimed that his patent of nobility – which introduced the 'von' before his name – meant little in his own eyes; and that's not surprising. In terms of family fortune and status back in Frankfurt, where the titled aristocracy were not part of the governing order, he had everything that a 'von' might have had elsewhere. However, it did make a difference in the eyes – or at least the habits – of others. Even in Weimar, when dining at court, Goethe as a commoner did not sit at the duke's table. The ennoblement changed that. More importantly, it allowed Goethe to be of greater use to the duke in quasi-diplomatic ways. Goethe would be much more acceptable as an emissary with a 'von'.

Disagreement about the meaning of Goethe's relation to high society finds dramatic focus in the events of a summer's day in 1812 when he went for a stroll with Beethoven in the spa town of Tepliz. As they walked they met a group of ladies and gentlemen – the Empress Josephine of Austria and her entourage. Goethe made a deep bow; Beethoven – it was later claimed – kept his hat firmly in place, and even deliberately pressed it down more securely; a kind of anti-bow, a gesture intended to be the opposite of respectful; then Beethoven is supposed to have berated Goethe for his pathetic, fawning obsequiousness.

This story has a vividness that makes it all too memorable. Goethe is the lackey of princes, Beethoven the defiant hero. In fact, historical evidence for the occasion is lacking; that Goethe bowed deeply is surely correct – quite what Beethoven did or said is not known, that was filled in later.

The more important corruption, however, lies in the interpretation. Suppose the event really did take place as described. What would it show? Naively we might take it as indicating that Beethoven was on the side of progress and the people, Goethe on the side of reactionary politics and social hierarchy. But the contrast is much less clear because of the ironies of history. Goethe in fact didn't support the Austrian Empire against Napoleon. Beethoven, who turned against Napoleon, was – in doing so – actually endorsing the Empire and Prussia, the principal beneficiaries of Napoleon's defeat. In the great celebrations of victory at the Congress of Vienna, Beethoven was an important contributor of music. Yet the meaning of the congress was not liberty or equality – but the victory of Metternich and the old ruling order.

Goethe's bow was an act of politeness, and recognition of the reality of power; not an expression of agreement. If Beethoven kept his hat on his head what good did that do?

Perhaps the reason that this anecdote – embroidered as it is – has stuck is not because it reveals some ugly truth about Goethe; but, rather, because it pins an ugly falsehood upon him. It therefore plays up to our longing to condemn those we fear. The fear is that Goethe is a reproach – the seriousness, the happiness and the success of Goethe's life make our own lives seem shabby and incomplete. What a relief if it turns out that Goethe was a callous, subservient man, a reactionary. We triumph easily over him on these points – never having been invited to serve a prince and not needing to be reactionaries in order to secure the benefits of a competent police force.

In his novel *Immortality* Milan Kundera returns repeatedly to this day in 1812. His view of Beethoven's supposed defiance is this: it is not political – after all, Beethoven was ready to accept patronage from princes. Rather, it was the expression of the distance between the realms of art and of worldly power. Perhaps Beethoven thought the courtiers should be bowing and curtseying to him. Within this perspective there is little to choose between Beethoven and Goethe – both stand for the same thing. The only difference is that Goethe's response is more polite. He too knows – or at least hopes – that Carl August's claim to fame will be that he was the patron of Goethe; just as the princes who paid for Beethoven's music are now known, if at all, only for that.

What Kundera hates is the way the episode is manipulated for self-congratulating ends which, in fact, run entirely against the assertion of the superiority of art to politics. 'Those who look at this allegorical picture – the bow, the hat squashed down – and hasten to applaud Beethoven completely fail to understand his pride: they are for the most part people blinded by politics. Who themselves give preference to Lenin, Guevara, Kennedy or Mitterand over Fellini or Picasso.'

And turning bitterly on a communist French writer who has made much of this episode and used it to humiliate Goethe, he adds: 'Romain Rolland would surely have bowed much more deeply than Goethe, if he had encountered Stalin on a path in Tepliz.'

Goethe's own view of the matter was expressed a few weeks later in a carefully worded letter to his friend Zelter: 'I met Beethoven in Tepliz; his talent is completely amazing; only he's a totally unbridled person; he's not entirely wrong in finding the world frankly detestable; but, honestly, he doesn't do anything to make things even a little more pleasant or bearable for himself or others.'

10

The Mad Sausage

The facts – and perhaps rather more than the facts – about Beethoven's hat are known because they were published much later (in 1839) by a woman called Bettina von Arnim. Bettina was born in Frankfurt in 1785 when Goethe was already in his mid-thirties and well after the time when he had considered Frankfurt his home. However, Bettina could easily be excused the deep-set conviction that she would play a major role in Goethe's life. As a youth Goethe had flirted with her grandmother, the accomplished aristocratic novelist Sophie von La Roche; as a young literary lion he had literally been thrown out of her parents' house for writing love letters to Bettina's mother shortly after her marriage to the Frankfurt banker Brentano.

Bettina became a close friend of Goethe's mother, learning many little stories about the great man's childhood. After Goethe's mother died in 1808 Bettina became the greatest living authority on the baby and boy Goethe (matters about which Goethe himself was, of course, slightly hazy). In fact childhood was Bettina's speciality and she was particularly adept at employing the spontaneity, carelessness and freedom of expression – which we associate with childhood – in her relations with august men. She first met Goethe in Weimar in 1807; when the rest of the world was inclined to treat him with extreme respect, Bettina was playful and coquettish.

For a while Goethe was fond of Bettina; she was also useful to him – as the repository of the anecdotes of his childhood – and, as such, a potential threat too. Could Bettina be relied upon to make appropriate use of such stories that might stick in the historical imagination of people trying to make sense of him?

In 1811 Bettina married; she was twenty-six: rather old by the standards of the day. Her husband was the thirty-year-old Achim von Arnim, a literary celebrity who had put together the first large collection of German folk songs in partnership with one of Bettina's (many) brothers, Clemens. Appearing between 1806 and 1808, the first of three volumes was dedicated to Goethe; not a surprising choice since not only was Goethe the most influential literary figure of the day but he had also shared this interest in folk tales and folk songs in his days as a student in Strasbourg, when Herder had persuaded him that the untranslatable and authentic spirit of German culture was to be found in such productions; ironically, this was an interest which Goethe had long left behind.

In the year of their marriage, Bettina and von Arnim spent a few weeks in Weimar, cultivating their relations with Goethe. It was September, the summer weeks at the spas were over; Bettina was pregnant, but still flirtatious – and she soon irritated Christiane. At that time, Goethe's long-standing friend and collaborator, the painter and art historian Meyer, was publicly exhibiting some of his pictures. Goethe sincerely approved of his work; what he admired was to some extent the lack of originality – he saw Meyer as the continuing servant of a good classical conception of art. (It was Meyer who had provided the copy of Titian's *Sacred and Profane Love* hanging in Goethe's formal dining room.)

Although Bettina admired Goethe passionately, she also admired the more recent movements in German art, which stressed sincerity and the individual vision of the painter. One morning while Goethe stayed at home Bettina and Christiane went to the gallery to look at the pictures; Christiane knew that her husband approved of the works and followed his line; Bettina, however, was in crisis – the central crisis of her life. She was confronted by a contradiction in her own mode of admiration. Goethe was a famous, great man – so she must attach herself to him; he admired the pictures, so they must be good. And she must admire them too; but the young artists were also great and famous men, and they were completely opposed to such works; and since she must follow the loves of great and famous men, she must condemn the pictures. They were good and bad: admirable and loathsome.

Finally, Bettina hit upon the solution – such paintings could not be – and she roundly declared them to be 'impossible'. Precisely: for what Bettina had to exclude was the fact that there could be principled oppositions among the men she admired, which revealed (all too horribly) that her admiration for them was not principled, but opportunistic.

Bettina's strange dismissal of the 'impossible' pictures enraged Christiane. As Bettina tried to make sense of her confusion by speaking more and more energetically, Christiane was facing a crisis of her own. Here was a young woman who flirted with her husband – who was extravagant in her show of affection; but now she was disputing the master's opinions. For Christiane, this was impossible; her own love for Goethe had involved a complete acquiescence to anything he might assert; her idea of love and devotion did not allow that one might love Goethe and not love whatever he said.

Christiane's confused anger found its target sitting on Bettina's nose. Bettina wore glasses – a relative novelty and a reliable target of Goethe's disapproval. Without giving adequate weight to the inconvenience of seeing a blurred world, Goethe held that glasses disturbed the look of the face and introduced a distortion into visual experience. Goethe himself suffered from short-sightedness and made use of a pair of hand-held spectacles – a lorgnon. Bettina's glasses were Christiane's salvation: since Bettina wore glasses, Goethe couldn't really find her attractive. As Bettina's attack on the pictures grew more complex and incomprehensible, Christiane lashed out, knocking the glasses from her nose, smashing them on to the floor.

Goethe sided with Christiane and broke off all dealings with Bettina. Later he warned off Carl August – when Bettina made an approach – describing her as a 'horse-fly'. Bettina was well able to cope, however; she would soon have the Beethoven episode up her sleeve with which to construct a painful caricature of Goethe; she had (as well) her own correspondence with him. In 1834, two years after his death, she published her correspondence with Goethe under a strangely misleading title: *Goethe's Correspondence with a Child* – although the earliest letter dates from 1807 when Bettina was in her early twenties. The title draws on the fact that Goethe refers to her as a 'child' – meaning sweet and childish. And no doubt while she was being sweet her childishness was charming; but to be childish and dogmatic about the philosophy of art is an immensely annoying combination.

Following the shattering of her glasses Bettina immediately trashed Christiane in Weimar society; this would not have been hard to do since Miss Vulpius – Frau von Goethe only since 1806 – didn't have anyone to support her; attacks on Christiane from an up-to-date visitor must have been welcome to any provincial Weimar hostess who could then justify her own contempt for Christiane as being not malicious and unkind, as she may have secretly feared, but as the smartest and most intelligent view of the matter.

Bettina cruelly described Christiane as 'a mad sausage'. Certainly, Christiane was no longer the seductive sex-nymph Goethe had tumbled into bed with twenty years before. But Goethe did not hesitate to side with his wife against the younger woman. He did not pretend that marriage had silenced his erotic or romantic imagination. He did not pretend that loving Christiane meant that he could never feel attracted to another woman. His views can be reconstructed from the fate of Eduard in *Elective Affinities*. Like Werther, Eduard is a vehicle for profound emotions but – again, like Werther – he is not a model for us to follow; rather, he is a warning. Eduard destroys his marriage by taking seriously his love for another woman. He believes that marriage should follow the path of passion – if passion declines, get a divorce; if you fall in love with another person, marry them instead. In the novel – as in life – our passions can destroy us. Marriage is uncomfortable because it requires that we renounce other loves; this is to acknowledge that there will be other loves, and yet to insist that they must be given up – if we are to be happy. It is the most natural thing in the world to suppose that following our instincts is the high road to a good life. But this is not the case for Werther or for Eduard.

Goethe remained intensely loyal to Christiane even though he was no longer romantically in love with her. The decision to marry her – after so many years together – was a kind of anti-divorce. It was a decision to assert the permanence of his relationship with her at a point when he was no longer motivated by a great passion. The theme of renunciation is painfully simple. To preserve certain important good things we have to give up on other longings (although we can't make those longings go away).

PART NINE

Happiness

I was born to see,
Looking is my vocation;
I am faithful to my watchtower,
And the world pleases me.
I gaze into the distance;
I see what is close to me:
The moon and stars,
The woods and the deer.
I find everlasting grace
In so many things;
And because I love them,
I am happy in myself.
My happy eyes
Have found great beauty in the world –
Though the world is as it is.
Goethe, The Song of Lynkeus the Watchman,
Faust, Part Two (1832), Act V

I

The Old Story

The complex, expansive and rather intimidating two-part drama *Faust* is, by title at least, Goethe's most famous work. Partly this is because of the preceding fame of the story, a story Goethe adapted, distorted and hugely expanded. Traditionally, Faust is the man who 'sells his soul to the Devil' in exchange for worldly pleasures and power. It seems, of course, like a wonderful deal at first. But the moment when the Devil comes to redeem the pledge – and take the soul of Faust – is so horrific that the former pleasures and glories seem worthless.

Such a story dramatizes one of the most basic and annoying features of the human condition. Anyone who has had a hangover knows only too well the feeling that the pleasures gained before seem shallow and silly when faced with the consequences of a burning head. 'Selling your soul' merely projects this sequence on to the larger canvas of eternity. You get a lifetime of pleasures and then you get the hangover from hell – in Hell.

To this purely prudential – but largely ineffectual – message, the traditional story of Faust has sometimes been given a more tender aspect. When Faust realizes that the fun is over and that he is going to have to pay the price, he has an agonizing vision of the sheer goodness, the moral beauty, of all those qualities which seek to make us mild and meek and which work against greed and acquisitiveness. Too late, he appreciates the qualities of character that resist the drive to pleasure. This is the point Christopher Marlowe brought out at the end of his play *Dr Faustus*. As Faustus is dragged down to Hell, he looks up to Heaven for a moment: 'See, see' – he cries in desperation – 'See where Christ's blood streams in the firmament!'

It is not the vision of heavenly glory – of the pleasure of Heaven that he is losing for ever – that moves him and the audience. It is not as if Faustus has merely miscalculated: stupidly choosing a bit of enjoyment now over endless enjoyment later. It is, rather, the image of someone who wasn't greedy, who didn't try to have everything, which now seems unbearably poignant. What's so moving about the blood of Jesus is precisely that it is a reminder of the willingness to suffer.

Marlowe's Faustus is like someone who has built up a big credit-card debt dining in fancy restaurants and, now unable to pay off the loan, sees a contented couple munching sandwiches on a park bench. If only he had realized this truth: the way to happiness is not through buying everything. He looked for happiness in the wrong place.

It's to these deeply humane and frightening stories that we attach the name of Faust. But if we read Goethe expecting a particularly brilliant representation of such themes we will be disappointed and disorientated. Goethe does touch on this theme in a couple of places; curiously when it does emerge it has nothing to do with Faust himself. Versions of the traditional 'Faustian bargain' are made only by others – by Gretchen in Part One and by the Emperor in Part Two.

A second major resonance of the traditional Faust story, though less familiar to non-German readers, emerges when we start asking why 'Dr' Faust, why not Mr Faust, or King Faust, or Jimmy Faust? Why is Faust a learned man, rather than Mr Average or some kind of potentate – given that the temptations of pleasure and power exist for everyone and, perhaps with special force, for those already partly hooked? In the old German stories on which Goethe was drawing, Faust was a dabbler in the occult – he sought illicit knowledge.

One story (which comes from a certain Zaccharias Hogel) relates how in the 1550s a Dr Faust turned up at the University of Erfurt and was sufficiently impressive to be allowed to lecture on Greek literature. Not content with simply talking about the extant works of the ancient authors, this Dr Faust went on to describe them as if on the basis of personal acquaintance – something he was able to procure given his ability to summon them up from Hades.

This aspect of sorcery, specifically relating to meeting the heroes of the past, was also a favourite of Cagliostro, the Sicilian swindler who made such an impression on Parisian aristocrats in the mid 1780s. Alexandre Dumas provides a witty fictional portrayal of Cagliostro at a grand dinner party, where he recounts his dealings with the great figures of history ('Let me tell you what Cleopatra was really like') and intimate knowledge of key events from the past – all of which he claimed to have witnessed in the first person.

In such a guise Faust stands for something really important to Goethe – the ideal of personal experience and the hope that literature or history could somehow pass on the next best thing – the experience of 'as if' encountering such people or really being there. But while art and literature necessarily fall short of this, the longing that drives those seeking this connection to the past pushes in the direction of sorcery. So Faust isn't just a representative of 'magic' or the occult – his aims are more noble and closely tied to the ambitions of art and culture: that we should come to possess an almost living acquaintance with, an intimate understanding of, the great people and events that have shaped our world. The bizarreness of the Erfurt literature course lay only in its means: raising the dead by magic; not in its aims: 'living' contact with the great writers of the past.

2

The Secular Bible

Goethe's play is a bewildering work. It belongs to that miserable list of canonical works which one glances at with hope, only to have it immediately dashed. The two parts are clearly intended to be considered as a single work, but they lack the coherence and continuity which would encourage the reader – or the rare theatregoer who sees it in its entirety – to grasp it as a single artistic whole.

The process of the writing of *Faust* gives some insight into its complex diversity. Goethe had been interested in the old, traditional story of Faust since childhood and had drafted ideas for scenes of a play on this topic in his early twenties. The story was to stay with him throughout his life. We briefly sight the developing text when Goethe is in Italy; later, there was encouragement from Schiller to keep going and finish it. Part One – which derives from the old story of Faust, was published in 1808 and very well received. Part Two was not completed until 1832, Goethe's last year, although some bits had been written decades before.

Before we actually get to see Faust on stage, Goethe provides three preliminary scenes. Each encloses the subsequent work in an interpretive shell – and though they might be slightly tedious to watch on stage because we keep on wanting the 'real play' to start, they vastly enrich the work.

Indeed this is a clue to the nature of the Faust work. It's a play, but in fact it's not always a play – there are lots of parts that seem impossible to stage, or others which, while beautifully written, have little dramatic force. The best model of comparison is probably the Bible – of course one of the books Goethe had known most intimately from childhood onwards. The Bible – in its conjunction of an Old and New Testament – in its status as containing the deepest truths about the human condition, although it is difficult to say what those truths are. The Old Testament brings together – as *Faust* does – narrative history, poetic cycles, proclamations of laws, advice on the practicalities of life, moral fables and a vast range of characters, some of whom are merely named. The Bible is at once 'the' book, the prototype of the literary work of art, and also unreadable in the fashion we suppose a book ought to be read: that is, more or less continuously from beginning to end. For writers perhaps the most intriguing aspect of the Bible is not the idea that it is divinely inspired, or sacred, but rather that it is intended to be read over and over again; it is to be taken to heart and read, in parts, across the whole length of a life.

Faust makes more sense when regarded in this way. We are not really invited to read it all through in one go – or even in a continuous fashion. There are many sections of the text which can be read entirely out of context, the contribution of which to the overall work is diffuse. *Faust* is Goethe's Bible – the foundational book for a new religion.

There's a device that Shakespeare uses in which he gets the actors to say: I hope you've liked our play – it was just a play. These are reminders that the play was put on by people who need to be paid, who have lives beyond the theatre.

In *Faust* Goethe provides a Prelude on the stage in which the manager who is responsible for the finances talks with a poet-playwright and 'a cheerful person': one who is going to be in the audience and wants a good evening's entertainment. Three perspectives are developed: theatre as a business; writing as the creation of the ideal; and plays as a form of entertainment. These characters dispute among themselves without reaching any resolution. They have divergent aspirations that, somehow, have to be contained in a single work. If the play is to succeed it has to turn a profit, has to be enjoyable and stimulating, and yet has to be a vehicle for the more noble ambitions of the poet. Goethe is addressing – from long experience – the core problems of the theatre as a cultural institution. The discourse suggests the ambition of writing the perfect play that would simultaneously satisfy these three demands. *Faust* in its entirety is not such a play. It might provide a very quick way of losing money; there cannot have been many 'cheerful people' whose idea of a jolly night out included a thirteen-hour production of Goethe's play.

But, in another sense, the Prelude can be read as giving a tripartite account of the soul. Each voice is a fragment of human nature – to live well we have to manage in all of these ways. We need practical competence, we need to enjoy ourselves and we need to articulate our ideals. A play that achieves such a balance might, however, seem unsuccessful when considered uniquely from any one of these points of view. These conflicting aims – which somehow have to be accommodated within a single life – set out the situation of Faust as a character in the play. Practicality, sensuous pleasure and noble ideals are – in the end – what Faust manages to bring together in himself; but (as we shall see) only through considerable difficulties which arise precisely from these very drives.

3

God and Mephistopheles

In the Prologue in Heaven, Goethe presents God the Father ('the Lord') on stage. The mighty angels praise the wonders of Creation: the sun, the ocean, thunder. Then Mephistopheles, the Devil, appears ('I like the old fellow; God's civil/When he chats to the Devil'). He is not entirely impressed by the world – and takes a particularly dim view of humanity.

> I've nothing to say
> About oceans and such,
> I only see how men go in
> For self-abuse;
>
> The little earth 'god'
> Hasn't learned
> A single thing
> Since time began.
>
> He'd be better off
> If you hadn't gone
> And given him
> A dim bit of light.
>
> He calls it Reason
> But its only use
> Is to find out how
> To be a perfect beast.
>
> He's a big grasshopper:
> Jumping about,

Singing only one
Terribly tedious tune;

Can't he stay still
For just a minute?
No, he goes and pokes his nose
In every piece of shit.

That's pretty much the sentiment. My translation aims at conveying the conversational lightness of the words Mephistopheles speaks; but it doesn't do any justice to the density and coherence of the phrases in German.

Take just one of the couplets, the one about the light of Heaven making people beastly:

> Er nennt's Vernunft und braucht's allein
> Nur tierischer als jedes Tier zu sein.

This is an incredibly tight construction. Not only is there a completely solid, full-bodied rhyme of 'allein' ('alone') and 'zu sein' ('to be'); but also each line divides into two and is vigorously structured. Consider the first line of the couplet: 'Er nennt's Vernunft' ('He calls it Reason') – with the 'it' contracted. 'Er nennt es Vernunft' would obviously be slower, more august, but with less force when delivered in a voice of amused contempt. And then the second half of that line repeats the same structure: 'und braucht's allein' ('and uses it only') – the 'braucht es' being contracted so that the whole line has a rum-te-tum-ty rhythm, which sounds awful put that way, but is a strong corrective to the view we might easily form of *Faust* as being characterized throughout by 'grand' diction just because its themes are so wide-ranging. In fact, it's very high-spirited.

The Devil is disgusted by humanity. Now this is not an altogether unreasonable view; and is one that has been shared by many rather distinguished thinkers – most notably Plato. What a paraphrase cannot do is show the way Goethe puts this into poetic form – so that the Devil's highly reasonable assessment of humanity reels and runs along with the kind of energy that we don't readily associate with lofty poetry, but which is continually present in *Faust*.

The verbal and narrative flow is like that of Goethe's younger contemporary Robert Burns: when you recite his verse the words seem to fly and yet the narrative is clear and easy – poetry is, here, not high flown, but speech coming into its own, mesmerizing in its drive. And yet, Goethe is producing work of the intelligence, the breadth of view, the scale and import of Milton.

Urbanely, God acknowledges that there is much in what Mephistopheles is saying, but suggests that there are at least a few people who are a little more noble than has been suggested – Faust, for example. Faust! says the Devil, he is a fool, he spends all his time on ridiculous intellectual ambitions. God agrees, but adds: at present Faust serves me only in a confused way, but soon I shall bring him into the light; in due course he shall bear fruit. And then Mephistopheles suggests a wager: would Faust really follow your path if he got the chance to follow mine? Very well, says the Lord, while he lives on earth do your best with him.

What is clear even from the brief scene in Heaven is that it's not really Faust who is making a wager here – and nor is it God. Faust stands as a representative of humanity. God's permission to Mephistopheles – that he may play with Faust during his time on earth as a cat plays with a mouse – is really just a description of the ordinary human condition. As God puts it: 'While a man strives, he must stray.' Human aspiration – multiply expressed in curiosity, desire, hope, longing for satisfaction – is good but it is inescapably connected to things going wrong. God's view of the human condition is pretty much the same as that espoused by Henry James: we cannot help but have the 'weakness of our strength'. And then the Lord goes on to voice what seems at first a strange sentiment: he isn't angered by Mephistopheles. As God puts it:

> Man often slumbers,
> He's too fond of rest;
> I'm happy he's got a mate
> To make him devilishly creative.

There's no wager between God and Mephistopheles, although the Devil angles for a bet. What we see, here, is the absorption of Mephistopheles into God's conception of human nature. Goethe's language for this is partly brilliant, partly provocative. When God creates woman, from the rib of Adam, she is described as his mate, his helper. Mephistopheles is presented in these terms too – the mate and helper of man. But 'helper' presumably in the same way as a woman helps a man – or a man a woman – enticing, goading, a spur to ambition, someone who (to put it at its most banal) keeps you on your toes. Thus, from the start we have no sense that Faust might be damned – that the issue is about whether Faust will end up in Heaven or Hell. Instead the focus is entirely upon how Faust will live his life; will the goad, the spur – and the opportunities offered through the agency of 'devilish activity' – lead Faust to live a good life or an empty one?

Basically, this is the question of the normal human condition. Do the ordinary troubles of life, our imperfect rationality, our sensuous desires, our frequently dashed, but often resurgent, longings for knowledge and happiness make life worthless – so that it would have been better never to have been born – or can they be seen as contributing to the good? Are they (despite first appearances) part of what a good life must contain?

The whole scheme of *Faust* is summed up in God's statement: I shall soon bring Faust into the light. God knows that Mephistopheles will do his best – or worst – with Faust; indeed he knows that the Devil is about to make his plea. So, Mephistopheles is – despite himself – the agent through which God is going to bring Faust into the light.

4

Frustration

At last we come to see Faust himself. He is in his study, surrounded by the objects and instruments of academic learning. Everything is dusty and gloomy. Faust is a great professor, a leading intellectual; and he is deeply frustrated. He has mastered all the official knowledge. And yet he feels he knows nothing worth knowing; its effect has been stultifying: 'all pleasure has been taken from me'. At the same time he laments his lowly place in the world; academic titles are little consolation: I haven't been able to buy a country estate, I'm not wealthy, I don't get respect and noble prestige in the wider world – not even a dog would want to live the way I do.

Rather than take to drink or try his luck in business, Faust turns to magic. But what is meant by 'magic' in this play? The spell he tries first is connected to the sign of the 'macrocosm'. This is an image that sums up the entire order of things – but considered at a high degree of abstraction. Everything is part of an ordered whole – there is a complete harmony of Heaven and earth. So it may be, but this vision is not much help to Faust. This is what Spinoza called 'the point of view of eternity', and it may be that from such a point of view all things are indeed well. But since we cannot live from this point of view it's not terribly helpful to us.

Faust's next effort brings forth the 'earth spirit' – and as this spirit speaks we get a clue to the kind of magic at work here: 'It was your soul's desperate pleading that brought me here.' It's not the ritual of a spell that's operative; the 'spirit' is – as it were – the imaginative object of Faust's emotion. He's summoning up within himself visions that might answer to his distress. But the 'spirit of the earth' is no consolation; instead of infinite harmony of the macrocosm, the earth spirit is 'a storm of life' – a perpetual repetition of birth and death. This is how life might look when considered from a mechanical point of view: atoms coming together, arranging themselves, separating, reuniting. Sublime, perhaps, but totally inhuman. From this point of view, no individual life has any particular importance. It's a horrifying spectacle and one that leaves Faust disconsolate.

Or so one might think from reading the text. Curiously Goethe provided an illustration for this scene which gives it a very different, and unexpected, aspect.

In this drawing the earth spirit is an unmistakably classical figure – radiant, naked – like a Greek sculpture, or perhaps a work by Bernini. What this suggests is something specific about Faust, rather than something fundamental to the earth spirit. Since, after all, Greek sculpture and the works of Bernini are not obviously unbearable – not things we cannot face. But the image, this kind of man, might be unbearable to Faust.

At this point he's interrupted by his 'Famulus' – a kind of live-in research assistant – named Wagner. This is probably a private joke; Wagner was the name of the duke's personal servant; this servant had a big black poodle, who soon makes an appearance, as the Devil in disguise. Wagner is still enamoured of the academic life and mentions to Faust how glorious it is that through diligent study we can come to possess the wisdom of all the ages. But Faust is in no mood for such consoling thoughts. After all, whatever wisdom you read is still only read by you – and if you're a fool it will only be wisdom as grasped by a fool that you possess. In any case, do we really learn anything of what people actually thought and felt? We know what they wrote – but that's the expurgated version. The few who have been truly honest about experience have been burned and crucified by the rabble. The truth about life – the truth about experience – is just unbearable to the majority of people.

Goethe once boasted that if he were to write a grown-up version of *Werther* – one based on mature experience rather than the limited knowledge of youth – it would 'make people's hair stand on end' in terror. We get a clue to what he had in mind in that extraordinary remark: 'There is no crime I have heard of that I could not have committed myself.' The imagination, the inner world, even of – perhaps especially of – someone as sensible, reasonable, reliable and pragmatic as Goethe is filled with nameless horrors and vices in embryo: the impulse to destroy, to kill, to seize, to pursue pleasure to its most insane excesses, to express unbounded vanity, to despotism – all this is within him. But suppose one tried to make this plain – that there's a Marquis de Sade, a Mussolini, an imbecile within – then this would appear too shocking, too unbearable, and like such characters one would be incarcerated or hung from a lamp-post.

Wagner finally heads off and Faust is scathing – how can it possibly be that Wagner keeps on going? He revels in rubbish, is enchanted by any old stale bit of nonsense – so long as it's got that musty smell of age; he thinks he's finding treasure and gets a thrill when he puts his hand on a pile of maggots.

This is Faust's lowest point. He feels that there is an impossible, unbearable split within his own nature. On the one hand he thinks of himself as 'made in the image of God' – that old biblical phrase. Meaning: that he aspires to huge creative activity, to knowledge of all things, to grasp the innermost secrets of reality. And at the same time he feels that he is a mere 'worm' – he lives a petty, trivial life, his great intellectual ambitions have given him no relief and brought no rewards. He is sick of life – sick of the horrible contrast between what he wants and what he is – and he resolves to poison himself. Faust has brought us to the key moment of the whole work. At this point he feels that life itself – the human condition (an appalling jumble of God and maggots) – is intolerable; that human nature is – as Schopenhauer, who deeply admired the play, later put it – some sort of mistake; humanity a botched creative attempt; a jug with a huge hole in the bottom: constitutionally incapable of doing the thing it was designed to do.

The real question here is whether – as Mephistopheles has asserted – humanity is one of God's mistakes; God's one big mistake. And at this moment, Faust feels that it is. The incredible reversal of expected logic that Goethe introduces starts here: it will be through Faust's 'bargain' with Mephistopheles that he will in the end come to feel that life is indeed worthwhile, despite all its inevitable shortcomings. We expect the story of Faust to show what's bad about people: we neglect our souls for the sake of power and pleasure. But Goethe's thesis is astonishing: it is partly through the pursuit of power and pleasure that our souls may be saved.

Just as Faust raises the poisoned cup to his lips, he hears the church bells ring for Easter Sunday. Presumably it is dawn – the time at which Christ's resurrection is described as occurring. Faust is not moved to religious faith himself: he feels only a painful gulf between his own thoughts and the simple certainties of unlearned people. But then the singing awakens a memory of childhood. Once, when he heard the Easter bells, he felt they announced the 'kiss of heavenly love' and he would weep with ecstasy. And now he weeps at this memory of a state so unlike his present condition, and puts away the poison.

This reliance upon memory of a time of innocence is brilliantly apt. Faust is a man of immense ability and yet he is about to kill himself.

The simple folk who lack his energy, his intellect and his education are secure and content. The very things that grace human life – subtlety, curiosity, doubt and imagination – are potentially destructive. One response would be to say that the 'poor folk' are simply better off than Faust: ignorance is better than knowledge. If this is wrong we have to work out why.

5

Mephistopheles

The scene shifts and Faust is out walking in the crowded streets with Wagner. We overhear the chatter of the ordinary world – the common townspeople, soldiers, servants: gossipy, teasing, mocking (and yet winking at) banal follies: beer, who's handsome, who's pretty. Their lives are – by the standards of Faust – idiotic, and yet they are full of life. Some old peasants recognize Faust and greet him with the greatest respect. Years before Faust and his father had attempted to cure the sick in a time of plague. He pleaded with God – in the hope that his plea would move God to mercy: in vain, of course. But later Faust claims that in fact it was poison he gave the infected peasants. 'The praise of the masses is like an insult; if only you knew what goes on inside me.' Obviously *Faust* is not a true story, so the issue here is not whether Faust should be understood as actually having murdered, as he says, thousands of peasants. Faust is a 'universal' not because he has killed thousands – that would make him insane – but because of what's inside him: namely, a deeply disturbing indifference to others, considered in the mass. Which indifference coexists with a longing to remove the suffering of others; a longing that the world should be more obviously governed by a benign and caring God.

The intellectual power of the drama is evident when one feels, again and again, that 'here' is the key to the work – and yet of course a work which has a 'key' at so many points cannot be at all simple. Everything seems 'meaningful' and yet we cannot sum up the meaning.

Goethe is here presenting two versions of what is called 'the problem of evil'. The first is better known: how could a loving God allow the world to go on as it does – why allow a plague to carry off so many people? The second is this: how do we as individuals cope with the fact that we have either done wicked things or recognize ourselves as, in some way, capable of evil? Both questions lead us to wonder about the possibility of 'salvation' within life – how could we live decently, how could we find life bearable, in the face of these two problems?

At this point Faust delivers a tender and lyrical expression of his own vision of happiness: life is terrible. We know most about the things that are unimportant to us; and what we do know does not make us happy; and yet happiness seems so obvious – look now at this lovely sunset, if only I could follow it for ever on its passage round the earth, in an eternal sunset with day always before me, night always behind.* This is what he wants – a serene, spirit-like existence – and what he knows he cannot have. The problem is that he also equally craves 'the world' and its physical pleasures. So nothing seems to satisfy him – the things that please one half of his nature revolt his other half. He feels as if he has 'two souls'. And it is not only the sensuous-spiritual distinction that matters here; there is a divide between passionate caring (praying that God will spare the victims of the plague) and sadistic cruelty ('I poisoned thousands'). While these immense themes are being evoked a large black poodle – in those times a breed favoured by students – joins Faust and Wagner and accompanies Faust back to his study.

In an attempt to find peace, Faust decides to translate the New Testament – starting with the opening sentence of the Gospel According to St John. The poodle becomes increasingly agitated as this pious task proceeds; in a gloomy corner, in the candlelight, its shadow seems to grow large and horrific. And from beyond Faust's door the demons complain that one of their number is trapped inside. The dog is now the size of an elephant, but Faust quickly casts a spell and orders the dog spirit to crouch at his feet.

The 'heart of the beast' turns out to be Mephistopheles, elegantly dressed as a travelling scholar. When Faust asks: 'What's your name?' Mephistopheles goes in for a bit of scholarly joking – you want to

* Faust would be flying from east to west, but looking east: that is looking backwards – in the opposite direction to his line of flight.

know my *name*? That's surely a mistake – it's not important to know what something is called – as a scientist you should surely ask: 'What is your essence?' Answering his own question, the Devil explains himself as a representative of the 'original darkness', the 'void' that preceded Creation – from which Creation emerged. His aim is to return everything to that original nothingness. This highly philosophical remark tells us more about Goethe's conception of 'evil'. Evil is, ultimately, the original condition of things – not an avoidable or escapable part of life. It is not evil in the conventional sense of being vicious or wicked – it is rather the aim of not living. Mephistopheles goes on about how he hates humanity – they keep on dying and yet they keep on breeding; their lives seem (to him) pointless and yet they don't stop. What he represents is complete inactivity – emptiness, black stillness. But, for the present, Mephistopheles has a more practical problem: in his earlier endeavours, Faust has drawn a sacred sign – the pentagram – on his floor and this prevents Mephistopheles from getting to the door; eventually he summons rats, lice and bats to gnaw away the doorposts, so he can make an exit.

But soon Mephistopheles is back – finely attired, a true gentleman in appearance, polite and witty as ever. Now it is Faust who is himself demonic in his hatred. He vigorously curses life – and all the things that draw us into it: cursed be patience for that enables us to go on living; cursed be money both because the desire for it spurs us to action and because the possession of it makes life pleasant – and therefore attractive; cursed be family pride, because it ties people to land and possessions and binds the generations; cursed be fame, because it inspires heroic action in those who seek it; cursed be sentimental memories because they console us and make us forget the horrors of the present.

By this point, Faust hardly needs to strike a 'bargain' with the Devil – he is already articulating the creed of Mephistopheles; and thus it makes sense to say that Mephistopheles is a part of Faust – a part of human character and intelligence. And what is so powerful and useful about Goethe's treatment of this theme is that he does not align the Devil with what we already consider vain and wicked – but rather with a condition into which genuinely good and intelligent people fall, and which might be taken as the antithesis of evil. Surely in denouncing money, pride, sentiment and the rest – all the things that make life bearable and take our attention away from its horrors – Faust is merely stating the opinion of modernity?

Mephistopheles agrees to serve Faust – to be his slave. But the 'wager' is presented by Faust in strange terms: 'If ever I give up longing, if ever I'm contented, that day can be my last.' There's no reference to Faust being drawn off to Hell – and we've already had some assurance, in the Prologue in Heaven, that Faust's soul is not to be bargained for. It is Faust's life that is in question. The thought here is that given the demonic powers that Mephistopheles has, Faust believes he will still never be satisfied, but – like the beautiful vision he had – that he will be able to chase the sunset for ever. Life will be both happy and yet, the appetite for life, for growth and development, will not wane.

The pair are just about to set off to explore the possibilities of happiness when a new student comes to Faust's door. Mephistopheles disguises himself as an academic. The student wants advice: in which faculty should he enrol – what should he study now he's at the university? In a lovely scene inspired by Molière, the Devil tells the student the truth about higher education.

First study logic – so as to turn all living questions into a mechanical game; then turn to metaphysics: this will lead you to spend a lot of time thinking about things you can't possibly understand, but never mind, you'll learn how to use pompous phrases. Law, however, you should avoid; lawyers turn common sense into nonsense, blessings into curses and have no interest at all in justice. So what about theology? The safe way here is just to concentrate on words. Student: but surely the words refer to something? Mephistopheles: oh yes, I suppose so, but don't worry about that. The advantage of words is that you can debate about them so much, construct systems, twist them about. But the best career is to be had through medicine. Your title, 'Dr', will lead people to trust you – especially women, and do remember to caress them; check their corsets aren't too tight; gaze deeply into their eyes. The student is much impressed by all this wisdom and takes his leave.

6

Gretchen

Given the support of Mephistopheles, the question for Faust – now – is: what does he want to do? The first efforts at enjoyment are not very successful. Mephistopheles takes him to a drinking party. The drunken guests are treated to a ridiculous display of magic – Mephistopheles provides each with his favourite wine, then turns the drinks to fire; then he makes them see things – the drunkards believe they are in a vineyard and seize each other's noses, taking them for bunches of grapes. On the stage this is a good pantomime; but Faust is not impressed.

They go on to a witch's kitchen, where Faust seeks a remedy for ageing. True to his spirit, Mephistopheles offers the soundest advice: work in the fields, live frugally, be as humble and accepting as a beast, have no ambitions, defecate outdoors – that's how to keep young. And the force of his point is just this: of course he's absolutely right, but Faust is incapable of doing this because he is ambitious, wants to enjoy life, is proud of his intelligence. The joy for Mephistopheles is that people are incapable of doing the things that would make them happy; instead they have to revert to magic – his speciality. Faust finds the kitchen loathsome, but in a magic glass – a mirror – he sees a contrasting vision: an image of perfect female beauty. The point is that it's in this revolting place – populated by raucous, rude half-human apes: perfect emblems of humanity, as seen by the Devil – that Faust turns with a real passion towards beauty. We learn about our longing for beauty not – as we might first expect – by being surrounded by beautiful things, but rather through disgust, to which beauty seems the necessary balm.

Faust and Mephistopheles return to the real world, where Faust meets and is immediately attracted to a sweet, innocent and naive girl called Margaret – or Gretchen. He is a grand gentleman, she comes from a poor but still just respectable family. She's very attracted to Faust but – like many readers – can't quite see what Faust sees in her. This really is a mystery – Gretchen is boring, to put it plainly. If it were merely sex Faust wanted Gretchen would be an uninspired choice. Perhaps her real significance is her trust and innocence – this is what makes it hard for Faust to have her, and it also exposes the limitations of Mephistopheles' powers; for, of course, merely to overcome Gretchen with magic – to create the delusion that she is married to Faust – would not produce the experience Faust is seeking. He wants to be genuinely loved by a trusting and innocent person.

The strategy Mephistopheles devises to bring this about could hardly be less satisfactory. He provides a treasure chest of jewels for Faust to give the poor young girl. Such an extravagant offering, utterly removed from Gretchen's emotional world and any possible route to her happiness, nevertheless manages to corrupt her. Resistant at first, she is entranced by the jewels. This is Gretchen's 'Faustian bargain'.

Although stimulated by expensive gifts, Gretchen's love for Faust is real. Goethe was lucky that Schubert set the poem in which Gretchen expresses her love to music – twice. The second version in particular, which deploys a repetitive, almost hypnotic, melancholy phrase (as Gretchen sits spinning and the spinning of the wheel seems to generate the music), is an emblem of romantic love: 'Mein Ruh ist hin' ('My peace is away') – she's unhappy and blissful; I could cling to him, faint with his kisses, but I'll never be happy ever again.

She and Faust are lovers; she conceives a child. In this condition, Gretchen is fetching water from the well one day and a friend tells her about another girl who is going to have a baby, fathered by her lover. The friend is deeply scathing about this. And won't the man marry her? Only if he's an idiot; in fact he's gone off already. Everyone is going to mock her – and she deserves it. This reminder of common inhumanity, cynicism and brutality terrifies Gretchen. She doesn't have any resource of counter-argument or moral independence. The only world she knows considers her actions evil and stupid. She is appalled at what she has done.

When her brother, a soldier, discovers the relationship he attacks Faust in the street. Protected by Mephistopheles Faust stabs the brother. As the brother dies, Gretchen runs out to try to comfort him, but he hates her to the end: my death is less painful to me than your loss of honour. His words, however, have for the reader an opposite meaning. The brother regards Gretchen's actions as evil; but an important source of evil here is his sense of honour – his morality, which would rather see them both dead than that Gretchen should have a child outside of marriage.

Goethe makes Gretchen bear an almost impossible accumulation of rejection. She goes to church but 'an evil spirit' – which might as well be called her conscience, guided by the dim lights of her brother and her friend at the well – torments her. She experiences herself as beyond salvation. She kills her mother and, when it is born, her child. Goethe drags Gretchen to the lowest condition. She is annihilated.

While Gretchen is in prison awaiting execution, Faust is led off by Mephistopheles to the 'Walpurgis night' – a demons' orgy which, we are told, takes place every year on the summit of the Brocken in the Harz Mountains. The name derives from that of a chaste Bavarian nun, St Walpurga. This scene – which has moments of deep obscenity worked into it involving mice, leeches and all the lower organs – presents the logic of sexual fantasy, striving after intense excitement and ultimately arriving at self-disgust. As with drunkenness, the idea is that Faust needs to know that he can pursue obscenity, can discharge his sexual imagination – just as he can get drunk if he wants to. This is the proper basis for developing his sense of what he is really after. But the issue of Faust's genuine ambitions is explored only in the second part of the drama. If Faust turns away from extreme sexual fantasy and drunkenness it is not out of prudishness – not because he thinks these are forbidden – but for the right reason: they do not on their own satisfy him.

There is a curious appendage to the Walpurgis-night orgy – a kind of 'masque' celebrating the golden wedding of Oberon and Titania. This scene is an obscure tribute to Shakespeare's *A Midsummer Night's Dream*, in which the wedding of the king and queen of the fairies is presented. This is the first point in the drama at which Goethe seems to give up on any plausible concern with staging. In the masque there are literally dozens of 'voices' who are clearly distinguished in the text but whose identity could hardly be grasped by anyone in the theatre who did not have the book open on their knees.

Part One ends with Gretchen in prison on the morning of her execution. Faust has contrived a means of escape, but Gretchen is beyond any such rescue; she chooses to remain and die, as there is nothing left for her to live for. At this point Faust utters one of the lines that goes to the heart of the whole drama: 'I wish that I had never been born.' The question is whether life – as it is – is worthwhile. Is it better, as the most pessimistic of the Greeks put it, 'never to have been born at all', because to enter into human life is to be humiliated and thwarted and tormented to no purpose? The extremism of Gretchen's situation obscures the general significance of the point. We have to see it in the light of Oscar Wilde's comment on the disgrace he brought upon his wife and children: 'yet each man kills the thing he loves' – not literally, but metaphorically. The condition of life is such that we almost always do bring wretchedness to others and to ourselves. Faust's betrayal of Gretchen is a symbol of that betrayal in its most horrific form.

But even as Faust despairs and Gretchen resolves to die, a voice from the clouds announces: 'She is saved.' But what kind of salvation is this? How are we to understand this intervention from above, which seems like the crudest version of the 'deus ex machina'? What are we to make of this 'god on the swing' being lowered on to the stage to provide a happy ending when the logic of the drama has brought everyone to the brink of disaster – a 'salvation' which was regularly criticized for making absurd the plays in which it occurs?

This is the end of Part One of *Faust* – this drama was published in 1808 to considerable public acclaim: it was the first really big literary success Goethe had had since *Werther*. And subsequently it was as the creator of *Faust* rather than of *Werther* that Goethe was known. Part Two developed very slowly over the following years and was not published until 1832. It is a much stranger production, and much less well known. But that some subsequent drama is required is obvious when we think of the weakness of the end of Part One. Goethe's basic question is just this: is Faust – and hence the human condition – essentially tragic or not? The logic of action, the horrific crushing and annihilation of Gretchen at the end of Part One seems to present life as tragic. But, at the same time, Goethe signals that he doesn't regard this as the right view: Gretchen is 'saved'. But what would one need to add to one's understanding of life to accommodate this? In what perspective would one have to see things in order to move on from what has happened to the poor girl?

It is crucial that this question is not about Gretchen but about Faust. Salvation for Gretchen is not possible – except by the agency of higher powers. The point is that we the audience are assumed not to be Gretchens, but rather Fausts. The audience is composed of those who have caused harm and suffering to others. The question is: how can we be redeemed in life?

7

The Emperor

Part One of *Faust* sticks, just, to a conceivable temporal sequence; it has 'characters' and tells a recognizable, though highly adventurous, human story. All this disappears in Part Two. Faust enters a species of dreamtime, where the dream is something like the history of classical culture from pre-Greek antiquity to the Renaissance and beyond – but this is extremely sketchy. Most of the action is set in a very hazy period, which might be around the end of the Roman Empire, or might be during the Crusades. This mixing of times is something like a representation of the mind of Goethe – in which all times can coexist imaginatively; Goethe can, like everyone else, think about history in a non-linear way, even though we can experience it only in an orthodox manner.

Faust awakens in the Elysian Fields, cleansed of memory or guilt relating to the appalling Gretchen episode. In the company of Mephistopheles he hastens to the court of 'the Emperor'. The generic, unspecified 'Empire' is in a bad way – mainly because there isn't enough money. The army is clamouring for pay and, out of control, is laying waste the country; crime is universal and the law courts a travesty; people have grown selfish and desperate. Even the fool has absented himself. At this point Mephistopheles offers to solve all their problems.

It is presumed that beneath the mountains of the Empire there is gold; well, if there is, says Mephistopheles, it belongs to the Emperor. Although no one can actually lay hands on it, it is still real – just as real as gold locked away in a safe that no one has permission to open. So, 'really', the Emperor is vastly wealthy. All he needs to do is offer bonds or notes backed by this subterranean bullion. One of the

Emperor's advisers suggests that this is the counsel of Satan, but the Emperor willingly makes this 'Faustian bargain'. He trades probity and prudence for immediate access to cash, power and pleasure.

This is an economic 'miracle' – a work of treasury magic – and it tells us something about the way Goethe conceives of magic or occult powers. This scheme can indeed create effects in the world – for the Empire suddenly has a great deal of cash at its disposal. The problem is that these effects are short term. The underlying issues are not really addressed. Superficially it looked as if lack of ready money was the cause of their difficulties – that is the analysis that the Emperor's advisers cling to and assert. But if they had been more acute they would have realized that the chaos of their society has other, more fundamental, causes.

Goethe was not naive – his experience in Weimar, as well as his family history, had given him great respect for money. The value of means depends upon the qualities of the person employing them – and the ends to which they are directed. Great means, on their own, are of no lasting worth. Further, preoccupation with economics gives a misleading account of the nature of the good society – even though affluence is, for Goethe, as for most people, a mark of the good society. But in Goethe's view we are inclined to draw the wrong conclusion. He sees affluence as a product of a good society; whereas the Emperor and his advisers suppose that money is the cause of the good society.

Magic, then, is essentially the name of a false, but tempting, short-cut: it is the general phenomenon of attempting to produce the desired effects without employing the real means. The 'occult' is just a very specific – very intense – version of this much more general phenomenon. Thus it is not surprising that Mephistopheles should be a specialist in magic. At first this seems merely a hangover from the old story – in which demons have access to genuine powers, powers akin to those of God, but which they direct to evil ends, retaining their angelic capacity, but directing it now to rivalry with God. But Mephistopheles is not demonic in this way. He is interesting because he hates something in humanity that many reasonable people are inclined to hate – our tendency towards 'wishful thinking', our desire to be happy without paying the price. So by intensifying this – by helping us take apparent shortcuts (giving the drunkard more to drink, giving the Emperor quick cash, letting us put our sexual fantasies into action) – Mephistopheles encourages the self-destructive aspects of human nature. Alchemy – the supposed knowledge of how to turn base metals into gold – is simply the crudest version of this. You want to be rich but you don't want to work hard or adapt yourself to the requirements of others, do things that other people want? You will the end (riches) but don't will the means (prolonged intelligent effort). Thus 'magic' is the name for the fantasy solution to a very normal problem.

The Emperor, however, is not completely satisfied. Mephistopheles is asked to summon up Helen of Troy – reputed to be the most beautiful woman in the world – for the Emperor's inspection. For some reason this task is beyond the powers of the Devil. But he knows what is required. Faust will have to descend to 'the mothers' and seek their assistance. The 'mothers' are presented as the deepest mystery – beyond comprehension, frightening.

Speculatively, we might consider that 'the mothers' carry two important burdens of meaning. In the Book of Genesis, after Adam and Eve have eaten the apple – and so acquired 'knowledge of good and evil', whatever that might really mean – God curses the pair and punishes them in the most ghastly way. He says to Eve: 'I will greatly multiply thy sorrow and thy conception; in sorrow thou shalt bring forth children.' The conception and birth of a child is, in the simplest sense, the most profound creative process that we encounter. And yet it is deeply strange – since it is not on the basis of intelligence or effort that the mother achieves this. Conception and birth go entirely against the grain of our assumptions about life and creativity. For the single greatest power of creation is completely unrelated to merit: the most deserving of people might be impotent or infertile, the worst of people may have many children.

The second speculative line concerns the nature of maternal love. Maternal love is, ideally – and certainly for Goethe in reality – unconditional. The mother does not love the child because it is good or beautiful or impressive – or even nice. Gretchen, in a remarkable little aside, mentions just how annoying it is to have to feed an infant at night – Goethe is not under any illusion about babies. But all the same – in spite of all the problems and difficulties, in spite of the fact that, as with Gretchen, a baby may, as God so unfortunately ordained, multiply a mother's sorrows – the love for the child is still unconditional.

And why should an encounter with 'the mothers' be a precondition for the raising of Helen – the ideal of perfect human beauty?

In fact Faust is able to summon Helen from the Underworld and present her, in a pageant, to the Emperor. Helen steps forth – Faust is entranced by her beauty. Mephistopheles regards her as 'pretty' but not really to his taste; perfect beauty is the antithesis of the Devil – why? Because the love of beauty calls us to life, it spurs ambition, feeds pride, but also seems to offer a vision of our intrinsic nobility. But the moment Faust tries to touch her – he seizes her – she disappears, there is an explosion and Faust is thrown to the ground.

We have now commenced an allegorical sequence of events. Faust is the representative of humanity – or, a touch less universal, the soul of European culture. Up to now he has been stranded in a kind of medieval limbo – and within a university. He has book learning and a broadly Christian conception of the world. But these have not satisfied him. Part One displayed Faust's yearning – for something: knowledge, land, high status. His encounter with Mephistopheles enabled him to live out his desires but (as Faust himself predicted) this has brought no sense of fulfilment – on the contrary Faust has been embroiled in the tragic sequence with Gretchen.

Now, the vision of Helen has come to be the focus of his desire. He has been able to evoke her ghostly presence – but she is still unattainable. The historical thesis is this: medieval Europe was able to recognize and long for ideal beauty, but was unable to grasp it in an embodied and living form. It could see ideal beauty only at a distance. The question for Europe – and the question for Faust – is: what do you need to do in order to turn the image of beauty into a living reality? And the answer – in the briefest possible term – is: have a Renaissance. And, as God suggested right at the start, the fulfilment of human life, the attainment of living beauty, required the participation of Mephistopheles. Meaning: it required the 'evil' aspect of mankind and also that mankind specifically have the very qualities that Mephistopheles hates. Here we see the doubling back of the Mephistophelean character – its tie to self-hatred. For as a desirable evil Mephistopheles represents the enticement of the qualities he himself professes to despise – and which he mocks. Therefore there is nothing more revolting to Mephistopheles than that someone should be attracted to him.

8

Creation

Faust returns to his old university office with Mephistopheles and they meet again the student whom the Devil had once advised on the course of study. The student is now a devotee of the latest fashion in philosophy. The university has turned him into a nationalist romantic – and something of a boor. A strange side emerges in the character of Mephistopheles: he can't stand the arrogance of youth; the student mocks experience: his professor – meaning Fichte – has told him there's no such thing. Mephistopheles is, the student says, just like any old man. Mephistopheles: how rude you are, how little you understand me. Student: politeness, for us Germans, is only lies.

Goethe confessed to Eckermann that he meant the student to represent 'the presumption which is in particular characteristic of youth, and of which we had such striking examples in the first years after the War of Liberation'. And he adds: 'Everyone thinks in his youth that the world is really only beginning with him, and that everything really exists only for his sake.'

Meanwhile, down in the cellars, Wagner – now promoted to Faust's old rank of professor – has been conducting some experiments. He is trying to create life out of inert matter and succeeds up to a point. In a bell jar he generates a little disembodied spirit – called 'the homunculus'. This product of art, an infant without a mother, is able to live only under glass. He pleads with his 'dearest father' Wagner to clutch him to his breast; but at once realizes that this is impossible.

The homunculus seems to represent something like an awakening yearning for the classical south. He is disgusted by the dingy Gothic chamber where he has been brought into existence. He has no fear of Mephistopheles, whom he regards as belonging to the north. And this seems to be one of Goethe's basic concerns here: essentially, Faust is a man trying to escape from the north to the south (to put it in geographical terms); from the Middle Ages to the classical Renaissance (to put it in historical terms).

Mephistopheles is only a 'Devil' when seen from the point of view of the medieval or Romantic imagination. From the classical point of view, Mephistopheles is a part of life: a part one can work with, without being destroyed by. In a sense the homunculus is sorry for Mephistopheles, since he sees Mephistopheles as a fragment of a man. And the homunculus leads Mephistopheles to a classical Walpurgis night: a classical version of the orgy on the Brocken that occurs in Part One. This scene resolves itself into an enactment of a Raphael fresco – the *Galatea*: 'the greatest evocation of paganism of the Renaissance'.

With the end of the homunculus, who is absorbed into the Raphael fresco, the scene is set for the reappearance of Helen. We have reached the point where we can encounter classical art; and Goethe invents a classical play of his own. It traces the return of Helen to Greece, after the fall of Troy, and her arrival at the palace of her husband, King Menelaus of Sparta.

The war against Troy was fought for the possession of Helen. And symbolically we might think that the sack of Troy and the recapture and homecoming of Helen would be a kind of apotheosis of an imagined Hellenic culture: now she is back in her true home, now all is well. But this is not what occurs. Menelaus intends to sacrifice Helen and he has ordered her to go before him to the palace and make preparation for a sacrifice, without telling her that she will be the victim. So, classical antiquity, in a sense, is about to destroy itself.

Faust comes in as the saviour of Helen. He provides refuge for her in his castle. Faust has become one of the vassals of the Emperor and been accorded states in Greece. The historical background to this is the history of Frankish kingdoms in Greece in the early Middle Ages; but it is quite obscure what difference this touch of historical credibility is supposed to bring with it to the play. Faust lives within the imaginative space of Goethe's culture, as if here he is playing out a kind of imagined life – a perfect genealogy, a perfect career – rather in the manner of his father, although with totally different content and completely unbounded by historical plausibility.

9

Salvation

Faust marries Helen: this is to be taken as symbolizing a union between the classical spirit as embodied by Helen and the world of Faust. His world is German and medieval, as we know from the early part of the play. So the marriage can be regarded as a cultural thesis: the modern world is or ought to be a conjunction of these historical epochs. If this is the right interpretation, it is a pity. For such large claims about the nature of history are always silly. To read *Faust* as a thesis about history is to take Goethe at his weakest. What does Goethe know about world history?

More importantly, it suggests a way in which through marriage Faust is making contact (not just intellectual contact) with the world of the classics: he is able to share his life with the classical spirit and with beauty. In other words, we should pay attention to the idea of marriage here. It is not so much a grand claim about the course of history as an analysis of the needs of a particular kind of person.

Faust and Helen have a son – Byron. But this child does not live long. He is too adventurous and, climbing a cliff, falls to his death.

Faust continues with his work reclaiming the lands from the sea; his kingdom is a kind of imaginative Netherlands. This project is symbolic – and of course also a realization – of the transformation of barren waste to fertile ground. Faust has started with an unpromising realm: just a coastal strip; now he is the lord of fields and towns. This is the right fulfilment for Faust and the point from which we can see the significance of the death of Byron. We can project another kind of ending; one in which Faust becomes a great writer, or in which, like

Byron, he dies fighting (or about to fight) for some noble cause. The whole point about Faust's later career is that he is no longer an academic; he is no longer involved with magic. He doesn't write about how to run a country, or how to reclaim land: he does it.

We should think back to a scene in Part One of the play, in which Faust is translating the opening sentence of the Gospel According to St John. Famously that text starts with the line: 'In the beginning was the word.' The suggestion being that it is words – or ideas – that have priority in life. Faust is deeply dissatisfied with this because he has spent his life dealing rather successfully with words and ideas – but the success has been merely official; he has become a professor, but it hasn't done him much good. To have Faust ending as a great writer would have been to follow a trajectory that has appealed to quite a number of other writers. The developmental goal of Stephen Dedalus, as recounted in *The Portrait of the Artist as a Young Man,* and of the narrator of *Remembrance of Things Past,* is literary. They are, at last, able to become great writers. The whole point about Faust's development is that he moves away from writing, from the word. In his translation he ends up preferring the line: 'In the beginning was the deed, the act.'

Mephistopheles had understood himself as having a bargain with God: the bargain was that if he could make Faust happy on earth he would have shown that man doesn't need God, and so Faust would belong to him. Faust had suggested that he could never be satisfied. And in this he was following a traditional view of life, perhaps best expressed by St Augustine. That was the view that earthly existence can never be satisfying to a human being; from which forlorn evidence was adduced the need of man for God; only God could satisfy man's yearning and need. This was the lesson that Augustine conveyed in his *Confessions.* Faust is a new Augustine. Augustine tried philosophy and literature; he tried the fleshpots of Egypt – much as Faust tried the first Walpurgis night. Augustine tried marriage. But none of this made him content. It was only in his admission to the Church and through his love of God that he came to satisfaction. It is as if Mephistopheles had been assigned to Augustine and had brought him to a condition of satisfaction with life before his famous conversion to Christianity.

So, when Faust admits that he wishes the moment to stay – when he acknowledges his satisfaction in life – it seems to Mephistopheles that he has won. Faust dies and the Devil and his agents prepare to carry him off to Hell. But then it turns out that Faust is saved after all and he is escorted to Heaven.

What has happened is that Mephistopheles has misconstrued the whole character of his engagement with Faust. Faust's satisfaction with life does not show that really he belongs with Mephistopheles. On the contrary, this is what makes him so very distinct from the Devil. The devilish view is not linked to happiness; rather, it is the view that life is inherently awful – that when seen aright one must find life unbearable. By a remarkable revision of the Christian conception – as it is conveyed by St Augustine – it turns out that it is the Devil who finds life unsatisfying. Mephistopheles is the one who holds, as Faust did in his moment of greatest despair, that it would have been better never to have lived at all. It was then that Faust was closest to the Devil. It is Faust's love of life – despite all his suffering and despite the suffering that he has caused others – that redeems him.

10

Faust and Everyday Life

Faust is Goethe's largest attempt to explain how he sees life. And in the broadest terms we can sketch that vision:

The God of the play occupies a special perspective upon life. God sees the whole of Faust's life – whereas Faust himself sees it only bit by bit. The redemption of Faust's soul isn't the act of an external God; rather, it is the conviction that, taken as a whole, life – including Faust's – is good. The act of salvation is Faust's conviction that life is good. The God of the play is essentially passive: he embodies contemplation and completeness; he is the spirit of the entire organized universe, which – as we are told at the beginning – has a vast coherent splendour. But this beauty is not closely concerned with human life, collectively or individually. Belief in the goodness of life has been achieved against the background of despair and cruelty, as they are played out in the early part of the drama.

Mephistopheles isn't an external agency seeking, for its own perverse ends, the downfall of an individual person. Rather, Mephistopheles embodies two things: clarity and energy. Before the coming of Mephistopheles, Faust is stranded in a dingy, limited world: he is bored, frustrated and weak.

Goethe's position here seems to be this: on to the names of God and the Devil we project two aspects of ourselves: contemplative and active. Of course these often end up in opposition. Pascal famously remarked that all the evil in the world comes from our inability to sit quietly in a room. It is activity that causes all our problems. Our appetites, our longing for possessions and for power, our desire to make things and impose our will: all of these are not surprisingly sources of trouble. Yet without them we are like Faust in his room at the beginning – feeling that life is not worth it, that it would have been better never to have been born. To sit, as Pascal suggests, quietly in one's room might be a way of avoiding trouble, but such a life could hardly be called good.

In order to 'redeem ourselves', that is, to feel satisfied with life, we have to embrace our appetites, longings and desire for power. We have to act. But, in so doing, we are going to end up committing all kinds of mistakes – sometimes very serious ones, as Faust does in his relationship with Gretchen.

The trajectory of Faust towards satisfaction involves a move from contemplative passivity to action and freedom. This is a path of correction: Faust needs to range freely through the world and head for the drinking dens, the brothels, the battles and the courts of power because this aspect of his nature is underdeveloped. For him this is the way to find – in the end – a satisfaction in existence which passive contemplation alone cannot yield.

It would, therefore, be quite foreign to Goethe's view of things if we thought that he was making a general pronouncement – go and taste, through the joys and terrors of the world. Maybe – if you have spent your whole life in a university studying law, theology and philosophy. But if you have spent your life in taverns and brothels it's not more of the same that you need.

In his *Divine Comedy* Dante is shown Heaven and Hell; these are, essentially, places of memory and retrospective justice. Every crime or folly or kindness or nobility enacted in life is perpetuated and intensified – nothing is forgotten, nothing is waived; the lesser sins are paid off in waiting rooms of purgatory.

By contrast, *Faust* contains one of the most astonishing – indeed troubling – moments of forgetfulness. At the end of Part One Faust is caught up in the Gretchen tragedy; he is not wholly guilty, but he certainly played a major part in her destruction. At the start of Part Two, he wakes without remorse and without, apparently, any memory of what has taken place. Certainly the poetry of the passage alludes

419

to the progress of time; this forgetting is not the work of a single moment. Nevertheless it is accomplished; Faust never has to pay for his neglect of Gretchen. Dante would have had him suffering through eternity.

We can make sense of the importance of this theme when we look back – across the decades of Goethe's life and work – to the tragedy of Werther. The problem Werther had was that he couldn't forget Charlotte. For the person paralysed by memory, forgetting is a liberation.

In 1815 Goethe wrote a short poem that encapsulates the thinking that went into the huge drama of *Faust*. This amazingly tender poem is entitled 'Es is Gut': 'It is Good'. It takes up the line repeated in the Genesis story of Creation in which God looks upon his daily labours and asserts that the world he is making is good. As with all of Goethe's poetry translation is hopeless, because in recreating the sequence of thought one cannot also capture the tone of the words. The idea is approximately as follows – but one has to add, imaginatively, the sleepy, gentle rhythm of the German lines.

In the moonlight in Paradise, Jehovah saw Adam sunk in a deep sleep. And God set into his side a little Eve, and let her sleep too. There they lay, in earthly smallness, God's two loveliest, most loving thoughts.

'Good!!!' he cried out to himself in recognition of his creative mastery, and could hardly bear to leave them.

And then the character of the poem changes and the lines develop a graceful flow: when we wake, and look freshly into the eye of the one who sleeps with us, and who looks lovingly back at us, we are drawn into that same moment of loving creation.

The key word here is God's self-praise, the 'Good' that he asserts. In the Book of Genesis this good is the prelude to the Fall, for however good the Creation itself may have been we have spoiled it by our knowledge of good and evil – primarily, in the traditional interpretation, by sexual desire: that was why Adam and Eve became aware of their nakedness after they ate the apple and hid from God. But in

Goethe's version the situation is quite different: the sexual union of the imaginary parents of the world is precisely what God has put in motion; and the scope of 'Good' is vastly widened. For creation is good – in the eyes of God – not only in the pre-sexual world of Paradise, but as a whole. And the 'Good' extends not only to Adam and Eve while they are obedient but also to human life as a whole, which includes desire and ambition and mistakes and work and sorrow.

PART TEN

Death

Moral value can be judged only by biography.
                                      Goethe, *Scientific Writing*

I

The Fall of Napoleon

After the defeat at Jena in 1806 Berlin was occupied by the French. The Prussian government fled to the east and attempted to continue the war in alliance with Russia. The fortunes of Napoleon were still rising and in June 1807 he defeated the Russian forces at the battle of Friedland. On 13 June the two Emperors, Alexander and Napoleon, met on a raft on the river Niemen at Tilsit, an event Tolstoy beautifully incorporates in the final sections of Book 2 of *War and Peace*. The *rapprochement* between the French and the Russians, which so confused Nicolai Rostov, left the Prussians isolated and vulnerable and with no sane option other than capitulation. Prussia was reduced in extent, halved in population, its army cut back; the state was required to garrison large contingents of French troops, provide recruits for Napoleon and pay a huge indemnity.

Napoleon, however, was not intending to occupy Prussia indefinitely. He hoped to reform the state and thereby transform it into a natural ally. Napoleon was an heir to the Enlightenment conviction that war between reasonable people was impossible; his conflict with Prussia was conceived as a war between modernity, which he represented, and old Europe. In Prussia he introduced the Code Napoléon and a new rational constitution, following his general recipe for the treatment of German states.

Napoleon's aims were not very different from those of many German reformers, who themselves wanted legal and administrative reform. However, the instrument that Napoleon employed was deeply inadequate. The most notorious failure was the territory of Westphalia, which Napoleon placed under the control of his brother

Jerome. Jerome felt obliged to reward his own supporters on a large scale and the nascent state was plundered and subject to corrupt rule; thus completely reversing the originally admirable logic of transformation. The result in Prussia was disastrous. Under Frederick the Great, Prussia had already been modernized to a large degree and was an inspiration for Napoleon's own conception of government. It was to a considerable extent the humiliation of defeat and the harsh terms of occupation that incited Prussian nationalism and an intense hostility to everything and anything associated with France.

This was doubly unfortunate because during the French occupation, important reforms were undertaken in Prussia under the guidance of Baron Carl vom und zum Stein. Stein organized the end of serfdom – although this was grandly symbolic as it left them largely free but penniless. He revoked the law which prevented aristocratic estates being sold to commoners. Under Stein's successor, von Hardenberg, the reforms continued, including the foundation of the University of Berlin under the guidance of Wilhelm von Humboldt – who had been a close friend of Schiller and was much influenced by Goethe. His brother, Alexander, was Goethe's ideal of the perfect scientist and, when not off taking the temperature of the Amazon, a great favourite of Carl August. Fichte was the first rector at the university and was succeeded by Hegel, both well known to Goethe from their Jena days.

But all this intelligent reform was to be submerged by world events. By 1812 the blockade of continental trade, initiated by France in the hope of harming England, was causing serious problems for some of Napoleon's major supporters at home. Russia, however, defied the embargo and provided an indirect trade route for British exports. To enforce the blockade, Napoleon enlisted a massive army and proceeded to the Russian border. He did not stop until he reached an abandoned Moscow; and was eventually forced to conduct an appalling retreat in the winter by the end of which his army was almost non-existent. Upon his return to Paris Napoleon was wildly defiant, insisting that he could easily raise new and larger armies. But his international enemies naturally considered that his position had weakened. The British forces in Spain under Wellington were making progress. The Russians decided to reclaim territory they had ceded after

Friedland and renewed their alliance with Prussia. The Prussians introduced military service, built up their army and declared war on France
in March 1813.

The Prussian mobilization was supported by the growth of nationalist
sentiment. This was not limited to Prussia but was taken up widely
and ardently in the German states: Prussia came to be regarded as the
conscience and soul of the German people. In some of its more extreme
forms German nationalism was explicitly hostile to the ideas of the
Enlightenment. It did not aim to produce a more reasonable or prosperous society or to enact wiser laws and enhance administrative
efficiency.

One of the leading voices of this new nationalism, Ernst Moritz
Arndt, extolled irrational power: 'The man of action will be guided
by something other than reason and will be guided by something else
through all eternity; he will be guided by the dark forces of the age,
and by a darker love for his people, its way of life, its language which
from childhood has become an inseparable part of the innermost
recesses of his being.' And the right way of enacting this dynamic
particularity, he proposed, was in violent struggle – the war with
France would not be a ghastly necessity but a wonderful opportunity.
It was the perverse side of Herder's theory of language and local
culture – the theory Goethe had heard all about long ago as he sat by
Herder's sickbed in Strasbourg. Arndt was a highly successful publi-
cist; he recast patriotism in religious terms, as a source of personal
salvation; he laments his own individual weakness, he accuses himself
of sins; but all of this is redeemed in the moments of national assertion
– at which point he loses his individuality and is purified and raised
to ecstasy: 'when a band of warriors passes by with flowing banners
and sounding trumpets, then I realize that my feelings and my actions
are not an empty illusion, then I feel the indestructible life, the eternal
spirit, and eternal God . . . like other men I am egoistic and sinful but
in my exaltation I am freed at once from all my sins, I am no longer a
single suffering individual . . .'

Goethe met Arndt in Dresden in 1812 – unsurprisingly the two did
not get on. Goethe taunted Arndt: 'rattle your chains to your heart's

content; you won't break them' – meaning, perhaps, you'll never see the overthrow of Napoleon. Not a very prescient remark and one can imagine how Arndt would have gloated in later years at his victories over Napoleon and Goethe. But there is another, more powerful, point that Goethe can be seen as making. Arndt's 'shackles' are internal: it is not the power of Napoleon that keeps him in chains, but the poverty of his thought and imagination. Even if Napoleon is overthrown, Arndt will still be the prisoner of his own rattling, constricting fanaticism. He can never be free no matter how many French emperors are disposed of, because he carries a tyrant within.

The forces combined against Napoleon at first suffered some reverses, but they had great strategic advantages. Their joint resources were immense; the Prussians and Russians were driven by an implacable need for vengeance. Their great moment came at the huge, prolonged battle of Leipzig, which started on 16 October 1813. Militarily defeated, Napoleon refused to surrender and six months later the allied forces entered Paris. Napoleon was exiled to Elba, and the Congress of Vienna, which was to reconfigure Europe, opened its lengthy and convoluted negotiations. Less than a year into his reign as Emperor in Elba, Napoleon was back and for a hundred desperate days attempted to break up the coalition arrayed against him. It ended, of course, at Waterloo on 8 July 1815, with Napoleon finally conceding permanent defeat a few days later.

2

Nationalism

After the battle of Leipzig, the then Jena professor of history, Luden, invited Goethe to contribute to a forthcoming journal entitled *Nemesis* – alluding to Napoleon's hubris – which was to be emphatically nationalist and anti-French. Goethe was not enthusiastic. Luden, who clearly rather liked Goethe, left a record of the conversation. 'Do not be persuaded,' said Goethe, 'that I am indifferent to the great ideas – freedom, Fatherland and People; they form a portion of our own being which no one can cast off. Germany is dear to my heart. I have often felt a bitter pain at the thought that the German people, so honourable as individuals, should be so miserable as a whole. A comparison of the German people with other peoples' – by whom he probably means the French and the English – 'awakens a painful feeling which I try to escape in any way I can; and in Art and Science I have found such escapes; for they belong to the world at large and before them vanish all the limits of nationality.'

Goethe's care for the German people does not aim at fostering a unique national identity – but rather at raising people to a love of art and science. And such devotion cannot possibly have a national focus, for such love – if it is genuine – will attach itself to beauty and truth wherever these are to be found. In making this point Goethe was being faithful to his own history. Half of his intellectual and emotional culture derived from France; how could a cultivated person be – in blanket fashion – anti-French? Luden – Goethe felt – was asking him to say that Molière was a useless dramatist, that Diderot was a fool, that Claude Lorraine was a bad painter.

*

At the time and for many years afterwards Goethe was considered reprehensible for his lack of enthusiasm for the national cause. Writing in 1855, Goethe's first English biographer, George Henry Lewes – consort of George Eliot – was still ambivalent about a man who could resist the call to serve his nation with his pen, and pleads that the reader not judge Goethe too harshly. Perhaps – he lamely suggests – Goethe was just too old; perhaps he simply didn't recognize that this was the authentic voice of the future that he was bound to serve.

Goethe in fact was replicating the attitude he had taken to the French Revolution and which had been well expressed by Schiller. Namely, that it doesn't matter how many revolutions you have or how ardent your beliefs or sincere your passions – none of this makes for a better society. We know how to make a better society; it will happen when 'everyone according to his talents, according to his tendencies and according to his position does his utmost to increase the culture and development of the people'. As things stand the people are not capable of participating in a really good society. All this enthusiasm will not result in things being better. Perhaps more than anything what Goethe couldn't stand was the illusory nature of the excitement – the endless assertions: if only we win this battle, if only we can throw off the foreign yoke, etc. To which Goethe is clearly thinking – well then you'll still be the boorish mass you always were; only you'll now be an exultant boorish mass. 'Is every agitation an elevation?' he asks.

Further, Goethe was deeply disturbed by the side effects of war – the destruction to private property and to public buildings – and the depletion of civic, personal and state wealth. This was not selfishness but a view based on a political principle which he cherished and which has great plausibility. The actual quality of existence of citizens depends upon the cultural wealth which has been accumulated by wise government – by fine parks, by rows of solid, comfortable and elegant homes, by art collections and libraries, by the continuous existence of universities; by the fact that money accumulated in one's lifetime can be securely passed on to subsequent generations so that they may have more liberal lives. The national zeal tended to make great play of sacrifice: we will give up all our wealth, abandon our farms, put everything to the service of the Fatherland – and then all will be well. But this is a dreadful equation: does the Fatherland really deserve everything?

Goethe hated the disturbance of war but, like many intelligent Germans, he was broadly sympathetic to Napoleon's conception of Europe – which was designed to provide peace and stability. In fact Napoleon had enjoyed fairly widespread popularity in Weimar: the people had put out their flags and been delighted by the social grandeur of Erfurt. Now the same people were furiously hostile to Napoleon – nothing could be too bad for this monster.

The Congress of Vienna had large consequences for Weimar. What had been the Holy Roman Empire was reorganized as the German Confederation. The number of states was drastically reduced – to a mere thirty-four together with four autonomous cities, of which Frankfurt was one. Prussia was a major beneficiary of the reorganiz- ation – having indeed taken a leading role in the removal of Napoleon. Many parties wanted a powerful Prussia, strong enough to provide security against any future French resurgence, but not so strong as to dominate the German Confederation. Austria also took a leading position in the confederation but lacked the economic and administrat- ive powers of Prussia. Nevertheless some balance between the forces was maintained by the lesser German states.

One of the provisions of the German Confederation was that each state should be given a constitution; this was not universally followed but Weimar did get a liberal constitution in 1816 – very much the doing of Carl August and strongly opposed by Goethe. The State of Weimar itself was enlarged and its population doubled; Carl August was made a grand duke.

3

West-East Divan

Throughout the second decade of the nineteenth century Goethe made regular, extensive summer visits to spas, mainly in Bohemia. The society he encountered there was far more cosmopolitan than that of Weimar. In 1814 and again in 1815 he broke with his usual pattern of summer trips and headed west to the region of his childhood. One day at the casino in Wiesbaden – not far from Frankfurt – an old acquaintance, a local banker named Willemer, came up to speak to him. He introduced Goethe to his long-standing mistress, Marianne Jung. She was then aged about thirty and had been a ballet dancer before she met the much older Willemer.

Goethe fell in love with Marianne, building an oriental fantasy around her and his relationship with her. She made him a pair of oriental slippers, arranged a turban on his head, and in the evenings he wore a flowing white robe. He thought of her as Suleika – the wife of Potiphar – and of himself as Joseph, son of Jacob. At other times he is the poet Hafis, who wrote of love in the disturbed time of Tamerlane. Marianne responded sympathetically to this fantasy. They wrote poems for each other inspired by Islamic prototypes. These poems were later to form the kernel of Goethe's *West-Eastern Divan* (1819). The term 'divan' is Persian in origin – meaning in fact a 'state council' and later a 'collection' (a kind of gathering) of poems. But it also came to stand for the cushioned bench upon which the councillors sat – hence its modern meaning as a 'daybed'.

Marianne's poems were included beside Goethe's – although it was assumed that he had written them until she revealed her authorship late in her life (she died in 1860). Willemer and Marianne married in

September 1814, but the banker was not exactly a possessive husband. He suggested that the three of them live together. Ironically, Goethe was at last presented with the chance of living the kind of relationship he had dreamed of in his youth. 'Sharing' a woman was the erotic arrangement suggested as a solution in both *Stella* and *Werther*.

Goethe's relationship with Marianne developed during the last spasms of Napoleon's military career. When Goethe headed west to see her in the summer of 1815 he found the roads infested with the allied troops marching to confront Napoleon. The turn to the Orient of his imagination, and to the past, was a deliberate strategy of escape. In one of the most philosophical of the *Divan* poems, Goethe elaborates a vision of 'the realm of poetry' that is distinct from the world of politics.

Put into prose the 'argument' of the poem goes like this: anyone who wants to understand poems has to go to the realm of poetry. The regions of the world are tearing themselves apart, empires are collapsing; thrones are tumbling to the ground. Let us go then (you and I) to the pure 'East' to breathe the 'patriarchal air'; to kiss and drink wine and sing – it will make me feel young again.

Goethe could hardly have chosen a worse word than 'patriarchal' to characterize the kind of life one might lead in the realm of the poets. 'Patriarchy' is now a technical term of feminist criticism: it names, in the most general terms, what feminism is opposed to. So Goethe's desire to take his lover off to enjoy the 'patriarchal air' is to present his own head on a plate to unkind critics.

In that land of poetry, Goethe finds essentially a simple life: one in which people live by 'God's teaching, communicated in easy, earthly words'; where people don't argue and interpret and 'break their heads' trying to work out what they should think or how they should live. In that imagined place – in that longed-for way of life – one's confidence in life is deep, but there's no need to think very much. And when you do speak your words have weight and sound serious – because you do not chatter but speak only from the heart.

In a sense it is easy to see that this is not so much a vision of how life used to be as a record of how it actually is when one is in the early days of mutual love. Your faith – or confidence – in the loved one, and theirs in you, is deep and easy and doesn't need to be understood in complex language. When you say 'I love you' or 'you are beautiful' the words – at that privileged moment – carry weight and ring true, and there is no need, no desire, in that state to construct theories about the nature of love or beauty or truth.

4

The Politics of Youth

In 1815 reform-minded and nationally enthusiastic students at Jena established a fraternity – a 'Burschenschaft' – that continued the themes of the nationalist opposition to Napoleon into the new era. The three basic principles which fired the students were: national unity – of the German states; 'freedom' – particularly in the face of the governmental reaction in some states which had occurred after their triumph over the French; and constitutional reform. The student society at Jena was particularly influential.

In 1816 – on 6 June – Christiane died; she would have been fifty the following year. She had been seriously ill for several weeks. It was a hard, distressing end, a sequence of agonizing seizures dragged out over her final week; the opiates she was given did little to reduce her suffering.

She had lived with Goethe for more than twenty-five years. Despite its early romantic character, the relationship had not been conventionally successful. That Goethe in some sense always loved Christiane is not in doubt; but the kind of love he had for her was limited. She was an important person in his life, but certainly not the centre of his life. Throughout her last year, Christiane's diary – a bare record of comings and goings in the Frauenplan house, rather than an intimate journal – has the almost daily remark: 'Mittag für uns': 'Lunchtime for us.' Meaning, that Goethe – whom she referred to as 'der Geheimrat' ('the privy councillor') – had given her a little part of his day. He deeply valued her warmth and naturalness – although this became harder to do as she lost her looks; she became fat and ugly. She drank too much and was not a particularly wise or careful mother.

It certainly does not amount to a modern ideal of married life; but one conclusion which cannot be drawn is that Christiane ever resented Goethe's mode of life, that she was angry or upset that he had romantic attachments elsewhere. The oriental ideal that Goethe develops in the *West-Eastern Divan* is essentially to do with the absence of erotic envy. In 'The Diary' he writes of a man – presumably himself – sharing the story of his erotic adventure with his wife. From all we know of her, Christiane would have been someone who could participate in this. She was not particularly possessive – to her Goethe was an incredible gift, an extraordinary arrival in her life. She may never have expected to be more than a 'bed-friend' (as Goethe's mother had called her).

As Christiane lay dying, very close to the end, Goethe himself fell ill. His collapse was surely connected to her impending death. He stayed in bed until she was buried and then got up and returned to his desk.

In 1817 the Jena students organized a festival to celebrate the fourth anniversary of the battle of Leipzig: the iconic national victory over Napoleon, France and the cosmopolitan conception of society. The festival was condoned by the archduke but got out of hand. Some of the students burned a few books – the Code Napoléon was particularly hated, presumably for its title and for being French rather than because of any disagreements about the principles of jurisprudence. Ironically, there was also much anti-Prussian feeling in the air. This was particularly muddled since the most probable beneficiaries of any move to German unity would be the Prussian state. The authorities in Weimar and Jena didn't bother themselves much about all this student rowdiness. These symbolic acts, however, irritated authorities elsewhere who regarded Weimar as unduly lax and hospitable to revolutionary elements. The students never constituted a mass movement – the whole student population in Germany was less than ten thousand, of whom only a few hundred were in Jena; the radical wing represented, in any case, only about one quarter of even that number. But they did attract attention.

A crisis came in 1818 when a radical student called Sand murdered the writer Kotzebue – whose books had been among those burned in 1817. He was an extremely popular author although loathed by Goethe, who suggested that the saints in Heaven would rejoice to see these works go up in flames. Kotzebue was the most performed of German authors, a great mainstay of the Weimar theatre and connected with reactionary Russian interests. Sand was soon arrested and executed: a few people regarded him as a martyr – the executioner sold the wood of the scaffold as relics. But as is generally the way the authorities got much the better of it. Obviously, Kotzebue was not hated by the very large numbers of people who went to his plays and it was easy to use his murder to justify aggressive action against student bodies – even though Sand was more of a demented individual than the agent of an organized movement.

Holidaying during that August of 1818 in fashionable Carlsbad the ministers of several states discussed and coordinated their actions at a series of elegant parties. External supervision of universities was established; suspect professors had to be dismissed at once and barred from ever being employed at any German university; liberal journals were suppressed; informers were recruited. In due course several of the Jena students were arrested and harshly sentenced. This was an aspect of the general reactionary politics of Austria, Prussia and Russia. Goethe was in an unusual position; he was by no means at one with Metternich (the guiding spirit of Austrian politics) or Hardenberg (still at the helm in Prussia); but he was not feared or opposed by such figures. They were, for example, quite happy to have Goethe appointed to oversee the University of Jena in their name – a position he did not care to accept.

Their trust in Goethe was personal rather than political: he had known Hardenberg since his teenage years when they had both been at Leipzig and had studied painting together. Goethe celebrated his sixty-ninth birthday that year at Carlsbad. In his loyalty to Carl August and his outward demeanour Goethe was unthreatening.

The policies put together over the dinner tables at the spa, the Carlsbad Decrees, were applied throughout the German Confederation. An early casualty was Wilhelm von Humboldt, who resigned from office in Berlin – since he regarded such measures as hugely impeding the development of higher education.

In fact Goethe really was not very impressed by the young men of the day. But the terms of his analysis were not exactly those of the high politicians. What Goethe found dismaying was the students' earnestness, their lack of sensuous delight. 'Short-sighted, pale, narrow-chested, young without youth; that is a picture of most of them. And if I enter into conversations with any of them, I immediately see that the things in which I take pleasure seem to them vain and trivial; they are entirely absorbed in the Idea and that only the highest problems of speculation are fitted to interest them. Of sound senses or delight in the sensuous, there is no trace; all youthful feeling and all youthful pleasure are driven out of them.'

He would have preferred them to be like his lovely Wilhelm Meister: falling for actresses, seeing the world, keen on fencing and dancing, bursting with delight in life. The young men – he now felt – were asking too much of the world: they wanted grand political change to make life wonderful; but that is not how life is improved. Goethe mocked them as 'waiting for a second Christ' and disdaining the actual, limited, things that could be done here and now. They needed, as Wieland had suggested decades before, to be saved by the cleavages of pretty girls.

Because Goethe was a great intellectual we might be surprised at the terms in which he condemns the education of the young intellectuals of the period: 'I cannot approve the requirement, in the studies of future statesmen, of so much theoretically learned knowledge, by which young people are ruined before their time, in both mind and body. When they enter into practical service, they possess indeed an immense stock of philosophy; but in the narrow circle of their calling this cannot be practically applied and must therefore be forgotten as useless. On the other hand, what they most need they have lost; they are deficient in mental and bodily energy, which is quite indispensable in practical life.'

Goethe's hard words can sound like the crabbed resentment of an ageing man: he hates young people because they are young. In fact Goethe's position is more interesting than this, when we consider the terms of his hostility. He criticizes an over-intellectual attitude to life and its two concomitants: neglect of the body and disdain for practical experience. He is concerned with effectiveness and happiness: he hopes that a better kind of education would give these people 'what they most need'; his attention is directed to their needs.

For all his wise words, Goethe's relationship with youth was about to undergo its most severe – and most personal – crisis.

5

Love's Elegy

In 1823 Goethe fell seriously ill – a problem with his heart. But it was also a time of good fortune. In that year Peter Eckermann, an impoverished (and not very accomplished) scholar, arrived in Weimar. He kept a record of his conversations with Goethe, together with many details of Goethe's domestic life, which were eventually published as the four volumes of *Conversations with Goethe* (1837). In these works we do not just hear what Goethe said, we accompany Eckermann into Goethe's house, we go to Goethe's parties, drop in during a dinner, sit with him in the evening over a bottle of wine.

For the summer Goethe went as usual – and, as it turned out, for the last time – to a Bohemian spa, to Marienbad. He had been there in the two previous summers. In Marienbad he normally lodged in the large house of a retired Prussian officer. The daughter of the house, Frau von Levetzow, was an old acquaintance whom he had first met at Carlsbad in 1806 when she was nineteen. She was now thirty-five. Divorced from a first husband, her second had died at Waterloo. She was by this stage separated from a third husband but intimately attached to Count Klebelsberg – an ambitious and rich local aristocrat. But that fateful year, 1823, the accommodation in her house – the best available in the town – was given over to Carl August, and Goethe stayed across the road at an inn. But he spent a lot of time on the family's terrace in the company of Frau von Levetzow and her three teenage daughters, who provided much loving attention.

Goethe was especially taken with the eldest girl, nineteen-year-old Ulrike. When they had first met he had been much attracted by her

440

natural charm. She had no idea of his reputation as a writer, and found his enthusiasm for rocks, which he collected on his daily walk, rather dry. He learned to put chocolates among the specimens for her to eat as he talked.

Goethe at seventy-four had visibly aged: his movements had become less sure; his eyes had lost something of their vitality; his face was less expressive – so thought Caroline von Humboldt, wife of Wilhelm, when she saw Goethe at the spa that year. He was still beautiful, but with an older beauty, she tactfully said. But a young girl who met Goethe that summer gives a revealing description. She was Lili Parthey, who had some connection with Goethe's old friend, the music master Zelter.

Lili was thrilled to see Goethe walking along the street or chatting to a prince, but she noted how old his mouth looked. When he spoke, though, when he was charmed – and charming – how he changed. He came across to her one afternoon, held her hand, and told her that she was beautiful – just as Zimmermann had said she was. In her journal she wrote that at such moments Goethe was as beautiful as Apollo. Having her hand kissed by Goethe was 'The happiest moment of my life; the climax of my existence.'

From a purely literary point of view, it is a great pity Goethe did not fall in love with communicative Lili; she would have left an intriguing journal. As it was, none of Goethe's loves left much – almost nothing at all – about what it was like to be loved by him.

That year Goethe fell in love with Ulrike. He was continually seen with the von Levetzow girls hanging on his arms; the upper-class tourists who hoped to be introduced to the great man took to courting Ulrike. Goethe's strength – if not his good sense – it was remarked, was returning.

He seriously considered marrying her – despite being fifty-five years her senior. He consulted his doctor – who assured him there was at least no medical reason not to go ahead. But Goethe certainly realized how strange this suggestion might appear to the girl and her family. He prevailed upon Grand Duke Carl August to formally present the offer of marriage. The duke even promised a very substantial pension of two thousand thalers a year for Ulrike when, as could only be expected, Goethe predeceased her – which he did, by sixty-seven years. But Ulrike showed no interest in marrying Goethe. The offer was formally refused by her grandmother.

But Goethe could not let the matter drop. He assured Ulrike that she would be much loved in Weimar – that August and his wife, Ottilie, would love her and be delighted to have her with them in the Frauenplan house. (It seems clear that Goethe never intended anyone to actually live with him – just in his house; and certainly not in his half of the house.) His behaviour was sufficiently worrying to lead Frau von Levetzow, who was immensely fond of Goethe, to take Ulrike and her sisters away to Carlsbad. But he soon followed them to Carlsbad, and took the rooms directly above theirs at the inn. This strained situation lasted for a few days before Ulrike's mother decided to leave. Goethe was abandoned; perhaps for the first time he was the one who was left.

In his carriage on the journey back to Weimar he wrote 'The Marienbad Elegy'. It was a cry of pain not just for the loss of Ulrike but also for his sense that love would never be open to him again.

> Once by the gate she caught me . . .
> The hasty kiss – how she ran and caught me,
> Pressed my mouth with an even laster last
> Still that living image of desire
> Burns in my heart a script of living fire.
>
> If ever love restored a lover's soul,
> . . .
>
> There's no self-concern, no self-importance
> Where she stands;
>
> As if I heard her say: 'Hour by hour
> Life gives itself, exuberant, unasked;
> Yesterday's meaning is a withered flower;
> Tomorrow! – who can live there
> Where is tomorrow hidden?
> But today . . .' She smiled

You and your pretty wisdom break my heart . . .

Tears are my only philosophy . . .

Years without her!
Her image haunts me a thousand ways:
Sun on her hair; dusk about her –

What good's all this?

 Ulrike was never to marry. She lived well into her nineties, dying in 1899. 'It was not love,' she remarked about her own side of things to those who inquired into her relationship to Goethe. She was another of those women – of whom Thomas Mann made Charlotte Kestner the moral advocate – whose lives became strained and difficult because of a brief encounter, serious though chaste, with a man who made use of his relationships as the material of his art.

On Tuesday 14 October 1823 Eckermann went to a large evening party given by Goethe. He arrived early and was delighted by the long series of brilliantly lit rooms opening one into the other. Eventually he found Goethe alone in the furthest room. They looked at a painting together. Soon the other guests began to arrive, gradually filling the suite of reception rooms. Eckermann had a chat with August about a recent play and noted that Ottilie would often come up to Goethe and give him a kiss. Eckermann complained to Goethe about getting bored at the theatre. Goethe argued that getting bored was a good thing: 'You are penetrated with the hatred of bad plays and that gives you a clearer insight into what a good play is.' Goethe then went off to join some ladies who were laughing and talking in a very lively manner. Later a courtier played some pieces by Beethoven and one of the ladies related details of the composer's life and character. At ten everyone left.

 The fame of Goethe – and of the intellectual culture that had grown up around him – drew many visitors to Weimar. They included William Thackeray (who later wrote *Vanity Fair*), who stayed some time and seems to have known Goethe quite well. Carlyle translated *Wilhelm Meister* and sent Goethe a copy, proclaiming himself in an accompanying letter as 'Goethe's disciple'; Goethe, he says, is his 'spiritual father', the man 'by whom I have been delivered from darkness'. Carlyle, in a sense, takes up where Schiller left off, presenting Goethe not just as a successful writer and poet but as a man who has something profoundly important to communicate to the world. Goethe never met Carlyle but corresponded affectionately with him and sent presents to Mrs Carlyle.

6

Death of the Grand Duke

Eckermann fell ill – not very seriously – in the spring of 1828. He told Goethe: 'I sleep badly, I have the most harassing dreams . . . I feel weak and unnerved in the daytime, without a wish or thought for intellectual activity' – and he frequently complained to Goethe about his condition.

Goethe suspected it was constipation and recommended drinking plenty of mineral water, a visit to a doctor and a cure at one of the spas. 'But do not linger,' he warned, 'attack it at once.' Eckermann, however, did nothing and the complaints only got worse. Eventually, Goethe lost patience: 'You are like the father of Tristram Shandy, who was annoyed half his life by a creaking door and who could not come to the resolution of removing the daily annoyance with a few drops of oil. But so it is with us all! The darkening and illumination of man makes his destiny.'

This observation is characteristic of Goethe – we spoil our lives by not addressing the practical things we could do to improve our lot. Instead of attacking straight away the things that interfere with our real concerns, we linger and live with them.

The essential thing about Napoleon was that he didn't do this. This, Goethe suggests, was the secret of his astonishing career – Napoleon's lesson for life, as it were; and here he's not praising Napoleon the political and military leader, but trying to imagine what a Napoleonic attitude to other aspects of existence might be. Clearness, energy and stamina are the qualities he is commending here.

*

Alexander von Humboldt, who had been an intimate of the grand duke for many years, was with him in Berlin and at Potsdam in the last days of the duke's life in June 1828.

Alexander described Carl August's last days: 'I'd never known him more lucid, mild, thoughtful and bright – although when combined with such bodily weakness and such advanced physical illness this is a terrifying phenomenon. The grand duke himself shifted from moments of hope to moments of expectation of death; he wanted to know about some granite that had been brought from Sweden, about the impact of a comet's tail on our atmosphere, why winter is harsher on the east coast of the northern European countries – and much else.

'He slept at intervals during his discourse and mine; was often restless; and then said – mildly and kindly, to excuse his inattention – "You see, it's all up with me now." Then he began to talk in a desultory way about religious matters.'

Goethe – now seventy-nine – was deeply affected by the death of the grand duke. Carl August had had an immense impact on Goethe's life and their mutual loyalty spanning more than fifty years was astonishing. The only serious strain in their relationship had come, in fact, towards the end. Goethe was responsible for the Weimar Theatre, and he took this duty seriously not just as an artistic director but also as a practical manager. He had tried very hard – in difficult circumstances – to create a professional spirit among the actors and particularly disliked it when actresses doubled as courtesans. This was impossible to prevent, however, when Carl August himself had an affair with one of the actresses. The actress then decided that she wanted to appear in a play with a dog, which Goethe regarded as absurd and completely contrary to all his principles. She no doubt made a fuss about this in the bedroom – who is in charge here: you (darling) or silly old Baron von G? Carl August ordered Goethe to allow the dog on stage; Goethe pleaded and argued – but to no avail. He resigned.

It was a bitter dispute, but both men were sensible enough to see that – however infuriating to either side – it was minor in comparison with their lifelong collaboration. Together they had made Weimar one of the most culturally and intellectually famous and respected places in Europe – an astonishing achievement given its tiny size and very limited means.

When Carl August died, Goethe headed off to the lovely castle at Dornburg, one of the duke's country places. He withdrew for a while from Weimar and tried to console himself with new activities. Eckermann sometimes came to visit Goethe, who, he said, 'seemed very happy, and repeatedly expressed his delight at the beautiful situation of the castle and gardens'.

'I enjoy here,' said Goethe, 'both good days and good nights. Often before dawn I am awake, and lie down by the open window to enjoy the splendour of the three planets at present visible together, and to refresh myself with the increasing brilliance of the morning-red at sunrise. I then pass almost the whole day in the open air and hold spiritual communion with the tendrils of the vine which say good things to me . . . If it were permitted, I should like always to remain here.'

It was deeply pleasing to Goethe – and a sign of his own constructive influence – that Carl August, 'one of the greatest princes Germany ever possessed', should have had Alexander von Humboldt, one of the most intelligent and knowledgeable men, with him at the end; and not merely as a chance witness, but as a close friend. This is central to Goethe's political philosophy: we need von Humboldts who can be friends with princes; and we need princes who appreciate and love such men and show them the highest possible honour, and who are eager to learn from them – in the areas in which they are competent.

Goethe's withdrawal after the duke's death was symptomatic of a general strategy of avoidance. Goethe did not merely hate and fear death, he seemed to need to avoid even acknowledging that it was possible. He could not bear to even hear about it. He did not go to Schiller's deathbed; nor to Christiane's; in his intimate correspondence with Zelter the death of August is passed over as rapidly as possible.

To gain some perspective on Goethe's attitude we might contrast it with the understanding of death found in the writings of Alexandre Dumas. Dumas came after Goethe, but his historical romances are set earlier. A central motif of all these stories is the idea that life is driven by devotion to ideals of conduct that may be served by dying in certain appropriate ways. For example, in *The Three Musketeers* (1844), one of the heroes is mocked for wearing a fanciful doublet; this slight to his honour can be avenged only by a duel. As it happens the heroes nearly always win their duels, but the point of the code of honour is that it makes sense to die in the act of upholding your honour. This is more important than carrying on living in dishonour. Service to one's feudal lord, or to one's mistress, has the same logic: a violent early death isn't a tragedy if it occurs in the service of these ideals.

In Goethe's mind there can be no such ideals: the point of life is self-cultivation: the harmonious development of one's character. To die for a feudal lord or to kill oneself for the sake of love are not noble or admirable – they cut short, rather than fulfil, the central business of life.

Dumas's immense popularity occurred in an era when such conduct was not only illegal but also very far from being admired anywhere except in works of fiction. The excitement is one of contrast – if in fact one lives in order to accumulate a fortune, pursue research or get elected and re-elected as a deputy or some other material end, then it is pointless to die for honour or out of loyalty to an ideal. Such projects can't be completed: they are open-ended and hence one could never die for their sake. In dying you can affirm, and fulfil, the demands of feudal loyalty or courtly love or honour. But you can't become wealthy or knowledgeable or a social success through death.

Goethe's position is not, however, the same as that of the readers of Dumas. Economic and social considerations – in relation to which death is always premature – are not ends in themselves. The purpose of life isn't to be knowledgeable or wealthy or to attain high status. These resources and advantages are enhancements of existence; in fact they may allow us to live more fully. The experience of power and authority may contribute to a more balanced view of the world; it may enrich aspects of personality – ideally we become more circum-spect, more responsible: mature. Money allows for freedom, for self-expression and self-realization; and the getting of money is, again, a fruitful engagement with reality. Knowledge is a natural foundation for wisdom. But, of course, all of these are only 'mays' and 'ideallys'. In other words, there is no causal link between money, knowledge and status and the flowering of life. Goethe is sure that, for most people, these are necessary conditions for a good life; but they are not on their own sufficient conditions.

Thus Goethe occupies a position of great modern relevance. He is critical of the feudal and later Romantic view that what matters most is the ideal – death may fulfil life; money, power, learning and status are chimeras. In this respect he is at one with the view of life most people accept – in practice – today.

7

A Lunch Party

On Saturday 11 October 1828 Eckermann went to a lunch party of Goethe's – arriving a little in advance of the others so that they could talk about an article Carlyle had written. It was full of praise for *Wilhelm Meister*, which Carlyle had translated. Goethe had read the piece that morning and was obviously much cheered by it – seeming 'in quite youthful spirits', wearing his elegant black frock coat which Eckermann thought made him look his best.

Wilhelm Meister had come in for quite a lot of abuse in Great Britain on account of its supposed immorality. Carlyle had faced the objection that 'no virtuous lady could read the book' and countered it – perhaps not very convincingly – with the fact that the late Queen of Prussia had studied it and was nevertheless generally held in the highest esteem. De Quincey – who wrote so honestly about his addiction to opium – denigrated *Wilhelm Meister* as a filthy and indecent work, lasciviously detailing the wickedness of all the women in it, just in case his readers have not yet had the chance to be shocked and disgusted by it themselves. Wordsworth hated it: according to Emerson, ' "It was," he said, "full of all manner of fornication. It was like the crossing of flies in the air." He had never gone further than the first part; so disgusted was he that he threw the book across the room.'

As Goethe and Eckermann discussed Carlyle's piece the other guests began to arrive and Goethe went over to greet them; he then turned back to Eckermann who mentioned, approvingly, Carlyle's suggestion that everyone should be made to read the book.

Goethe drew Eckermann aside, into a window recess. 'My dear fellow,' says Goethe, 'I'll tell you something which I think will help you – and which might simplify your life in later years' – that is, when I am dead and you are an advocate of my work – 'My work simply cannot be popular. Anyone who thinks it can be – and who tries to win popularity for it – is making a mistake. I haven't written for people in general – for people en masse. I've written for individuals – people who are looking for something that engages with their individuality (with what makes them not part of the crowd, with what makes them lonely) and whose minds tend in roughly the same direction as mine.'

Goethe was going to say more but a young lady came up, started chatting and drew him away to another conversation. Soon they went through to the formal dining room to eat. Eckermann could not follow the general conversation – he could not get Goethe's words out of his mind; words which, of course, touched on the meaning of his life since he saw himself as someone who could bring Goethe to wider appreciation.

A few years before there had been a fire at the Weimar Theatre and Eckermann had been particularly moved by the sight of one of the theatre musicians weeping over the remains of his violin, which had been severely damaged. Now Eckermann's vision of Goethe as universally popular was going up in flames.

Everyone else was jesting and talking, and eating the excellent lunch, Eckermann contributing only the occasional monosyllable – hardly even thinking of what he was saying. Until one woman asked him a question and his reply was so distracted and pointless that everyone started laughing at him. Goethe steps in to rescue him and a little later, when some very fine grapes were brought in, Goethe divided them and passed Eckermann a particularly nice bunch across the table. 'I highly enjoyed the grapes from Goethe's hand, and was now quite near him both in body and soul.' It was a touching moment. If Goethe was not to be universally popular it made this intimate moment all the more special – and now, for those readers who do come to love Goethe, it is the symbol of our relationship to him.

Eckermann tried to imagine the kinds of people who would find Goethe's work useful and attractive. He decides they would be people who are themselves engaged in trying to do something serious and creative – artists, poets, scientists. It would be a limited, but a serious and devoted, audience: 'all that is great and skilful exists with the minority. Passions and feelings may become popular; it is not to be imagined that reason can ever become so.'

If Goethe had come to terms with the fact that he would never be a 'popular' author – in the sense of being the favourite reading of a wide audience – he had not given up other ambitions; he had an alternative conception of success.

In these later years Goethe often talked about what he called 'world literature'. This was partly envisaged as counter to any nationalist idea of writing. However, the notion of world literature was not – as we might easily imagine – just about being interested in writing from other places. It was not that Goethe desperately wanted people in Russia or Spain to read an author like Kotzebue, who was highly popular in Germany. Or that Germans should read middling Spanish or Russian works. That would be to see world literature as a global lowest common denominator. World literature was not envisaged as writing for a universal audience; rather, it was the idea that the best writing will never have a large readership at any particular place and time; yet it is able to hold its own in quite different places and times from that in which it was created.

The audience for such writings is the communion saints or the society of noble spirits; or, rather, such writing helps constitute a society of this kind out of the otherwise isolated individuals who are not quite at home in their own place and time. It is Goethe's attempt – perhaps the only conceivable attempt – to resolve a paradox in his view of life. Proper development is essentially individual; but, for an individual to live well, it is not sufficient to be oneself alone. Groups are deeply appealing because of the way they embody community and security; but usually this comes at the terrible cost of the suppression of individuality; we become creatures of the group – our ideas are clichés, our sentiments fashionable, our fears and hopes are commonplace. World literature creates a society of like-minded members who are part of that group *because* of their individuality.

452

8

Goethe's Death

Goethe was once asked to write a line or two in an album belonging to a certain Frau von Spiegel – an extremely common request. Many famous writers had already signed this lady's album, including a writer called Tiedge – who had become something of a celebrity on account of his book *Urania*, from the Greek for 'Heaven'. Goethe noticed some words from this man in the album. 'In one moment of insolence, I was just about to write something directly about Tiedge – but I'm glad I didn't. It wouldn't have been the first time I'd disgusted good people by rash expressions.'

Goethe was, however, really rather annoyed by Tiedge, whose ideas he found simpering and silly. 'Wherever you went you found *Urania* on the table . . . Let him who believes in immortality enjoy his happiness in silence; he has no reason to give himself airs about it; and such incomprehensible matters should not be a theme for daily speculation, or gossipy chatter.' Goethe frequently encountered enthusiastic readers of *Urania* who were delighted by its promises of immortality – which they regarded with pride, almost as if living for ever was a special and personal achievement. They always wanted to know what Goethe thought about this great issue – did he expect to go to Heaven? They were not pleased with the answer Goethe standardly gave: 'I should be well pleased if, after the end of this life, I were to discover that I was about to have another. Only I rather hoped I wouldn't have to meet any of the people who had ardently insisted that there would be another life. I would be tormented. Think of what they'd be like – the pious would crowd round me saying "We were right, we were right," and so the next life would be even more trying than this one.'

Concern with immortality, he came to think, was a preoccupation of idle people. 'A competent man with something sensible to do down here – who has to work hard every day to accomplish it – he lets the future world take care of itself.' Thoughts about immortality are good, though, for people who are not all that successful down here. He concluded that Tiedge must be both idle and a failure – if he had a nicer life he would not have written that silly book but would have had more useful thoughts instead.

Goethe was exceptionally lucky in that his health and mental clarity held out to the end. He read the new literature: Sir Walter Scott and Victor Hugo; he reread old favourites: Plutarch's *Lives*. He maintained his correspondence with old friends – especially Zelter and Sulpiz Boisserée, the wonderfully cultivated collector of Early Netherlandish paintings, who did much to soften Goethe's attitudes to Romanticism by his obviously sensible mode of life. Goethe was visited

by travelling royalty and much enjoyed the company of his grand-children.

This 1831 portrait shows Goethe – aged eighty-one – dictating to his secretary, Johann August John. Goethe is standing in his work room and if we could look out of the window we would see the large rear garden of the Frauenplan house. Goethe is wearing his marvellously stylish house coat and stands elegantly. A miniature portrait of Carl August is visible above the drawers on the right. It is twenty-five to twelve; Goethe will work a little longer before lunch.

In fact, Goethe continued working until just before his death. The second part of *Faust* was completed in the summer of 1831. After that he slowed down. He made his last visit to the lovely garden-house across the river Ilm in February of 1832. Some English admirers sent him a little model of a steam train – and told him about the Liverpool–Manchester line, which had just opened.

On 16 March he felt ill and took to his bed. He died a few days later on 22 March 1832. His doctor reported the horror of his last day as Goethe struggled with the violent pain in his chest. He was terrified of dying. He died at noon, in the armchair by his bed. Unable to speak, his fingers traced letters on the rug around his knees, still – we are told – careful in his punctuation.

The devoted Eckermann recorded a last impression: 'The morning after Goethe's death, a deep desire seized me to look once more upon his earthly garment. His faithful servant, Frederick, opened for me the great chamber in which he was laid out. Stretched upon his back, he reposed as if asleep: profound peace and security reigned in the features of his sublimely noble countenance. The mighty brow seemed to har-bour thoughts. I wished for a lock of his hair; but reverence prevented me cutting it off. The body lay naked, wrapped only in a white sheet; large pieces of ice had been placed near it, to keep it fresh as long as possible. Frederick drew aside the sheet, and I was astonished at the divine magnificence of his limbs. The breast was powerful, broad and arched; the arms and thighs were full and softly muscular; the feet were elegant and of the most perfect shape; nowhere on the whole body was there a trace either of fat or leanness or decay. A perfect man lay in great beauty before me; the rapture of the sight made me forget for a moment that the immortal spirit had left such an abode. I laid my hand on his heart – there was a deep silence – and I turned away to give free vent to my suppressed tears.'

9

Afterlife

After his death, Goethe became an icon of humanity, a symbol of bourgeois selfishness, a totem of German nationalism and – to most people – a name standing for very little. This is, of course, to record what Goethe has been for others. But the secret question – the important question – is what might he be for us – for me? And certainly it is the question that would have most interested him.

When I started to think about this book I felt daunted by the mass of information about Goethe, by the vast range of his own work and by his august reputation as a canonical figure of Western culture. One evening I was feeling particularly anxious and despondent and I tried to imagine, as vividly as I could, what Goethe would say if he could walk into the room and sit beside me on the sofa and hear out my worries. This is how I imagine his response:

'Remember how I felt when Schiller wrote his first, long letter to me – explaining how he saw me? Remember how moved I was by what he said? Was that the whole truth about me? Did Schiller know the details of my life? Of course not; but he saw something to love in me, and that drew us together. Of course you will make mistakes; think of my own dear Wilhelm Meister – the favourite child of my imagination – his life was a sequence of mistakes; how would he have written about me? That is what I should most like – to be judged by Wilhelm. When I felt lonely at first in Italy, I imagined myself talking to Palladio: was I right in the way I imagined him? I don't really know; only I cannot believe that he would have turned from me, or left me to my distress.

Remember that day when I handed Eckermann the grapes, when I told him my work would never be popular? I liked him very much and felt very close to him. I felt isolated in my time; I liked formality and the old ways, but I also liked ease and modern comfort; I liked my fine rooms, but I also liked simplicity; I was always high-minded, but I loved drinking and flirting. I felt no contradictions in myself – the girls of Venice, the temples of Rome, the fields and the mountains, the library, the laboratory, the inns, the palace – how much I liked them all.

'My aim in life, and in my work, was – how did I put it? – to undertake "a mission to healthy people". We learn about how to deal with problems when things go badly; but I was interested in cultivating the happiness of those who are well. They need help too – although of a different kind. I could see folly and violence and greed at work all around me; but I learned not to waste my life being saddened by it; that was extremely difficult for me; I always wanted to put things right, to teach people, to point them in a better direction. But if I could not succeed, what was the point of being miserable? So I did not seek to convert, but to encourage – not to add to despair but to strengthen those who might already be attracted to a simple, noble view of life. What is it important to know in life? How to be happy, how to be useful and helpful to others, how to cope with difficulties.

'Perhaps you see: it is that mission that matters to me. And it is a simple mission, not a complex one. What would I like people to know of me? Just whatever will help them to cultivate their own strengths, to be cheerful and kindly. My mother, you know, was my greatest inspiration. She was active, constructive, serene and wise; I wanted to be like that, and I hoped my work would communicate that ideal. I have met so many clever people whose cleverness served no constructive purpose that I could see; people who could, with remarkable sophistication, make themselves hate the world and hate themselves, could make themselves unsatisfied with every good thing. People who persuade themselves that every simple and natural good is an illusion, that there is one great thing which will save them or transform the world.

*

'Perhaps you know a poem I wrote, a little allegory about a banquet? I imagined myself arranging the nicest lunch, in a beautiful room – the loveliest things I could think of. Then – so it goes – I invite some people (my contemporaries, really); but they walk past what I have laid out for them; and so I have to eat alone. And although I was alone, I could still enjoy the feast. All the same I would rather have others there with me. That was the secret meaning I had in mind when I gave Eckermann the grapes – although I never told him. It was to show him he was with me at the imagined table.

'When I wrote Mignon's song of longing for Italy, remember she imagines the lovely house – where the statues look fondly upon her and speak with such tenderness: wanting to comfort and protect her? It's a theme I stole from Virgil; it is the dream of Aeneas pointing to the future foundation of Rome; and I mean that grandeur to be there, as well as the warmth and sweetness of the regard the household gods have for Mignon. To me, this theme is deeply appealing: the home that the princely, favoured Aeneas dreams of is also the place of refuge for confused, loyal, sad and lovely little Mignon. I am both the person seeking that place and one of the household gods, one of the statues.'

10

The End and the Beginning

THE CROOKED TIMBERS
OF HUMANITY

Goethe's good fortune in his upbringing and in the generally benign pattern of his career – the early success of *Werther* and the wonderful support he received from Carl August – did not cut him off from suffering. But it did give him sufficient strength to look at the human condition without disgust. He was secure enough to think seriously about unhappiness, about death, about failure and the things that we may need to face in order to make the best of our lives.

Although Goethe stressed the importance of cheerfulness and considered happiness the normal and sane goal of existence, he was under no illusions about the general character of the human world. Listen, he advises us, 'to a physician with a large practice; and he will whisper to you tales that will horrify you at the misery, and astonish you at the vice, with which human nature is visited and from which society suffers'.

Goethe was under no illusion that such people were essentially different from him: he might have suffered such misery, practised such vices: 'There is no crime I have heard of that I could not have committed myself.'

But at the same time, Goethe is not a pessimist – he doesn't think that these facts entail the destruction of human achievement or make it pointless to build nice avenues or lay out parks. This is part of Goethe's sanity – the fact that he isn't hysterical about the human condition, while not being naive.

However, to face these facts about ourselves and the world – and still make life interesting, pleasant and productive – we need to be strong. One of the points he keeps on making is that we need to master ourselves. To live well we need to be able to say 'no' to ourselves – but this is not a life-denying, fearful attitude to pleasure. On the contrary, it is a discipline which allows us to do the larger things that are important to us, to allow our more worthwhile projects to be undertaken and to enjoy what pleasures we can without being ruined by them, without finding that all of our time is taken up with them, or that we are endlessly combating the ill-consequences of our moments of gratification.

THE VALUE OF ART

This general attitude to life led Goethe to particular conclusions about the task of art. He was particularly critical of poets – or other artists – who write or paint 'as if they were ill and the whole world were a lazaretto. They all speak of the woe and misery of this earth and the joys of a hereafter; all are discontented, and one draws the other into a state of still greater discontent. This is a real abuse of art, which was given to us to hide the little discords of life and to make man contented with the world and his condition. But the present generation is afraid of all such strength, and feels poetical only when it has weakness to deal with.'

This is a central statement of Goethe's position. Since this world is the only world we can live in we have to make the best of it. What's the value of being discontented? None – if it is not connected to some genuine progress, some real improvement. But that is not the case here. The artists he berates imagine that it is somehow virtuous, special and admirable to go on about how bad everything is. But this is a reflection of their own weakness, not a fair statement of the condition of the world. And this is a kind of negative version of culture – skill and intelligence devoted to making life more painful, rather than better; and people encouraging and supporting each other in this project. The point of culture, on the other hand, is to 'arm men with the courage to undergo the conflicts of life' – not of course any old conflicts, but those conflicts that are unavoidable in the pursuit of really valuable goals. 'Most modern productions are romantic, not because they are new, but because they are weak, morbid and sickly. And the antique is not classic because it is old, but because it is strong, fresh, joyous and healthy.'

THE TASK OF LIFE

At the start of Book 16 of *Poetry and Truth* – when Goethe is well advanced in his task of giving a lucid and coherent account of his early life – he suddenly remarks: 'No one has ever understood another person; I never understand others, and no one has ever understood me.' It is in part a despairing admission: I have been trying to explain myself and I have to face the fact that I won't succeed. But it is also a message to anyone who aims at understanding him: you're not going to succeed.

And he is right; not because there is something strangely obscure about Goethe himself: every individual life is unfathomable. But it's hardly a disaster that Goethe, in the end, eludes our grasp. For the purpose of life is not that we should become experts on Goethe: there will always be many details of his life that we will not know unless we devote the whole of our existence to mastering the record of his.

For the message Goethe is trying to send us isn't a plea to understand him, or the impotent command that we become like him, but rather, that like him we should take courage in an infinitely more worthwhile task – that of becoming ourselves.

Notes

SOURCES

When it comes to Goethe's life, the sources of information are almost inexhaustible. I have been hugely conscious of my dependence upon the work of distinguished scholars and biographers and three in particular have guided my thinking. *The Life of Goethe* by George Henry Lewes was first published in 1855. It was reissued in Everyman's Library in 1908; although no longer in print, the Everyman edition is often available in second-hand bookshops. *Goethe: His Life and Times* by Richard Friedenthal was first published in 1963, reissued by Weidenfeld & Nicolson in 1993 and has been reprinted. These are engaging narratives but from a scholarly point of view the outstanding biography is that by Nicholas Boyle: *Goethe: The Poet and the Age*, published by Oxford University Press, of which two volumes have so far appeared. *Volume I: The Poetry of Desire* considers the period from 1749 to 1790; *Volume II: Revolution and Renunciation* carries the story on to 1803. The bibliographic sections of these volumes provide excellent guidance to Goethe scholarship. I have also been much influenced by the short and sweet volume on Goethe by T. J. Reed in the Oxford Past Masters series. This was first published in 1984 and is a compelling response to the question: why is Goethe important to us now?

Goethe intrigued me for a very long time before his own works made much of an impression. In my late teens I had tried to read *Faust* but found it baffling and boring (although I could not quite admit this to myself). I read *Werther* a few years later with some admiration but little real enthusiasm. Some years later still I looked at the *Italian Journey* with only moderate enjoyment. Goethe only really came alive for me when I was working on Schiller: the friendship between Goethe and Schiller became an obsession. Then I read *Wilhelm Meister's Apprenticeship* and this was the first book by Goethe that gripped me; I found Wilhelm deeply sympathetic. Returning to *Werther* when I was writing a book on the topic of love, I began to appreciate the intelligence of Goethe's treatment of that experience. With these secure points of attachment in place I found the rest of Goethe's work much more approachable.

In 1999, for an essay on the 250th anniversary of Goethe's birth, I read his autobiographical narrative *From My Life: Poetry and Truth* and the much shorter *The Campaign in France* and *The Siege of Mainz*. The latter two – which are certainly among Goethe's less well-known writings – particularly impressed me. They bear comparison with the war sections in *War and Peace* but, for me, they extended the range of what I took to be Goethe's personality – filling out his experience of life in unexpected ways. This occurred to me when I first saw images of the houses Goethe had lived in in Frankfurt and Weimar. I wanted to live there; and this is a metaphor, or an extension, of what draws me to a writer: wanting to live in their view of the world (even if only from time to time).

In working on this book I was surprised by how much I liked some of Goethe's works that I feared I would have to read merely from a sense of duty. In particular the plays *Egmont* and *Tasso* struck me as really wonderful. I delayed reading *Faust* for as long as possible, finally getting round to it during a family winter holiday at a small coastal town. It was a revelation and brought me to the most standard of conclusions that *Faust* in its entirety really is Goethe's masterpiece.

Because Goethe has been the object of scholarly effort for such a long time, the most important source material has been conveniently collected – although it is mostly not available in English.

Three collections of his correspondence are especially important: the letters to Frau von Stein, which were written during Goethe's first period in Weimar when he was in his late twenties and his thirties; the exchange of letters with Schiller from the period 1794 to 1805, commencing almost exactly on Goethe's forty-fifth birthday; and his correspondence with the Berlin composer Zelter, which covers the last three decades of Goethe's life. Triple-volume editions of each of these collections are published in German by Insel.

Reference to these letters is straightforward; citation of a letter to Zelter, for example, refers the reader to the standard edition of the letters – arranged by date; so mention of when the letter was written enables one to check the reference. Sometimes, if there are few letters in a particular period, then merely saying 'as Goethe wrote to Zelter that summer' when the year is obviously 1812 will allow the letter to be identified at once – Goethe wrote only one letter to Zelter between May and November 1812.

Supplementary information about Goethe's childhood can be gleaned from *Goethe's Correspondence with a Child*. Published in 1834 this is the exchange of letters between Bettina von Arnim and Goethe's mother and between Bettina and Goethe himself. I am not aware of an English translation.

Goethe's later years were extensively recorded by his assistant Johann Peter Eckermann; *Conversations with Goethe*, translated by John Oxenford in 1850, was reproduced in Everyman's Library in 1930. This delightful volume is long out of print but I have seen many second-hand copies.

In addition, there is a three-volume collection of contemporary letters written about Goethe; this marvel of scholarship, edited by Wilhelm Bode and published by Insel, is never likely to be translated into English.

The single most revealing book on Goethe and his environment is not a biography but a work of fiction: Thomas Mann's *Lotte in Weimar*; this wonderful novel is unfortunately marred – for a modern audience not already deeply in awe of Goethe – by its very slow start. Ideally one would read it in reverse. I loved the idea of it: it tells the story of Charlotte Kestner – whom Goethe had loved, briefly, in his twenties and turned into a celebrity by making her the 'Lotte' of *Werther*. But the opening fifty pages are so unrewarding that I gave up, reading it as a whole – with growing excitement – only when I felt I had to in the course of writing this book. The 1940 translation by Helen Lowe-Porter, published by Knopf and reprinted by Penguin in 1968, is admirable.

A wonderful source of information about Goethe across his whole life was compiled in the late 1940s by Ludwig Lewisohn, and published by Farrar, Straus and Company. This two-volume work, *Goethe: The Story of a Man*, draws together extracts from Goethe's letters and biographical works, along with comments on him by many of his contemporaries.

Goethe appears as a character in Milan Kundera's *Immortality*: the discussion of Goethe's relations with Beethoven, Napoleon and Bettina von Arnim (three figures striving, with greater or lesser success, for immortality) is compelling – I have been strongly influenced by it. Translated by Peter Kussi, *Immortality* was published by Faber & Faber in 1991. I'm grateful to my brother, Joe, for sending me a copy.

For Goethe's works I have generally made use of existing translations, but – quite often – I have used my own translations. Almost all of Goethe's poetry that I quote is in my own translation. Scholars of German will have to excuse certain liberties: my aim was to reproduce the character of the meaning – rather than the verse structure or the literal meaning.

The principal translations I have used are:

Early Letters of Goethe, ed. Edward Bell [1884], facsimile reprint with introduction by Christopher Schweitzer (Rochester, NY: Camden House, 1993)

Johann Wolfgang von Goethe, *Early Verse Drama and Prose Plays*, eds. Cyrus Hamlin and Frank Ryder, trans. Robert M. Browning, Cyrus Hamlin and Michael Hamburger (New York: Suhrkamp, 1988):

    i. *Egmont*, trans. Michael Hamburger

    ii. *Clavigo*, trans. Robert M. Browning

    iii. *Stella*, trans. Robert M. Browning and Frank Ryder

    iv. *Brother and Sister*, trans. Frank Ryder

    v. *Prometheus*, trans. Frank Ryder

    vi. *Jery and Betty*, trans. Frank Ryder

    vii. *Proserpina*, trans. Cyrus Hamlin

Johann Wolfgang von Goethe, *Elective Affinities*, trans. R. J. Hollingdale (London: Penguin Books, 1971)

Johann Wolfgang von Goethe, *From My Life*, eds. Thomas P. Saine and Jeffrey L. Sammons (New York: Suhrkamp, 1987):

    viii. 'Poetry and Truth', Parts I–III, trans. Robert R. Heitner

    ix. 'Poetry and Truth', Part IV. *The Campaign in France. The Siege of Mainz*, trans. with an introduction and notes by Thomas P. Saine

Johann Wolfgang von Goethe, *Maxims and Reflections*, ed. Peter Hutchinson, trans. Elisabeth Stopp (London: Penguin Books, 1998)

Johann Wolfgang von Goethe, *Scientific Studies*, ed. and trans. Douglas Miller (New York: Suhrkamp, 1988)

Johann Wolfgang von Goethe, *Verse Plays and Epic*, eds. Cyrus Hamlin and Frank Ryder, trans. Michael Hamburger, Hunter Hannum and David Luke (New York: Suhrkamp, 1987):

    i. *Iphigenia in Tauris*, trans. David Luke

    ii. *Torquato Tasso*, trans. Michael Hamburger

    iii. *The Natural Daughter*, trans. Hunter Hannum

    iv. *Pandora*, trans. Michael Hamburger

    v. *Hermann and Dorothea*, trans. David Luke

Johann Wolfgang von Goethe, *Wilhelm Meister*, trans. Thomas Carlyle (Edinburgh, 1824)

REFERENCES
Part One: Luck

Section 2. The principle sources for Goethe's childhood are the early books of *From My Life: Poetry and Truth*, and Bettina von Arnim's exchange of letters with Goethe's mother and with the elderly Goethe (in *Goethe's Correspondence with a Child*). Bettina herself enters the story in Part Eight, section 10. Goethe's descriptions of family life in two of his novels – in Book 1 of *Wilhelm Meister's Apprenticeship* and the early sections of *Wilhelm Meister's Theatrical Mission* – are compelling, and have some connection to Goethe's personal experience.

Section 4. The house was destroyed during the Second World War but has been fully reconstructed and furnished with some of the pieces and pictures which it held during Goethe's lifetime and others in keeping with the original style, so we can get a fairly good idea of what it was like during the many years Goethe lived there. The German publisher Insel has produced a detailed documentary book on the Goethe family house in Frankfurt.

The Connolly quote comes from *The Unquiet Grave* (1944–5).

Section 5. Nietzsche set this quotation as the opening line of *The Uses and Abuses of History for Life* (1874).

Section 7. The description of looking out over the neighbouring gardens comes from *Wilhelm Meister*, Book 1. The whole account of childhood and youth in that first book is strongly autobiographical in flavour.

Section 8. The description of Käthchen comes in a letter from Goethe to his boyhood friend J. A. Horn, from Bell's *Early Letters of Goethe*.

Part Two: Love

Section 3. The reply to Zelter is dated 3 December 1812.

Section 4. The long letter by Kestner is in the Bode collection of letters (no. 115). The translation is my own.

Section 5. The account of the relationship with Lili is from *Poetry and Truth*.

Section 6. There is a detailed biography of Cornelia by Sigrid Damm, published by Insel in 1992. Simply entitled *Cornelia Goethe*, it tells the sad story of her life from a feminist perspective – rather along the lines of Virginia Woolf's essay 'Shakespeare's Sister'. It is a heroic task – Cornelia's life really was dreary – because it is hard to determine to what extent inequality of gender was Cornelia's problem, as opposed to some more elusive spiritual distress.

Section 7. The word 'genius' was eventually brought to heel by Kant – although only some twenty-five years later. Genius is the capacity to form new rules. Hence it's not at all that the work of genius is undisciplined (as the Stolbergs thought) but that it introduces a new discipline, through which fresh areas of experience can be understood. The point of *Werther* wasn't to do away with conventional narrative but to convey an internal drama rather than an external one; it's the story of how Werther's mind changes, rather than the story of what he does. And to tell such a story Goethe had to move away from established narrative forms.

Section 9. Goethe borrowed the basic idea of *Stella* from a novel by Christian Gellert, who had been professor of poetry when Goethe was a student at Leipzig. *The Swedish Countess* (1747–8) is, in fact, far superior to Goethe's play and still a delight to read – which cannot honestly be said of *Stella*.

Part Three: Power

Section 1. The letter to Lavater was written in September 1780. It was T. J. Reed who coined the memorable line about Byron joining the civil service.

Section 7. The description of sitting in the garden listening to the sounds comes from a letter to Augusta von Stolberg (end of May 1776).

Part Four: Art

Section 1. From the start of his journey to Italy Goethe scribbled notes about what he saw and what he was thinking. These diaries, together with letters he wrote later in the trip to his friends back in Weimar, provided the material for the *Italian Journey*, which Goethe wrote and published much later as part of his large autobiographical project. And it is from this source that we can recapture some of the immediacy of his experiences.

In general I have followed the 1962 translation of the *Italian Journey* by W. H. Auden and Elizabeth Mayer, published by Collins and reprinted by Penguin in 1970. However, I have fairly often adapted the translation to capture the spontaneity and freshness of Goethe's prose. Most of the passages quoted are easily located in the text, either by date or place – since the *Italian Journey* is organized like a journal, with the entries arranged by date, and usually mentioning the place where they were written.

Section 2. Goethe discusses Palladio in entries relating to his time in Venice, not only because a few of Palladio's most impressive buildings are in that city, but also because he'd bought some books in Vicenza (where most of the villas are), which he was reading and thinking about while in Venice.

Section 4. All the letters mentioned can be found in the Bode collection.

Section 5. Insel's *Goethe and Tischbein in Rome* is a documentary handbook which neatly draws together the visual images and passages relating to Goethe's time in Rome.

Section 10. The lines that open this section were written on 23 August 1787, a few days before Goethe's thirty-eighth birthday.

Part Five: War

Section 1. The story about Goethe seeking Christiane in the night – and her seeking him – was told by Goethe to Eckermann.

Section 7. The last quote in the section – about the effect of art – is from the 'excursus' added to the end of *The Campaign in France*.

Section 10. Quotations are from *The Siege of Mainz*.

Part Six: Friendship

Section 9. The final quotation is from *Wilhelm Meister*, Book 8.

Part Seven: Nature

Section 1. A fine recent book on Goethe's interest in science is Matthew Bell's *Goethe's Naturalistic Anthropology: Man and Other Plants* (Clarendon Press, Oxford, 1994).

A representative figure was Alexander von Humboldt. Today, Alexander's brother, Wilhelm, is more famous as the originator of the university of Berlin, which now bears his name. Alexander's magnum opus was *Cosmos*: a vast work that sought to present literally everything that was known about the natural world. In later life, after many years of research in South America, Alexander von Humboldt became a Prussian administrator and was mocked by the courtiers as 'Mr Know-all'; but he was a delightful man and latterly a very good friend of Carl August, who died in his arms talking about lightning and the depth of the oceans.

Section 4. Goethe describes his response to Bayle's article in *Poetry and Truth*, Book 16.

Part Eight: Peace

Section 1. Extracts from *On Germany* describing Goethe can be found in *Major Writings of Germaine de Staël*, trans. Vivian Folkenflik (New York: Columbia University Press, 1987).

Thomas Mann's painful defence of German militarism, written in 1918, can be found in *Classical Readings in Culture and Civilization*, ed. John Rundell and Stephen Mennell (London: Routledge, 1998).

Part Ten: Death

Section 4. Goethe's partial distancing from the younger generation: it was only ever partial – Goethe was universally held in high esteem and objection to any particular position he adopted at this stage or which might be attributed to him, was regarded as the decline of age. For example, on 27 August 1827 (some years later than this), Hegel's birthday, his university students attended a high-spirited feast at which they drank many toasts to Hegel, and continued drinking to Goethe after midnight. A high point of praise for their liberal hero Hegel was the assertion that he had done for philosophy what Goethe had done for German literature.

Section 8. The comment about Tiedge was written on 25 February 1824.

Section 10. The statements are recorded by Eckermann.

Acknowledgements

This book was conceived in discussion with Gillon Aitken on an exceptionally wet spring day in London four years ago. I am deeply grateful to Stefan McGrath and Paul Elie for their early support for the project. Helen Conford has been an inspiring editor. Most of the writing has been undertaken in the congenial surroundings of the Melbourne University Philosophy Department; I am particularly indebted to Graham Priest, Christopher Cordner and Graeme Marshall for their continuing support. In Berlin, Ursula Roos has been wonderfully generous and imaginative.

My interest in Goethe was shaped – often indirectly – by my parents, Ann and Anthony Armstrong, and more explicitly by David Mayers and Alain de Botton; collectively they allowed me to feel that I could address a canonical, much-researched figure on my own terms. My children, William and Charlotte ('Lotte'), have been alarmed to discover that they are both named after characters in the novels but have acquired a breezy curiosity about 'silly old Goethe'.

I would never have written about Goethe – or indeed about anything – had it not been for my wife, Helen Hayward; I owe whatever fragments of adult personality I have to her. In a truly Goethe-like spirit she has tried to get me to see that life is more important than any book.

Thematic Register

As a reader I rarely make use of a conventional Index but I often find myself making a record (on the back page) of themes and key phrases. Here is my own Thematic Register for this book.

475